REA

This study of James Joyce's fiction as a response to Irish and European history exemplifies Fredric Jameson's injunction, "Always historicize!" James Fairhall examines the effects of colonialism, nationalism, and World War I on Joyce's work; and he explores significant absences in his treatment of women, the lower classes, and the Irish countryside. He maintains that Joyce's great problem was his desire to transcend the artist's subject position within history. Joyce responded to the difficulties of being an artist in Ireland by going into self-exile; but in his work he grappled increasingly with the constraints of all history, any history. Drawing on a wide range of critical theories Fairhall argues that Joyce opened up seemingly closed possibilities by destabilizing the boundary between history and fiction, and the notion of an undivided subject.

JAMES JOYCE AND THE QUESTION OF HISTORY

JAMES JOYCE AND THE QUESTION OF HISTORY

JAMES FAIRHALL

DePaul University, Chicago

CAMBRIDGE
UNIVERSITY PRESS

Published by the Press Syndicate of the University of Cambridge
The Pitt Building, Trumpington Street, Cambridge, CB2 1RP
40 West 20th Street, New York, NY 10011–4211, USA
10 Stamford Road, Oakleigh, Melbourne 3166, Australia

© Cambridge University Press 1993

First published 1993

Printed in Great Britain at the University Press, Cambridge

A catalogue record for this book is available from the British Library

Library of Congress cataloguing in publication data
Fairhall, James
James Joyce and the question of history / by James Fairhall.
p.   cm.
Includes bibliographical references (p.   ) and index.
ISBN 0 521 40292 1
1. Joyce, James, 1882–1941 – Knowledge – History. 2. Literature and history
– Ireland – History – 20th century.
3. Ireland in literature. 4. Historicism. I. Title.
PR 6019.09Z533375   1993
823'.912 – dc20   92-37271   CIP

ISBN 0 521 40292 1 hardback

For Elaine Siegel

Contents

Illustrations

Preface

While James Joyce was in the last stages of composing *Ulysses*, he confessed to an impulse to tie a chain around Leopold Bloom and throw him into the River Seine. In the course of writing this study I experienced a similar impulse, and was tempted to fling Joyce, or at least his books, into Long Island Sound. I didn't. But it was a close call.

What kept me going, among other reasons, was a belief not only in the value of a historical approach to Joyce, but in the value of his writings as a catalyst for investigating and interrogating history. What *is* history, anyway? Something that happened in the past, or an account of that thing? How true are historical narratives? How do they differ from fiction? How firm, controllable, and even referential is that common medium of history and fiction, language? Joyce's works – grounded in a dense historical reality, yet at the same time free-floating in a universe of endlessly signifying, interconnected words – provoke such questions.

No single book can examine in depth both Joyce and the nature of history. Thus, rather than attempting any original treatment of history or historiography myself, I draw on the ideas of Hayden White, Fredric Jameson, and other theorists. Against the backdrop of their thoughts I investigate Joyce's handling of history, especially Irish history, and situate him in his own historical moment.

Another way of looking at this book would be to see it as an ideological study. Ideology may be what Joyce called "one of those big words which make us so unhappy" (*CW* 87), yet the word has a broader meaning than that which we are used to hearing on the seven o'clock news. In its broadest sense, which is a neutral one, it means socially derived beliefs and values. In this study I analyze Joyce's ideology, conscious and unconscious, as expressed in his major writings.

History and ideology are two different things, needless to say. Yet we can scarcely analyze one without the other. Ideology actuates the makers of history – the masses of ordinary citizens no less than their leaders (even if they deny the influence of ideology, preferring to think that they are moved by transcendent laws or values). At the same time, ideology grows out of history. It is produced by wars, famines, modes of economic organization, technological advances, and so on.

This brings us to what Stephen Dedalus in *Ulysses* calls the "nightmare" (*U* 34/2.379) of history. As an Irish Catholic and a European living in the late nineteenth and early twentieth centuries, Joyce was well aware of the violence of history. He also understood the connection between history and ideology – the fact that, in many respects, history is ideology enacted. The central problem in Joyce's life, perhaps from the time when he gave up his position as prefect of the Sodality of the Blessed Virgin Mary at Belvedere College, was that of situating himself in relation to history. Inevitably, this entailed situating himself in relation to ideology, or ideologies, as well. In each case he sought a magic circle – that of art – in which he could take refuge from the nightmare and undo its power with a wave of his "lifewand" (*FW* 195.5).

Joyce, in his fiction, attempted to subvert history, which he saw as both a chronicle of violence and oppression, and as a fixed past that had ousted other possible pasts and thus delimited the present. He also attempted to subvert those ideologies which underlie the violence and the oppression. Both *Ulysses* and *Finnegans Wake* attack, or rather destabilize, the very basis of modern history – the idea that historical narratives can somehow tell "the truth" about a complex event, can recount what "actually" happened. These books destabilize, too, the linguistic basis of ideology, undermining binary notions such as "race," "people," and "nation" which depend on defining something or someone else as the Other.

Joyce's subtle, brilliant attack on received history offers lessons from which most of us, not just literary specialists, could profit. Imagine a United States whose people understood the ideological nature of history and the historicity of ideology. Certainly such a country would not have stepped unreflectively, with slogans as its justification, into Vietnam or Panama or the Persian Gulf. I mention actual conflicts because Joyce responded in his art to equally real conflicts – the whole chronicle of Irish–English relations, the Boer War, World War I, and the Irish Civil War – and because the stakes involved in establishing an understanding of history and ideology are so high, even after the end of the Cold War.

Yet Joyce made his attack, inevitably, from a position within history. He, like the rest of us, was conditioned by his own history – by his birth in 1882 in Ireland, by his family's gradually declining position in the Catholic middle classes, by his father's Parnellism. He rebelled against the ideologies of Irish Catholic nationalism and nineteenth-century European imperialism, but held through his life unexamined opinions (on women, for instance) derived from both. A reformist impulse runs throughout his fiction, from *Dubliners* on, yet the challenges posed to the reader by his writings after *A Portrait of the Artist* drastically restrict the audience on which that impulse could act.

The critic's task, then, is to analyze not just the success of Joyce's rebellion against history but its limitations. We must step outside the magic circle of his art and examine its assumptions; we must ask those questions which his art does not acknowledge as questions. In my attempt to do this, I am, I admit, limited by my own position within history (not to mention my position within language, whose limits and lack of limits *Finnegans Wake* underscores). Nevertheless, we must make the effort. If we do not historicize our reading of texts, then how can we achieve an awareness of our own historicity?

❋

This study grew out of a dissertation. I owe special thanks to Michael Sprinker, not only for his invaluable suggestion that I read Jameson's *The Political Unconscious*, but for his close readings and other help. Paul Dolan gave me the idea of beginning with the "Eumaeus" episode in *Ulysses*, which in turn led me to the Phoenix Park murders. Karl Bottigheimer welcomed my foray into his own field, history, with advice and encouragement. Though not a reader, David Sheehan aided me, with his usual good-humored efficiency, in other ways. Tom Flanagan steered me toward a broader treatment; the sense of Irish history that pervades his novels is reflected, I'd like to think, in my own work. Kevin Taylor, of Cambridge University Press, advised me well on selecting a title and on other matters. Finally, I must thank Ellen, who always believed in my writing.

Abbreviations

Works by James Joyce

CP	*Collected Poems*
CW	*The Critical Writings of James Joyce*
D	*Dubliners*
E	*Exiles*
FW	*Finnegans Wake*
L I, II, III	*Letters of James Joyce*, Vols. I, II, and III
P	*A Portrait of the Artist as a Young Man*
SH	*Stephen Hero*
U	*Ulysses*

Other abbreviations

JJ	*James Joyce* (Richard Ellmann)
JJQ	*James Joyce Quarterly*

Introduction: What is history?

> History, the articulated past – all kinds, even our personal histories – is forever being rethought, refelt, rewritten, not merely as rigor or luck turns up new facts but as new patterns emerge, as new understandings develop, and as we experience new needs and new questions.
>
> Robert Penn Warren, "The Use of the Past"

I have no original answer to the question posed by my subtitle. But I would like to explore some of the issues in the voluminous debate about the status of history and historiography so that we can better understand Joyce's own implicit but rich contribution to that debate.

History comes to us most often in the form of a narrative, a story. Unlike fictional narratives, historical ones are supposed to be true: "The one describes the thing that has been," as Aristotle wrote, "and the other a kind of thing that might be."[1] The historian deals with truth, facts, a past reality; the poet or fiction writer makes something up. Yet the English word "history" did not always register this dividing line, as we see in the *Oxford English Dictionary*'s first definition: "A relation of incidents (in early use, either true or imaginary; later only of those professedly true)." During the Renaissance, the writing of history was viewed not as a scientific inquiry but as an exercise in the art of rhetoric.[2] As late as 1828 Macaulay could write: "History, at least in its state of ideal perfection, is a compound of poetry and philosophy."[3] Only in the nineteenth century did historiography take on the status of a social science and sharply differentiate itself from story-telling.

But what is this science of history? The *OED* defines it as "That branch of knowledge which deals with past events, as recorded in writings or otherwise ascertained." Past events, however, can no longer be experienced – a fact which opens historical knowledge to the charge that it is a construction as much of imagination as of thought, and that its authority is no greater than the power of the historian to persuade his readers that his account is true. This places historical discourse on the same level as any rhetorical performance; it becomes a textualization no more authoritative than literary discourse.[4] Yet history (past events) "is *not* a text, not a narrative,"[5] as Jameson takes pains to point out. And history (an account of past events) has a referent that is not merely imagined but real. Aristotle's distinction, then, holds. The problem for the historian, which Aristotle does not address, is an epistemological one that can be condensed into a few questions. First, how do we gain knowledge of past events when we can no longer experience them? Second, how do we gain knowledge of aspects of the past which have shaped our lives without our awareness and which make themselves felt to us as givens, as Necessity? Third, how does the discourse of history mold those events which it attempts to represent?

Leopold von Ranke (1795–1886), the pioneer of "scientific" history, might have been puzzled by these questions. His goal was simple: not to judge or evaluate the past, but to tell "only what actually happened" ("wie es eigentlich gewesen"). He had tried, he said, "to extinguish my own self ... to let the things speak and the mighty forces appear which have arisen in the course of the centuries."[6] Ranke's co-founder of early nineteenth-century German historicism, Wilhelm von Humboldt, saw the historian's task in a similar light: it is "to present what actually happened." He added a twist, though, pointing out that an event

is only partially visible in the world of the senses; the rest has to be added by intuition, inference, and guesswork ... The truth of any event is predicated on the addition ... of that invisible part of every fact, and it is that part ... which the historian has to add ... Differently from the poet, but in a way similar to him, he must work the collected fragments into a whole.[7]

J. G. Droysen, too, recognized the historian's role in bringing out the undersurface of historical facts. Historians, he declared, "must know what they wish to seek; only then will they find something. One must question things (*Dinge*) correctly, then they give an answer."[8] Writing in the early twentieth century, Eduard Meyer, a historian of the Romantic idealistic school whose ideas were adumbrated by Humboldt, turned Ranke's concept of scientific objectivity on its head. He denied that historiography is a systematic discipline, claiming: "The historian's subjective judgment [is] decisive. The historian has the right to demand that in this respect he is not judged differently from the artist."[9] Meyer's credo brings us back to Aristotle and the question of how the historian differs, or does not differ, from the poet.

During the first half of the twentieth century the English philosopher-historian Robin Collingwood also grappled with this question. He observed that the historical imagination cannot operate as freely as the poet's or fiction-writer's because it must work from "evidence." This evidence does not have to consist in written records alone; it can be derived from archeology, paleography, philology, numismatics, and so on. In the case of textual evidence, "history finds its proper method when the historian puts his authorities in the witness-box, and by cross-questioning extorts from them information which in their original statements they have withheld."[10] He acknowledged, though, that evidence cannot be easily separated from the argument or interpretation built upon it: we recognize evidence as such only when (as Droysen implied) we're already working from a system or hypothesis which invests it with significance. The historian's imaginative and creative faculties, therefore, are involved in the very foundations of his work.[11] For this reason Collingwood found history (accounts of past events) to be the record of human thought. But history (the past events themselves) is also an expression of thought. The human agents of historical events acted as they did because of their conscious or unconscious ideas and beliefs. Thus "wrong ways of thinking are just as much historical facts as right ones,"[12] at least insofar as they gave rise to actions, events, regimes, and ways of life.

Collingwood not only considered history to be thought, but felt that "all historical thought is the historical interpretation of the present."[13] Because evidence changes with the nature of our questions, and the questions change as time brings about new historical perspectives, "every new generation must rewrite history in its own way."[14] This is not an argument for relativism, but rather a recognition that the value of reconstructing the past depends on what we do with it in the present.[15] Thus, while Collingwood does not advocate a particular social program, he does tie the writing of history to its effects on present-day thought, both in itself and as translated into action.

To revert to the first of my questions posed above – how do we gain knowledge of the past when we can no longer experience it? –

Collingwood felt that we cannot fully know past events. He never questioned their reality, yet avoided falling into what Barthes saw as scientific history's error of taking the signified for the real.[16] Acknowledging that an account of past events does not equate with the events themselves, he stressed the imaginative and time-bound aspects of such an account. The knowledge we gain of the past is partial not only because evidence may contain gaps or be doubtful, but because our point of view conditions it. Collingwood posited a kind of historical parallax, according to which the position of the observer in a given culture plays a key part in forming her view of a past culture. The questions we ask about the past are determined by our own particular present, and the resulting answers – while never yielding full, absolute knowledge – can illuminate the past in terms of the present and vice versa. Emphasis falls on illuminating the present, which is why Collingwood has been called "the philosopher of history as a strategy for asking questions about ourselves."[17]

Yet how do we know what to ask about ourselves? Collingwood might well have agreed with the premise of my second question – that the past has helped form our present lives in ways unknown to us which manifest themselves as Necessity – but he didn't raise this question. He recognized that past writers of history unconsciously withheld certain information which historians today must extort from them "by cross-questioning." As to what we withhold from ourselves, though, he remained largely silent. Apparently he assumed that this blank space in our self-knowledge is small enough so as not always to prevent us from directing our inquiries about ourselves and history in the right direction.

A crucial concept absent from Collingwood's thought, which relates to that gap in our historical self-awareness, is ideology. Both in general and Marxian usage, "ideology" has three primary meanings:

  (i) a system of beliefs characteristic of a particular class or group;
  (ii) a system of illusory beliefs – false ideas or false consciousness – which can be contrasted with true or scientific knowledge;
(iii) the general process of the production of meanings and ideas.[18]

Collingwood clearly had (ii) in mind in writing of "wrong ways of thinking." He also used the first sense in suggesting that each generation has its own perspective, its own way of thinking. And he recognized that (iii) takes place in a specific cultural and temporal context, with the resulting limitation that meanings and ideas never contain full, absolute truth. Yet his failure to grapple head-on with the concept of ideology barred him from systematically exploring the problem of how historians, caught in their own historical moment, can avoid wrong ways of thinking and unconscious omissions such as they detect in their predecessors' work.

A later historian, M. I. Finley, embraces the missing word which ties together so much of Collingwood's thought. Citing a definition of "ideology" from the *Shorter Oxford English Dictionary* that roughly matches (i) above, he states: "The study and writing of history . . . is a form of ideology." He dismisses the possibility of objectivity, such as that which Ranke professed, and observes that the selection and arrangement of events in any historical narrative implies a value judgment. It is the historian who "must ask the right questions [of historical evidence] and provide the right conceptual context." Further, we must begin by asking of any written evidence, "why was it written? why was it 'published'?" This is paramount because "what any given society asks or fails to ask, records or fails to record, by itself offers an important clue to the nature of that society."[19]

Finley goes beyond Collingwood, at least insofar as he names and conceptualizes the beast – ideology – that lurks in the margins of Collingwood's texts. Yet both he and Collingwood fail to explore sufficiently the implications for people who write about history (be they novelists or historians) of the limits and relativity inherent in ideology in all its senses. To say that each generation must find its own historical truth, or that the historian must consciously articulate his "conceptual context," provides little in the way of theory or a program for action.

Fredric Jameson, an American cultural critic, offers both the theory and the program. Though a Marxist, he implicitly rejects the claim that Marxism furnishes a scientific means of attaining the truth about the past – that it explodes the "false consciousness" of earlier ideologies (ii), yet remains immune itself to the conditioning effects of making its observations at a certain point in history. Rather, he finds that Marxism can transcend other ideologies precisely because it takes history (that is, ideology enacted) as its object of study. All ideologies (i) contain elements of truth and, indeed, resemble Marxism in that they express at bottom a salvational or Utopian impulse. But they are "strategies of containment,"[20] not because they limit salvation or citizenship in Utopia to the chosen, but because they keep certain matters from consciousness. This unconscious material, as it affects behavior, assumes the guise of Necessity. It seems, in spite of its historical origins, to be given – simply "the way things are." Society, through ideology, works hard to maintain this illusion; for when repressed material breaks through, instability or chaos can result.

Jameson's adaptation, in *The Political Unconscious*, of Freudian psychoanalytic theory to a cultural context is restricted to method. For Jameson, Freudianism is not a body of timeless truths; rather, its continuing value lies in Freud's insights into the mechanism of repression, and in his development of an interpretive system to ferret out and bring to light what has been repressed or denied. The Freudian analyst, far from accepting at face value the patient's statements about himself, looks for latent meanings in them. Such meanings spring up when a repressed set of drives or energies (the unconscious) exists in a troubled, antagonistic relation to an overt structure (consciousness) that has the task of keeping the repressed invisible and masking or containing its eruptions. We never see the unconscious directly, but instead infer it from what can be seen and analyzed. By coming to an awareness of previously unknown influences on our behavior – in other words, by discovering the causes of Necessity and thereby unmasking it as such – we gain the possibility of freedom from such internal determinants. They may still affect but no longer need determine our actions. We can choose.

The person who wins such potential liberation through psychoanalysis exists not just as an individual, though, but as a member of society, and so remains subject to social (as well as natural) Necessity. Jameson posits a collective unconscious – we might call it a cultural or ideological as well as a political unconscious – which accounts for the given and seemingly necessary on the social level. It consists in repressed energies derived from historical contradictions which are unacknowledged or denied in a society's conscious existence. Again, we cannot look at this unconscious directly as an object of study, yet we can infer its nature from the inevitable signs and symptoms of repression. Jameson derives this kind of "symptomatic analysis" not only from Freud but from Marx – whose genius, according to Engels, lay in treating as questions what everyone else took to be solutions – and ultimately from Hegel, whose dialectic of thesis and antithesis presumes that any solution or resolution must always be incomplete. As with Freudian psychoanalysis, though, the goal is to reveal the roots of outwardly causeless imperatives and to enable us to make choices not even seen as existing before. Thus Jameson offers an answer to the question, scarcely addressed by historians because scarcely perceived, of how we gain knowledge of the past when it has shaped our present in ways unknown to us which we experience as Necessity.

Jameson assigns narrative a key part in his analytic procedure. History (past events) comes to us through the medium of history (accounts of past events). Even unwritten historical evidence, for Jameson, has an implicit narrative structure. If we perceive the world in the shape of stories, then there arises the issue of interpretation. We cannot read narratives without interpreting them, and interpretation cannot occur without a framework provided by ideology. As remarked by Droysen, Collingwood, and Finley, we cannot recognize evidence as such without a pre-existing conceptual system that invests it with significance. Hence the problem of getting around or going beyond the system. Sensing this problem, Collingwood advocated cross-examining one's authorities to "extort" from them information they did not originally intend to yield, and Finley prescribed stepping "behind the text" to ask questions that the text itself fails to pose. In a much broader context, dealing with reality in general as well as history books, Jameson outlines a technique for doing this. We unmask the givens and uncover the hidden assumptions of any ideology (history being, for both Collingwood and Jameson, human thought or ideology [i] enacted) by interpreting or reinterpreting its narratives in terms of their latent rather than overt meanings. This results, to be sure, in another narrative. But to make such a narrative involves a re-emplotting and hence a transforming of the past, with significant consequences for both present and future. Although we never quite attain absolute historical truth – history, ultimately, is for Jameson a transcendent category which no narrative can comprehend[21] – we can to some extent free ourselves of the chains of our past.

Concerning the implications of Jameson's thinking on narrative, Hayden White comments:

Human beings can will backward as well as forward in time; willing backward occurs when we rearrange accounts of events in the past that have been emplotted in a given way, in order to endow them with a different meaning or to draw from the new emplotment reasons for acting differently in the future from the way we have become accustomed to acting in our present.[22]

To put it in psychoanalytic terms, the patient, having brought to light and understood some of the unconscious causes of his actions, re-emplots his life history so as to change the meaning not only of those actions but of the entire context in which they occurred.[23] Thus he becomes able to avoid neurotically repeating the past, and can live a truly new plot in the present, devoting to it that formidable flow of energy formerly channeled into repressing an awareness of threatening conflicts or contradictions in his thoughts and behavior. Jameson sets as a goal a similar process on the communal level. We cannot touch, look at, or directly engage the unconscious and absent causes of a society's history, but we can infer them by analyzing the succession of narratives they have generated, including overarching master narratives. The resulting new narrative does not free us of the past or causality in any absolute sense. It does, though, represent a past we have chosen, rather than one determined for us by unknown causes, and it makes possible a different, far more consciously created future.

Jameson's thinking invests with great, almost unbearable importance the role of the historian or literary critic or any analyst of the narrativized past. Such an analyst is, potentially, a liberator – a participant in what Jameson's master narrative depicts as "the collective struggle to wrest a realm of Freedom from a realm of Necessity."[24] But, as critics of Jameson have pointed out, there are problems with his totalizing vision of Marxism as the science of history. This vision (like that conceptual framework which Droysen, Collingwood, and Finley cite as a prerequisite for historical thought) is a priori; it requires belief before it can be used to analyze and subsume competing ideologies. Without such a belief, we can applaud Jameson's injunction "Always historicize!"[25] yet must recognize the potential limitations of the historicizer, who arguably cannot see (or see clearly) everything within the horizon of history because of the shadow cast by her position within her own historical moment.

Another problem with Jameson's theory has to do with language. Even though he describes his predominant practice, interpretation, as "an essentially allegorical act, which consists in rewriting a given text in terms of a particular interpretive master code," he nonetheless relies on the potential of words to represent reality accurately or adequately. The "problem of representation, and most particularly of the representation of History ... is essentially a narrative problem, a question of the adequacy of any storytelling framework in which History might be represented."[26] That is, we can properly represent historical events and characters by locating them within the right master narrative. Yet historical narrative, though its referent (the past) can be seen as existing or having existed beyond the realm of words, is itself contained within language. This fact raises, as White points out, the issue of the rhetoricity of history. Moreover, history (accounts of the past) can even be said to originate in language. And language, as demonstrated by Jacques Derrida, is a far more slippery thing than the rhetoricians ever dreamed: no word or series of words has a single, unitary, absolute meaning, but rather is defined in relation to other words in an endless sequence of differing meanings (*différance*)[27] which cannot be made to stand alone through reference to a reality outside language. For a deconstructionist no storytelling framework, such as Jameson's Marxian master narrative, can solve the problem of representing history, since all stories and histories remain trapped within the airless closure of language. History, from this point of view, is not a transcendent category; and historical discourse, regardless of the investigative methods behind it, is caught forever in a cloud of linguistic uncertainty, unable to break free into the sunshine of clear fixed truth.

One could, however, turn on its head this view of the post-structuralist prisonhouse of language. Instead of closure, we might see an infinite semiotic openness; instead of entrapment, we might see freedom – at least a freedom from absolutist concepts and ideologies. It is this idea of freedom or liberation which links Joyce's attitudes toward history and language, and provides a common ground for both Jamesonian and Derridean perspectives on his work. Joyce struggled throughout his adult life to wrest a realm of freedom from history; though this was above all a struggle to save himself, we do find, in his fiction from *Dubliners* to *Finnegans Wake*, a liberating impulse directed toward the consciousness of his readers. Jameson's theories provide a tool for investigating the successes and failures of this monumental war of liberation. At the same time, however, Joyce's works increasingly localize (and universalize) the conflict within language. From the "Sirens" episode of *Ulysses* on, the word tends to become the world, and referentiality becomes ever more problematic. Stephen's desire in *A Portrait* to escape the nets of family, country, and religion, whose effects on his growing mind are precisely delineated, is replaced in the second half of *Ulysses* and in the *Wake* by a generalized desire to escape the authority of the word and the imprisonment of narrative. Here Joyce's project contradicts Jameson's, since the latter implies that, without narrative, the possibility of freedom (through reconstructing the past) would not exist.

We have arrived at an impasse, then, which is still being argued passionately today in a debate that Joyce's art prefigures. I myself lean toward a program of ideological activism, based in part on Jameson's theories, that aims to change our lives (and our descendants' lives) by changing the way we think about history. Like many other readers, I feel reluctant to accept the all-encompassing horizon of his Marxian master narrative; yet his major theme – the struggle to achieve freedom – seems to me as irresistible as the human need for a narrativized system of beliefs. We cannot, in contrast, speak of the master narrative of deconstruction, which is a method of interrogating idealist philosophical ideas and practices; nor can we speak of its program of action. Because of its focus on language, it has been charged with a denial of history; and because of its refusal to take a position of its own or do anything but subvert other positions, including those which oppose the established order, it has been charged with a tendency to foster political paralysis. But deconstruction has other political implications that potentially lend it to left-wing activism. It emphasizes

plurality over authoritarian unity, a disposition to criticize rather than to obey, a rejection of the logic of power and domination in all their forms, an advocation of difference against identity, and a questioning of state universalism. It ... argues for the flawed and structurally incomplete, if not contradictory, nature of all attempts at absolute or total philosophic systems.[28]

Thus no discourse can be accorded ontological privilege. Any position – that of Marxism or Catholicism or any other – is self-divided, and its claims to authority are self-contradictory.

How to reconcile these seemingly contrary implications of deconstruction – and of Joyce's art – is beyond the scope of my book. So, too, is the question of how to frame a discourse, deprived not only of any "transcendental guarantees"[29] but of a clear relation to history, which nonetheless can powerfully, self-confidently intervene in history.[30] I will, however, attempt to trace the evolution of Joyce's own narrative interventions in history, which began with the word's attempt to change the world and ended with the collapsing of the world into the word.

CHAPTER I

The murders in the park

It has been said that although God cannot alter the past, historians can.

Samuel Butler, *Erewhon*

At sunset on the sixth of May 1882, an Irishman and an Englishman strolled together beside a carriageway in Dublin's Phoenix Park among crowds of citizens enjoying the warm Saturday evening. A group of four men approached and parted to let them pass. Then, with the cry "Ah, you villain!" one of the four stabbed the tall, gaunt, gray-haired Irishman in the back. Other blows followed. The four men leapt onto a red jaunting car which took off at a furious gallop towards the Chapelizod Gate. Their two victims lay on the roadway, the Irishman dead, the tall, dark-bearded Englishman dying. Within minutes they were identified as Thomas Henry Burke and Lord Frederick Cavendish. The latter had been sworn in that afternoon as Chief Secretary for Ireland; his companion and deputy had been for many years Permanent Under-Secretary. Perhaps, as they strolled, the two had been discussing their duties as Ireland's top administrators.

The assassination of high officials was unheard of in Ireland at that time, although it had been for several years a well-publicized menace in many European countries, resulting fourteen months earlier in the death of Czar Alexander II. Black-bordered cards thrust into the letter-boxes of three Dublin newspapers bore the message: "Executed by order of the Irish Invincibles." But who were the Invincibles? The newspapers, which rushed out special editions, didn't know; nor did the authorities in Dublin Castle, seat of England's colonial government in Ireland. Many people witnessed the murders; but most of them thought they were seeing a scuffle and remembered few details – some of which proved inaccurate. Rumors flew. American Fenians were immediately suspected, partly because of the theory that the long, sharp weapons used were bowie knives, partly because of eyewitness accounts that the assassins resembled Americans. At the same time, though, the weapons could have been butcher knives; this possibility plus the fact that Burke's throat had been cut led police to investigate all Dublin butchers with Fenian connections.

Actually, confusion and rumors notwithstanding, Detective Superintendent Mallon had a shrewd idea of who the killers were from the start. By chance he had visited the park an hour before the murders occurred. He was on his way to meet an underworld informant, from whom he had received an urgent message, when he stopped to talk to a plain-clothes man; the latter reported that he had spotted several nationalist extremists among the crowds. Worried about walking into a trap, and in any event feeling pinched by his new boots, Mallon left his informant waiting in the park and went straight home.

The extremists noticed by the plain-clothes man included James Carey, Patrick Delaney, and Joe Brady. These three and a handful of nearby loiterers made up about one quarter of the Irish National Invincibles – a tiny band that had no official ties with other nationalist groups, including the Fenians. (I use the term "Fenian" loosely, outside the context of the 1858–67 movement, to refer to advocates of armed revolution; in 1882 it would have designated chiefly the Irish Republican Brotherhood.) Though undoubtedly influenced by the upsurge of European terrorism, the Invincibles were a homegrown product. They ranged in age from twenty to fifty and belonged largely to the lower-middle classes. Most were craftsmen and tradesmen; the two young men who wielded the knives, Joe Brady and Timothy Kelly, were a stonecutter and a coachbuilder, respectively. An exception, James Carey, was a prosperous middle-aged builder and an owner of slum tenements who six months later would be elected on a nationalist platform to the Dublin Corporation as a town councillor.

The three-man, London-based Directory which organized the Invincibles began recruiting in Dublin around the beginning of 1882. A key member, Frank Byrne – Secretary of the British branch of the Land League, a nationalist agrarian organization – helped the gang procure some surgical knives with twelve-inch blades, which his pregnant wife smuggled across the Irish Sea concealed in her skirts. The Invincibles' first target was Lord Frederick's stern, much-hated predecessor as Chief Secretary, William "Buckshot" Forster (so nicknamed because he ordered constables to use buckshot in lieu of regular ammunition). Their several attempts on his life during March and April failed through a combination of bad luck and ineptitude. They made up for these failures on 6 May by killing Burke and Cavendish. Ironically, Cavendish was a far more flexible and conciliatory man than Forster, and he had brought with him Prime Minister Gladstone's promise of better things to come for Ireland – a result of secret negotiations with Charles Stewart Parnell, leader of the nationalist Irish MPs, a key minority in Parliament.

Superintendent Mallon, who perhaps could have prevented the murders had he stayed in the park long enough for the conspirators to spot his well-known face, slowly pulled in a dragnet that ensnared most of the Dublin Invincibles by the end of January 1883. The Crown's case appeared to be mainly circumstantial. Then one of the two Invincible drivers, Michael Kavanagh, in whose jaunting car Brady, Kelly, and two others had escaped, became an "approver" and testified against his fellows. A week later the prominent James Carey T.C. followed suit.

At this point the popular view of the trial shifted. The chief issue, in spite of the general distaste for the crime itself, became betrayal. Carey was seen to be working for the English oppressor against a band of brave if misguided patriots. *The Irishman* called Joe Brady "a sincere lion-hearted enthusiast" while describing Carey as "a Hypocrite and a cunning coward."[1] In contrast to the turncoat, Kavanagh, stood the true-blue figure of the other getaway driver, "Skin-the-Goat" Fitzharris.

Hangings – five in all – began with Brady's on 14 May 1883 and ended three weeks later with that of the twenty-year-old Kelly. Foreshadowing the aftermath of the Easter 1916 Rising, this prolonged series of executions aroused much sympathy for the victims and indignation against the authorities. Their deaths transformed them from villains into nationalist heroes. The detested Carey sailed for South Africa; an Irish American Fenian who happened to be aboard discovered his identity, shot him to death, and was later hanged for this much-applauded act. Unlike Irish popular opinion, the English attitude towards the Invincibles did not evolve. It continued to be one of fascinated horror; and in late Victorian times visitors to Madame Tussaud's wax museum had the opportunity to stare, shivering, at "a tableau of the Phoenix Park murders displaying the true jaunting car purchased from the informer Kavanagh and . . . a pair of 'long dissecting or amputating knives' bought from the London surgical supply house that had sold the murder weapons themselves."[2]

NO DEFINITIVE ACCOUNT

I have drawn most of my information above from Tom Corfe's book (1968) on the Phoenix Park murders. I tried to give a straightforward account based on as many hard facts as possible. Still, even my first paragraph contains the surmise: "Perhaps . . . the two had been discussing their duties." Nobody really knows the subject of the deep conversation in which, according to witnesses, the two men had been engaged. This is hardly an important detail of the murders; but, as the event was reconstructed by investigators at the time and by Corfe eight decades later, many other details – some crucial – remained obscure. Was there a link between the Invincibles and the leadership of the Irish Parliamentary Party? Had they planned to kill the new Chief Secretary or just Burke? Were they trying to sabotage the improved prospects of constitutional nationalism implied by the Kilmainham treaty?

Even today we know little more than that shrewd detective, Superintendent Mallon, eventually uncovered. Consider Corfe's comment on the information available: "It is evidence riddled with doubt and untruth, vagueness and confusion, evidence which permits of no definitive account . . . and which leaves much still hidden in mystery."[3] Much of Corfe's book, in fact, plumbs these ambiguous depths, so that his account becomes a practical exercise in historical epistemology even while he attempts to tell a coherent story and base on it a broad conclusion.

Take the role, both in history and historiography, of the mysterious Invincible "Number One" (as he was called briefly in the headlines), Patrick Tynan. After fleeing to America, Tynan wrote one of the two inside accounts of the Invincibles. It advanced three propositions. He portrayed himself as a master plotter and a hero of the war against England. He maintained that the assassination of Cavendish was a gambit in that war and not, as most people believed, a tragic accident. And he accused the Home Rulers in Parliament, Parnell's Irish Party, of betraying a vigorous organization, the Invincibles, which they themselves had inspired and backed.

The medium Tynan used to convey his message was a fluent, melodramatic prose, full of portentousness and invective, that requires quotation to be appreciated. Consider his account of Mrs. Brady's visit to her son on the day before his hanging:

The lying slanders circulated by the usurper's detectives and hirelings, against these imprisoned Irishmen, had horrified this Spartan Irish mother. The supposed eagerness of these men to supply the enemy with information that would lead to future captures, and aid him in breaking up the INVINCIBLE organisation ... caused her patriot soul to recoil with indignation at the vile slander. When final leave-taking came, and she was taking her last look upon her heroic offspring, struggling with her grief, she cried out to him: "Joe, if you know anything don't tell it; bring your secret to the grave." Joseph Brady was worthy of such a mother; Mrs. Brady deserved such a noble son.[4]

We can scarcely judge the substance of Tynan's argument by its style, yet we cannot separate the two, either. The style suggests a lurid, highly partisan sensibility. At the same time his perspective seems as privileged as that of an omniscient narrator in a novel. How did Tynan, who was in America at the time, know what Mrs. Brady felt or said? *The Irish National Invincibles and Their Times* purports to be history – it isn't simply a record of one patriot's thoughts and feelings, such as John Mitchel's *Jail Journal* – but its style and its wide, undocumented range of information and assertions indicate it to be something else.

Not surprisingly, Corfe, an academically oriented historian who provides his readers with notes and a bibliography, attacks Tynan's book. He begins by demonstrating the shallowness and vagueness of its evidence. Then he offers an alternative picture of Tynan – who "was short, plump, round-faced and bewhiskered, and ... wore a pince-nez"[5] – as a drab commercial traveler with a vivid imagination who was enlisted by the Invincibles at a late stage to carry messages to and fro across the Irish Sea. Understandably, his argument relies on intelligent speculation rather than documents (as he observes, secret terrorist societies do not keep detailed records). He also bolsters his argument rhetorically by appealing to the reader's sense of the ludicrous in dwelling on his subject's unheroic appearance and social insignificance.

As for the alleged involvement of the Irish Parliamentary Party,

Corfe points out that Tynan's sole contact with the Invincible Directory in England was the Land League Secretary, Byrne. Again he emphasizes Tynan's vanity and impressionability. He admits that Patrick Egan, in charge of the Land League's Paris funds, probably provided the Invincibles with money. And the reins of the League, to be sure, were held by the Irish Party's leader, Parnell. But he cites the findings of the British Special Commission which, in spite of a strong will to do otherwise, exonerated Parnell of any intimacy with the Invincibles. Perhaps, he suggests, Parnell's ambiguity on the topic of violent nationalist action encouraged Egan and Byrne to go off on their own. He makes a convincing if ultimately unprovable case.

Tynan's proposition that Lord Frederick was murdered on purpose, which contradicted popular opinion, prompts Corfe to take a surprising tack. He points up the slenderness of the facts supporting the "accidental" theory and "the legend . . . that Cavendish had been killed because he gallantly leapt to defend his companion with his umbrella."[6] He explains why Irish and English public sentiment, for different reasons, favored this theory, and why the Irish police and Gladstone embraced it. He shows how James Carey may well have found it expedient to testify that he was "astounded when he heard that it was Lord Frederick Cavendish who was killed."[7] Then, after posing two questions which the "accidental" theory does not address, he concludes:

It is impossible . . . to say with a certainty that Cavendish's death was an accident; there would seem to be much that is more easily explicable if one assumes that the story of Tynan, despite its absurdities and pomposities, has a basis of truth, and that Lord Frederick Cavendish was the victim of a deliberate and successful plot, albeit one that had been hastily improvised at the last moment. If we accept this as a possibility it becomes necessary to consider whether the crime was intended as a deliberate answer to the new Anglo-Irish understanding, a blow aimed at the Gladstone–Parnell rapprochement.[8]

In other words, Tynan – that self-glorifying go-between whose "evidence is of very doubtful value"[9] – may have been essentially right on a key point. At this juncture Corfe reconstructs the day before the murders, trying to separate the truth from the misperceptions of Tynan's account. That "eager little man"[10] and the Dublin Invincibles received a message that day. Although it no doubt emanated from Byrne, they assumed it had come from high-level members of the Irish Party, and they misread its words of general encouragement to mean that Chief Secretary Forster's departure did not change the Invincibles' assignment to assassinate Castle officials. They didn't know that Parnell, just released from Kilmainham jail, had joined Gladstone in a tentative agreement – the so-called Kilmainham treaty – to take constructive steps toward Home Rule for Ireland. In any event, they certainly would have opposed such an agreement. Further, they were enraged by news that day of the "Ballina massacre" – the shooting by constables in County Mayo of boys parading with tin whistles and cans to celebrate Parnell's release. For these reasons, Corfe argues, it is likely that they formed a last-minute plan to murder Cavendish as well as Burke.

Corfe, in admitting one of Tynan's main propositions, is plainly doing more than just searching for the truth, which he acknowledges cannot be pinned down. He needs to show that the Phoenix Park murders were not just another of the spectacular yet impotent acts of violence punctuating Irish history. The Invincibles, he writes, "helped to ensure that the hated enemy would remain in control of their land for another forty years."[11] If they killed Cavendish intentionally, and if they were hostile on principle to the sort of gradual, limited emancipation presaged by the Kilmainham treaty, then we have a clear-cut conflict between two primary currents of Irish nationalism – a conflict between assassins and politicians, between advocates of physical force and advocates of constitutional change – that would be muddled were the Chief Secretary's murder an accident. This conflict provides Corfe with a central theme, summarized in his final paragraph:

We can never know what would have come of Kilmainham. The men of sane vision on both sides, the men who believed in a new Ireland to be made by Irishmen working in co-operation with Englishmen, were given no chance ... to work out their plans. That this was so, that their momentary glimpse of a harmonious future for Ireland so quickly vanished, was a result of the actions of the Irish National Invincibles and of the murders in Phoenix Park, a classic demonstration of the utter futility of assassination as a political weapon.[12]

We see that Corfe's theme, which shapes his book and results in this conclusion, relies on a relationship between the may-have-been and the might-have-been. He draws on a discredited account, Tynan's, to support the likelihood that the Invincibles murdered the new Chief Secretary in order to thwart constitutional nationalism. He then speculates on the possible "harmonious future" which might have come into being from the Kilmainham treaty except for Cavendish's assassination. In other words, the Phoenix Park murders may well have changed the long-range course of Irish history.

May have. We don't know, of course; neither does Corfe, as he acknowledges. In fact, though his book does not mention this, the Kilmainham treaty continued in effect after the murders, and Gladstone did introduce a Home Rule bill four years later. The House of Commons voted it down; what effect, if any, lingering memories of the Invincibles had on this defeat we cannot say. A few years later, a greater drama than that of Phoenix Park unfolded – the fall of Parnell. This debacle split the Irish Party and its backers, and, according to most historians, injured the prospects for Home Rule far more gravely than the actions of the Invincibles had done. But, if Parnell had not fallen, would he have achieved Home Rule for Ireland in the end? This much-debated question leads us back into the realm of the might-have-been to which students of history, especially Irish history, so often make side excursions. Again, we just don't know. It is hard enough to determine in all its detail what *did* happen and why it happened.

It is disconcerting to turn from Corfe's book to the chapter called "Bakhunism in Phoenix Park" in Malcolm Brown's *The Politics of Irish Literature*, which appeared a few years later. First, there are the minor discrepancies. Joe Brady, a "paviour" and an "unskilled labourer"[13] for Corfe, becomes a "stonemason" and an "artisan"[14] for Brown (presumably due to differences in interpreting Brady's job as a cutter of paving-stones for the Dublin Corporation). Both authors recount in detail the escape route of Kavanagh's jaunting car; for Corfe it ends at "Davy's tavern in Upper Leeson Street,"[15] while for Brown it ends at "Davis' public house in Leeson Park."[16] Corfe lists twenty-six accused Invincibles rounded up by the police during January and February 1883; Brown tells us that twenty-seven were arrested in January. Small beer, perhaps. More serious are differences between the two accounts of the murders. Brown presents as fact – "When Cavendish tried to rescue his companion, he too was stabbed to death"[17] – what Corfe asserts to be "legend."[18] Further, he bypasses Corfe's vexed issue of whether the Invincibles intended to kill Cavendish. Finally, he concludes that the murders, far from quelling an unprecedented opportunity for constitutional nationalism, merely proved a temporary setback: "Though strained, the Kilmainham treaty ... survived the Phoenix Park crisis."[19] (Máire and Conor Cruise O'Brien offer a third view: "It is possible that this 'Kilmainham treaty' might have seriously injured Parnell's authority with the Irish majority ... had it not been for the shock administered by the Phoenix Park murders.")[20]

I do not intend here to apportion degrees of historical truth among Tynan, Corfe, and Brown or to discuss their differing perspectives – that of a participant and imaginative memoirist, that of a historian, and that of a professor of literature. But I want to emphasize the slippery, protean nature of the thing – history – which they try to capture and render into a fixed form. And I would like to point out certain consistencies among their accounts, themes they have in common despite their differences. For all three the commanding, enigmatic figure of Parnell is the principal offstage player in the drama of the murders. The incubus of English rule motivates the drama. The tight sequence – Kilmainham treaty/murders/Irish Party denunciation of the murders – embodies at once the close ties and the long-standing conflict between constitutional nationalism and physical-force nationalism. There hovers a sense of cyclical violence, stemming from the remotest past, between the representatives of Irish nationalism and those of British colonialism. However ambiguous and malleable this past may be, certain basic aspects of it – the defeat of James II at the Battle of the Boyne, the Famine, the killings in Phoenix Park and the ensuing hangings – are in themselves stark and unchangeable and overwhelmingly negative. The only escape from them leads into the realm of legend, fiction, and the might-have-been. In different ways, Tynan, Corfe, and Brown all concern themselves with this realm, which has a close connection with Irish history.

THE INVINCIBLES IN *ULYSSES*

Approximately three months before Joe Brady's surgical knife passed between Under-Secretary Burke's ribs and pierced the left ventricle of his heart, May and John Joyce had their second child. He grew up in an atmosphere charged with politics and with family and national history. While Ireland was still languishing in the problematic colonial status brought about by the Act of Union

(1800), he began his most famous work of fiction. It was published seven years later on his fortieth birthday in 1922. By that time, the Easter 1916 Rising, World War I, and the Anglo-Irish War had occurred, and the new Irish Free State was about to be shaken by civil war.

The Phoenix Park murders first enter Leopold Bloom's thoughts after he has stepped into All Hallows Church in "Lotus Eaters":

> That fellow that turned queen's evidence on the invincibles he used to receive the, Carey was his name, the communion every morning. This very church. Peter Carey, yes. No, Peter Claver I am thinking of. Denis Carey. And just imagine that. Wife and six children at home. And plotting that murder all the time. (*U* 5.378–82)

Twenty-two years have passed since the murders, which took place when Bloom was sixteen. Not surprisingly, his memory is faulty. He forgets James Carey's first name and confuses him with his brother, Peter, a belated, minor member of the Invincibles. Then, aware of his trouble in remembering, he compounds the confusion by imagining that Peter Carey's name has occurred to him because of its similarity to Peter Claver, the Jesuit saint, of whom he was thinking a little earlier.[21] Yet he is quite correct in general and even in the detail of the six children. A couple of hours later, at lunchtime, he even hits on the right first name – "that Peter or Denis or James Carey that blew the gaff on the Invincibles" (*U* 8.442–43) – although he forgets it again in his wee-hours fatigue at the cabman's shelter.[22]

The Invincibles' fading exploit is recalled with similar correctness and confusion in the newspaper episode. The garrulous old editor of *The Evening Telegraph*, Myles Crawford, reminisces to Stephen Dedalus about Ignatius Gallaher's scoop in using a code to cable the route of the getaway vehicle to a New York paper:

> That was the smartest piece of journalism ever known. That was in eightyone, sixth of May, time of the invincibles, murder in the Phoenix park ... I'll show you.
>
> He pushed past them to the files.
>
> —Look at here, he said turning. The *New York World* cabled for a special ... Where it took place. Tim Kelly, or Kavanagh I mean. Joe Brady and the rest of them. Where Skin-the-Goat drove the car. Whole route, see?
>
> —Skin-the-Goat, Mr O'Madden Burke said. Fitzharris. He has that cabman's shelter, they say, down there at Butt bridge. (*U* 7.631–42)

After an interruption, Crawford uses a newspaper ad to chart the escape route:

—F to P is the route Skin-the-Goat drove the car for an alibi, Inchicore, Roundtown, Windy Arbour, Palmerston Park, Ranelagh. F.A.B.P. Got that? X is Davy's publichouse in upper Leeson street. (*U* 7.667–69)

Then two other characters delightedly note the summonsing of some street vendors in Phoenix Park after the Lord Lieutenant's wife, Lady Dudley, "thought she'd buy a view of Dublin ... [a]nd it turned out to be a commemoration postcard of Joe Brady or Number One or Skin-the-Goat" (*U* 7.702–03).

Though close to the truth, the editor gets almost all of his details wrong.[23] The murders occurred not in 1881 but 1882, and Gallaher couldn't have managed his scoop until early 1883 after Invincible approvers started talking to Superintendent Mallon. Tim Kelly – Crawford has the name right the first time, then falls into error – was one of the two killers. Michael Kavanagh, in his jaunting car, drove the circuitous getaway route; Skin-the-Goat Fitzharris acted as the decoy and used his four-wheeled cab (not a jaunting car) to carry a group of Invincibles other than the murderers straight back into downtown Dublin.

In "Eumaeus," Bloom and Stephen visit the cabman's shelter mentioned by O'Madden Burke. Bloom does not exactly confirm Burke's second-hand report that Skin-the-Goat (fifty at the time of the murders, sentenced to life imprisonment, and released after many years thanks to the Amnesty Association) is alive and well, and in charge of this establishment. Rather, he whispers to Stephen that "the keeper [is] said to be the once famous Skin-the-Goat, Fitzharris, the invincible, though he could not vouch for the actual facts which quite possibly there is not one vestige of truth in" (*U* 16.323–25). Later, when a conversation about knives leads to the park stabbings, the keeper's "inscrutable face ... conveyed the impression that he didn't understand one jot of what was going on" (*U* 16.598–600). The Bloomish narrator remains poised in doubt throughout the episode, referring to "Skin-the-Goat, assuming he was he" and "the licensee of the place rumored to be or have been Fitzharris, the famous invincible" (*U* 16.985, 1043–44). When the keeper spouts revolutionary rhetoric in an argument with the sailor, W. B. Murphy, the narrator doubts the identities of both men and even suspects the keeper of being an instigator who might inform on people siding with him.

The flesh-and-blood Skin-the-Goat (so named because of how he used a pet goat to pay off a debt) was "an ugly, whiskery, jaunty, picturesque figure in a shabby black overcoat, a jarvey's waistcoat, and a red neckerchief"[24] whom the newspapers described as "looking like Father Christmas"[25] because of his white whiskers and ruddy nose. Hardly a nondescript person. Middle-aged and older Dubliners who had followed the Phoenix Park case presumably would have been able to make a shrewd guess as to the identity of the celebrated Invincible had he really returned to civic life in the guise of the keeper of a cabman's shelter. Reasonably, Bloom doubts that this is the genuine article. And, by imagining him as a possible provocateur, he turns the keeper into an antiself of the real Fitzharris, who steadfastly defied the authorities. Still, he never decides once and for all that this isn't, this couldn't be Skin-the-Goat. The possibility remains open.

Joyce, as Robert Adams remarks, delighted in having his characters display their imperfect historical memories, especially when they come to the right conclusions anyway. That is how the Phoenix Park murders enter *Ulysses* – through the faulty recollections of the aging editor, Crawford. The realm of historical fact, which we are taught to regard as firm and fixed, becomes somewhat fluid in Crawford's reminiscences. Bloom, too, often remembers his history hazily. But the introduction of "the pseudo Skin-the-etcetera" (*U* 16.1070) in person injects a new element – living history or, rather, pseudo-history. Like the shadowy Number One, Tynan, he seems to be "another of those dubious Irish hero-claimants, floating in limbo between imposture and honor."[26] He is real and unreal, factual and fictional, and cannot be explained away as can Bloom's confusion over James Carey or Crawford's muddling of dates.

Skin-the-Goat's reincarnation bothers Bloom, who would have preferred finality: "He ought to have died naturally or on the scaffold high. Like actresses, always farewell positively last performance then come up smiling again" (*U* 16.1071–73). He is also bothered by the keeper's patriotic peroration, delivered in a windy style befitting the Citizen, on Ireland's natural resources and England's imminent downfall. The bold, colorful Fitzharris who stood in the dock in 1883 was not recorded to have been a blatherer. Nevertheless, his bombastic revenant in 1904 is an alter ego, another self who coexists with and enters into dialogue with the original. What were the "real" Fitzharris's opinions, anyway? Perhaps, had he voiced them, they would have sounded as banal as those expressed by the keeper. Perhaps the sort of person who joins a terrorist group and takes part in violent, spectacular actions typically has a narrow, second-hand world-view. Joyce's portrayal of this suspect Skin-the-Goat redux – a fictional character whose identity as a historical personage is doubted by a largely reliable narrator-character – tends to engender such speculations. Bloom wonders if the keeper is really who he is supposed to be. We may well wonder if the "formidable cab-driver Fitzharris,"[27] the prisoner who knew how to hold his tongue, was really what received historical memory depicts him to be. In any case we sense that Joyce was out to destabilize this historical memory.

Setting aside his doubts as to the 1904 Skin-the-Goat, Bloom thinks admiringly of the 1882 version as

a man who had actually brandished a knife, cold steel, with the courage of his political convictions (though, personally, he would never be a party to any such thing), off the same bat as those love vendettas of the south, have her or swing for her, when the husband ... inflicted fatal injuries on his adored one as a result of an alternative postnuptial *liaison* by plunging his knife into her. (*U* 16.1058–65)

He has forgotten for a moment that Skin-the-Goat was one of the drivers and not one of the stabbers. Still, though the passage does not apply properly to Fitzharris, it does link two other figures in the Phoenix Park affair, Joe Brady and Charles Stewart Parnell, through its intertwining of love, politics, and murder.

The symbol assigned to the "Eumaeus" episode is the sailor, but it might more appropriately be the knife. The motif begins when the self-described rover, Murphy, tells of seeing a man stabbed in the back in Trieste. He displays a "dangerouslooking claspknife" (*U* 16.578) to illustrate his story. The narrator refers to it as a stiletto, which prompts an unnamed speaker to recollect one of the initial rumors concerning the assassinations of Burke and Cavendish: "That was why they thought the park murders of the invincibles was done by foreigners on account of them using knives" (*U* 16.590–92). Later Stephen asks Bloom to take away a table knife; associating it with Julius Caesar, he says, "I can't look at the point of it. It reminds me of Roman history" (*U* 16.816). That "stab-in-the-back touch" (*U* 16.865) figures once more in "Eumaeus" before Bloom expresses his mistaken admiration for Skin-the-Goat as a man who has brandished cold steel on political principle.

Joe Brady and Tim Kelly, to be sure, wielded the steel in question. Of the two, the solemn, barrel-chested, hugely strong Brady seems to have best captured the public's imagination, as suggested by the "commemoration postcard" mentioned in the *Evening Telegraph* office. Unmistakably he caught Joyce's imagination. He makes his major appearance in *Ulysses* in "Cyclops" when Joyce gives the grim subject of Brady's hanging a scabrous fictional twist. One of the pub hangers-on recounts the story that the corpse, on being cut down after the drop, exhibited a remarkable "upwards and outwards philoprogenitive erection *in articulo mortis per diminutionem capitis*" (*U* 12.477-78). Two narrative flights embellish this story over the next several pages. In the first one Bloom (transformed into a quack scientist) tenders a plausible medical explanation of this nonexistent phenomenon. The second, much longer digression details the preparations for the execution of a "hero martyr" with a "muscular bosom" (*U* 12.609, 638).

Admittedly, this figure represents more than just Brady. There are suggestions of Tim Kelly – the youthful former choirboy who spent his last night singing ballads such as "The Memory of the Past"[28] – in the Citizen's toast to "The memory of the dead" and the sweetheart's farewell to "her hero boy who went to his death with a song on his lips" (*U* 12.519, 644–45). And there are suggestions of Robert Emmet, victim of the most celebrated execution in Irish history, in the details of the hero's faithless sweetheart and the grisly disembowelling appliances.

It is Emmet who paves the way for Brady in the two preceding chapters, "Wandering Rocks" and "Sirens."[29] He appears first in the ironic context of Tom Kernan's thoughts. A converted Catholic but an Orangeman at heart, Kernan is en route to admire the cavalcade of the personification of British power in Ireland, Lord Lieutenant Dudley, when he spots the site where Emmet was punished for having led an abortive uprising in 1803: "Down there Emmet was hanged, drawn and quartered. Greasy black rope. Dogs licking the blood off the street when the lord lieutenant's wife drove by in her noddy" (*U* 10.764–66). Later, after supping at the Ormond restaurant, Bloom gazes at "a gallant pictured hero" (*U* 11.1274), Emmet, in a display window; his farts punctuate his reading of Emmet's famous last words.

Conflated with Brady in "Cyclops," Emmet's image undergoes further indignities when Joyce parodies the sentimental legend of his romance with Sarah Curran. Curran's refusal to flee with him to America contributed to his capture, and she assuaged her broken heart two years after his death by marrying an English officer. She provides the model for the "blushing bride elect" who flings herself on Brady–Emmet's bosom –

The hero folded her willowy form in a loving embrace murmuring fondly, *Sheila, my own.* Encouraged by this use of her Christian name she kissed passionately all the various suitable areas of his person which the decencies of prison garb permitted her ardour to reach. She swore to him as they mingled the salt streams of their tears that she would ever cherish his memory ... (*U* 12.639–44)

and then accepts an engagement ring in the form of a shamrock from "a handsome young Oxford graduate" (*U* 12.658–59).

Brady had no such sweetheart to titillate the popular imagination. But, as the virile leading man among the Invincibles, he himself caught the public eye. The gathering of emotional crowds outside Kilmainham prison on the morning of his hanging is reflected in the execution scene (absurdly inflated and melodramatically reported in a style rather like Tynan's) in "Cyclops"; and his physically imposing masculinity underlies the report, invented by Joyce, of his graphic potency after death. The whole episode brings out and undermines the union effected by sentimental patriots of hero-worship and eroticism – that is, "heroticism."[30]

The theme of heroticism, embodied in part by Brady, reaches its literal climax in "Circe" when the execution prepared in "Cyclops" takes place. This time the victim is identified as "the croppy boy" – hero of a ballad by that title about a rebel betrayed and hanged after the rising of 1798. It is this tune which Kernan, on his way to watch the viceregal cavalcade, is humming when he notes the site of Emmet's execution; and it is this song which the narrator of "Sirens," while Bloom sits in the Ormond restaurant just prior to his evocation of Emmet, mixes with highly sexualized thoughts and imagery, such as:

On the smooth jutting beerpull laid Lydia hand, lightly, plumply, leave it to my hands. All lost in pity for croppy. Fro, to: to, fro: over the polished knob ... her thumb and finger passed in pity: passed, reposed and, gently touching, then slid so smoothly, slowly down, a cool firm white enamel baton protruding through their sliding ring. (*U* 11.1112–17)

In "Circe" the croppy boy, already associated with Emmet, merges with both Emmet and Brady into a composite figure. The scene begins with a reminder of the gruesome *coup de grâce* dealt by Brady to Burke when the Citizen calls on God

To slit the throats
Of the English dogs
That hanged our Irish leaders.

Rumbold, the hangman-barber (modeled after the hangman
Marwood, exterminator of the Invincibles), reappears from
"Cyclops" to preside. He jerks the rope. As if to confirm the barfly's
report about Brady, a *"violent erection of the hanged sends gouts of sperm
spouting through his deathclothes on to the cobblestones"* (*U* 15.4548–49).
Three souvenir collectors (ironically, Anglo-Irish ladies who would
belong to Lord Dudley's set) recall the reverent souls who dipped
their handkerchiefs in Emmet's blood by using their own handkerchiefs to sop up the victim's semen. This scene highlights the
visceral horror overlooked by sentimental expressions of the nationalistic "death mystique";[31] it also reveals the sterility of the hero-
martyr.[32] The sexually charged violence inflicted by the authorities
on the patriot results in spilling the seeds of life, which frenzied
death-worshipers mop up. Wasted, too, are the seeds of the future –
the result of reenacting past violence and reliving the nightmare of
history from which Stephen Dedalus says he is trying to awake.

HISTORY AND FICTION

The Phoenix Park murders lie at the center of *Ulysses*, at least insofar
as Joyce uses the novel as a vehicle for a meditation on the nature of
history and of Irish history in particular. Though I have hardly
exhausted their ramifications in *Ulysses*, I have said enough to
consider the implications of Joyce's fictional treatment of them in
juxtaposition with the nonfiction accounts outlined above.

Let us go back now to Dublin's Phoenix Park on the evening of
6 May 1882. What happened there was real – all too real – even
though we have no direct, empirical knowledge of it. My opening
paragraph thus has a referent in reality which does not owe its
existence simply to my own or others' words. But I was able to
approach the murders of Cavendish and Burke solely through their
"prior textualization"[33] – that is, through the narratives of Tynan,
Corfe, Brown, and Joyce. (There are other "narratives" on the
assassinations – newspaper accounts, the attorney-general's speech
to the jury at Brady's trial, Superintendent Mallon's memoirs, etc. –
which I didn't use but would have done had this event been my
main topic.)

The only one of my authors with any immediate experience of the Phoenix Park affair, Patrick Tynan, spun a story around three themes having to do with his own importance, the purposefulness of the Chief Secretary's killing, and the intimate ties between the Invincibles and their treacherous sponsors, the Parnellite Home Rulers. Though he did not witness the murders, he wrote, as far as the Invincible conspiracy in general goes, a first-person participant history. Much of his impulse to write came as a reaction to prior narratives. The narrativization of the event had begun immediately after its occurrence with the eyewitness accounts taken down by detectives and with the rumors spread by word of mouth and in the press. The particular narrative that incensed Tynan and inspired his own, as he declares in his "Introduction," was that of Parnell in denouncing and disavowing the Invincibles. He also wanted to correct the reiterated story of Cavendish's accidental death. He saw his own story as a revolutionary one, recounted by a revolutionary hero:

In sending into the world a book of this nature, the writer ... expects to meet the usual opposition which prejudiced convictions will always array against the daring spirit who ventures to combat settled forms of thought. It was so with Galileo ... it was so with Columbus ... If it has been so with these immortal leaders ... how much more with the Irish Nationalist, who would try to draw his country's cause from the mass of misconception and falsehood that is struggling to smother it![34]

But Tynan's book falls down as history in a Rankean scientific sense because we suspect him of perpetrating his own misconception and falsehood. He fails because he does not support his main points with verifiable evidence – Collingwood's criterion for distinguishing the constructive imagination of the historian from that of the writer of fiction. We might also say that he fails to persuade us – a reminder of the Renaissance view of history as an exercise in rhetoric – in large part due to his feverish, unscholarly style. Yet the style can hardly be centrifuged out of the substance, and in any case a more useful procedure than criticizing it might be to look for what White calls "the content of the form." We would find, I think, a naïve expression of bourgeois nationalist ideology modeled after the narratives of third-rate editorials and political speeches and, to a lesser extent, shilling shockers.

Consider Tynan's description of the evening of the murders. It borrows the language and thus the world-views of a variety of discourses.[35] These range from an Irish tourist guide's hype – "Few cities have such beautiful and varied surroundings for enjoyment as the capital of Ireland" – to political polemic – "Peace and joy ruled there but for the myrmidons of a foreign power" – to the melodrama of a thriller, as seen in Tynan's novelistic contrast between the idyllic scene before the murders and the horror felt afterwards:

The young grass was fresh and springy, here and there speckled over with pink-eyed white-rimmed daisies, and dotted ... with golden-yellow butter-cups ... Numbers of people were walking about, enjoying the balmy air and luxuriating on the springy turf.

The sun had scarcely descended behind the western horizon when a strange rumour arose among the citizens. Weird and wildly tragic was this awful story.[36]

Unifying this description and the book as a whole in both form and content is a plot, borrowed from earlier narratives of the physical-force faction of Irish nationalism, of courageous but doomed action by lonely heroes in the centuries-old war with England. If we look beyond the obvious problems with Tynan's evidence to the hidden contradictions in this narrative, we learn more than he wants to tell us. One of his story's premises is that only dramatic, violent, heroic acts – not political palaver – can free Ireland. Yet the murders in the park end like earlier deeds of this nature in death or imprisonment or exile for the doers. What then is being celebrated if not failure? Heroic failure, especially that which leads to martyrdom, represents success in this narrative, which unconsciously discounts its professed aim, "the complete and absolute Independence of Ireland."[37] Such success can occur only within the context of an Ireland dominated by England.

Other latent meanings lie in this supposedly revolutionary narrative. We can dig up some of them by searching for the contradictions and problems masked by the givenness of its manifest goal. What does "the complete and absolute Independence of Ireland" mean? Does it mean freedom from the English language and its concepts (such as that of "law") which have shaped Tynan's book? Does it mean freedom from the English narrative models (for instance, the novel) which also have shaped his book? And does it mean freedom not just from all the hegemonic aspects of English culture in Ireland, but from European bourgeois culture in general? A current of Irish nationalism, institutionalized as the Gaelic League, did recognize the fact of English cultural domination and see the necessity of fighting it. But this recognition went only so far. It did not extend to dismantling the English-derived legal system and its laws protecting property. Nor did it extend to the economic emancipation of the masses of urban poor so caught up in the struggle to survive that nationalism in any form scarcely touched them at all. Sean O'Casey – that rare bird, an Irish Marxist nationalist – gives us a vignette of this class in his description of young Sean digging with navvies:

Not one of these brawny boys had ever even heard of Griffith or of Yeats . . . A good many of them had done seven years' service in the British Army, and now served on the Reserve, for sixpence a day wasn't to be sneezed at . . . What would the nicely-suited, white-collared respectable members of the refined Gaelic League branches of Dublin do if they found themselves in the company of these men?[38]

If Dublin's poor wouldn't have known or cared much about Number One or even about Joe Brady, Patrick Tynan didn't know or care much about them. They had no part in his petty-bourgeois Irish nationalist narrative; and it is precisely their absence that generates one of the latent meanings of this narrative.

Unlike Tynan, Corfe, a scrupulous writer of history whom Collingwood would have respected, takes pains to document his statements as much as possible. He draws a line between verifiable fact and imaginative interpretation. When he speculates, he tells us so, and he confesses disarmingly what he does not know or cannot absolutely confirm. He puts his cards on the table as to the "doubt and untruth, vagueness and confusion" of the evidence available. His awareness of the epistemological limits of the historian's work might be summed up in the conclusion:

The hard fact is that the full truth about the assassination – in the sense that there is an objective and verifiable truth – will never be known . . . More to the point, the past may be as unknowable as the future. One may guess at what has already happened with greater and lesser degrees of accuracy . . . But in many of a nation's affairs, as in many of an individual's, truth can never be known, and even the important questions cannot be settled one way or another beyond a reasonable doubt.[39]

The quotation comes from another historian writing about a different pair of murders – John F. Kennedy's and Lee Harvey Oswald's. It could have been Corfe's, though, and represents an often-voiced, admirable admission on the part of a social science which Barthes accused of confusing discourse with reality – of taking accounts of past events to be the copies or equivalents of the events themselves.[40] Yet in addition to being seekers of an elusive or unknowable truth and arguers of cases based on imperfect evidence, historians such as Corfe and John Kaplan are spinners of stories that can be seen as adaptations of prototype narratives[41] based on pre-existing conceptual frameworks. They do not simply present and weigh the evidence, leaving readers to draw their own conclusions. Indeed, they cannot. By arranging data, "facts," and prior interpretations of these data and facts into patterns, they inevitably narrativize their material. They also inevitably exclude from their narratives material that doesn't strike them as constituting "evidence" (in Collingwood's sense). When such material has been repressed by the ideology out of which a prototype narrative has grown, then it exists, as a latent contradictory meaning and subtext, in uneasy relation to any (hi)story embodying that narrative.

Corfe points out the death mystique and unconscious defeatism of Tynan's book and of violent Irish nationalism in general. He cites the Phoenix Park killings as an illustration of the uselessness of assassination as a political tool; and, while acknowledging the problematic nature of some of his evidence, he builds his thesis on the possibility that the Kilmainham treaty might have led to Home Rule if only the Invincibles had not deliberately sabotaged it by murdering Gladstone's emissary, the new Chief Secretary. He thus endows the Phoenix Park murders with an overall meaning by placing them in the context of the long-standing dialectic between moderate and radical Irish nationalists, between advocates of constitutional change and advocates of armed rebellion. The people in the white hats, of course, are the moderates, aided by progressive Englishmen such as Cavendish; and the ones in the black hats are the revolutionaries, abetted by reactionary members of the *ancien régime* such as Forster. The prototype narrative here, I suspect, is one that grew out of the reactions of liberal European historians to the French Revolution. And Corfe, in arguing for the superiority of reformism over violent revolution, follows this narrative in falling silent on the subject of the relations between the formerly oppressed but finally victorious middle classes and landless workers. He speaks of the destruction of the moderates' vision of "a harmonious future for Ireland," but does not speculate as to how that future would have prevented the ruthless exploitation of workers by bourgeois nationalist employers which led to the Dublin strike of 1913. Clearly, his focus on a chapter in the struggles of Irish nationalism omits precisely that issue which most nationalists themselves ignored or glossed over when it was raised. It did not fit into their story or his.

To discuss in turn Tynan and Corfe and Malcolm Brown is to move from a half-educated, fervid mixer of history and memoir and political polemic to a competent historian to a brilliant if not entirely reliable – what shall I call him? – exponent of literature and history. It doesn't serve my purpose to explore Brown's occasional carelessness with minor facts or his tendency to make catchy but not always cogent generalizations. And I'll content myself with observing in passing that he shares Tynan's and Corfe's blind spot – and that of Irish nationalism – in regard to the plight of the urban lower classes who were doubly disenfranchised by foreign colonialism and native capitalism. What interests me about *The Politics of Irish Literature* is its double premise that juxtaposing history with art is an illuminating exercise and that "felt history" can be a more important influence on literature than "formal history."

Some defining of terms might be in order. Implicitly taking history (past events) as something real yet not directly examinable, Brown approaches it through the narratives it has generated – the stories of poetry and fiction, the stories of formal or academic history, and the stories of felt or popular history. He explains that he turned to felt history because of the gulf between Irish historical monographs and Irish literature. He bridges "their parallel unfolding chronicles" with the pages of

the Irish nationalist press, the only source known to me that undertook to treat – as elements of a single consecutive thread – the concurrent political and cultural history of the country ... Much of [my] narrative ... is therefore drawn from ballads and popular sarcasms, from the passionate topical responses of hustings and newspaper office, from old wives' tales, from the savory style of chance episodes, and from the color of local personalities ... insignificant in formal history, but extremely important carriers of true meanings and genuine affections in "felt history."[42]

Let's call these "true meanings and genuine affections" expressions of ideology – purer and more naked expressions than those of formal history, which may be shaped by the same local ideology but is more self-conscious and subject to influence by broader ideologies. The narratives of this felt history influence later events, in Brown's view, both in helping to cause them and in providing a framework for interpreting them. A complex process of cross-fertilization takes place by which ideology – not only thought but thought enacted – reinforces and perpetuates itself. Thus, for instance, the neurotic reproduction in Ireland of hero-martyrs and tales of hero-martyrs. We must keep this process in mind when we turn to Joyce, who, in different ways, at once exposed and embodied it.

❊

Collingwood distinguished between the constructive imagination of the historian and that of the poet or fiction-writer by noting that the historian must stay within the bounds of evidence. By this standard, among others, we judge Tynan's, Corfe's, and Brown's accounts of the park murders. It does not apply in Joyce's case since the artist's imagination can roam free, conjuring up Aristotle's "thing that might be" as opposed to "the thing that has been." Yet this freedom remains a relative one, especially in dealing with past events. It is not simply that the artist's imagination is affected by documented facts, such as William of Orange's victory over James II at the Battle of the Boyne. Another powerful influence is that of the narrativized event, documented or not. A novelist, for instance, might imagine Julius Caesar writing his memoirs in retirement on a sun-drenched estate in Tuscany, having plotted with his supposed assassins to have a stand-in die for him, but cannot in the end dispel from memory Shakespeare's image of Caesar on the Ides of March falling under knife blows in a blood-soaked toga. Even more than the scholar's researched, footnoted history, felt history refuses to be undone or forgotten. It reminds us that another restriction on the poet's or fiction writer's freedom is that of ideology – meaning not a given monolithic system of beliefs, but rather an ongoing dialectic among various coexisting and historically determined ideological practices.[43] What kind of freedom, if any, can the artist win from this process that defines and encloses all of us? More specifically, how does Joyce's fictional treatment of the Invincibles, apart from the limited liberty we accord it as art to break the bounds of historical evidence, differ from nonfiction treatments?

  Let me start to address these questions by reconsidering the motif of the knife in *Ulysses*. The huge surgical knives used by Brady and Kelly caught the public's imagination. If in Ireland the visceral horror of the killings became overshadowed by the issue of betrayal and then by the drawn-out hangings that assured the Invincibles' transformation into hero-martyrs, it nonetheless continued to be felt. Joyce, too, was struck by the brutality of the assassinations. But they were more than brutal; they foreclosed certain historical possibilities, as Corfe emphasizes, and their instrument – the knife – symbolizes this closure in *Ulysses*. Imagery of knives and stabbing appears throughout the "Eumaeus" chapter and links up with images of violence in other episodes, notably "Nestor." Stephen's inability to look at the point of a table knife because it reminds him of Roman history harks back to his ruminations at Mr. Deasy's school on the deaths from cold steel of Pyrrhus and Julius Caesar:

They are not to be thought away. Time has branded them and fettered they are lodged in the room of the infinite possibilities they have ousted. But can those have been possible seeing that they never were? Or was that only possible which came to pass? (*U* 2.49–52)

Suggestions and images of ancient battles involving steel and blood – a general leaning upon a spear "above a corpsestrewn plain," "spearspikes baited with men's bloodied guts" (*U* 2.16, 318), and so on – fill the chapter. For Stephen history is not just "a tale like any other too often heard"; he has a strong sense of its nightmarish referent, both in world history and Irish history, which he construes as a series of violent events ending in an apocalyptic explosion like the one imagined at the outset of "Nestor": "I hear the ruin of all space, shattered glass and toppling masonry, and time one livid final flame" (*U* 2.46–47, 9–10). Even Stephen's powerful imagination cannot undo such past events. He feels oppressed by them much as he feels oppressed by genetic history:

I was ... made not begotten. By them, the man with my voice and my eyes and a ghostwoman with ashes on her breath. They clasped and sundered, did the coupler's will. From before the ages He willed me and now may not will me away or ever. (*U* 3.45–48)

Both Stephen and his creator, as Seamus Deane observes, are "hostile to fact, to history, to what has happened, to the restriction which the past has placed upon possibility ... History is a betrayal of possibility."[44]

An idealistic young man raised in the Irish Catholic nationalist tradition, who knew by heart Ireland's record of failed rebellions against British oppression, and who left the country for good "at the bottom of a dreary political downswing"[45] – such a man might well have seen Irish history as a succession of possibilities usurped by an intolerable reality. The downfall of Parnell, seemingly on the verge of leading Ireland to Home Rule, was only the most recent in a centuries-long chain of tragedies and catastrophes and fiascos. But popular history since the rise of cultural nationalism in the mid-nineteenth century had coped with this reality by celebrating the glorious, doomed heroism of Irish defeat and so turning it into victory. As Deane comments, "imagination figured powerfully as true what fact could not provide. The crowned king of Ireland, Edward VII, is a sorry figure beside the uncrowned king, Parnell."[46] Similarly, the moral and physical horror of the Invincibles' crime and punishment became overshadowed by their sea-change into hero-martyrs. Hence that young idealist who put distance between himself and Ireland in order to write about her, who was a nationalist yet rejected the claims of the Irish nationalism which he knew, had to acknowledge both the nightmare of his country's past and the nationalistic tales (that is, "felt history") which reinterpreted and in part repressed that past. Yet he also had to find or create a realm of freedom. Politically, he sought it beyond the existing European order in a vague, anarchistic socialism that had no chance of being realized. Artistically, he sought it beyond the existing narratives of his country's history – English, Anglo-Irish, and Irish Catholic – in fiction and, ultimately, in language itself.

Going back to the motif of the Phoenix Park murders in *Ulysses*, we can see that Joyce was attempting to expose and subvert Irish popular culture's received notion of the Invincibles. This by no means involved his adopting the English view evoked in a *Punch* cartoon of 20 May 1882 that depicted a giant, caped, chimpanzee-faced figure clutching a bloody knife.[47] Rather, he exposed the assumptions of both sets of attitudes by exaggerating them and carrying them to absurd extremes in imagined enactments. Thus the satirical "British Beatitudes" in "Oxen of the Sun" – "Beer, beef, business, bibles, bulldogs, battleships, buggery and bishops" (*U* 14.1459–60) – are set against parodic Irish virtues in "Cyclops" such as "chivalry" and "manly strength and prowess" (*U* 12.289, 911). Thus, too, the cruel yeoman is set against the croppy boy, H. Rumbold against the Citizen, Edward VII against Old Gummy Granny, and so on. The covert complicity of the opposing sides in producing each other's history and fables of history is suggested in "Cyclops" when all parties – hangman and victim, Englishman and Irishman – cooperate in the preparations to execute the "hero

martyr" (*U* 12.609). I have already outlined the development of this
figure, a conflation of Brady and Emmet and the croppy boy, and
his embodiment of heroism, death, and eroticism. Though clever,
Brown's borrowed term "heroticism" leaves out the middle element
of this triad, whose worship Joyce saw as characterizing an
especially unhealthy strain of Irish nationalism (which his former
Gaelic teacher, Padraic Pearse, spectacularly enacted in 1916).
Ulysses magnifies and literalizes this characteristic, chiefly in the
story of Brady's potency after death, the grisly-romantic scene
before the unnamed hero's execution, and the depiction of the
women who sop up the croppy boy's semen after he has been
hanged. Thus exposed and subverted, the trait becomes both absurd
and horrifying. Yet the exposure is never simple or one-sided; and
we are reminded again of the other side's complicity in Irish
excesses, for instance, by the fact that the three sperm-collectors in
"Circe" bear Anglo-Irish names.

Ulysses does more, though, than simply unmask the morbidity
underlying the great funeral marches and many of the poems and
songs and other expressions of Irish nationalism from Thomas
Davis's day to Joyce's. In the case of the Phoenix Park murders,
Joyce set about portraying the process by which history (past
events) becomes history (accounts of past events), especially in
popular culture. Imagine the story of the Trojan War – or that of the
Trojan War hero, Odysseus – being passed down from poet to poet
in archaic Greece and being heard and discussed by their various
audiences. Everyone "knows" the story, yet certain details become
hazy or change, and emphases shift. So Myles Crawford and Bloom
think of the assassinations from their different points of view,
emphasizing the getaway and the actual stabbings respectively, and
make small errors of fact which we can check by resorting to the
evidence of formal history. To the reminiscing old editor the event
appears mainly as an episode in the annals of journalism, that is,
Gallaher's clever scoop of cabling the escape route in code to a New
York newspaper. Bloom thinks of it ambivalently in connection with
the subject of his ill-fated conversation with the Citizen – "Force,
hatred, history, all that" (*U* 12.1481) – admiring a man able to kill
on political principle, but abhorring the act itself. To Alf Bergan,
one of the barflies in Kiernan's pub, the event provides a titillating
anecdote about Brady's hanging. And the Citizen, that embodiment
of gusty popular nationalism, sees the Phoenix Park affair as a

chapter in the saga of the ancient conflict between England and Ireland. Immediately after the discussion of Brady

he starts gassing ... about the invincibles and the old guard and the men of sixtyseven and who fears to speak of ninetyeight and ... all the fellows that were hanged, drawn and transported for the cause [and] the brothers Sheares and Wolfe Tone ... and Robert Emmet and die for your country. (*U* 12.480–500)

Thus *Ulysses* shows us a past event transformed into felt or popular history – a many-faceted narrative, made up of fact, fiction, error, and speculation, whose emphasis in the telling depends on the tellers' varying perspectives and the nature of the dialogues in which they are engaged.

Take away the words "fiction" and "error" and the above definition could apply (ideally) to scholarly history such as Corfe's account of the Invincibles. Joyce's principal target was popular history, which had a monopoly among nationalists in Ireland due to a strong oral tradition and the absence of a large educated audience for the few Irish Catholic historians (both by-products of colonialism, in particular of the denial to Catholics under the Penal Laws of state-supported schooling). But he obviously viewed formal British histories of Ireland, such as those of Carlyle's disciple Froude and others which the Oxonian Haines might have read, as being no less biased or conditioned by ideology. And his introduction into "Eumaeus" of the fictional/historical Skin-the-Goat, taking his examination of the Phoenix Park murders further, questions the claims to truth of both kinds of history and even the validity of any authoritative portrayal of a historical figure.

As I have argued above, the appearance in *Ulysses* of a patriotic blowhard, who may possibly be the former Invincible in old age, raises doubts about the received memory in Irish popular culture of Fitzharris as a brave, simple, taciturn hero. The keeper's blustery words interrogate the cabdriver's silence. Had the latter given voice to the thoughts that prompted his actions, would he, too, not have sounded like the Citizen? Was his involvement in the murders as futile an expression of nationalism as his alter ego's rhetoric? Bloom's suspicion that the "pseudo Skin-the-etcetera" (*U* 16.1070) may be a Castle provocateur brings to mind the murkiness, remarked by Corfe, of that realm of history inhabited by revolutionaries, terrorists, spies, and double agents. But it also suggests the more general complicity of colonial oppression and nationalistic violence in producing and reproducing each other – the unconscious complicity, say, of Buckshot Forster and the Invincibles. In this context the flesh-and-blood Fitzharris, though not an approver, was indeed an unwitting accomplice of the most reactionary enemies of Irish nationalism. If he assisted at the birth of a new set of hero-martyrs, he also made possible the reincarnation of the murderous, ape-visaged Irish nationalist pictured in *Punch*.[48]

We might say of Skin-the-Goat Fitzharris what Brown writes of Joe Brady: "He was dead or alive an equivocation."[49] In any case, the ambiguous identity of the keeper of the cabman's shelter – Invincible or impostor? hero or fool? – raises questions that tend to destabilize the received historical memory of his original. It is not that Joyce substitutes one Skin-the-Goat for another, a fictional character for a historical figure. Rather, the two Skin-the-Goats coexist as contradictory yet non-cancelling realities, suggesting the limitations of any narrative of history that echoes Ranke and says, in effect, *This* is what happened or *This* is what that person was really like. There is no denial of the reality of history (past events). Rather, there is a recognition that we interpret this reality in histories (accounts of past events) which take on a reality of their own, regardless of their validity in terms of historical evidence. *Ulysses* acknowledges the nationalist version of Skin-the-Goat, but offers us a means of deconstructing – rather than destroying – this version by presenting an alter ego whose identity is so ambiguous that we are impelled to ask questions about the "real" Fitzharris. Naturally most readers don't go to the length of doing research on the Phoenix Park murders. But Joyce's depiction of "Skin-the-Goat, assuming he was he" (*U* 16.985) – this historical figure who may be a fiction within a fiction – acts as a potential maieutic device that begins by making the reader a little uneasy through its subversion of traditional notions of history and fiction and even identity. If we start to recognize the problems inherent in representing an actual person, such as Fitzharris, then we must sense the even more problematic nature of a hypostasized concept such as "Ireland" or "Dublin" that is represented as an individual actor in a historical narrative.

Deane tells us that Joyce rebelled against the doneness, the immutability of history (past events) in much the same way that Irish nationalism did. That is, he created an alternative reality

which otherwise would have no existence and in which the external reality ... would be only one ingredient among others. He had learned from Irish nationalism the power of a vocabulary in bringing to existence that which otherwise had none except in the theatre of words. Joyce, we may say, discovered the fictive nature of politics.[50]

As a model of liberation, however, Irish nationalism took Joyce only so far. He rebelled against both its vocabulary and its history (accounts of past events), as we have seen in connection with the park murders. Its roll call of hero-martyrs may well have made possible the Easter Rising and the Free State, but these were not entirely good things from the point of view of a nationalist who was also a pacifist and, for many years, a socialist of sorts. Joyce sought liberation from the nationalist tradition itself. In his art he set about doing this through a procedure of exposure and subversion, not just of Irish nationalist history but potentially of all histories, revealing to us the shaky foundations of any representation of the past that claims to be authoritative. At the same time, he revealed the liberating potential of language and narrative to reshape history by reshaping our consciousness of history. One implication of this procedure is the possibility of attaining a limited freedom to choose the future through our recognition that the past is not given or inevitable or unquestionable, but culturally determined and reinterpretable.

Joyce's innovations in style and technique, Deane suggests, arose out of his ongoing effort "to find new relationships between author and audience through language, so that language (and author) could escape from history ... yet at the same time be rooted in history."[51] Thus *Ulysses*, in its fictive reconstruction/deconstruction of the park murders, at once roots itself in Irish history and denies the authority of that history – denies its claims on the behavior of the living. In doing this, Joyce's novel achieves a liberating openness denied to the historical narrative that strives to give the reader a single, coherent, thematically directed account of the past. This is true no less of Corfe's fairly sophisticated analysis than of Tynan's naïve memoir. If Corfe does not fall for the hero-martyr story of the Invincibles, he does fall for narrative itself, unselfconsciously fitting the assassinations into a narrative framework that neglects to acknowledge its own origins or limits.

Yet Joyce, in spite of his ability to subvert received history, hardly escaped history – his own or Ireland's. Though immune to the mystique of the hero-martyr as embodied in Emmet or Brady, he was not immune to it as embodied in Parnell. Nor was he unaffected by his middle-class Catholic upbringing, even if he surmounted it enough in his youth to embrace socialism. Hence, for instance, most of his fictional characters belong to the petty bourgeoisie; and hence the designated story of politics in *Dubliners* revolves around the ghost of Parnell, the aristocratic leader of a middle-class nationalist movement, rather than the living socialist, James Connolly. But that's another story, which I shall tell in later chapters.

CHAPTER 2

Literary politics

History is past politics, and politics present history.
Sir John Robert Seeley, *The Growth of British Policy*

Seeley is better known for his remark on the English people: "We seem, as it were, to have conquered and peopled half the world in a fit of absence of mind."[1] An exaggeration, to be sure. Though the ideology actuating British imperialism may have been half unformulated and half unconscious, the minds of its agents were by no means blank, even if many would have explained their purpose through catchphrases and scraps of poetry:

I mete and dole
Unequal laws unto a savage race.[2]

Take up the White Man's burden.[3]

"Play up! play up! and play the game!"[4]

Ideology in this sense – the ideas and beliefs of a society or group – always has political ramifications; it mystifies and justifies a given power structure. And if human history is thought or ideology enacted, then indeed "History is past politics, and politics present history." In a rebellious colonial possession such as Ireland – where England expanded and maintained its hold through state policy – this statement applies all the more. The conflict between nationalism and imperialism overtly politicizes activities whose political nature might otherwise remain disguised and latent. This holds especially true among the intelligentsia of such a country, who cannot retreat to the imaginary high ground of neutrality or objectivity without determined efforts being made to pull them down into the political fray. Even a complex, intelligent partisanship becomes difficult under these circumstances. This brings us to the problem of Joyce's politics, in particular his mixed feelings toward Irish nationalism. In art as in life, political tensions shaped his view of Ireland; only if we're aware of these tensions can we appreciate both his insights and his blind spots.

Ambivalence marked most of Joyce's attitudes toward his native land, not least his attitude toward its would-be liberators. On one hand, his writings reveal a deep-seated contempt for British imperialism and the viceregal regime in Ireland. On the other hand, his fictional portrayals of Irish nationalists of all stripes are sometimes scathing and at best reservedly sympathetic. Ireland and things Irish permeate his books from *Dubliners* through *Finnegans Wake*. Yet, except in elliptical allusions, he appears to have virtually ignored the Easter Rising, the Anglo-Irish War, and the Irish Civil War – events which occurred during his prime and which inspired Yeats, O'Casey, and other Irish writers. On the surface, these are striking contradictions; but underneath them we can trace a certain consistency in Joyce's ambivalence toward Irish nationalism. This ambivalence, in short, stemmed partly from a political mythology inherited from his Parnellite father, partly from his "socialist" and pacifist beliefs, and partly from a need to establish his independence not only of Irish nationalism but of any organized political group, movement, or institution. (I place "socialist" in quotation marks since this term – though no other serves as well – covers what was in Joyce a rather diffuse and protean political radicalism.)

The earliest literary expression of Joyce's Parnellism was "Et Tu, Healy," a poem composed as a nine-year-old on the fall of Parnell. This dramatic and traumatic event in Irish politics contributed to a less dramatic, but no less traumatic event in the Joyce household – John Joyce's dismissal from a patronage post no longer controlled by the Parnellites. John Joyce did not view this as just a turn of the political wheel of fortune; he inflated it into a turning-point in his own life. If Parnell had been betrayed, so too his loyal follower. Thus the Joyces' financial and social decline from 1891 on became linked, in a family mythology, with political betrayal (*JJ* 33–34).

The young Joyce realized soon enough that his father's drinking and spendthrift habits had something to do with the family's downhill slide. But the key association was Parnell, as indicated by an allusion to "Et Tu, Healy" in *A Portrait*: "The morning after the discussion at the Christmas dinnertable [Stephen tried] to write a poem about Parnell on the back of one of his father's second moiety notices" (*P* 70). These fictional demands for payment suggest the

real-life economic troubles into which John Joyce lurched after
losing his well-paid job as a rate collector for Dublin City and
County.[5] Though his Parnellite allies couldn't intercede for him, his
wife did, and secured him a pension which was "a generous proportion of his salary for ten years' unsatisfactory service [and] a nice
start for a man aged forty-two if he were prepared to undertake
other work and conduct his affairs with reasonable prudence."[6]
Nevertheless, he found it convenient to feel stabbed in the back, and
conveyed a sense of this to his favorite son ("he became slowly aware
that his father had enemies" [*P* 65]). For James Joyce, betrayal in
his own life and in Ireland's national life became a fixed idea.
Parnell had been betrayed; he, too, would see himself as having been
betrayed by friends, colleagues, his wife Nora, and Ireland herself.

It is hardly surprising that, at the age of nine, Joyce accepted
uncritically the Parnellite martyrology which his father passed on to
him. But in 1912, at the age of thirty, he still was propagating the
legend. In an article, "The Shade of Parnell," he described an Irish
"Moses" who had engineered the first Home Rule bill (1886) and
who had led his people "to the verge of the Promised Land"
(*CW* 225) when, in 1890, the treachery of his own Irish MPs and of
the Church struck him down over an insignificant issue. This issue
was the naming of Parnell as the lover of another man's wife in a
divorce suit. Joyce does not concede the impact of this news in
Catholic Ireland; nor does he concede the possibility that the former
associates and allies who turned against Parnell in Committee Room
15 at Westminster had solid patriotic, if not moral, grounds for
doing so.

In fact, the anti-Parnellites saw their choice as lying between the
man and the cause. Personal loyalty to Parnell, they insisted, was
not worth losing their alliance with Gladstone's Liberal Party and
thereby forfeiting Home Rule.[7] Though the anti-Parnellites were by
no means all high-minded statesmen, Joyce ignored the basic issue
when he charged in another article, "Home Rule Comes of Age,"
that the majority of the Irish Party sold their leader" (*CW* 196) to
Gladstone without securing domestic liberty in exchange. One
wonders whether he would have regarded Healy and his cohorts as
traitors if Gladstone's second Home Rule bill (1893) had not been
vetoed in the House of Lords. In any case, Parnell's ruination
represented to Joyce the most recent act of treachery in a long series
of such acts darkening Irish history. He placed his own perceived

betrayal within this tradition, referring to Ireland in his broadside, "Gas from a Burner" (1912), as

> This lovely land that always sent
> Her writers and artists to banishment
> And in a spirit of Irish fun
> Betrayed her own leaders, one by one.   (*CW* 243)

The theme of betrayal runs throughout Joyce's writings. In *Dubliners* the theme emerges most plainly at the end of "Ivy Day in the Committee Room." Hynes, a die-hard Parnellite and amateur versifier, ascribes the Chief's fall and death to

> coward caitiff hands
> That smote their Lord or with a kiss
> Betrayed him to the rabble-rout
> Of fawning priests – no friends of his.   (*D* 134)

In *A Portrait* another version of Hynes, Mr. Casey, also denounces "the priests and the priests' pawns" who "broke Parnell's heart and hounded him into his grave" (*P* 33–34). Later in the novel Stephen reminds Davin, a member of the Gaelic League and the Gaelic Athletic Association, of the ubiquity of Irish informers, telling him: "No honourable and sincere man . . . has given up to you his life and his youth and his affections from the days of Tone to those of Parnell but you sold him to the enemy or failed him in need or reviled him and left him for another" (*P* 203). In *Ulysses* Stephen seems to have cast off his Parnellism, if not his preoccupation with betrayal; but the Bloomish narrator of "Eumaeus" voices good Parnellite dogma in stating: "It was . . . a stoning to death on the part of seventytwo out of eighty odd constituencies that ratted at the time of the split" (*U* 16.1731–32). Joyce obviously did not always endorse his characters' sentiments, yet his own youthful Parnellism and his never-outgrown fear of betrayal underlie this theme.

Another primary theme arising out of Joyce's literary Parnellism was that of Irish paralysis, an idea central to *Dubliners* and implicit in later works. Prominent among the different forms of paralysis portrayed in *Dubliners* is that of political life; evidence of this, usually in association with economic decline and foreign domination, appears throughout the book. We find it in the biting opening of "After the Race":

The cars came scudding in towards Dublin, running evenly like pellets in the groove of the Naas Road. At the crest of the hill at Inchicore sightseers had gathered in clumps to watch the cars careering homeward and through this channel of poverty and inaction the Continent sped its wealth and industry. Now and again the clumps of people raised the cheer of the gratefully oppressed. (*D* 42)

We also find it, more typically, in quiet but telling details such as the Northern Irish accent of Farrington's superior in "Counterparts," the inscription "*A Present from Belfast*" on Maria's purse in "Clay," the London address of Mr. Kernan's firm in "Grace," and the Dublin Castle or police – hence British – affiliations of relatively well-off characters such as Messrs. Doyle, Power, and Cunningham.

The most striking expression of this motif occurs in "Ivy Day," which depicts the paralysis of Irish constitutional politics on the eleventh anniversary of Parnell's death. Home Rulers and Conservatives have formed an uneasy alliance to oppose a Labour candidate in a municipal ward election. They bicker and backbite, debating in particular the merits of Ireland's dead "uncrowned king," Parnell, and her living, actual king, Edward VII. The debate goes on against a background of economic, social, and political stagnation. Significantly, only Hynes, the true-blue Parnellite turned Labourite, draws the reader's sympathy. Yet he, too, is ineffectual. Not a call to action but a lament, his poem evokes a vanished past, a past full of hope and high purpose and action, against which the paralysis of the present is measured. A similar nostalgia for fallen greatness pervades the Christmas dinner scene in *A Portrait*. And in *Ulysses*, several characters pay homage to the legend at Parnell's grave and in the cabman's shelter. In both novels, as well as in *Dubliners*, the days of glory for Irish nationalism lie in the past. They are dead and buried with Parnell in Glasnevin cemetery. (References to Parnell in *Finnegans Wake* are harder to interpret, but some clearly tie in with the themes of betrayal and a great man's fall.)

As shown by Cruise O'Brien, F. S. L. Lyons, and others, the interval between Parnell's death in 1891 and the "terrible beauty" of Easter 1916 was hardly the lacuna of paralysis and demoralization depicted in Joyce's fiction. These symptoms did, to be sure, exist in abundance. They could be seen especially among the Irish Party during the ten years, beginning in 1895, of Conservative prime ministers hostile to Home Rule. Not by coincidence, the young Joyce left Ireland in 1904 at the nadir of this sorry interlude, which served as a model for his portrayals of Irish politics even after the situation in Ireland had changed visibly.[8] The action of the stories in

Dubliners, of much of *A Portrait*, and the whole of *Ulysses* takes place during this period, when parliamentary nationalism and violent rebellion alike appeared to be dead ends.

Other flourishing forms of nationalism at this time included the Land League, the Gaelic League, the Gaelic Athletic Association, and the Irish Literary Theatre. For mixed reasons, Joyce slighted or resisted all of these organizations. Except for brief allusions in *A Portrait* and *Ulysses*, we would scarcely realize from a reading of Joyce's works that Michael Davitt and the Land League even existed – let alone that the League scored its greatest victory in 1903 with Wyndham's Land Act, which provided financing for tenants to purchase landlords' estates. We would also scarcely realize that two-thirds of Ireland's population then lived in the countryside, and that Irish and English attention long had been focused on the political struggle there.

Two organizations that came after Parnell – the Gaelic League and the Irish Literary Theatre, founded in 1893 and 1899, respectively – did interest Joyce. The results of this interest, however, were for the most part mockery or criticism that established his distance from these groups. He stopped taking Irish lessons from Padraic Pearse because of Pearse's linguistic chauvinism. He welcomed *The Countess Cathleen*, the first play performed by the Theatre, but wrote an article, "The Day of the Rabblement" (1901), protesting what he saw as the Theatre's turn to parochialism after it announced plans to put on a play in Gaelic by Douglas Hyde and a play by Yeats and Moore taken from Irish heroic legend. In a book review (1902) he slated a volume of patriotic verses by William Rooney, a co-founder of Sinn Fein, on artistic grounds. Once he began writing fiction his reaction became even harsher. "A Mother" reduces the language movement to the level of a middle-class fad, and portrays the cultural revival in terms of a comical, low-brow series of concerts that includes the singing of "Killarney." In *A Portrait* Stephen mocks Davin, the Gaelic Leaguer and G.A.A. sportsman, for wanting to make a "rebellion with hurleysticks" (*P* 201). In *Ulysses* the "Cyclops" episode parodies one of the founders of the G.A.A., Michael Cusack, in the person of the Citizen, and gives a wickedly absurd pseudo-report on a Gaelic League meeting. Throughout the *Wake* Irish politics ("our wee free state") and culture (the *"cultic twalette"* [*FW* 117.34, 344.12]) suffer mocking pinpricks and worse.

Joyce's motives, conscious and unconscious, were as always complex. After all, he created the character of Rumbold, the egregious English hangman, in the same chapter in which the Citizen fulminates. And he had the anti-chauvinist Stephen comment, in *A Portrait*, on his sense of English as a foreign tongue. At least in part, his quarrels with the Irish Theatre and the Gaelic League stemmed from his belief in an art which was national but not patriotic – to use Yeats's distinction – and from a feeling that the nationalistic rhetoric issuing from many Gaelic Leaguers was obnoxious and not to be taken seriously in comparison with the efforts to free Ireland made in the past by Parnell or even by the Fenians. He also needed to align himself with European literature and justify his subject matter, petty-bourgeois urban life, in a country where "the countryside is often taken as the imagination's proper territory."[9] Before Joyce the literature of Dublin consisted almost entirely of "histories, street directories, and guidebooks ... and novels about dueling playboys by Charles Lever and Sheridan Le Fanu."[10] He knew that he was working against the overwhelmingly rural bias of the cultural revival. No doubt his own leeriness of the countryside is reflected in Stephen's diary entry about the old man in the mountains – a speaker of Irish and Synge-accented English ("Ah, there must be terrible queer creatures at the latter end of the world" [*P* 251]) – with whom he fears he must grapple to the death. Terence Brown comments:

Here Stephen ... is repelled and horrified by the forces that generated both the Gaelic revival and the Anglo-Irish literary movement ... But Joyce, Stephen's creator, had his revenge on both their houses in *Ulysses* when he made epic of a petit-bourgeois world they would both have sought to exclude in their definitions of the essential Irishry.[11]

Another facet of Joyce's ambivalent Irishness was his attitude toward Fenianism, a movement that appeared quiescent if not dead at the turn of the century. He certainly did not bathe it in retrospective glory – witness his portrait in "Proteus" of the broken-down old Fenian, Kevin Egan, in exile in Paris. But references to Fenianism and violent nationalism abound in *Ulysses*. I have already discussed the Phoenix Park murders. Another motif is the jailbreak and getaway to the Continent of James Stephens. Above all, the Clerkenwell explosion resounds throughout the novel.[12] This huge, fatally miscalculated blast was set off by a splinter group of Fenians called the Dynamitards, who, in 1867, blew down a prison wall in

London during an attempt to free their comrades. Stephen imagines the scene through the eyes of Kevin Egan: "He prowled ... under the walls of Clerkenwell and, crouching, saw a flame of vengeance hurl them upward in the fog. Shattered glass and toppling masonry" (*U* 3.246–49). The imagery links this event with Stephen's vision of apocalypse in "Nestor" (*U* 2.9–10) and with his own violence at the climax of "Circe" when he uses his ashplant to smash a lamp in Bella Cohen's brothel: "*Time's livid final flame leaps and, in the following darkness, ruin of all space, shattered glass and toppling masonry*" (*U* 15.4244–45). Possibly this imagery alludes to the devastation of downtown Dublin during Easter 1916. Such an allusion does occur a little later during Stephen's encounter with the two privates.[13] Shortly after Major Tweedy and the Citizen salute each other "*with fierce hostility*" (*U* 15.4623–24) – and shortly before Old Gummy Granny urges patriotic martyrdom on Stephen – voices cry, "Dublin's burning! Dublin's burning!" "Troops deploy," and fires spring up amid the sounds of galloping horses, artillery, and Gatling guns (*U* 15.4661–63). Then the soldiers disappear, replaced, after a rain of dragons' teeth, by mutually embattled heroes who turn out to be various types of Irish nationalists. This futile sequence of conflict, which prefigures the Civil War of 1922–23, suggests a recurrent pattern in Irish history of rebellion and internecine fighting. In any case, it is in *Ulysses* that Joyce takes note of the violence which has punctuated Irish struggles against England and which figures only peripherally in *Dubliners* and *A Portrait*.

Joyce's late-blooming interest in Fenianism may have been triggered by World War I and the 1916 uprising, and perhaps reflects a recognition of violent nationalism's ability to bring about change even in Ireland. But the redrawing of maps in Ireland and on the Continent in the aftermath of war, although it resulted in the independence of a few formerly oppressed peoples, very likely did not seem worth the candle to him. He expressed nostalgia for the *laissez-faire* Austro-Hungarian Empire, under which he had lived in Trieste, after its collapse. His brief exhilaration at the founding of the Irish Free State turned into skepticism and disappointment, reflected in his comment in 1932: "They are doing many things much more efficiently, I am told, than was possible under the old régime but any semblance of liberty they had when under England seems to have gone – and goodness knows that was not much"

(*JJ* 643). Emphasis, for him, always fell on Blakean spiritual liberation and, during his socialist years, on economic liberation.

Underlying Joyce's preference for these kinds of revolution was
his deep-seated pacifism. He expressed this belief in a muddled
fashion in his schoolboy essay on "Force" (*CW* 17–24) and with
lacerating irony in his poem "Dooleysprudence" (1916). In the
latter he asks:

> Who is the man when all the gallant nations run to war
> Goes home to have his dinner by the very first cablecar[?]
>   . . .
> Who is the funny fellow who declines to go to church
> Since pope and priest and parson left the poor man in the lurch
> And taught their flocks the only way to save all human souls
> Was piercing bodies through with dumdum bulletholes?
> > It's Mr Dooley
> > Mr Dooley,
> > The mildest man our country ever knew
> > "Who will release us
> > From Jingo Jesus"
> > Prays Mr Dooley-ooley-ooley-oo.   (*CW* 246–47)

The Dooleyesque Mr. Bloom similarly rejects "Force, hatred,
history, all that" (*U* 12.1481). He declares his credo to Stephen: "I
resent violence and intolerance in any shape or form. It never
reaches anything or stops anything. A revolution must come on the
due instalments plan" (*U* 16.1099–101). Pointedly, the only con-
summated act of personal violence depicted in *Ulysses* is the knocking down of a pacifist Irishman, Stephen, by a British soldier. This
occurs in a context of futile patriotic violence created by interactions
among the hallucinatory figures of the croppy boy, the hangman
Rumbold, Old Gummy Granny, Edward VII, Major Tweedy, and
the Citizen. Stephen's statement of his philosophy regarding such
violence, which he makes shortly before Private Carr hits him,
sounds like both Bloom's and Dooley's. He tells the private: "You
die for your country. Suppose . . . Not that I wish it for you. But I
say: Let my country die for me. Up to the present it has done so. I
don't want it to die. Damn death. Long live life!" (*U* 15.4471–74).

If Joyce's pacifism and Parnellism led him to reject both violent
and constitutional forms of Irish nationalism, there was one movement that attracted him as an alternative. The Sinn Fein program of
working toward independence by means of extra-parliamentary

agitation and boycott entailed neither fighting England nor collaborating with her.[14] Moreover, Sinn Fein stressed individual self-reliance and did not depend on a single charismatic leader who, Joyce felt, inevitably would be betrayed.[15] In his article "Fenianism" (1907) he traced the history of the double struggle, during the nineteenth century, between Ireland and England and between the moderate patriots and the advocates of physical force. He found Sinn Fein to be the last and "most formidable" (*CW* 191) phase of Fenianism. Other articles and letters reveal his approval of Sinn Fein's doctrines of separatism and economic nationalism and its hostility to John Redmond's Irish Party. He also approved Arthur Griffith's support of James Connolly and other Labour candidates during the Dublin Corporation elections in 1902 and 1903. At the same time, though, he criticized Griffith for "educating the people of Ireland on the old pap of racial hatred whereas anyone can see that if the Irish question exists, it exists for the Irish proletariat chiefly" (*L II* 167). In another letter, he predicted that a success by Sinn Fein "would be to substitute Irish for English capital" (*L II* 187); and he took exception also to Sinn Fein's insistence on the Irish language.

"HE CALLS HIMSELF A SOCIALIST"

Joyce's socialism, which helped distance him from Sinn Fein, was, together with his pacifism and his bedeviled nationalism, the third strand of what we might call his public politics – that is, his belief in goals such as national self-rule, peace, and economic equity that he shared as broad principles with large numbers of other people. The term "socialism" must be immediately qualified, however, since we cannot identify Joyce with a particular socialist party or movement as we can identify, say, George Bernard Shaw with the Fabians. In dealing with Joyce's life as well as with his work, we are impelled to re-examine some of "those big words which make us so unhappy" (*CW* 87). Although he described himself more than once as a socialist, what that meant to him proves hard to pin down. He himself admitted to Stanislaus: "Of course you find my socialism thin. It is so and unsteady and ill-informed" (*L II* 187). Yet, since the word "socialism" does have meaning in specific, historical contexts, we must explore what it meant – and did not mean – in a Joycean context.

Like all of Joyce's important allegiances, his socialism had roots in his youth. In 1901 he translated Gerhart Hauptmann's play, *Vor Sonnenaufgang*, which features an idealistic socialist in the leading role. In 1903 he "attended occasional meetings of a socialist group in Henry Street, where prophets of the new day milder than Marx were discussed" (*JJ* 142). His brother recalls: "He ... frequented meetings of socialist groups in back rooms in the manner ascribed to Mr. Duffy in 'A Painful Case.' I sometimes accompanied him to these dimly illuminated, melancholy haunts and listened to un-convincing arguments."[16] Though Stanislaus cites no dates for these meetings, the brothers must have attended them sometime between 1901 and 1904. Joyce's interest in socialism continued to grow during this period. The conclusion to "A Portrait of the Artist," an essay composed shortly before his twenty-second birthday, adapts from Marx's *Critique of the Gotha Programme* a description of a future communist society.[17] An entry in his brother's diary dated 13 August 1904 observes: "He calls himself a socialist but attaches himself to no school of socialism."[18] During the next three years, while he was working on *Dubliners* and *Stephen Hero* in Pola, Trieste, and Rome, his intellectual involvement with socialism peaked. He termed himself in May 1905 "a socialistic artist" (*L II* 89). His letters to Stanislaus included long, tortuous arguments on behalf of social-ism and against "tyrannies of all kinds" (*L II* 148). He made friends among Triestine workers, and devoured book after book by socialists and allied radicals. During his sojourn in Rome he followed the proceedings of the Italian Socialist Party congress, which took place there in October 1906; and he became a regular reader of the party's satirical weekly, *L'Asino*, and its daily paper, *Avanti!*, whose views are reflected in his letters at that time.[19]

In March 1907, however – less than half a year after the Socialist congress had ended – Joyce seemed to turn away from politics. He informed Stanislaus:

It is months since I have written a line and even reading tires me. The interest in socialism and the rest has left me ... Yet I have certain ideas I would like to give form to: not as a doctrine but as the continuation of the expression of myself which I now see began in *Chamber Music*. These ideas or instincts or intuitions may be purely personal. I have no wish to codify myself as anarchist or socialist or revolutionary. (*L II* 217)

His mood of world-weariness undoubtedly contributed to his sudden professed dismissal of socialism; but, even if his aboutface was not total, from this time on his interest in "isms" of any kind declined. As his fame developed he became known as an esthete, an apolitical artist. Even his close friend Frank Budgen commented: "On one subject he was more uncommunicative than any man I know: that of politics ... An occasional vague reference to the pacific American anarchist, Tucker, was the only indication I ever heard of a political outlook."[20]

Yet, during those early years in Europe before his disillusionment, exactly what kind of socialist was Joyce? A friend in Rome described him as "un po' di tutto" – a little of everything (*L II* 183). Exploring the protean, undoctrinaire nature of Joyce's socialism during this period, Dominic Manganiello isolates syndicalism and anarchism as the two currents that attracted him most. Arturo Labriola, the Italian syndicalist leader who took part in the 1906 Socialist congress, advocated industrial unionism, particularly the weapon of the general strike. His opposition to parliamentary socialism appealed to Joyce, who scorned the Irish Party which (in his eyes) had let Parnell down. It was a similar hostility to constitutional reformism that drew him to Sinn Fein; he wrote to Stanislaus that Labriola reminded him of Arthur Griffith (*L II* 173–74), although Griffith opposed political action through unions. Curiously, he did not mention James Connolly, who pioneered the idea of industrial unionism in Ireland and who much more than Griffith was ideologically in tune with Labriola.[21] (I attempt to account for Joyce's puzzling, pregnant silence on Connolly in Chapter 3.)

Anarchism appealed to Joyce even more than syndicalism, and he was familiar with the writings of many anarchists. They "fascinated [him] because, whereas Marx dictated an impersonal class warfare, they sought to liberate the individual from those forces that smothered human potentialities."[22] In this respect, their aim meshed with his as an artist – as one of that class of "subversive writers" (*P* 78) whose liberating influence we see on Stephen Dedalus. Needless to say, he preferred pacifistic anarchism, such as Tolstoy's and Benjamin Tucker's, over the better-known violent variety. Thus (although he found *Das Kapital* absurd) he would have agreed with Marx and Engels in condemning the "stupid" Fenian explosion at Clerkenwell along with the "Bakuninist" and "purposeless"[23] murders by the Invincibles in Phoenix Park. Yet, as Ellmann suggests, Bakunin may well have been the paramount influence on Joyce's politics. Joyce resisted and attempted to expose what

Bakunin saw as the hidden alliance between the materialism of the State and the idealism of the Church.[24] And, generally, he was attracted by the Russian's "moral anarchism [which] sees the individual as a law unto himself."[25]

Liberalism also interested Joyce: he knew Ruskin's works well and owned a copy of Mill's *On Liberty*. Sidney Feshbach has suggested that left-wing liberalism, more than anarcho-syndicalism, actuated him politically. This tradition, in European history,

begins with John Ruskin and John Stuart Mill, continues through the left-wing liberalism of 1890–1900 . . . and includes the more radical Continental expressions of liberalism, a liberalism illuminated by the anarchism and socialism of 1880–1910.[26]

But Joyce mocked Ruskin's road-building project, calling him "a pompous professor . . . leading a crowd of Anglo-Saxon adolescents to the promised land of the future society – behind a wheelbarrow" (*CW* 202). He also declared in 1918, "As an artist I am against every state,"[27] whereas both Ruskin and Mill, in spite of their reservations about governmental interference in private lives, still thought the State necessary as an external authority.[28]

Whatever influence radical liberalism exercised on Joyce, he detested other kinds. Gladstone's Liberalism he accused in 1907 of being, together with Vaticanism, one of "the most powerful weapons that England can use against Ireland" (*CW* 195). Its philosophical relative, Arnoldian liberalism, did provide him with what Irish cultural nationalism also provided – namely, the concept of "the heroism of the extraordinary individual who, confronted by the mob, must create a distance from it and, in doing so, develop a kind of chivalry of the intellect."[29] Like Yeats, he adopted this trope, yet differed from Yeats in his ability to treat it ironically, to expose it in his art as culturally determined role-playing of the sort in which Stephen engages. (Stephen takes his role models from parallel prototype narratives which we might call "Celt vs. Saxon" and "Artist vs. Philistine." One of his and Joyce's problems was that the Celts turned out to be Philistines.) But Arnold's liberalism represented to Joyce a truly hostile force, as Deane argues, because it repressed the energies of sexuality and anarchy. Its concept of culture – or monoculture – did not leave room for pluralism or letting a hundred flowers bloom; certainly *Ulysses* would have been considered a rank weed by the guardians of such a culture, as the reaction to it of a would-be guardian, Sir Edmund Gosse, indicates. Coupling Joyce's "sheer indecency" with his literary iconoclasm, Gosse pronounced: "It is an anarchical production, infamous in taste, in style, in everything" (*JJ* 528).

In making this conjunction, Gosse hit upon a genuine nexus in Joyce's politics. The literary rebel was a sexual rebel. As Joyce told one of his Paris friends, Church and State impose on the individual's life a historically determined pattern intended to suppress the "eternal qualities [of] the imagination and the sexual instinct"; against this pattern the "writer must maintain a continual struggle."[30] As part of this struggle, he cohabited with Nora for over twenty-five years until the need to legitimize their children – a nod toward the State – resulted in a civil ceremony. Over and over, he attacked the mystification of sex and linked the ideal of sexual purity to sexual disease, which he turned into a metaphor of moral disease – the syphilisation" (*U* 12.1197) of both Ireland and Europe. In his correspondence with Stanislaus in 1906, he proclaimed venereal disease to be "like any other disease, caused by anti-hygienic conditions." Aroused by Oliver St. John Gogarty's and Arthur Griffith's nationalistic criticisms of the venereal excess of English soldiers, he denounced "lying drivel about pure men and pure women and spiritual love" and wished that "some unkind person would publish a book about the venereal condition of the Irish" (*L II* 170, 191–92). In his art he was less straightforward and more satirical and parodic, although the early essay, "A Portrait of the Artist as a Young Man," does end on a visionary note: "To these multitudes, not as yet in the wombs of humanity but surely engenderable there, he would give the word ... [A]mid the general paralysis of an insane society, the confederate will issues in action."[31] Here "a socialist vision and a medical definition of the terminal stage of severe syphilitic infection are combined."[32]

We recognize the artist of this vision – whose seminal word is the seed from which a politically sane and sexually healthy society will arise – in the protagonist of *Stephen Hero*. Stephen takes delight both in flouting his society's repressive code of sexual purity and in pointing out its widespread, covert violations of the code. Thus he provokes the Gaelic Leaguer, Madden, with the information that one of his medical professors is "the landlord of a whole street of brothels" (*SH* 65). He declares to Lynch the superiority of the "woman in the black straw hat" – who offers him her body in exchange for money – over Emma Clery, whose price is a wedding ring and who rejects his proposition that she give herself for nothing. Marriage he denounces as "a simoniacal exchange" because "a human being's love and freedom is not a spiritual asset of the State" (*SH* 202). In contrast, the Stephen of *A Portrait* never quite attains such dogmatic self-assurance as a sexual rebel: instead he oscillates between unrealistic loathing and unrealistic longing, thereby embodying some of the attitudes his precursor criticizes. The Stephen of *Ulysses* has other things on his mind besides desire or romance; in that book it is the androgynous Bloom, a "womanly man" (*U* 15.1799), who assumes the artist's role of subverting middle-class sexual morality.[33] Other passages in *Ulysses*, such as the preparations in "Cyclops" for the hero-martyr's execution, parody the nexus of values – "[s]exual purity, gentlemanly conduct, military valour, group loyalty" – which Irish nationalism shared with English liberalism and turned into "a myth of chivalry."[34] In *Finnegans Wake* the hero, who is everyone as well as a tavern keeper in Chapelizod, is accused of that direst of middle-class sexual transgressions, incest. A single word used in the *Wake* in connection with the Rising of Easter 1916 – "Surrection" (*FW* 593.2–3) – conflates erection, insurrection, and resurrection, and illustrates the key fact that "[t]he political, the religious, and the sexual are always interrelated for Joyce."[35] They had to be interrelated, of course, since they were so closely tied together in the society against which Joyce was rebelling and which he sought to reform by giving its people "one good look at themselves in my nicely polished looking-glass" (*LI* 64).

A LITERARY REVOLUTIONIST

Admittedly, Joyce's political beliefs are difficult to label. He was a pacifist all his life, yet stood aloof from organized expressions of pacifism (much as Stephen spurns MacCann's petition for universal peace [*P* 194–98]). He hated British imperialism, yet took no part – his brief attraction to Sinn Fein notwithstanding – in organized expressions of Irish nationalism. Although his letters to Stanislaus reveal a genuine concern with social issues and a deep intellectual interest in left-wing politics, he failed to enlist under the banner of any of the factions of socialism (discouraged, perhaps, by their "endless internecine warfare"[36] which struck him during the 1906 congress).

Still, now that Ellmann, Manganiello, and others have dispelled the myth of Joyce's indifference to politics, critics continue to look for a unifying principle in his political attitudes. Colin MacCabe asserts: "Joyce's politics were largely determined by attitudes to sexuality. Central to his commitment to socialism was his ferocious opposition to the institution of marriage, bourgeois society's sanctified disavowal of the reality of desire."[37] This claim has much truth, yet it strikes me as being overstated – as being the sort of effort to impart identity to multiplicity which MacCabe himself describes Joyce as resisting. Feshbach argues for the influence of radical liberalism; at the same time, though, he finds Joyce's politics to be "entirely subordinate to his personal moral concerns, which are consistently 'defensive': whatever he felt impinged on his freedom he fought off."[38] But the dividing line between political concerns and "personal moral concerns" does not seem altogether clear to me.

The key distinction, I think, lies between kinds of political action. Both Joyce and Yeats, for instance, expressed – directly and indirectly, consciously and unconsciously – political beliefs in their writings. Unlike Yeats, however, Joyce didn't care to combine the life of an artist with that of a politician (even though he modeled his stance as an Irish artist – as a lone, noble, persecuted would-be liberator of his people – after a man who was a politician to his fingertips). Feshbach is right about his fighting off any threat to his freedom, and he plainly perceived political movements and groups of any sort as being such a threat. Hence his interest in anarchism, with its emphasis on individual freedom and its distrust of politics as "involving either the exercise or restraint of power."[39] Hence, too, his interest in Oscar Wilde's "The Soul of Man under Socialism," which he considered translating into Italian in 1909. Wilde writes:

People sometimes inquire what form of government is most suitable for an artist to live under. To this question there is only one answer: ... *no government at all*. Authority over him and his art is ridiculous ... There are three kinds of despots. There is the despot who tyrannises over the body. There is the despot who tyrannises over the soul. There is the despot who tyrannises over soul and body alike. The first is called the Prince. The second is called the Pope. The third is called the People.[40]

Wilde's declaration appears to be echoed in Stephen's answer to Haines, during a conversation on religious dogma and free thought, that he is the servant of three "masters" (*U* 1.638). A similar anarchistic philosophy seems implied in Joyce's early declaration to

Nora: "My mind rejects the whole present social order and Christianity" (*L II* 48).[41] As a man whose creed was not only art but the unfettered growth of his own soul (to which he dedicated his first play), he couldn't embrace any institutionalized form of nationalism, pacifism, or socialism. Even though he detested the forces against which they were reacting, he needed to distance himself from their potential restrictions on his intellectual freedom. Thus his departure from Ireland into self-exile, and thus his gradual adoption of a posture of esthetic indifference, which had begun to grow into a mask by the time he started writing *Ulysses*. The madness of World War I impelled him to drop the mask in "Dooleysprudence," where he calls for a plague on all the belligerent nations, but normally he kept his views to himself except insofar as they are filtered through his main characters, all three of whom are pacifists with negative attitudes toward patriotism. Stephen rejects Old Gummy Granny. Once relatively radical, Bloom now thinks of Sinn Fein, the latest manifestation of Irish nationalism, with middle-aged caution.[42] Remembering a protest against the Boer War, he speculates that the student demonstrators will, in time, become pillars of the established order. In the same passage he unflatteringly mixes up Sinn Fein with the Fenians, musing: "Sinn Fein. Back out you get the knife. Hidden hand. Stay in. The firing squad." Arthur Griffith, he concedes, is "a squareheaded fellow," but he mistrusts Griffith's tendency "to gas about our lovely land" (*U* 8.458–64). As usual Molly gets in the last word. Recalling Bloom's youthful Parnellite enthusiasm, she thinks: "Wasnt I the born fool to believe all his blather about home rule and the land league." She also dismisses his more recent talk about "the coming man Griffiths"; we learn, in this context, that she has hate[d] the mention of politics" (*U* 18.1187–88, 387–88) ever since her first lover died in the Boer War.

❊

Politics, nationalism, death. Writing *Ulysses* during and after World War I and the violence out of which the Irish Free State arose, Joyce hardly could have avoided this linkage. As a Parnellite, a pacifist, and a socialist of sorts, he had always been ambivalent toward Irish nationalism. Seemingly he had rejected nationalism altogether by the time the war forced him to move from Trieste to Zurich. Yet his very silence on the subject of politics, which so impressed Budgen, suggests denial – especially in wartime Switzerland, which "had some of the character of a beleaguered town" and whose citizens "all ... talked war strategy and politics."[43] In any event, though he remained a neutral in both Irish and European politics, he did not become an apolitical artist. He shared Shelley's belief in the poet's importance to society[44] – "Poets are the unacknowledged legislators of the world"[45] – and, as a young writer, he paraphrased Shelley in having Stephen declare: "Every age must look for its sanction to its poets and philosophers. The poet is the intense centre of the life of his age to which he stands in a relation than which none can be more vital" (*SH* 80). Throughout his career he belonged to "the literary-revolutionary school" (to borrow his own term for the early Romantic movement) and engaged, like Blake, in a "spiritual rebellion against the powers of this world" (*CW* 215).

The instrument of Joyce's rebellion was the written word. Very early in his life he learned the political significance of the word, both oral and written. He grew up in a city of three languages – English English, Irish English, and Gaelic – then moved to Trieste, another city where three languages interacted and reflected a history of conflict and subjugation.[46] His awareness of language as a reflector of the human past can be seen in his essay, written at the age of seventeen, on "The Study of Languages": "In the history of words there is much that indicates the history of men ... [S]ometimes the advent of an overcoming power may be attested by the crippled diction, or by the complete disuse of the original tongue, save in solitary, dear phrases, spontaneous in grief or gladness" (*CW* 28). In *A Portrait* Stephen remarks bitterly, "My ancestors threw off their language and took another" (*P* 203). But their new language, English, does not belong to him fully or give him a viable identity any more than does the resurrected Irish of the Gaelic revival, as his encounter with the dean of studies makes him realize. Though a Catholic convert and "a poor Englishman in Ireland," the dean represents the conquering race and authoritatively calls a "funnel" that which Stephen knows only, in Irish English, as a "tundish." Stephen thinks:

The language in which we are speaking is his before it is mine. How different are the words *home*, *Christ*, *ale*, *master*, on his lips and on mine! I cannot speak or write these words without unrest of spirit. His language, so familiar and so foreign, will always be for me an acquired speech. I have not made or accepted its words. (*P* 189)[47]

Most of all, the Maamtrasna murders, reflected in the Festy King episode of *Finnegans Wake*,[48] exhibit Joyce's awareness of the life-or-death political importance of language. Joyce first referred to this case, which involved the trial and hanging of an Irish speaker by an English-speaking court for a crime he had not committed, in a Triestine newspaper article in 1907. He described the interaction between the accused, an old man "almost beside himself with the anguish of being unable to understand or to make himself understood," and the indifferent interpreter, who dryly translated long, emotional outbursts of Gaelic into monosyllables. Then, after sketching the scene of the hanging, where the victim didn't comprehend the executioner's instructions, he summed up:

The figure of this dumbfounded old man, a remnant of a civilization not ours, deaf and dumb before his judge, is a symbol of the Irish nation at the bar of public opinion. Like him, she is unable to appeal to the modern conscience of England and other countries. The English journalists act as interpreters between Ireland and the English electorate ... Abroad there is no talk of Ireland except when uprisings break out ... Skimming over the dispatches from London ... the public conceives of the Irish as highwaymen with distorted faces, roaming the night with the object of taking the hide of every Unionist. (*CW* 198)

The problem Joyce puts his finger on here includes but goes beyond language. It is that of having one's history misrepresented in the hegemonic narrative of a conquering power – the problem, in short, of the stage Irishman and the ape-faced Irishman of *Punch*, those "old stale libels" (*SH* 65) which the Gaelic revivalist, Madden, accuses Stephen of voicing. The usual response to such a narrative involves the creation of a contrarily distorted counter-narrative that also aspires to hegemony, at least among members of the oppressed race. Espousing the counter-narrative of Irish nationalism, Madden mistakes Stephen's attempt to break free of any dominant discourse for advocacy of the English and Anglo-Irish view of Ireland. In a foreshadowing of *A Portrait* and *Ulysses*, Stephen finds himself caught among competing narrativized expressions of ideology corresponding to the three "masters" (*U* 1.638), who, his later self tells Haines, lay claim to him. These threaten not only his soul but, potentially, his body. To speak the wrong language, and to tell the wrong story, can prove fatal. This was the case with the victim of British justice in the Maamtrasna murder trial – a man bearing the name of Joyce, Myles Joyce. For his namesake he became an emblem of Irish inarticulateness in the face of English cultural domination and an embodiment of the ultimate consequence of such domination, backed up as it was with brute force. Joyce himself feared being silenced – by indifference, by censorship, and even by murder, though he was afraid of death at the hands of Irish nationalists rather than of English imperialists. His fear of physical harm if he returned to Ireland stemmed (a touch of paranoia aside) from his awareness of the hostility aroused by heretics and rebels who challenge established orders with subversive narratives. Myles Joyce – whose statement on the scaffold, "I am going" (*tá mé ag imtheacht*), echoes throughout the *Wake*[49] – was not even a rebel; he simply spoke the tongue of a subjugated culture.

Self-protectively moving into exile in 1904 and adopting Italian as his domestic language, Joyce thereby distanced himself from the threats and claims to which he felt he would be subject in Ireland or anywhere in the British Empire. Though continuing to write in English, he turned *Dubliners* into an instrument of subversion against the powers of this world by eschewing any "dominant discourse" or "meta-language controlling the other discourses."[50] The stories work paratactically, placing one event after another, without allowing us to draw any authorized conclusions. Except for rare satirical passages, the neutral-sounding narrative voice in the third-person stories which we might identify with the author (or implied author) of *Dubliners* does not give us authorial guidance. Instead of "monological unity,"[51] we find a diversity of voices or "heteroglossia," different languages with different points of view on the world engaged in dialogue with each other. "The author is not to be found in the language of the narrator ... but rather, the author utilizes now one language, now another, in order to avoid giving himself up wholly to either of them."[52] In *A Portrait* Joyce went further, developing his protagonist through a series of languages and world-views ranging from baby talk to poetics and from a hellfire-and-brimstone sermon to sexualized esthetic longing. To apply Bakhtin's comment on *Little Dorrit* to *A Portrait*, the entire text is

everywhere dotted with quotation marks that serve to separate out little islands of scattered direct speech and purely authorial speech, washed by heteroglot waves from all sides. But it would have been impossible actually to insert such marks, since ... one and the same word often figures both as the speech of the author and the speech of another – and at the same time.[53]

Again, but more radically than in Dickens, there is no dominant or transcendent discourse; all relations of dominance are undermined.

Joyce carried his "revolution of the word" (to borrow Eugene

Jolas's phrase [*JJ* 588]) even further in his last two books. With regard to *Ulysses*, Bakhtin serves once more as the best commentator, noting that heteroglossia in the comic novel is marked by two distinctive features:

(1) Incorporated into the novel are a multiplicity of 'languages' and verbal-ideological belief systems – generic, professional, class-and-interest group ... tendentious, everyday ...

(2) The incorporated languages and socio-ideological belief systems, while of course utilized to refract the author's intentions, are unmasked and destroyed as something false, hypocritical, greedy, limited, narrowly rationalistic, inadequate to reality.[54]

In *Ulysses* the discourses of British colonialism, Irish nationalism, low-brow popular magazines, the Celtic twilight, Catholicism, and other belief systems all have their say, yet all are unmasked and demonstrated to be "inadequate to reality." The critic trying to identify Joyce with any particular discourse faces an impossible task, since no one discourse is privileged or indeed has any meaning except in dialogue with other discourses.

By the time he conceived the idea of *Finnegans Wake*, Joyce had found the English language itself – by implication, any given language – to be inadequate in its ability to evoke the world. "I cannot express myself in English without enclosing myself in a tradition," he said. "I'd like a language which is above all languages, a language to which all will do service" (*JJ* 397). Hence in the *Wake* he created an English-based, international portmanteau language, not free of tradition but full of different traditions, in which even individual words cannot be assigned single, authoritative meanings. The result is not a Tower of Babel but polyphony at the level of the word, virtually endless dialogism, both macrocosmic and microcosmic. The *Wake* thus points to the limits of any national language and of nationality itself. As MacCabe comments on Joyce's writing in general, "all positions are constantly threatened with dissolution into the play of language."[55] It is because *Finnegans Wake* in particular calls into question all monologic, officially sanctioned forms of identity and all communities short of humanity as a whole that Philippe Sollers terms it "the most formidably anti-fascist book produced between the two wars."[56]

A key source of Joyce's subversive literary politics was a book called *La Scienza nuova* by the eighteenth-century philosopher and jurist, Giambattista Vico. Vico's "New Science" develops a combined theory of history and language with far-reaching political implications. Language, for Vico, arises out of and reflects human history; it is the vehicle by which the spirit of a nation enters the soul of the person who learns it. Further, "the world of civil society has certainly been made by men, and . . . its principles are therefore to be found within the modifications of our own human mind."[57] In other words, both language and history are human products, and the interpreter of history (past events) actually makes that history (accounts of past events) in the process of writing it.[58] This brings us by "a commodius vicus of recirculation" (*FW* 3) back to Jameson and the problems of historiography touched on in my introduction. As Vico claimed in his *Autobiography*, he discovered "a new critical method for sifting the truth as to the founders of the nations from the popular traditions of the nations they founded."[59] This "New Critical Art" rejects the notion of history as a collection of significant names, dates, and events – that is, the history Stephen is supposed to teach his class at Mr. Deasy's school. Because it is authorized by the winners of wars and powerful vested interests, this kind of history cannot be trusted. Instead, through a comparative study of civilizations, religions, and mythologies, the New Critical Art seeks to uncover that "mental language common to all nations, which uniformly grasps the substance of things feasible in human social life and expresses it with as many diverse modifications as these things may have diverse aspects."[60] That is to say, Vico's hermeneutics takes as its goal the revelation of something resembling the modern concept of "ideology" (in its original sense expounded by Destutt de Tracy) as it is embodied in institutions, language, and ideas.

In rebelling against official history, Vico turned to myth, which he saw as *vera narratio*, for expressions of that international "mental language":

Mythologies, according to Vico, often narrate those forbidden "true stories" which have been systematically suppressed and omitted from the official, homogenous histories of nations, religions, social and political institutions, and so forth. Heretic beliefs, revolutionary movements, rebellious heroes, and other subversive forces, he saw, have found no recognitions in the authoritative accounts of the past, but they have left their traces in such counter-historical accounts as folk-tales, carnivals, [and] songs.[61]

In interpreting Greek and Roman myths, Vico attempted to uncover repressed facts concerning sociopolitical conflicts in Athens and Rome. Thus he ascribed the account of Mars's rebellion against Jupiter to the plebeians, who wanted to counter patrician myths and indirectly claim civil rights for themselves. Vico in this respect was a forerunner of Nietzsche and Foucault: all three set about "decoding or deconstructing the established historical traditions in their respective Ages of Reason."[62]

Toward the end of his life Joyce said, "My imagination grows when I read Vico as it doesn't when I read Freud or Jung" (*JJ* 693). He had begun reading *The New Science* as early as 1911 or 1912, when one of his Triestine pupils discovered his passionate interest in the Neapolitan thinker, and perhaps earlier.[63] We see in Joyce's writings a hostility to official history similar to and, at least in *Ulysses* and *Finnegans Wake*, influenced by Vico's own rejection of such history. *The New Science* also may have reinforced Joyce's Irish Catholic bias in favor of popular or felt history. Clearly it gave him a theoretical justification for his use of such history, much as it justified his obsessive concern with heretics and rebels. For both Vico and Joyce, history was "a system of restraint,"[64] and Joyce followed Vico's example in turning to mythology as a liberating counter-reality. Mythology not only puts human experience into an alternative perspective, but actualizes those "infinite possibilities" (*U* 2.50–51) which history (past events as well as established accounts of past events) has ousted. Both real and imagined, it breaks down Aristotle's distinction between poetry and history.[65] The "thing that might be," mythology, assumes equal (if not superior) ontological status in relation to the "thing that has been," history, which Joyce and Vico in their different ways reveal to have an imagined component also. Myth can significantly affect the present as well as the past. T. S. Eliot recognized this in finding the mythic framework of *Ulysses* to be "a way of controlling, of ordering ... the immense panorama of futility and anarchy which is contemporary history."[66] But Eliot overemphasized the controlling and ordering aspects of Joyce's use of myth and overlooked its subversive effect on the very traditions he wished to uphold. For Joyce, like Vico, sought freedom from tradition, from received history, and from linguistic convention. Both "set themselves up not only as diviners and rebels but as virtual divinities and Creators ... determined to remake the world through language."[67]

Thus, for Joyce, writing was both a creative act and an act of liberating.[68] He wrote at once to make history and to free himself from it. Though he sought freedom from Irish history in particular – from its hard, fixed, oppressive facts and from the vying colonialist and nationalist interpretations of those facts – he nevertheless attempted to forge "the uncreated conscience" (*P* 253) of his race in his own (hi)story and his own language. The model he followed in doing this may well have been not only Vico but (as suggested in Chapter 1) the rhetorical tradition of Irish nationalism, which illustrates the power of the word and the imagination to give birth to reality.[69] From this point of view, he remained under the influence of Irish nationalism even after going into exile to remove himself from it. Although he never visited the Free State, he continued to write about Ireland and to be involved with her both emotionally and politically. But, however we try to define his ambivalent, elusive politics – nationalist, left-wing liberal, socialist, anarchist, Vichian, and so on – he was in any event not a passive esthete, but a literary revolutionist for whom writing represented the supreme political act.

CHAPTER 3

The paralyzed city

My intention was to write a chapter of the moral history of my country and I chose Dublin for the scene because that city seemed to me the centre of paralysis.

> Joyce, letter to Grant Richards, 5 May 1906

Dear Stannie I sent you yesterday copies of the F. J. containing fuller accounts of the Abbey riots ... Of course just the very week I wanted it most Aunt J did not send *Sinn Fein* ... I feel like a man in a house who hears a row in the street and voices he knows shouting but can't get out to see what the hell is going on.

> Joyce, letter to Stanislaus Joyce, 11 February 1907

In 1907 an Anglo-Irishman named Samuel A. Ossory Fitzpatrick published his "historical and topographical account" of Dublin. It includes this sketch of recent progress:

The nineteenth century has added to Dublin most of its parish churches, Protestant and Roman Catholic, has seen the foundation of many more public institutions and some important additions to its public buildings, the rebuilding and alteration of four of the six previously existing bridges over the Liffey, and the erection of four new ones, the completion of a new and magnificent water supply, and the creation of a splendid system of internal communication. In addition, numerous statues and other memorials have been erected in the leading thoroughfares, the Phoenix Park has been laid out, and enriched with one of the finest zoological gardens in Europe, and a very complete system of main drainage and electric lighting practically completed. The construction of railways has brought Dublin into direct communication with every provincial centre, and the continuous growth of the suburbs and the erection of artisans' dwellings has raised considerably the standard of comfort of the middle and lower classes.[1]

Politics enters this "historical" account mainly as a series of public works honored in ceremonies involving Queen Victoria, Prince Albert, Lords Ardilaun and Iveagh, various Lord Mayors of Dublin, and similar figures. A dissonant note – "the cowardly and purpose-less assassination of Mr. Thomas H. Burke ... and Lord Frederick Cavendish" – is muffled within the context of a history of places. We move in successive sentences from "the much-needed South City Markets" to the Phoenix Park murders, "perpetrated within sight of the windows of the Viceregal Lodge," to the opening of the Killiney Hill Park by Prince Albert. As part of a narrative progress, the murders almost seem enlisted in an ameliorative historical progress that continues, in the early twentieth century, with the estab-lishment of an electric tram system "which now renders Dublin in respect to internal communication second to no city in Europe."[2]

In that same year, 1907, a 25-year-old Irish Catholic completed his own portrait of Dublin. Three years earlier he had announced his aim: "to betray the soul of that hemiplegia or paralysis which many consider a city" (*L I* 55). Later, in a query sent to a publisher, he pointed proudly to "the special odour of corruption which, I hope, floats over my stories" (*L II* 123). He won a contract; then the publisher demanded revisions to avoid offending the Dublin public. In his arguments against revising, he cited both his lofty purpose and his faithfulness to reality:

It is not my fault that the odour of ashpits and old weeds and offal hangs round my stories. I seriously believe that you will retard the course of civilisation in Ireland by preventing the Irish people from having one good look at themselves in my nicely polished looking-glass. (*L I* 63–64)

He held to his purpose throughout a seven-year battle with Irish prudishness and censorship. Finally, in self-exile ...

The story's a familiar one – so familiar that we tend to take it for granted. *Dubliners* eventually did appear, to mixed reviews, on 15 June 1914 in an edition of 1,250 copies; it sold badly. Joyce's genius slowly won recognition as little magazines published installments of *A Portrait of the Artist as a Young Man* and then *Ulysses*. Decades later, after the publication of *Finnegans Wake* and after Joyce's death, American professors of literature rediscovered *Dubliners*. The year of awakening (disregarding Levin and Shattuck's wild-goose chase after Homeric analogues and a handful of minor essays) was 1956. Writing separately, Brewster Ghiselin, Hugh Kenner, and Marvin Magalaner and Richard Kain all discerned in the stories a remark-able formal unity whose key is the theme of paralysis. Ghiselin traced a symbolic pattern that turns the book's separate "histories" into one essential history, that of the soul of a people which has confused and weakened its relation to the source of spiritual life and cannot restore it.

In so far as this unifying action is evident in the realistic elements of the book, it appears in the struggle of certain characters to escape the constricting circumstances of existence in Ireland, and especially in Dublin, "the centre of paralysis."[3]

Kenner, comparing the city in its "present paralysis" to a "ghost," evoked Joyce's Dublin as "a shell of grandeur populated by wraiths."[4] Magalaner and Kain blamed Ireland's moral paralysis on "the enervating Dublin climate of fifty years ago"; Joyce's subject, they wrote, "was determined for him by the only life he knew – a sordid, poverty-ridden, monotonous day-by-day existence in a city whose former greatness seemed in eclipse."[5]

The ensuing flood of *Dubliners* criticism followed the path, primarily, of these treatments. Joyce's admission that his stories were less than accurate reflections of the reality he had known – "I have reproduced ... none of the attraction of the city" (*L II* 166) – was often quoted and yet, in practice, ignored. Overlooked was the description in Gorman's authorized biography, written in consultation with Joyce, of the artist in Rome beginning his third year of exile and feeling isolated because of news from home that

impress[ed] upon his mind the exhilarating effect of the strong yeast that was fermenting in his native city. Dublin, according to all accounts, was one of the liveliest and most pleasant places in which to live during this transitional period of time when the rest of the world's great cities appeared content to doze in a sort of midsummer lethargy. There was sparkling excitement over art and politics in the air above the Liffey.[6]

This picture of Dublin can be criticized as less than the whole truth, as can the opposite picture drawn in *Dubliners*. But it did not register. As a consequence, Joyce's one-sided presentation of turn-of-the-century Dublin became, for most of his non-Irish readers, *the* Dublin – or the only one that mattered.

It would have greatly startled Samuel A. Ossory Fitzpatrick to hear in 1907 that Dublin was paralyzed – a mere shell inhabited by ghosts and the living dead of whom he was one. This is not to say that he wouldn't have recognized the city depicted in *Dubliners*. A reader for a publisher which rejected Joyce's manuscript – a man with a social background similar to Fitzpatrick's – knew quite well what he was dealing with:

Most of these stories treat of very lower-middle class Dublin life. They are never enlivening and often sordid and even disgusting. There is a faded, musty odour about them: the scenes are in gloomy back streets, in houses with dust-stained fan-lights and windows, in rooms with battered prints on the walls and only a coal of fire in the grate, in the bars of Public Houses. Most of the characters are too fond of drink, and nearly all are physically repulsive. It is a dismal and depressing world, this.[7]

Major Dermot Freyer did not object to Joyce's stories because of their lack of artistry or their lack of realism. He simply didn't care for Dublin's largely Catholic lower-middle classes, either in life or in art. They were not a fit subject for art; and, in Fitzpatrick's eyes, they undoubtedly were not a fit subject for his history of Dublin except in relation to outrages (the Phoenix Park murders) or good works (artisans' dwellings). To turn things around, Joyce had no artistic use for the Anglo-Irish and little use for Dublin's lower classes. Yet his Dublin and Fitzpatrick's do not cancel each other out, any more than they sum up Dublin between them. On the contrary, they intersect in interesting ways, as when Maria in "Clay" rides on the city's fine tram system or when the characters in "Two Gallants" walk past a series of Ascendancy landmarks. We could illuminate both "histories" – Joyce's and Fitzpatrick's – by analyzing such intersections. We could analyze them, too, in terms of significant absences – those aspects of Dublin which one or both leaves out. But in any case, we would be looking at narrativized facets of a reality which those persons who experienced it would have recognized, with differing levels of awareness, as being many-faceted.

That brings me back to the American formalists whose interest in *Dubliners* helped inspire the burgeoning of Joyce studies. Joyce's fictions at once resist and lend themselves to formal analysis; not for nothing did he adopt as his youthful pseudonym the name of a fabulous Greek artificer. Seemingly beginning to fulfill Joyce's wish to "keep the critics busy for three hundred years" (*JJ* 703), the formalists rose to the challenge of his increasingly elaborate texts and turned out a body of interpretation that, at its best, thoroughly maps the internal and cross-relations of these texts and the techniques used to create them. But the New Critics' work also tends to blur or elide the difference between Joyce's Dublin and its historical referent. Not that this referent is a simple, single ingredient missing from their interpretations. Rather, we might sum up the problem by asking: What sense do these critics give us of any textualization other than Joyce's of that complex set of ideological tensions which was known, in the first decade of the century, as Dublin?

Ironically, the ahistorical bent of the first postwar generation of Joyce critics deprived them of historical evidence that supports his fictionalized view of Irish paralysis. Cruise O'Brien was the first of two distinguished Irish historians to place this view – actually an extreme form of a widespread Irish perception – in context. In 1960 he wrote:

> In the summary historical retrospect which we all acquire at school ... this period 1891 to 1916 forms, I think, a sort of crease in time, a featureless valley between the commanding chain of the Rising and the solitary enigmatic peak of Parnell. It was a time in which nothing happened; nothing except ... a revolution in land ownership, the beginning of a national quest for a lost language and culture, and the preparation of ... two successful rebellions. Yet despite these momentous events it is not only to us with our memories of school history that the period seems empty: it seemed so to many contemporaries.

O'Brien remarks of both Joyce and his opposite, the Ascendancy writer Edith Somerville, that they saw through the pretenses of the official expressions of Irish nationalism – the Gaelic League, the Gaelic Athletic Association, and so on – but did not see through them to anything living and growing:

> They could have taken to themselves the majestic words of the English statesman of the day: I was never present while a Revolution was going on. In a sense indeed, most of the population was absent while the Revolution was going on. What, for example, did the Gaelic League mean to the working people of Dublin? ... And as for the middle class ... there is some reason to believe that on Easter Monday, 1916, the main focus of its interest was not the G.P.O. but Fairyhouse Racecourse.[8]

O'Brien sets beside the revolutionary tradition of modern Ireland, which its citizens are taught to accept as their heritage, the "Fairyhouse tradition" – that is, the massive, continuous indifference that forms the background against which any tradition stands out. For every enthusiast who took Gaelic lessons or wielded a hurley stick there were hundreds of people who did not; for every armed rebel in the G.P.O. there were thousands of able-bodied men who stayed at home, not merely indifferent but angered by the disruption of everyday life. It is this counter-tradition, he suggests, which we should keep in mind in assessing the contradictions of a period that struck contemporaries as being paralyzed, yet, at the same time, alive with political and cultural energy.

Ten years later, F. S. L. Lyons's article on "James Joyce's Dublin" took aim at literary critics who apparently had learned nothing from O'Brien. Lyons begins with a discussion of the intellectual excitement attending the birth of the Irish Literary Theatre; then he turns to Joyce's view of Dublin, which

> has so imposed itself on ... critics and commentators ... that it is almost impossible to see [Dublin] as other than drab, impoverished, servile ... It almost seems in fact as if "that special odour of corruption" which he hoped floated over his stories floated also over the entire city.

> To the historian such a view ... is totally unacceptable, and he cannot avoid asking a few inconvenient questions. Was the Abbey Theatre, were the plays of J. M. Synge, the product of paralysis? Did Yeats's poetry proceed from paralysis? Was George Moore's *Hail and Farewell* a study in paralysis? ... At a different level – were the emergence of Sinn Fein, the growth of the Gaelic League, the rise of organised labour, symbols of rebirth or of paralysis? Above all, was the city which, just 10 years after Joyce's letter [naming Dublin "the centre of paralysis"] was written, burst into a flame of revolution, not quenched until the Union with Britain was dissolved, really in the grip of an inexorable paralysis?

Lyons concludes that the prevailing trait of Dublin during the early twentieth century was not paralysis, but tension. The rest of his essay flows from the questions: What were the origins and nature of this tension? And why did Joyce react to it so differently from everyone else caught up in the city's cultural life? Lyons proceeds to examine Dublin's social and topographical divisions:

> The south bank was prosperous, professional, governmental; the north was commercial, clerical, and all too conscious of its decline from the great days of the eighteenth century. It was not so much that a lot of it was a slum area – Dublin slums spread impartially on either side of the river – but rather that many of its streets and squares were sliding from a desperate kind of shabby gentility to real delapidation.[9]

Joyce was born a south-sider; his family moved across the Liffey because of his father's calamitous inability to manage his affairs. Here, on the north side, Joyce found "those brown brick houses which seem the very incarnation of Irish paralysis" (*SH* 211) – not in the bustle of Grafton Street or the opulence of Merrion Square.

But Joyce's perception of Dublin as a paralyzed city did not arise simply out of his family's slow fall from the Catholic upper-middle classes to a perch just above the destitute poor. This perception was related to his political attitude – "a bad case of arrested Parnellism" – and to his alienation from the Irish literary movement, which "was the creation of the Anglo-Irish, mainly Protestant, Ascendancy."[10] Thus the theme of paralysis may be traced both to Joyce's ambivalent nationalism and to his strong sense of identity as an Irish Catholic. Identifying with the fallen, "betrayed" Parnell, and thereby adopting one of the (hi)stories of Irish Catholic nationalism, he nevertheless rejected other expressions of that ideology. At the same time he rejected the Anglo-Irish literary movement, in part because of its seeming surrender to the dictates of narrow-minded patriotism, but ultimately because its history of Ireland – the Ireland of Burke and Grattan and Swift and Emmet, to paraphrase Yeats – was not his own.

For the Anglo-Irish, history was the record of their dominance. But for Joyce, history, Irish history, was the nightmare from which he was trying to awake. History for him meant Catholicism, meant subservience to the Ascendancy, meant subordination to Britain, meant isolation from Europe, meant a small island turned in upon itself, meant the fall of Parnell and every kind of national ignominy.[11]

Joyce needed to escape those snares of nationality, language, and religion, Lyons argues, which to the Anglo-Irish were external problems only – not bred in the bone. He had to leave Ireland, whereas Yeats and Lady Gregory and members of their circle could remain without suffering the pressures of an intolerable history and without, particularly, being caught between the conflicting demands of artistic integrity and those of nationalism.

Lyons's historical argument offers a corrective to formalist criticism yet has its own flaws. He exhibits a curious blind spot in missing Joyce's deep intellectual involvement as a young man with socialism. Indeed, socialism contributed to that "tension" which Lyons points out as the major characteristic of turn-of-the-century Dublin. So, too, did the slums – a problem dismissed because, "although an essential part of Joyce's Dublin, they do not enter very directly into his work."[12] Here Lyons accepts as a given a significant absence that, if explored, might shed light on what is present. He seems to take for granted also that "flame of revolution" which broke out in 1916 and eventually led to the Free State. His figurative language perhaps should put us on our guard: both language and attitude are those of triumphant Irish nationalism which sees its own history as a teleologically ordained progress – a movement "towards one great goal" (*U* 2.381), as Mr. Deasy describes human history, and not simply the actualization of one of several possibilities. Thus Lyons, in his own narrative of "Joyce's Dublin," relies briefly on what Joyce so vigorously resisted – the narrativized history of the Irish revolutionary tradition. He takes at face value a manifest text – here the success story of Easter 1916 and ensuing events – which should be questioned precisely because it is manifest and therefore hides or omits something of importance. He also overlooks the "Fairyhouse tradition," in light of which his statement that Dublin "burst into a flame of revolution" appears simplistic and misleading. And he forgets his own words on the ambiguities of historical parallax:

There was not one Dublin, but several different Dublins, and how they looked depended upon the eye of the beholder. Viewed from Eccles Street the city might well appear to be the centre of paralysis; yet from the new theatre, or Moore's house in Ely Place, or half a dozen other points, life and movement and excitement seemed its most obvious characteristics. But to find a balance between these different definitions and arrive at some notion of what the city was really like is not easy.[13]

To be sure, we can never find out in any absolute, Rankean sense what Dublin "was really like." But in telling a story about what it might have been like, one must be careful to question not only the claims but the silent assumptions of previous narratives. It isn't enough to rebut Joyce's picture of a paralyzed city simply by citing, as if the facts spoke for themselves, the 1916 Rising – yet another expression of Irish nationalism's hero-martyr complex – and the ensuing violent events which led to the birth of an isolated, repressive, truncated Irish state.

✻

Apart from his preoccupation with paralysis, one limitation of Joyce's stories as a historical picture of Dublin stems from his focus on the Catholic petty bourgeoisie to the virtual exclusion of other important classes – not only the slum-dwellers but also the Anglo-Irish (almost a fifth of the city's population). Even the down-at-heel protagonists of "Two Gallants" have petty-bourgeois backgrounds. The barfly Lenehan feels out of place in a workingman's cafe, while the jobless Corley impresses his girl by saying that he works at Pim's, an eminently respectable dry-goods store. The only working-class characters – children, two servant-girls, and a caretaker – have walk-on parts or speak briefly.

Although small by English or French or American standards, the petty bourgeoisie in turn-of-the-century Ireland was steadily growing in numbers and affluence.[14] The characters in *Dubliners* follow what can be viewed as a cross-section of urban middle-class occupations so long as we remember that the cross-section is skewed toward the lower end of the scale and that the legal and medical professions are absent from it. Eveline and Mr. Kernan eke out livings in sales. The scrivener Farrington teeters above the gulf of joblessness. Little Chandler, however, with his pretty furniture bought on the hire-purchase plan, represents a more prosperous kind of clerk, one in whom class consciousness and vague cultural longings intermix. The higher reaches of the civil service remained a mostly Protestant preserve, but increasing numbers of "Castle Catholics" like Power and Cunningham enjoyed well-paid positions of influence. Municipal government also offered opportunities, both small ones – M'Coy has become secretary to the City Coroner – and large ones: the post of Town Clerk is implied in "Grace" to carry considerable clout, as in fact it did.[15] Among the ranks of the self-employed, the grocer Fogarty scrapes along, while Mr. Doyle senior is *nouveau riche*. Two reporters in "A Mother" and two university teachers in "The Dead" represent the intellectual professions; other characters from these stories represent the musical arts. Fathers Flynn and Purdon belong to the Catholic clergy which, from the revocation of the penal laws onward, had occupied a privileged position among the middle classes.[16] In 1900 there were approximately 14,000 priests, monks, and nuns out of a Catholic population of little over three million.[17] The priesthood, as Flynn's progress from the slum of Irishtown to the Irish college in Rome indicates, was an avenue of social advancement. It also was a means of economic and political influence, as suggested in the discussion of the Jesuits in "Grace" and Henchy's mention of Father Burke in "Ivy Day."

We catch only glimpses of proletarian Dublin in Joyce's stories. If several of his characters must scrimp, they do make ends meet, whereas only a quarter of the male labor force earned more or less adequate wages. Ireland at the turn of the century was an agricultural satellite of metropolitan Britain, with a single industrial region (around Belfast) and a few trading centers among which Dublin ranked foremost. The two biggest businesses in Dublin were Guinness's brewery and Jacob's biscuit factory. Most workers, however, could not rejoice in the security of jobs at these two atypical enterprises. Except for those in skilled trades, most working-class men were dockers, porters, carters, or navvies who found employment when and where they could. Unemployment among unskilled men may have reached 20 percent; it may have risen much higher among working-class women in the job market, most of whom were competing for positions in service.[18]

Lyons sketches living conditions for the city's poor:

About thirty per cent (87,000) of the people in Dublin lived in the slums which were for the most part the worn-out shells of Georgian mansions. Over 2,000 *families* lived in single room tenements . . . without heat or light or water (save for a tap in a passage or backyard) or adequate sanitation. Inevitably, the death-rate was the highest in the country, while infant mortality was the worst, not just in Ireland, but in the British Isles. Disease of every kind, especially tuberculosis, was rife and malnutrition was endemic.[19]

Even the Earl of Dudley, the Lord Lieutenant whose cavalcade traverses Dublin in *Ulysses* and the embodiment of a regime often blamed for Ireland's ills, could state that he "had seen the misery of Irish peasants in the West, but nothing compared with what existed at their own doors in Dublin."[20] In short, the Dublin slums – a "pestilence,"[21] as that hard-headed mystic AE called them – rivalled the worst in Europe.

Joyce, of course, had no moral obligation to depict working-class Dubliners in his art, any more than he had an obligation to depict the Anglo-Irish. He hardly could have undertaken to encompass the whole of that many-faceted social reality, Dublin, in any single work. As Henry James has written: "Really, universally, relations stop nowhere, and the exquisite problem of the artist is eternally but to draw, by a geometry of his own, the circle within which they shall happily *appear* to do so."[22] Precisely because relations stop nowhere, and because the magic circle of Joyce's art is an illusion, we must look beyond the circle to history and historical narratives in order to better understand that art.

COUNTRY AND CITY

Thanks to the patronage of George Russell, the earliest printed version of "The Sisters" appeared on 13 August 1904 in a rural magazine called *The Irish Homestead*. The first of two pages devoted to the story also offers the reader part of a nostalgic poem, filled with images of merry girls, hay-making, bees, daisies, and birds, which ends: "And, O, God of Grace, it was fine to be / In beauteous Ireland at that time!" A small advertisement for Cantrell and Cochrane's mineral waters occupies the foot of the first page; an ad for "Dairy Machinery and Appliances of Every Description" takes up slightly over half of the second page and, because of its boldface type and relatively striking layout, dominates the page. Both advertisers cite appointments to "His Majesty the King." An odd and yet appropriate setting for the literary debut of "Stephen Daedalus" – one that signaled Ireland's colonial status, her predisposition toward piety, patriotism, and sentimentality, the economic and imaginative pre-eminence of the Irish countryside, and the existence of a middle class with enough money to imbibe "SPARKLING MONTSERRAT" ("The Drink for the Gouty & Rheumatic") or dilute its whiskey with club soda or "royal" seltzer. All these phenomena posed threats to Stephen Daedalus's creator, and in order to deal with them in his fiction he had to distance himself from them in his life. He took this step a few months later by boarding a boat at the North Wall and sailing into self-exile. His uneasy relationship with Ireland, especially rural Ireland, is thus presaged by his first publication, which in the context of the *Homestead* (the "pigs' paper" [*U* 9.321]) enters into uneasy dialogue with a world of cream separators and butterflies among thistles which "Stephen Daedalus" clearly has judged and found wanting.

The countryside that was so central to readers of *The Irish Homestead* barely exists in *Dubliners*. This might seem a peculiar omission since the closest model for Joyce's collection was George Moore's *Untilled Field* (1903), set largely in rural Ireland. Further, Dublin was "a glorified market town where droves of cattle [could] still be seen in the streets and which [was] populated by an imperfectly urbanized peasantry."[23] Granted, this sketch by Frank O'Connor disregards the city's eighteenth-century heritage and its history of public works in the nineteenth century, yet it contains sufficient truth to point to a significant absence in *Dubliners*. I don't mean simply the absence of the countryside in the sense that Joyce should have included a couple of rural stories (or should have written his projected companion volume, *Provincials*) as Moore included a couple of Dublin stories in *The Untilled Field*. Rather, the recent history that drove many country dwellers to the city is missing from *Dubliners*. In 1901, 33 percent of the citizens of Dublin had been born elsewhere. They were not all of rural origin, but "migrants from the countryside flocked to the city in the 1890s and 1900s" and filled the ranks of the shop-keeping classes in particular.[24]

Hence many petty-bourgeois Dubliners, the class depicted by Joyce, either were rural migrants themselves or were their children or grandchildren, and would have had relatives with first-hand memories of the great hunger of the 1840s. Nora Barnacle was one such refugee. Her native Galway, surrounded by ocean, mountainous bogland, and farmland owned by absentee landlords, was a tiny city (15,471 people in 1881) "of great poverty and misery" from which not only she but eventually all her siblings would flee. The workhouse there, which doubled as the city hospital where she was born in 1884, had been built in 1840

in an effort to feed, clothe, and shelter the poor and destitute, who roamed the streets of the city or flocked into the city from surrounding districts whenever famine or pestilence stalked the land. Famine ravaged the land, not just in the years of Black Famine like 1847, 1852 and 1873, but was also known each year in the period between May and August [when] the fruits of the previous year ran scarce and the new crops were not yet harvested.[25]

Given this history, which was also Nora's history and accounted for her presence in Dublin on 10 June 1904 when Joyce first met her, it seems twice remarkable that the characters in *Dubliners* reveal no awareness of what we might consider their predictable antecedents beyond the pale of Dublin. Perhaps, by portraying them without any past or future other than Dublin's, Joyce was evoking not simply the paralysis of a perpetually entrapped present, but the repression of something nightmarish in the intertwined history of city and country in Ireland.[26] At any rate, his citizens are curiously rootless, and it is instructive to try to fill in the gaps in their history.

The few direct references to the countryside in *Dubliners* can be listed quickly. Eveline's brother Harry, "who was in the church decorating business, was nearly always down somewhere in the country" (*D* 38). One of Gallaher and Little Chandler's cronies has "a good sit ... in the Land Commission" (*D* 75), the agency in charge of transferring farmlands from landlords to tenants in accordance with the 1891, 1896, and 1903 Land Purchase Bills.[27] Cunningham alludes to the rural roots of many constables – "thundering big country fellows" (*D* 161) – of the Dublin Metropolitan

Police. Like Nora Barnacle, Gretta Conroy, put down by Gabriel's mother as being "country cute" (*D* 187), comes from the rural West of Ireland. "The Dead" closes with a vision of snow falling on a lonely country churchyard.

We can also find a few oblique references to the countryside that Joyce may or may not have made consciously. In "An Encounter," the skirmish between the boys and the ragged children ends with the children screaming after them, *Swaddlers! Swaddlers!* because they associate the silver badge of a cricket club on Mahony's cap with Protestants. The derisive term "swaddlers" refers especially to Catholics who converted to Protestantism for the sake of food or clothing during famines.[28] In "Grace," Pope Leo XIII's feat of writing Latin poetry leads to a recollection of humbler rural Irish schooling:

—We didn't learn that, Tom, said Mr Power ... when we went to the penny-a-week school.
—There was many a good man went to the penny-a-week school with a sod of turf under his oxter, said Mr Kernan sententiously. (*D* 167)

The countryside's history of hunger lurks behind this sentimental reminiscence of schoolboys carrying their own fuel supplies to lessons with a private teacher insofar as these penny-a-week schools "were finally broken up by the famine of 1847."[29] So, too, does the oppressive history of the Penal Laws, since the penny-a-week schools had grown out of the hedge-schools, which provided clandestine education for Catholics during the early eighteenth century.

A more oblique allusion is made with the help of an offstage character in "Eveline." Joyce tells us next to nothing about his protagonist's mother and her "life of commonplace sacrifices closing in final craziness" (*D* 40), but her dying words may point to a historical event that helped shape her self-denying life and exercises a continuing influence on her daughter's life. These words – "Derevaun Seraun! Derevaun Seraun!" – sound like Gaelic yet are not; they have posed a minor mystery for Joyce scholars. The consensus seems to be that they are corrupt Gaelic or West of Ireland dialect (perhaps resulting from Joyce's shaky Irish), and they have been variously rendered into standard Irish Gaelic.[30] But whatever they denote, the point of these words may be that they are "one language ... recalled within another, a problem which diachronically involves the largest perspective of nineteenth-century Irish history, the displacement of Gaelic by English as the vernacular language."[31] Associated with this displacement is the central trauma of rural nineteenth-century Ireland, famine, especially the hunger of the 1840s, which disproportionately affected Gaelic-speaking areas in the south and west. Thus Mrs. Hill's puzzling utterance constitutes a rare link between Joyce's Dublin and rural Ireland. Her words are one of those "solitary, dear phrases" of a supplanted tongue, "spontaneous in grief or gladness" (*CW* 28), described by Joyce in his schoolboy essay on languages. In this light, we may see Eveline's mother as deliriously exclaiming words half remembered from her parents' or grandparents' native Gaelic, a language displaced by English when the family moved from country to city in response to socioeconomic forces including the periodic threat of famine. Hence the cry "Derevaun Seraun!" reflects a traumatic history repressed by Joyce's Dubliners, who barely acknowledge the existence of the site of the trauma (notice the vagueness of "somewhere down in the country" [*D* 38]).

The slavey in "Two Gallants," with her outlandish clothes and "Frank rude health" (*D* 55), exemplifies the many domestic servants who had migrated to Dublin to escape the countryside's poverty and lack of marital opportunity.[32] Like Eveline and Eveline's mother, she too is exploited, both by individual males and by patriarchal society in general. Of special interest is the economic nature of this exploitation, which can be traced back partly to the same rural history that lies behind Mrs. Hill's dying words.

The final irony of "Two Gallants" springs from the revelation of the economic goal of Corley's courting, embodied in the gold coin he has wheedled out of the slavey. Lenehan sees women in a similar light. After feeling sorry for himself during a solitary meal at a restaurant, he imagines the balm of domesticity: "He might yet be able to settle down in some snug corner and live happily if he could only come across some good simple-minded girl with a little of the ready" (*D* 58). The absence of sex from this vision is balanced by the presence of cash that, presumably, will finance his pub crawls while his wife keeps their snug corner warm until he lurches home.

The male Irish stress on the economic side of sexual relations was by no means limited to lowlifes such as Joyce's two gallants. Séan O Faoláin quotes a letter from a 38-year-old man "in no hurry to get married" who, when ready to take the plunge, "will inform ... the priests ... that I am a bachelor of some substance who requires a

wife with a dowry of a certain minimum figure."[33] Even in the 1960s
an observer could write that Ireland "is perhaps the one place in the
world where men most effectively manage to continue their bachelor
pursuits (which have little to do with sex) after marriage."[34] Florence Walzl draws on Arensberg and Kimball's *Family and Community
in Ireland* to link this syndrome – that of a society marked by rampant
celibacy and by late, economically calculated unions – to the
famines of the late 1840s. Prior to 1845 men and women married at a
"normal" age by European standards, and Ireland maintained the
high birth rate that had turned certain rural areas into "Congested
Districts." But the deaths, emigrations, and socioeconomic dislocations of the famine years ushered in a century-long depression.
For those who remained, jobs were scarce, salaries low, and chances
for promotion infrequent. Since the famine had ravaged the Congested Districts, where the land had been subdivided into tiny plots,
with unusual ferocity, survivors learned a lesson: families could be
raised only on a sound economic basis. Most men therefore delayed
marriage until they were thirty-five to forty-five and had become

established in a secure position or had inherited family land, money, or a
business ... Women began marrying in significant numbers only after
thirty ... Meantime ... there might be "understandings" or engagements
for as long as ten to fifteen years, but more commonly men avoided any
commitments, preferring the company of their own sex. Moreover, the
statistics show that most women who reached forty-five and men who
reached fifty-five without marrying would remain single all their lives.
Bachelors outnumbered spinsters ... though the percentages of both continued to be the highest in the world.[35]

Small wonder, then, that even Corley looks good to the slavey.

The protagonist of "Clay," a story that takes place on Hallow Eve
and ends with a divination game, often has been transformed by
critics into a witch or hag or spirit. Margot Norris views such
symbolic enlargements of Maria as a response to "the powerful
working of desire in human discourse and human lives," in particular Maria's "desire for the recognition and prestige that would
let [her] maintain her human status in paralytic Dublin." Norris
depicts Maria as a "scullion" who likes to think of herself as "a
well-bred, middle-class maiden lady living on a small but independent income."[36] A contrary reading by Walzl cites historical evidence that a real-life equivalent of Maria, working at the Dublin by
Lamplight Laundry which inspired Joyce's fictional laundry (*L II*

192), would have held a "supervisory position ... as an Assistant Matron with housekeeping duties"[37] – one of the few middle-class occupations open to Irishwomen.

Walzl goes on to relate Maria's situation to the calamities of the 1840s; and this move allows us to reconcile some of the divergent readings of "Clay." Critics who discern a ghost or dolorous spirit in this Halloween story, or a discourse of desire, should perhaps consider the influence of the 1840s on Joyce's Ireland. If Maria exaggerates her contentment at the laundry, it seems likely that she does so less to hide the lowliness of her post there than to compensate for the sex and romantic love and family of her own that are absent from her life. Like thousands of actual women in turn-of-the-century Dublin, she embodies the unhappy consequences of the hagridden history of the Irish countryside – a history whose chief terror, famine, was caused not only by a canker of the potato blossom, but also by colonialism, *laissez-faire* capitalism, and racism. This history, which made unfulfilled desire the theme of so many unmarried Irishwomen's lives, is the true ghost or specter in "Clay."

WOMAN AND HOME

On 10 September 1904 *The Irish Homestead* printed a short story, "Eveline," dealing with a young woman's debate over whether to elope with her sailor lover on a boat to Argentina. In October the writer, a young man known for wearing a yachting cap, eloped with his sweetheart on a boat to England. Joyce and Nora Barnacle made good their escape from Dublin; the girl in "Eveline" draws back at the last moment. Revolving around the theme of leaving home, the story considers the meaning of doing so in the context of turn-of-the-century Dublin. It also considers, together with other stories in *Dubliners*, the special meaning of "home" for women, and reveals Joyce's ambivalent attitudes toward the social position of women, which in some ways conflicted and in others coincided with middle-class Irish attitudes.

In his letter to Nora of 29 August 1904, Joyce said this on the subject of "home":

My mind rejects the whole present social order and Christianity – home, the recognised virtues, classes of life and religious doctrines. How could I like the idea of home? My home was simply a middle-class affair ruined by spendthrift habits ... My mother was slowly killed, I think, by my father's ill-treatment ... When I looked on her face as she lay in her coffin ... I understood that I was looking on the face of a victim and I cursed the system which had made her a victim. We were seventeen in family. (*L II* 48)

The words "home" and "house" occur eighteen times in "Eveline" as the protagonist ponders the decision she must make.[38] She balances the pros and cons in a rational manner, but finally, in a fit of emotion, the two most important opposing factors emerge: her promise to her dying mother "to keep the home together" and her desire to live. Frightened by the memory of her mother's sacrifice of her own life, she seems to choose: "Escape! She must escape! Frank would save her. He would give her life, perhaps love, too" (*D* 40).

Joyce recognized the significance for a young woman of eloping without any certainty of marriage or love or financial support. He sent a worried note to Nora on 19 September, following up their apparently tense conversation that day:

My object ... was to find out whether with me you would be deprived of comforts which you have been accustomed to at home ... You ask me why I don't love you, but surely you must believe I am very fond of you ... Your people cannot of course prevent you from going if you wish but they can make things unpleasant for you. (*L II* 55)

In his story he makes clear why Eveline would contemplate such a momentous step. For one thing, she dislikes her job at "the Stores" (*D* 37). Though he does not state this explicitly, he knew, as his Dublin readers would have known, that employment as a shop assistant entailed long hours for low wages. None of the few occupations open to women were unionized. Not until 1911 did Jim Larkin, together with his sister Delia and Helena Molony, form the Irish Women Workers Union. Delia Larkin, in her column in *The Irish Worker*, commented on the term "women workers": "To the employing class [it] has a sweet sound. They know that in these workers they have an extraordinary cheap means of producing wealth."[39] James Connolly described the female worker as a double slave: in the cities she is driven out "to become the chief support of the house ... at the earliest possible age" by laboring under oppressive conditions "in mills, shops and factories," then returns home at the end of each day's work to become "the slave of the domestic needs of her family" and to be exploited by male relatives who give her "never a penny as reward."[40]

"Eveline" illustrates Connolly's comments. Eveline's father, an alcoholic bully, appropriates her meager earnings and expects her to perform all the domestic work unpaid:

She always gave her entire wages . . . but the trouble was to get any money from her father. He said . . . that he wasn't going to give her his hard-earned money to throw about the streets, and much more, for he was usually fairly bad of a Saturday night. In the end he would give her the money and ask her had she any intention of buying Sunday's dinner. Then she had to rush out as quickly as she could and do her marketing . . . returning home late under her load of provisions. She had hard work to keep the house together and to see that the two young children who had been left to her charge went to school regularly and got their meals regularly. (*D* 38)

When her father forbids her to see what appears to be her first serious suitor, he cites the hackneyed dangers of walking out with a sailor, but we can readily infer that he wishes to keep her at home to replicate his dead wife's subservient role.

Sexual oppression, symbolized by her father's blackthorn stick,[41] is not the least of Eveline's reasons for wanting to elope, and is a motif throughout *Dubliners*. In his relationship with Eveline, Mr. Hill brings to mind Corley and the slavey, the stick-carrying James Duffy and Mrs. Sinico, and other self-important male characters in the stories who dominate or use women. Joyce's portrayal of this relationship perhaps draws on the situation in Synge's one-act play, *The Shadow of the Glen*, which Joyce probably attended or at least heard of when it was performed in Dublin in 1903. At the end of this dark comedy, the heroine, Nora, a lonely young woman desperate for more out of life, leaves her jealous, elderly husband and the security of his house to go wandering with a tramp. Arguably, when he composed "Eveline," Joyce must have seen the rough parallel to his own Nora's circumstances: she had fled Galway to find a better life and to escape her overbearing uncle, who had thrashed her with his "big walking-stick" (*L II* 73) for spending time with an unsuitable (Protestant) young man, and was now considering an uncertain future in foreign parts with her ardent but strange new lover.[42] In any event, both Synge's play and Joyce's stories reflect the hard choices Irishwomen faced in matters of love and marriage.[43]

The colored print of the twelve promises made by Christ to the Blessed Margaret Mary (and so to all followers of the Order of the

Sacred Heart) is one of the few details Joyce added to the *Irish Homestead* version of "Eveline." Known for self-denial even in childhood, Margaret Alacoque spent most of her adult life in a convent where she had visions of Christ in which he named her his instrument to propagate the devotion of the Sacred Heart. There are parallels between the seventeenth-century French girl and the self-denying Eveline,[44] but more striking is the ironic application of the dozen promises to Eveline's troubled, strife-ridden home life. The print emphasizes the Order as a family devotion, and includes promises to grant believers grace, sow peace in their families, and console them in their difficulties. One of two verses shown on the print – "Come to Me all you that labour, and are burthened, and I will refresh you" (Matt. 11:28) – seems especially ironic in view of Eveline's fatigue from serving the two masters, capitalism and patriarchy. One wonders if Joyce did not have in mind, when he revised "Eveline," Marx's adage that religion is the opiate of the masses. In any case, the print of the Sacred Heart reinforces the virtues held up by Irish society for young women – piety, self-renunciation, chastity – and helps explain Eveline's failure to complete a rebellious leap toward self-fulfillment.

Another working woman, Mrs. Mooney, owner of a boarding house, appears to be less victim than victimizer. But, though she and her daughter exploit a hapless male boarder, Joyce implies the economic insecurities behind this behavior. Walzl explains:

Many fathers set up their children in a business like their own, but usually in other neighborhoods. This seems precisely the situation of Mrs. Mooney, who had married the foreman in her father's butcher shop. Subsequently, her father had set up the newly wed couple in a butcher shop in Spring Gardens. Provident fathers were often concerned for their daughters, since the marriage rate for women in Ireland was so low.[45]

After separating from her abusive, alcoholic husband, who had ruined their trade, Mrs. Mooney needed another source of income. The business of letting rooms was one of the few feminine economic niches. (*Thom's Directory* for 1904, as Walzl remarks, shows all boarding and most lodging houses in Dublin as being run by women.) Joyce describes Mrs. Mooney as "a woman who was quite able to keep things to herself: a determined woman" (*D* 61). Yet we can see her as "determined" in another sense: her identity as a tough, shrewd businesswoman has been determined or shaped by her history as a Dublin woman of the shop-owning class who knows the dangerousness and weakness of men, but recognizes their importance as a means of acquiring goods and power.

For Nanny and Eliza, Father Flynn's sisters, devotion to a man has resulted in blighted lives. Their brother's attendance at the Irish College, which accepted forty students a year, implies that he was regarded as an outstanding candidate for the priesthood."[46] This represents a remarkable social leap for a poor Dublin boy, which would have required not only intelligence and hard work but the steady support of his family. What remains of this family in 1895 is two elderly sisters. Having served their brother in life – "God knows, we done all we could, as poor as we are" – they now provide for him after death: "All the work we had ... getting in the woman to wash him and then laying him out and then the coffin and then arranging about the Mass in the chapel" (*D* 16). Joyce may have named the story after them to highlight their own unfulfilled lives, so bound up with their brother's failure. An impecunious candidate for the priesthood

might expect two of his sisters to earn money and help put him through his training. After serving as his housekeepers as he went up the ecclesiastical ladder, [they] might expect their rewards: a decent chance at good marriages. We know of Father Flynn's accomplishments and learning, yet we are also made aware of his sisters' flat accents and malapropisms. The conclusion must be that his scruples, his breakdown, and then his strokes have been the wreck of all his promise and their rewards, since the Flynn sisters had to care for their brother until his death and are left ignorant, near-destitute, aged spinsters.[47]

The sisters' "unassuming shop," with its tiny stock made up "mainly of children's bootees and umbrellas" (*D* 11), typifies the kind of enterprise run by widows and single women in Dublin's marginalized, male-dominated colonial economy.[48]

In "Two Gallants," another story of sexual exploitation, the aptly called "slavey" or maid-of-all-work is employed at the lowest level (save prostitution) of urban occupations open to women. Most likely she would have been paid £6 or £7 a year.[49] Comparisons are problematic since she receives room and board as well, but a report for 1895 by the St. Vincent de Paul society defined "decent employment" (meaning that the worker's family did not require relief) as paying "from 20/– to 25/– a week" or £50 to £65 per annum; and by 1900 all employees of the Dublin Corporation, including the unskilled, earned a minimum of £1 a week.[50] By these measures, the

sovereign extracted from the slavey by Corley represents an enormous portion of her miniscule income or, if she has stolen it, an
enormous risk. Either way she is a victim, for she obviously takes
Corley's attentions seriously and recognizes the slimness of her
chances of leaving service except through marriage.

Music represented a middle-class occupational field in which
women, as teachers and performers, claimed over half the positions
listed in *Thom's Directory* of 1904. Four characters in *Dubliners* give
lessons: Mrs. Sinico's daughter, M'Coy's wife, and Kate Morkan
and her niece, Mary Jane. Kathleen Kearney, whose mother is
grooming her to be a singer, serves as a (partially) paid accompanist
in a concert series.[51] But, in terms of prestige and remuneration,
these and other feminine occupations were marginal in Irish society.

In the absence of financial necessity, with or without young
children, Joyce's women remain at home. The aunt in *Araby*, who
seems not to control so much as the two-shilling coin which the boy's
uncle gives him for the *Araby* bazaar, apparently belongs to this
group. So do Annie Chandler, Ada Farrington, Mrs. Sinico, Mrs.
Kearney, Mrs. Kernan, and Gretta Conroy. These women stay at
home not only because they lack outside employment, but because
their primary sphere of activity and influence is the domestic one.
The professions, skilled crafts, managerial or administrative positions in business and government, politics, religion, and even largely
the arts are masculine preserves. In the sole instance of a woman
intruding into such a preserve, Mrs. Kearney loses her reputation as
"a lady" (*D* 149). Julia Morkan, a singer in her church choir, has
recently been deprived of even that limited means of self-fulfillment
by papal decree.[52] Her sister Kate denounces this masculine fiat
before half-heartedly submitting: "O, I don't question the pope's
being right. I'm only a stupid old woman" (*D* 194–95). The pope in
question, Leo XIII, described man as "the chief of the family and
the head of the woman." He stated: "Nature destines [woman] to
domestic tasks ... which safeguard admirably the honor of her sex
and [are necessary to] the good upbringing of her children and the
family's prosperity."[53] In 1903 Father Nicholas Walsh, a Dublin
Jesuit, propagated similar notions in *Woman*, a study recommending
St. Monica (St. Augustine's mother) as a model and concluding:
"The Lord likes to see a woman busy at a useful task, holding a
needle or distaff in her hand."[54] Thus, in portraying his female
characters as he does, Joyce gives us a fairly representative picture of

middle- and lower middle-class women in Dublin whose lives have been shaped by economic and ideological forces (patriarchy, colonialism, capitalism, Roman Catholicism) which they seem to accept as Necessity.

The question is: does *Dubliners* treat these forces as Necessity also? There *were* other kinds of women in Dublin, for instance, the one who replied to Walsh's treatise in the *United Irishman* under the name of Femina: "Father Walsh does not seem to be desirous or capable of considering woman as a distinct being who should above all be consecrated to herself."[55] Joyce knew a few of these women and had entrée into their circles. While at Belvedere College his social life after school, "apart from sporadic visits to Nighttown, seems to have centered chiefly around the home of David Sheehy, M.P." (*JJ* 51). Unlike his own, the Sheehy family appears to have been a happy one, and the six children, including four daughters, were lively, intelligent, and interested in the arts and politics. Joyce had a long-lasting crush on Mary Sheehy, who later married his talented contemporary at University College, Thomas Kettle. Hanna Sheehy married another UCD contemporary, Francis Skeffington, who attempted unsuccessfully to enroll Joyce under the banner of women's rights. Kathleen Sheehy may have contributed to Miss Ivors in "The Dead," "for she wore that austere bodice and sported the same patriotic pin" (*JJ* 246–47).

Only in "The Dead" does Joyce tentatively depict women who are more than passive victims and objects of masculine fantasies and control. Many critics have pointed out that "[t]he road leading to the destruction of Gabriel Conroy's inflated ego is lined with a succession of women."[56] Unlike the slavey in "Two Gallants," Lily, the housemaid, has a voice. She responds to Gabriel's patronizing question about her marital prospects with the disconcerting retort, "The men that is now is only all palaver and what they can get out of you" (*D* 178). He again loses his composure when Molly Ivors twits him about being a West Briton and urges him, instead of visiting the Continent, to see his own country, preferably the West, a suggestion his wife eagerly seconds. Much later, after Gretta's revelation of an early love affair has quenched his sexual desire, he seems finally shorn of his usual sense of superiority. His ambivalent feelings toward women, his country, and life and death appear to achieve resolution in his drowsy vision of the snow falling over Ireland.

"The Dead" reflects Joyce's own ambivalence, during his first years in Italy, toward Nora, Ireland, and his vocation as a writer. The parallels between Joyce/Nora and Gabriel/Gretta have been well established (*JJ* 243–47). Critics tend to order them into a series of oppositions such as male vs. female, intellect vs. emotion, and Dublin vs. the West of Ireland. Gabriel's vision of the snow falling on all the living and the dead seems to establish a communion in which such oppositions dissolve, and Joyce's own union with Nora overshadowed the differences between them. Nevertheless, Gretta remains, at the end of "The Dead," caught in a subordinate, distinctly feminized position. An object rather than a subject, she depends for representation on Gabriel's masculine consciousness, just as in her marriage she is entitled to act only with her husband's approval (even within the traditionally feminine sphere of the home, Gabriel, who has his own ideas about child-rearing, undercuts her authority). Her real-life counterpart fared no better. Nora, in spite of Brenda Maddox's effort to establish her as Joyce's strong, independent equal, depended on him economically; and she was even more tied to her home, or series of homes, than she would have been in Ireland. Her sphere of action was extraordinarily limited.

The questions of why Joyce chose Nora as his companion in life, and why he chose to depict a representative but unnecessarily narrow range of women in *Dubliners*, have something to do with the brief appearance of his most atypical female character, Molly Ivors. Molly is Gabriel's intellectual and economic equal, a fellow university teacher who can question his words far more authoritatively than Lily or Gretta. She knows Browning, yet is a nationalist and an Irish-language enthusiast. A single woman, she dresses primly, yet is emancipated enough to come to the party alone and leave it early, refusing Gabriel's offer to escort her and eliciting a puzzled response from the more conventional Gretta. Gabriel is relieved to see the back of her.

Perhaps Joyce shared Gabriel's relief. Only once more would he portray a well-educated professional woman capable of dealing with men as an equal. Beatrice Justice, a 27-year-old music teacher in his play *Exiles*, is emotionally involved with Richard Rowan, who has recently returned to Ireland from Italy. During most of his nine-year exile they have carried on an intense correspondence, including chapters of his now-published book; she understands him as his wife Bertha, an intuitive, passionate woman with little interest in intellectual matters, cannot. Add to this triangle a fourth character,

Robert Hand – Beatrice's first cousin and former fiancé, now hungering after Bertha – and we would seem to have the makings of a captivating drama. But one reason why the play does not entirely satisfy has to do with Joyce's depiction of Beatrice as an incomplete woman. Richard chides her:

You were drawn to him as your mind was drawn towards mine. You held back from him. From me, too, in a different way. You cannot give yourself freely and wholly. (*E* 22)

At the outset we realize that the two will never have an affair, and Beatrice quickly fades out of the play, returning only for an anticlimactic confrontation with Bertha in the third act. Joyce fretted over her absence and her unattractiveness; he jotted in his notes: "It will be difficult to recommend Beatrice to the interest of the audience, every man of which ... would like to be ... Bertha's" (*E* 114). Another note compares her mind to "an abandoned cold temple" (*E* 119). The implication is clear: intellectual women are flawed – that is, they are frigid. He could see neither the absurdity of this patriarchal cliché nor its injurious effect on his play.

Joyce was attracted to pretty, non-intellectual women like Nora, and he sympathized with women like his mother who were victims of patriarchy; but he did not much respect either sort. He seems to have been uneasy with women who, like the Sheehy sisters or Sylvia Beach, were intelligent, cultured, and strong. Perhaps his discomfort with such women accounts in part for their virtual absence from his writings. In any event, this absence suggests that he shared some of the assumptions of the "system" which he blamed for his mother's death. In art as in life, he felt most comfortable with women who were dependent on males and bound to the home.

THE CHURCH

Joyce's two sketches of religion in *Dubliners*, "The Sisters" and "Grace," have generated a cottage industry of allegorical and symbolic readings by critics. Not until 1962 did Robert Adams make a ground-breaking historical approach to "Grace," juxtaposing documented facts with the errors and half-truths of the felt history of the Church which furnishes bedside conversation for Tom Kernan and his friends.[57] A later essay by Donald Torchiana examines the careers of the public figures mentioned in "Grace." For instance,

Father Tom Burke, whose oratory Cunningham and Kernan praise, was well known for his skill in sermonizing on topics such as "Drunkenness the Worst Degradation – Temperance the Greatest Blessing of Man" and "No Salvation outside the Catholic Church";[58] he also was known for his nationalism and his attacks on Darwin and women's rights. Archbishop John MacHale was another patriotic and skillful, but intellectually sloppy, orator. The model for Purdon, Father Bernard Vaughan, was a popular, flamboyant English preacher who spoke often in Dublin. An admirer of businessmen, Vaughan described himself as a drummer for Christ, and advertised a retreat in San Francisco as the "'Golden Gate' Limited Express" bound for the "Paradise of the Soul."[59]

Torchiana's research supports Adams's view of "Grace" as a comedy in which the main characters are innocents compared with Dublin's worldly spiritual authorities. Both essays complement other interpretations which suggest that Joyce scathingly portrays the Church in *Dubliners* as a powerful, worldly institution whose ceremonies lack religious feeling and whose activities support a materialistic middle-class social order. I agree with this overview, but would like to take a look at the role of religion in the story from a different historical perspective, focusing on the Church in relation to social classes in Ireland.

Joyce depicts religion in Dublin unfairly in that no doubt most priests were not as worldly as Father Purdon, who equates commercial values with spirituality, nor as neurotic as Father Flynn, who fetishizes the outward forms and rituals of the Church in the absence of inward faith. Nevertheless, we can also say that Joyce overlooks one of the Church's prime defects, namely, its attitude toward the poor. Purdon's flattering of his middle-class audience signifies more than his failure as their spiritual guide. It should suggest to us the alliance in "Ivy Day" between the Church and the petty-bourgeois nationalist establishment in Dublin, implied by the presence in Purdon's congregation of "Mr Fanning, the registration agent and mayor maker of the city, who was sitting immediately under the pulpit beside one of the newly elected councillors of the ward" (*D* 172). But, though Joyce exposes the venal partnership between the Church and a certain class, he does so as if its chief consequence were a vague moral malaise or "paralysis" and not the injury and oppression of another class.

The Irish Church tended to see the masses of Dublin's poor as an inevitable, ever-present problem that called for the application of Christian charity rather than a reformation of the social order. The Church provided material relief on several levels: through local convents, monasteries, and parish churches; through institutions such as orphanages and homes for distressed gentlewomen; and through the well-known Society of St. Vincent de Paul, which ministered to people in their own homes.[60] We see an example of such assistance in *Ulysses* in the form of peasoup that Maggy Dedalus attributes to "Sister Mary Patrick" (*U* 10.280). Perhaps Dr. Walsh, Archbishop of Dublin, was right in claiming that "[t]he clergy and nuns of Dublin have been providing for years past food and clothing for the children of the poor ... at an extent totally unknown by the ordinary citizen."[61] But he didn't assert that these efforts, or even the combined efforts of Dublin's numerous charitable agencies, met the needs of most of the city's swarms of poor children, let alone destitute adults. And the Irish Church, despite Pope Leo XIII's advice in *Rerum Novarum* (1891) on the importance of adequate wages for workers, had no agenda for improving the economic condition of the working classes: the "major social problems discussed in the leading Church journal, the *Irish Ecclesiastical Record*, in the closing years of the 19th century were alcoholism and the threats posed by socialism."[62] The rise of mass trade unionism and the Dublin Lockout of 1913 brought out the worst in the Church: allied with the nationalist employers, priests helped prevent the sending of strikers' starving children to atheist (that is, English Protestant) homes, and *The Irish Catholic* newspaper excoriated the strikers as "members of the very lowest and most degraded section of the unemployable class who came out from the slums attracted by plunder."[63] The Church's lack of sympathy toward the urban working class abated somewhat after the Lockout. It remained, however, a middle-class organization, strongly oriented toward the peasantry and the countryside.

Both Catholic and Protestant relief usually had a religious as well as a material purpose. The former took precedence when the two impulses came into conflict. Daly quotes the 1912 report of a conference (or branch) of the Society of St. Vincent de Paul responsible for the depressed area of the quays:

So numerous were the applications for relief that the members were inclined to look to the temporal needs of their friends to the entire exclusion of their spiritual necessities. Bearing in mind that the object of the Society was not to remove poverty but to raise the moral tone, both of the visitors and the visited, the Conference therefore, adopted no new cases but devoted itself to the spiritual interests of the families whom they had already on their books.

Running through these reports, she observes, is an "implication that material benefits in the form of employment or greater prosperity will follow from closer attention to religious duties."[64] Another limitation on the Society's relief efforts arose from the localization of raising and spending funds in individual parishes. Middle-class parishes could afford to be very active (presumably that of the Church of Saint Francis Xavier, chosen by Joyce for the retreat in "Grace" and "noted for its well-heeled and fashionable congregation,"[65] belonged to this category). But the poorest parishes found their resources spread thin. The conference attached to St. Mary's Pro-Cathedral complained:

Owing to the increase in the population of the poorer classes in our district and to the continued exodus of the moneyed classes to the fashionable south side of the city the demands upon our resources have increased while the sources of our income ... have become seriously reduced. We are now constantly in the habit of giving relief to destitute Roomkeepers who occupy the houses from which we formerly received generous contributions towards our work.[66]

In 1905 one conference suspended relief for lack of funds. In general, religion and class appear to have played important parts in the Society's decisions as to who received help and who did not.[67] The principal irony of the Church's attitude toward the poor relates to that symbol of Catholic emancipation, the Pro-Cathedral in Marlborough Street, mentioned above. St. Mary's was designated a provisional cathedral because the Church of Ireland occupied (and still occupies) both of Dublin's medieval cathedrals, Christ Church and St. Patrick's.[68] Nevertheless, "its opening was a triumph. Very few years after the passing of Emancipation this, the first great church built for the Catholics as a distinct denomination in Dublin, was opened. Daniel O'Connell, the Liberator, was ... conspicuous in the ceremony. But the centre of it was the Catholic Archbishop Murray." The Pro-Cathedral became one of "the high places of Catholic worship"[69] in Dublin, and it is fitting that the class-conscious Mrs. Mooney of "A Boarding House" goes there for Mass. Yet in 1900 *The Freeman's Journal* observed: "In no other district of the city is there such a teeming population of poor children – with such limited resources to meet their needs – as in the Pro-Cathedral parish."[70] The contradiction looms: how could the Pro-Cathedral be at once "a landmark in the story of the resurrection of a race"[71] and a center of vast, persistent, tolerated poverty? This contradiction was not just local or limited to Joyce's day. In 1968 a journalist wrote of the "meek acceptance of poverty and suffering" and the

strange lack of awareness by political and religious leaders of just how primitively the nation was caring for the sick, the handicapped, the mentally ill, the delinquent young, the orphaned, the widowed, the itinerant families, and all the others who lived desperately in what de Valera chose to describe as "the foremost Christian nation in the world today."[72]

The triumph of Irish Catholicism, symbolized by the Pro-Cathedral, can be seen or represented as such only from a middle-class perspective that overlooks or denies the significance of lower-class poverty and suffering. Joyce, admittedly, wished to portray the failure of Irish Catholicism – its paralysis. But he did so from his own middle-class perspective, and in his writings he neglected the failings of the Church with regard to Dublin's poorest citizens for the same reason that the Church tended to neglect these citizens in life: they belonged to a lower class.

POLITICS

All Joyce's stories deal with politics. Even the date of Father Flynn's death, 1 July, reverberates politically, for on that day in 1690 William of Orange defeated James II in the Battle of the Boyne. This Protestant victory quelled one of Catholic Ireland's most serious bids for national and religious liberty; afterwards it was annually celebrated (on 12 July) in Irish towns, as still happens in Northern Ireland, by Orangemen marching to the triumphant sound of drums and pipes. Thus Father Flynn's demise resonates with political as well as spiritual failure, bringing to mind turn-of-the-century Ireland's continuing status as a colony.

Background details in other stories convey a similar message. In "Eveline" the "soldiers with brown baggages" (*D* 40), who fill the station at the North Wall, belong to the British Army. Signs abound of a depressed colonial economy: the housing development put up by a presumably Protestant (hence British-allied) "man from Belfast" (*D* 36), the removal of the Waters family "back to England" (*D* 37), Harry's work in "the church decorating business" (*D* 38), and Frank's emigration. In "After the Race" the city wears "the mask of a capital" (*D* 46) – a reference to the 1800 Act of Union that closed down the Irish Parliament. Corley and Lenehan, Joyce's "Two Gallants," walk past a series of Dublin landmarks of the Protestant Ascendancy (roughly, the period from the Battle of the Boyne in 1690 to Catholic Emancipation in 1829) which suggest a parallel between their own debased gallantry and that of the past.[73] Reprimanded at work by his Protestant boss, Farrington, the legal clerk in "Counterparts," slouches home "in the shadow" (*D* 97) of a British Army barracks. Maria's purse bears the legend "*A Present from Belfast*" (*D* 100). Gabriel Conroy tells an anecdote about an Irish horse walking in circles around the equestrian statue of William of Orange and then bids good-night to the statue of the would-be Irish liberator, Daniel O'Connell.

There are many such details, which could be discussed at length, but I shall concentrate on Joyce's one overtly political story. "Ivy Day in the Committee Room" depicts the fallen state of Irish politics a short time after the three nationalist factions resulting from the "Split" over Parnell's leadership had been reunited under the Parnellite, John Redmond. Critics have dwelled on the contrast between the characters in the story, a lackluster group of canvassers working unenthusiastically for a small-time, shady politician, and the towering but absent figure of Parnell. Although this contrast is crucial, my interest lies in another historical personage, whose offstage presence in the story gives a different slant to its presentation of Irish political "paralysis."

Joyce made no recorded reference to James Connolly. This is surprising, and it seems to me even more surprising that there should not be a powerful connection between Connolly and Colgan, the Labour candidate in "Ivy Day." To explore this connection we have to examine not so much the politics of Parnellism or of Ireland vs. England, but rather the social – and socialist – aspects of the local election campaigns on which Joyce based this story. His brother Stanislaus tells us that he got almost all his material from Stanislaus' account of working with their father during the latter's stint as an election agent and canvasser.[74] Joyce, however, was himself in Dublin during the municipal campaigns of 1902 and 1903

(*JJ* 93–94, 116–19). My thesis is that he followed these campaigns, like many other citizens, attentively, and required little more from Stanislaus than a few inside details. Further, I think that the facts concerning Connolly's participation in the 1902 and 1903 Dublin elections are embedded in "Ivy Day" as a subtext which reflects not only the conflict between Irish middle-class nationalism and Irish labor, but the contradictions between Joyce's own Parnellite and socialist allegiances.

The action of "Ivy Day" undoubtedly occurs in 1902, since the characters debate Edward VII's coming visit to Ireland, which he made during the summer of 1903. The death of Ireland's "*Uncrowned King*" (*D* 134), who led his country seemingly to the verge of Home Rule, is thus eleven years in the past. There is no need here to repeat the familiar outlines of Parnell's career. His fall from the leadership of the Irish Parliamentary Party in 1890 split the party and ushered in a dismal period of divisiveness that continued after his death the next year. Only in 1900, after the cause of Home Rule had become a dead letter due to a change of government in England, did the Nationalist MPs and their local allies achieve unity under Redmond. The stage was set for the institutionalization of Parnellism and for the little drama to be played out in Joyce's imaginary committee room in Wicklow Street.

The characters in "Ivy Day" embody the major political parties, though by no means all the political movements, of Ireland in 1902. Henchy and O'Connor work for the Nationalist candidate, Richard Tierney, who is vying to represent the Royal Exchange Ward in the Municipal Council of the Dublin Corporation. Tierney's official sponsor very likely would have been the United Irish League, which functioned as an arm of the Parliamentary Party in local elections and supported the latter's goal of Home Rule. (I use the upper-case in "*N*ationalist" to distinguish the Parliamentary Party and its local allies, who dominated Dublin politics, from *n*ationalists with ties to other groups such as Labour or Sinn Fein.) Crofton and Bantam Lyons belong to the Irish Conservative Party, allied with the English Conservatives in upholding the Union with England, but, since their candidate threw in the towel, they have been canvassing for the Nationalist as "the lesser of two evils" (*D* 131). Hynes works for the Labour candidate. Although the story does not make this clear, labor as a national political movement scarcely existed in Ireland at the turn of the century. Of the hundred odd Irish seats at

Westminster, the Nationalists held the lion's share, while the remainder were divided mainly among Conservatives and other Unionists. Irish labor had not a single seat.

At the municipal level the picture differed. The Local Government Act of 1898 vested a sizable portion of the working classes with the right to vote in city elections. In Dublin several trade unions, under the aegis of the Dublin Trades Council, vigorously contested elections for the three councillors and one alderman allotted to each ward. In 1899 seven candidates endorsed by the council won seats, as did five Nationalists with union ties. Alarmed, Redmond's Parliamentary Party and the United Irish League urged union leaders not to form a separate political organization that might hurt the Home Rule movement; the Nationalists, they claimed, were the workingman's proper representatives. Labour did well again in the 1900 elections. In 1902, though, Labour candidates were rebuffed; and in 1903 they were routed, never to pose a serious electoral threat again.

The Unionists, though not hampered by an identity problem, had long been declining and also posed no threat to the United Irish League. Indeed, the Nationalists were "in many respects an alternative Irish Establishment to the Vice-Regal Lodge and Dublin Castle";[75] their hold on the Corporation, dating from the early 1880s, would last until 1920 when it was broken by a more radical nationalist party, Sinn Fein.[76] Still, for the first five years after the Local Government Act, the Nationalists feared a political challenge from the unions. Such a challenge appeared real even on the brink of Labour's debacle in 1903, when Labour candidates ran in slightly over half of fourteen ward elections and provided highly publicized opposition to the United Irish League in the politicking for the Lord Mayor's job. The prospect of an independent Labour party troubled the Nationalists; it also troubled the beleaguered Unionists, who knew that their traditional foes at least wouldn't sponsor any dramatic social reforms. Hence the uneasy alliance, in "Ivy Day," between Home Rulers and Conservatives.

The opposition to the Nationalists of a Labour candidate suggests the ever-present economic aspect of Irish politics. Actually, two economic issues are raised in "Ivy Day": first, the unequal relationship between England and Ireland; and second, the relationship between haves and have-nots within Ireland herself. The first issue, which dominates the foreground of the story, constituted a chronic grievance for Irish politicians of all shades. Almost a century after the Act of Union,

the Irish metropolis was no longer the proud second city of the empire ... As municipal councillors were to complain before the Select Committee on Industries in Ireland in 1885: "There is no other large city in Europe that has declined so rapidly of late as Dublin" ... The situation in Dublin ... was only one instance of the regressive nature of the colonial relationship.[77]

The second issue, less obvious, was also chronic:

After 1872 or thereabouts every attempt was made to focus attention on the social ills of the capital, in particular on the woeful lack of proper housing for over one-third of the city's population. The various official investigations from 1876 onward performed a valuable service in their delineation of the city's social and structural decay. Sanitary inspectors, medical officers, clerics, and reformers all bore witness to the fact that thousands of families existed ... on the borderland between habitual privation and absolute destitution.[78]

Many readers know something of the ever-present distress of working-class life in Dublin from Sean O'Casey. Joyce's stories, however, reveal little of that life. There is just a glance here and there, as when the narrator of "A Little Cloud" points out a horde of grimy children" (*D* 71) from the tenements of Henrietta Street which his petty-bourgeois protagonist ignores. Politically, there was scant contact between the middle classes and the poor, if only because the latter were still disenfranchised and more concerned with survival than politics. But workers in skilled trades (fewer and better off than their unskilled, nonunionized brethren) did hold some beliefs in common with the Catholic middle classes. Generally, they supported Home Rule and opposed the English and Anglo-Irish viceregal regime. They accepted capitalism (as did virtually everyone in Ireland). And most of their union officials would have echoed Mr. Henchy's call for an influx of capital to create more jobs in Dublin.

The problem with this attitude, as James Connolly recognized, lay in its lack of provision for social change. Catholic employers took no less advantage than Protestant ones of workers who "suffered long hours and low wages in a city where ... the loss of a job could often mean ... emigration or the workhouse."[79] Further, no guarantee existed that Home Rule, or even the pipe dream of complete independence, would bring the millenium any closer for Irish workers. Connolly's solution was to graft socialism onto nationalism in the form of the Irish Socialist Republican Party. Born in May 1896, this tiny party loudly voiced the growing awareness of organized labor that the needs of workingmen might be served better by a distinctive Labour party rather than, as hitherto, by the Nationalists.

James Joyce was only fourteen years old when Connolly founded the I.S.R.P. Within a few years, though, as early as 1901, he expressed his independence of his conservative instructors at Belvedere and University Colleges by taking an interest in socialism. He and Connolly both left Dublin after the 1903 elections; later that year Connolly left Ireland for an extended stay in America. Still, the chances are excellent that Joyce heard him speak, either during his two election campaigns or at his regular soapbox appearances, which have been described as

John Mitchel and Karl Marx taken neat, bouquets for politicians and the millenium for the multitude, every Sunday evening outdoors in summer, inside in winter, in Foster Place, near the Bank of Ireland, a small room in Abbey Street, nearby.[80]

One of the fine set-piece descriptions in O'Casey's autobiography evokes "the squat, swaying form of Connolly speaking from his box" in Foster Place while a disciple hawks pamphlets on socialism and Arthur Griffith listens grimly on the fringe of the small crowd.[81] The socialist community in Dublin at this time was miniscule, and Connolly and the I.S.R.P. were highly visible within it. Connolly had won notoriety for having led protests against the celebration of Queen Victoria's Diamond Jubilee and against the Boer War. On one occasion he seized the reins of a carriage transporting speakers, among them Arthur Griffith and Maud Gonne, to a prohibited antiwar demonstration and drove through a police cordon. (This exploit inspired another of O'Casey's vignettes.[82]) His campaign against the war aroused public opinion and reduced to a trickle the flow of Irish recruits for the British Army.

These doings alone would be solid grounds for assuming Joyce's familiarity with Connolly's career and principles. But we might also adduce the Joyce family's connection with Dublin politics – in particular, John Joyce's friendship with Timothy Harrington, the Nationalist Lord Mayor, whose character reference his son took with him to the Continent in 1902 and 1904. Harrington was much distrusted by Labour ... When he ran for an unprecedented third year in 1903, the Labour party put up its own candidate (Alderman Dowd, a registered plumber) to contest the mayoralty. Harrington's success ... elicited murmurings about the hegemony of the United Irish League.[83]

Perhaps Harrington's sharpest critic was Connolly, who attacked him frequently in the pages of the I.S.R.P. newspaper, *The Workers' Republic*. Connolly made a typical swipe in an editorial (1901) on "Home Rulers and Labour": "Mr. Tim Harrington M.P., and Lord Mayor of Dublin by the intrigues of the Home Rulers, is the gentleman who is notorious for having declared that sixteen shillings a week was enough wages for any working man."[84] Thus Joyce had personal as well as political reasons for following the 1902 and 1903 elections, in which Connolly stood as a candidate for councillor in the Wood Quay Ward, with special attention.

Backed by the Dublin Trades Council, on which he represented the United Labourers' Union, Connolly ran against two Nationalists in January 1902 and garnered 431 out of about two thousand votes. In 1903, with the support of Griffith's *United Irishman*, he again ran against two Nationalists, but this time finished even further behind the winner. The same issues cropped up in both elections. In his speeches and in *The Workers' Republic*, Connolly sounded his old theme that the Nationalists were "the party of the middle classes, the agriculturalists, the house jobbers, slum landlords, and drink sellers."[85] His opponents hit back, using three weapons unavailable to him – religion, alcohol, and money.

Clerical influence in Irish politics was pervasive. In the Dublin elections of 1902 at least nine priests, canons, and archdeacons were among the nominators; and this does not count the clergymen who served on election committees. In general, they supported, and often actively worked for, chosen Nationalist candidates. Three members of one such United Irish League committee – Fathers O'Brien, Staples, and M'Gough – told the Wood Quay electors that no Catholic could be or vote for a socialist, and called Connolly an anti-Christ. Connolly reportedly described the voters as "priest ridden"; but, as a socialist, he would have received rough treatment at the hands of the priests anyway. Nationalist candidates were "assured of the powerful influence of the Catholic clergy ... especially if it was to protect the wards from socialist infiltrators."[86]

The power of priests in politics, which worked against Connolly in

his two election campaigns, manifests itself in Joyce's fictional campaign also. Recounting his meeting with a resident of Aungier Street
named Grimes, one of the Nationalist canvassers, O'Connor, tells his
colleague Henchy: "He asked me who the nominators were; and I
told him. I mentioned Father Burke's name. I think it'll be all right"
(D 123). Since it was commonplace for a priest to act as a nominator
in a Dublin election, Joyce may not have had a particular model for
Father Burke in mind. Still, it's interesting to note that the same
Reverend Staples who attacked Connolly was a nominator for the
Nationalist candidate in the Royal Exchange Ward – the contested
ward in "Ivy Day" – and that his address was No. 56, Aungier
Street, next door to the Nationalist who was opposing Connolly in
the adjacent Wood Quay Ward.[87] It is also unclear if any specific
person was the original of Father Keon. But the appearance in the
committee room of this shady, mysterious priest or ex-priest "on a
little business matter" (D 126) underscores what Joyce saw as the
unholy mixture of religion and politics in Ireland. Keon shows up in
search of Mr. Fanning – no doubt the Fanning identified in "Grace"
as "the registration agent and mayor maker of the city" (D 172) and
modeled by Joyce after an actual official (JJ 43). It is with Fanning
that Tierney is confabulating and with whom, Henchy implies, he
has been colluding as to the election of the Lord Mayor. A moment
after Keon's departure O'Connor remarks that he and Fanning
seem "very thick" (D 126). The precise nature of their involvement
Joyce leaves to the imagination, but he implies the porousness of the
boundary between religion and politics in Dublin.

  Another issue of both Connolly's 1902 and 1903 election campaigns and Joyce's story is that of the influence of drink and
drinksellers in politics. Daly comments on the "significant" role of
free drink in local elections and quotes a working-class auto-
biographer who recalled "hearing that in Johnny P's public house
free beer was to be got by promising to vote and work for Johnnie in
the elections."[88] Free booze was not the deciding factor in Connolly's defeat, but it did play a part. On the eve of the 1902 election,
more than 300 pints of porter were quaffed gratis at the public house
of the Wood Quay Ward's Nationalist alderman; and on election
night itself, one of the Nationalist candidates gave away drinks at his
own pub.[89]

  In his election address in 1903 Connolly declared: "There can
never be ... clean, healthy or honest politics in the City of Dublin,

until the power of the drink sellers is absolutely broken."[90] He scarcely exaggerated the economic and political clout of this group. The city had a good 800 licensed pubs, almost half that number of "off license" spirit grocers and beer dealers, and "an untold number of illegal 'shebeens'."[91] The drink trade made up the largest single occupational block within the Corporation, where, not surprisingly, it looked after its own interests. It also was an indispensable source of funding for the Irish Parliamentary Party.

The drinking of alcohol thus had serious ramifications that made it a chronic public issue in Ireland. For Connolly and the more radical labor leaders, it represented a tool of capitalism, which enriched publicans while keeping workers docile. For others, it was a moral issue with nationalistic overtones. Lyons notes that the Irish temperance movement was often

equated with liberation from English domination. "With fell design," said one preacher, "England suppressed our commerce, our factories, our mines, our industries, and left us only the distillery."[92]

At the urging of Archbishop Croke, the Gaelic Athletic Association banned drink from its meetings and spurned the sponsorship of publicans. Later Arthur Griffith advocated temperance as part of the Sinn Fein program and castigated the "whiskey ring" he saw dominating the Dublin Corporation. Connolly went along with the temperance lobby, as he did with the nationalists, only so far: the key program for him remained that of economic liberation, which could be achieved only under socialism.

We know that Joyce himself ("Ireland sober is Ireland stiff" [*FW* 214]) was never an exemplar of abstinence. Yet *Dubliners* reveals a sharp awareness of the social damage caused by drinking. Drinking figures prominently in several stories and peripherally in most of the others. Linking colonialism, alcohol, and child abuse, "Counterparts," for instance, could have been used as an exemplum not only by the nationalist temperance movement but by the National Society for the Prevention of Cruelty to Children, which emphasized "that drunkenness was the main factor in the majority of cases which it handled."[93]

The harm to family life caused by alcohol is suggested in "Ivy Day" by the old caretaker's unconsciously ironic lament that his teenage son, already a drunkard, "takes th'upper hand of me whenever he sees I've a sup taken" (*D* 120). Reinforcing this irony,

Mr. Henchy later gives a bottle of stout to the teenage delivery boy from the Black Eagle; the latter downs it, causing the two men to predict an alcoholic future for him. But the emphasis in the story falls on the interrelationship between drink and politics. The proprietor of the Black Eagle is Tierney, the Nationalist candidate. The "mayor maker" Fanning and another politician, Alderman Cowley, are both reported to be at the Black Eagle, to which Father Keon repairs so that he can do business with Fanning. Mr. O'Connor remarks of this last-mentioned pair, "They're often in Kavanagh's together" (*D* 126) – Kavanagh's being an actual pub which "was located just north of the City Hall and the Castle and was a gathering place for Dublin politicians and for those in search of political favors."[94] The dozen of stout promised by Tierney as a refreshment repeatedly occupies the canvassers' attention during the second half of the story. Its arrival amounts to a major event taking up over a page, and a series of poks made by the corks flying out of the heated bottles punctuates the remaining pages. These "apologetic" (*D* 131) explosions not only pay ironic tribute to Parnell, underscoring the futility of Irish politics after his death, but serve as a reminder of the politically and socially unhealthy alliance between the Nationalists and the drink trade that helped defeat Connolly and that – we may surmise – will help defeat Colgan.

A related issue in both the real 1902 and 1903 election campaigns and Joyce's fictional campaign is the complex one of money, corruption, and politics. For Connolly, the two most pernicious influences among the Nationalists on the Municipal Council were the drink-sellers and the slum landlords. He recounted in his 1903 address to the voters of the Wood Quay Ward – an area full of alley tenements since the end of the eighteenth century – "how Mr. Byrne of Wood Quay told the surrounding tenants that 'if Mr. Connolly was elected their rents would be raised.'"[95] Repeatedly he charged that many Nationalist councillors and aldermen were tenement owners or their allies, and that they ignored sanitary codes and used political office for personal advantage.

The Dublin Corporation was notorious for malfeasance. Two weeks before the 1903 elections an official report seemed to bear out this reputation: it accused the Corporation of "fraud and deceit," in particular of paying full wages to no-show employees and featherbedding on a grand scale.[96] Mary Daly and Joseph O'Brien downplay the city government's corruption, finding it to be unspectacular. Yet Daly concludes that the Corporation was "a body whose dominance by drink sellers and tenement landlords did little to articulate any broader goals for municipal government, other than narrow political gain and survival in office."[97]

Dublin's noxious tenements were the Corporation's heaviest burden. The city did carry out small-scale housing projects, "but the slums from which people were re-housed ... were left standing to receive their further complements of the hungry poor."[98] Furthermore, even if solving this huge problem lay beyond the city's resources, evidence shows that its Nationalist rulers failed to use those resources and laws available to them. The Dublin Housing Inquiry of 1913 revealed sensationally what Connolly had been charging for years. Sixteen members of the Municipal Council (only one a Unionist) turned out to be owners of eighty-nine tenement and second-class houses. Three Home Rulers possessed the bulk of these properties; almost all were in poor repair – some being classed as unfit for human habitation – even though rebates of rates had been granted, supposedly for making improvements. A parliamentary report criticized the Dublin Corporation for "a want of firmness in the enforcement of the ordinary Public Health Laws with regard to housing."[99] Yet, only weeks after the inquiry, a resolution to bar future ownership of slum property by city officials fell on deaf ears. Daly comments on the inquiry's findings:

Perhaps the most appalling case concerned the collapse of a tenement house in Townsend St. in 1902, resulting in one death. This house was the property of Alderman Gerald O'Reilly, a local publican and had been condemned as unsafe by the sanitary department ... This did not prevent [him] being elected Lord Mayor in 1908. Corporation members obviously used their influence to prevent the enforcement of regulations against their properties.[100]

A decade before the Housing Inquiry, Connolly had editorialized: "whenever a house falls in Dublin it will be found to be the property of a town councillor."[101]

No houses fall in "Ivy Day." Still, an odor of corruption floats over the story, with personal economic interest being the driving force instead of public spirit. O'Connor and Henchy voice keener concern over the lateness of their wages than over electoral issues. Tierney's ability to pay up seems a virtue to old Jack, the caretaker, as opposed to the presumed impecuniousness of the Labour candidate; and he scorns the Lord Mayor (in 1902, Harrington, known for his humble background and simple tastes) for being frugal. Since Jack is the only lower-class character in "Ivy Day," this strikes an especially ironic chord. (His preference for the party with money and patronage suggests the problem faced by Labour nominees in general and Connolly in particular: the economic and ideological hold of the Nationalists on those members of the lower classes who voted.) Another question raised in the story is that of jobbery. Assailing the Nationalist candidate, Hynes asserts: "This fellow you're working for only wants to get some job or other" (*D* 121). We would perhaps be justified in dismissing this as a partisan judgment except that Tierney's own supporters echo it. Referring to his employer's conferences with an alderman and some other politician – probably the power-broker, Mr. Fanning – O'Connor infers: "There's some deal on in that quarter." Henchy comes closer to the point: "I think I know the little game they're at . . . You must owe the City Fathers money nowadays if you want to be made Lord Mayor" (*D* 127). The idea appears to be, as Joyce reminisced to his son in 1935, that "the Lord Mayor was elected by members of the corporation to whom he owed money so that they could get a garnishee order on his salary" (*L III* 346). Joyce may have passed this on to Giorgio with tongue in cheek, or he may have based it on an anecdote drawn from his father's inside experience. But Henchy, in any case, speaks both seriously and cynically. The possibility of venal goings-on does not shock him or his listeners, who all seem to accept the spoils system on which they depend for their own ill-paying but undemanding jobs.

If "Ivy Day" does not take us into any of Dublin's pestiferous tenements, it does suggest what Connolly charged and presages what the 1913 inquiry would prove as to slum-owning, tax-fixing Home Rulers. Look at Mr. Henchy's pitch on behalf of his nominee to a Conservative voter:

But isn't your candidate a Nationalist? said he. *He's a respectable man,* said I. *He's in favour of whatever will benefit this country. He's a big ratepayer,* I said. *He has extensive house property in the city and three places of business and isn't it to his own advantage to keep down the rates? He's a prominent and respected citizen,* said I, *and a Poor Law Guardian, and he doesn't belong to any party, good, bad, or indifferent.* (*D* 131)

Absurd on the face of it, Henchy's denial of party affiliation shrewdly affirms ties of class – ties Connolly stressed in his attacks on the Nationalists, whom he saw as sharing the Conservatives' unwillingness to give organized labor and the laboring classes their due. The alliance in "Ivy Day" between these long-time enemies reflects the actual situation in at least one ward in 1902 where "the Home Rulers solicited the support of the Tory against the Socialist."[102] Moreover, the phrase *"extensive house property"* can be nothing other than a euphemism for tenements. Of course Tierney would want to keep taxes down. Henchy's description of him to the well-to-do Tory puts him among the ideal candidates for whom the Houseowners and Ratepayers Association urged its members to vote during the January 1903 campaign – "men of standing and position ... who would have a personal interest in the reduction of the present city rates."[103] Such an exhortation did not in itself imply chicanery. Nor did the Conservative preference for a commercially active Lord Mayor (in this case, John Joyce's friend) which a letter writer to *The Irish Times* expressed as follows:

In course of conversations occurring daily between Unionist electors the following is about what occurs ...

—A. "Do you see what a dodge is being attempted by those rascally City Councillors? Why they want to run in Harrington as Lord Mayor for the third time."

B. "Yes, but he is better than that Labour man Dowd, and, after all, he is a good business man."[104]

But class interest rather than individual corruption as a source of injustice was always Connolly's main text, and it is Joyce's subtext. The "P.L.G." (*D* 119) following Tierney's name on his election cards signals his class allegiance. Poor Law Guardians, elected by the tax and tithe payers of their parishes to administer the Poor Law, typically cared little for the disenfranchised poor. Tierney stands for those Nationalists who were slum-owners and publicans, or were allies of those groups and of the property-owning classes in general.

❈

Plainly, then, Joyce's imaginary election of October 1902 invokes or assumes the circumstances and issues of the actual municipal elections of January 1902 and 1903, in particular Connolly's campaigns in the Wood Quay Ward. We do not have to subscribe to the simplistic equation Connolly = Colgan. Connolly (though a manual laborer in his youth) was not a bricklayer – the only personal detail we're granted about Colgan. In addition, most Labour politicians were not socialists, and other members of the I.S.R.P. besides its leader stood for office in Dublin elections. But beyond doubt

Connolly's solid, historical reality underlies the vague, absent figure of the Labour candidate in "Ivy Day."

Colgan comes to our notice only when Hynes defends him against old Jack and makes a series of short, propagandistic comments to the effect that the workingman "gets all kicks and no halfpence" and "it's labour produces everything" (*D* 121). The question must be asked: why do he and the entire working-class population of Dublin (save the compromised caretaker) remain offstage in this political story written by an increasingly radicalized socialist? One reason, perhaps, why Joyce chose not to portray them directly is that the unity of *Dubliners* depends in part on its focus on a single (if variegated) social class. Another reason may be that he was largely a stranger to the world of the Dublin masses, and that he saw Dublin through middle-class eyes. Thus "Ivy Day" is first an expression of the petty-bourgeois Parnellism which he learned from his father, and only secondarily a reflection of the social and socialist issues of turn-of-the-century Dublin politics. Ultimately, it could be pointed out that all Joyce's fictional views of Ireland are subject to a kind of ideological parallax, as a result of which the thing observed is modified by the observer's position in a certain social class and culture. Although Joyce designated "Ivy Day" as his representative story on politics in Dublin, his deep-rooted Parnellism and the pre-eminence of the Nationalists who had claimed Parnell's mantle seem to have led him to focus on the contrast between the great leader and his unworthy, venal, ineffectual successors. This contrast gradually comes to occupy the foreground of the story. Colgan and the one-third of Dublin's citizens who lived in the slums linger out of sight in the wings.

Yet Joyce the socialist understood that "the Irish question ... exists for the Irish proletariat chiefly" (*L II* 167). Even a triumphant Parnell scarcely would have addressed this question, any more than did Sinn Fein, which Joyce saw in 1906 as Ireland's best, but deeply flawed, hope since Parnell. He predicted accurately that "either *Sinn Fein* or Imperialism will conquer the present Ireland" and that the former's success would "substitute Irish for English capital" (*L II* 187). The Parliamentarians, Sinn Fein, the Irish Republican Brotherhood – all fostered petty-bourgeois nationalism. Connolly's socialism was a "subtext" in Irish politics. After he merged his Citizen Army with the Irish Volunteers in April 1916, even this subtext and its unlikely possibilities were written out of existence.

His death at the hands of a British firing squad added drama but not substance to the crucial move he already had made; there would have been at best a token position for him in the conservative Free State which arose in 1922. So, to revert to my question of why Colgan and the laboring classes remain offstage in "Ivy Day," I think that Joyce, consciously or unconsciously, was impelled to represent them by a significant absence. They exist in a subtext which reflects not only the situation of Connolly and the Dublin masses in a country dominated by middle-class nationalism, but also what Deane calls "the major political dispute in [Joyce's] mind and in his work ... between a nationalism which he repudiates and a socialism which he cannot link with or conciliate with those ... authentic qualities which he thinks that nationalism, despite all its distortions, nevertheless enfolds."[105] Joyce could not reconcile Parnell and Connolly. Both leaders – the heroic nationalist and the heroic socialist – suggest alternatives to the miserable political scene depicted in the story. But they are mutually cancelling alternatives, and Joyce's ideological bias caused him to focus on one while relegating the other to a shadowy subtext that reflected political reality all too well.

THE IRISH FRANKENSTEIN.

"The baneful and blood-stained Monster * * * yet was it not my Master to the very extent that it was my Creature? * * * Had I not breathed into it my own spirit?" * * * (*Extract from the Works of* C. S. P-RN-LL, M.P.

1 "The Irish Frankenstein," *Punch*, 20 May 1882. The English view of the Phoenix Park assassins.

2 "The Sisters," *The Irish Homestead*, 13 August 1904. Note the context – a bucolic poem, agricultural machinery, and appointments to H.M. the King – of Joyce's first published fiction.

3 A contemporary engraving shows victims of the potato famine of 1846 at a workhouse gate. Joyce's works rarely mention the famines.

4 Crowds viewing damage to General Post Office, Dublin, Easter 1916. Joyce was writing *Ulysses* during the Great War and the Easter Rising.

THE PROCLAMATION OF
POBLACHT NA H EIREANN.
THE PROVISIONAL GOVERNMENT
OF THE
IRISH REPUBLIC
TO THE PEOPLE OF IRELAND.

IRISHMEN AND IRISHWOMEN : In the name of God and of the dead generations from which she receives her old tradition of nationhood, Ireland, through us, summons her children to her flag and strikes for her, freedom.

Having organised and trained her manhood through her secret revolutionary organisation, the Irish Republican Brotherhood, and through her open military organisations, the Irish Volunteers and the Irish Citizen Army, having patiently perfected her discipline, having resolutely waited for the right moment to reveal itself, she now seizes that moment, and, supported by her exiled children in America and by gallant allies in Europe, but relying in the first on her own strength, she strikes in full confidence of victory.

We declare the right of the people of Ireland to the ownership of Ireland, and to the unfettered control of Irish destinies, to be sovereign and indefeasible. The long usurpation of that right by a foreign people and government has not extinguished the right, nor can it ever be extinguished except by the destruction of the Irish people. In every generation the Irish people have asserted their right to national freedom and sovereignty ; six times during the past three hundred years they have asserted it in arms. Standing on that fundamental right and again asserting it in arms in the face of the world, we hereby proclaim the Irish Republic as a Sovereign Independent State, and we pledge our lives and the lives of our comrades-in-arms to the cause of its freedom, of its welfare, and of its exaltation among the nations.

The Irish Republic is entitled to, and hereby claims, the allegiance of every Irishman and Irishwoman. The Republic guarantees religious and civil liberty, equal rights and equal opportunities to all its citizens, and declares its resolve to pursue the happiness and prosperity of the whole nation and of all its parts, cherishing all the children of the nation equally, and oblivious of the differences carefully fostered by an alien government, which have divided a minority from the majority in the past.

Until our arms have brought the opportune moment for the establishment of a permanent National Government, representative of the whole people of Ireland and elected by the suffrages of all her men and women, the Provisional Government, hereby constituted, will administer the civil and military affairs of the Republic in trust for the people.

We place the cause of the Irish Republic under the protection of the Most High God, Whose blessing we invoke upon our arms, and we pray that no one who serves that cause will dishonour it by cowardice, inhumanity, or rapine. In this supreme hour the Irish nation must, by its valour and discipline and by the readiness of its children to sacrifice themselves for the common good, prove itself worthy of the august destiny to which it is called.

Signed on Behalf of the Provisional Government,

THOMAS J. CLARKE,
SEAN Mac DIARMADA,   THOMAS MacDONAGH,
P. H. PEARSE,   EAMONN CEANNT,
JAMES CONNOLLY.   JOSEPH PLUNKETT.

5 Proclamation of the Republic, Easter 1916. An attempt to transform an imagined nation into a legal one.

SACKVILLE St.DUBLIN. 1269 W.L.

6 Dublin trams, c. 1900. Though Dublin was a European backwater, its tram system provided state-of-the-art public transportation.

CHAPTER 4

Growing into history

Ideology interpellates individuals as subjects.
Louis Althusser, "Ideology and the State"

Stephen begins growing into history, and into his story, at the outset of *A Portrait of the Artist as a Young Man*. In the first sentence, which starts with a traditional opening of made-up narratives, "Once upon a time," a moocow comes down along the road and meets "a nicens little boy named baby tuckoo." If we have read the epigraph, which quotes Ovid's statement that Daedalus devoted his mind to unknown arts, then we might think of the tale of Pasiphaë and Daedalus' wooden cow.[1] The moocow may suggest too, in connection with Stephen's special destiny, cows that play a part in another mythology, that of Celtic Ireland:

The book starts out in the manner of the *shenachie*, the Irish teller of tales, and the first pages speak of two Irish heroes, Davitt and Parnell . . . Now, if we have Irish hero tales on our minds, we may recall lots of moocows led down many roads. Not least are the moocows of the Ulaid driven by the armies of Queen Maeve in *Táin Bó Cúailnge*, which climaxes the Ulster cycle of heroic tales. The "nicens little boy" whom the raiders met on that occasion was Cú Chulainn (who is generally presented as being both smaller and younger than his heroic colleagues, as Stephen is at Clongowes).[2]

The immediate source of the moocow was John Joyce, who asked his son in old age: "I wonder do you recollect the old days . . . when you were Babie Tuckoo, and I used to tell you all about the moocow that used to come down from the mountain and take little boys across?" (*L III* 212). In this story, still told in Ireland, a supernatural cow carries children to an island where "they are relieved of the petty restraints and dependencies of childhood and magically schooled as heroes before they are returned to their astonished parents and community."[3] Similarly, the youthful Cú Chulainn travels to an island where a supernatural woman warrior completes his tutoring in his vocation as hero; and Stephen crosses a bridge to the island of "the Bull" where, inspired by "the great artificer whose name he bore" (*P* 170), he discovers his own heroic vocation.[4]

Thus the first sentence of *A Portrait* encompasses elements of many stories: Greek and Irish myths, the story of Stephen's development into an artist, John Joyce's retold tale of the magical cow, and James Joyce's story of his own development into an artist. History and story, life and art intermingle. We see the artist at work already, "forging anew in his workshop out of the sluggish matter of the earth a new . . . being" and "recreat[ing] life out of life" (*P* 169, 172). The artist's material here is his own life, his history, which he transforms into a story of his growth into self-awareness.

The novel's second sentence – "His father told him that story" – reminds us of the fabricated nature of the first. The moocow is imaginary: a story within a story. Yet in the next paragraph we learn that the "moocow came down the road where Betty Byrne lived: she sold lemon platt." Here this made-up animal bumps into history, for *Thom's Directory* shows that one Elizabeth Byrne, a grocer (who typically would have sold, among other foods, confections such as lemon platt), did business at 46 Main Street in Bray, a small town where Joyce lived between the ages of five and ten.[5]

Baby tuckoo's song also mixes life and art:

> *O, the wild rose blossoms*
> *On the little green place.*
> He sang that song. That was his song.
> *O, the green wothe botheth.* (*P* 7)

The original, a sentimental Victorian song called "Lily Dale," relates the death of a young girl who is buried in a "little green grave" over which "the wild rose blossoms."[6] Deaths of children were common in this era, and the Joyce family lost several infants as well as Joyce's younger brother, George. Whether or not they sang "Lily Dale," the Joyce children had their own special songs, and in the happy days of Joyce's early boyhood the house often filled up with music (*JJ* 27). This is the historical background of Stephen's song. But it becomes significant because of how he transforms it: "*O, the green wothe botheth.*" Someone else created the magic cow, but here he makes his own imagined object, a blossoming green rose. The image recurs a few years later at Clongowes Wood College, where the badges of the two sides in a maths contest, white and red roses, distract him from his team's losing effort. His musings on the "beautiful colours" of roses spark a memory of "the song about the wild rose blossoms on the little green place." He recollects his own contribution and reasons: "But you could not have a green rose. But perhaps somewhere in the world you could" (*P* 12). His retreat from the reality at hand – the maths competition – is thus not mere escapism, for he has discovered that the creative imagination can bring into the world what did not exist there previously.

Stephen repeats this sequence of "withdrawal, imagined ideal, and return-to-world"[7] several times. He daydreams about Mercedes, from *The Count of Monte Cristo*, preferring her as a companion over other children. He longs "to meet in the real world the unsubstantial image which his soul so constantly beheld"; in this encounter he "would be transfigured" (*P* 65), like the wild rose metamorphosed into a green one. Later, at Belvedere, he withdraws from his classmates and masters, feeling happy only "in the company of subversive writers" and "intangible phantoms" (*P* 78, 83) of his own mind. About to enter University College, he again pulls back from everyday reality, choosing Europe over Dublin and the bird girl over his fellow students. He formulates his artistic aims at the end of his university career: "I desire to press in my arms the loveliness which has not yet come into the world" (*P* 251). This "loveliness," as he prepares to make his grandest flight from Ireland and the ordinary world, becomes "the uncreated conscience of [his] race" which he, as Daedalus' son, will "forge in the smithy of [his] soul." Hence the imagined green rose at the outset adumbrates the not-yet-created loveliness and national consciousness of the last pages, and baby tuckoo's claiming "his song" adumbrates Stephen's claiming his vocation as artist.[8]

Making a green rose is one thing; forging the conscience of a race, another. The artist, in attempting the latter, must confront history. Stephen, at Clongowes, cares little about the brutal internecine Wars of the Roses signified by the flowers in the arithmetic contest; taking sides is not yet for him a serious matter. But as a university student he wards off a flower-seller, a representative of Ireland who identifies herself as "your own girl" (*P* 183). Ireland's own civil conflicts are suggested on the first page by Dante Riordan's two brushes: "The brush with the maroon velvet back was for Michael

Davitt and the brush with the green velvet back was for Parnell."
Later Dante will rip the velvet off Parnell's brush, and the passions
still simmering since his death will boil over at the Dedalus family's
Christmas dinner. As a very young child Stephen knows nothing
about nationalism; he learns fast, though, that authority will pounce
on him if he deviates from expected conduct. He hides under the
table after saying that he will marry Eileen, the Protestant girl next
door, a statement for which his mother and Dante demand apology.
The issue here is religious, but there are political implications as
well, for it was his relationship with a woman that caused Parnell to
run afoul of the Church. The Christmas dinner scene, with its
quarrel over the role of priests in public life, gives Stephen a lesson
on the interpenetration of religion and politics in Ireland. A non-
partisan observer, he watches the adults exchange verbal blows,
staying on the sidelines as he had done while his fellow football
players skirmished at Clongowes. Later, at Belvedere College, he
cannot escape involvement and is beaten for championing a
"heretic" and "immoral" (*P* 81) writer. The repeated command,
"Admit" (that Byron was no good), echoes the command, "*Apolo-
gise,*" which as a child he had interwoven with Dante's threat
vis-à-vis marrying Eileen:

> *Pull out his eyes,*
> *Apologise,*
> *Apologise,*
> *Pull out his eyes.*
>
> *Apologise,*
> *Pull out his eyes,*
> *Pull out his eyes,*
> *Apologise.*

Stephen's rhyme, embodying his ability to make art out of a
frightening experience, ends the first section of Chapter 1 on a mixed
note. Conjuring up a green rose as baby tuckoo was a joyous exercise
of imagination. The rhyme is creative, too, but its regular, rigorous
shape and incantatory sound imply its function as a counter-charm
against evil and reflect the rhymer's changed relation to the world.
Stephen is fearfully hiding under a table – our last view of him in this
opening sketch. He has been introduced to history, in particular to
his prescribed story as an Irish Catholic, which requires that he
behave in a certain manner – for example, not marry a Protestant.

His intention to live his own, unsanctioned story has led to a traumatic conflict with authority. His response is significant not only because he resorts to art, but because he resorts to hiding. The vexed issue of the artist-hero's relationship to society is raised. The eagles invoked by Dante to pull out his eyes suggest the fate of another rebellious hero, Prometheus, whom Zeus punished for having stolen fire from heaven by sending an eagle to rend his liver. As a young man, Stephen decides he must save his soul through "silence, exile, and cunning" (*P* 247). Hence his childhood response to a conflict with authority – hiding and making a rhyme – foreshadows his adult decision to pursue his art abroad. Unlike Cú Chulainn or Prometheus, this artist-hero is a prudent fellow who wishes to be neither warrior nor victim. His heroism lies in forging his own and his people's history amid the loneliness and exigencies of exile. This, at any rate, is the conclusion of a dialectic that commences with a little boy hiding under a table. Joyce thus endows Stephen's departure from Ireland with an appearance of inevitability: he has no choice but to flee a repressive society hostile to him and his art.

Let me make a last observation about the way in which this opening section of *A Portrait* anticipates, like an overture, later themes. It mentions five females (one a moocow) who all give Stephen good things. Besides being associated with real cows, which supply milk, the moocow bears children to a magical place of empowerment. Betty Byrne sells sweets. Mrs. Dedalus is the nice-smelling caretaker who puts on the oilsheet when he wets the bed and, more importantly, plays music for him to which he sings or dances. Dante rewards him with pastilles for minor services. What Eileen does remains vague, but she is a pleasant enough playmate for Stephen to think of marrying her. Yet this wish provokes orders and threats from his mother and Mrs. Riordan. Both women and the girl become ambiguous figures, coercive or attractive but danger-ous. Later he connects them with the Church, which, especially through the Blessed Virgin Mary, offers him its strong embrace. E. C., another ambiguous figure who replaces Eileen as the object of his desires, inspires further artistic efforts from him, but yields satisfaction neither as muse nor as temptress. He associates her with both the Church and Ireland, neither of which offers the conditions he requires for sexual and artistic fulfillment. Hence the problem of the artist-hero's position in relation to Irish Catholic society is reflected in his problematic dealings with women. The ambivalence toward women he develops as a child, crystallized in his confusion over whether or not to kiss his mother, parallels his ambivalence toward Ireland. He arrives at the same solution in each instance – to put distance between himself and the source of conflict.

THE ARTIST, THE ARTIST'S STORY, AND HISTORY

Joyce's identity as an artist preoccupied him long before he composed his overture to *A Portrait*. He tied this identity to the idea of exile. Written mainly in Trieste, both *Stephen Hero* and *Dubliners* justify his decision to leave Ireland with Nora and pursue his art on the Continent. *Stephen Hero*, or the large fragment we have of it, asserts its protagonist's heroism in opposing an incorrigibly Philistine society; though we don't know the ending, it would seem impossible for Stephen to remain in such a world. *Dubliners* depicts a stultified society whose unheroic citizens seem unable or unwilling to escape it. The stories can be seen as fictionalizations of Joyce's experience of growing up in Dublin and his possible future experience had he remained there as an adult. If the boy's situation in the opening stories does not seem hopeless, it is because he still has the opportunity to quit Ireland. Not having done so, later protagonists (except perhaps Gabriel Conroy) suffer from an irremediable paralysis; they are stay-at-homes caught up in oppressive histories, both Ireland's and their own, alterable only through silence, cunning, and exile.

Life turned out to be more complicated than art. Trying to live his own counter-history as expatriate artist and rebel during his early days in Pola, Trieste, and Rome, Joyce, in letters to Stanislaus, alternately questioned and justified the giant step he had taken. He chevied his brother for materials from home and quicker, longer responses to his letters, deploring "the martyrdom my life is here [Trieste] and its dullness." Having wondered anxiously in February 1905 if his "writing ha[d] suffered any change," he asked in July if it was merely "a caricature of Dublin life" (*L II* 89, 90, 99). The difficulties of living in exile and living with Nora led him to contemplate terminating both situations before the end of 1905.

A long, revealing letter composed in July, during the torrid Triestine summer which left Nora prostrate and caused sweat to stream down Joyce's face as he worked on "The Boarding House" and "Counterparts," captures the 23-year-old writer's ambivalence. He introduces a "serious matter" by declaring:

You will remember the circumstances in which I left Ireland nine months ago. Like everything else that I have done in my life it was an experiment. I can hardly say ... that it ... has failed seeing that in those nine months I have begotten a child, written 500 pages of my novel, written 3 ... stories, learned German and Danish fairly well, besides discharging the intolerable ... duties of my position and swindling two tailors. (*L II* 92–93)

He goes on to describe Nora's unhappiness with Trieste and, less directly, their unhappiness with each other. Then he comes to the point: as an "experiment" – that defensive word again – he, Nora, and Stanislaus "might take a small cottage outside Dublin in the suburbs" for a year. At once he draws back, expressing reluctance on three counts, the last of which "is that I have proposed so many things which are now considered follies of mine and done so few of them that I am beginning to think it is not right for me to expect people to help me out in my notions." He ends on a note of embarrassment mixed with relief, citing his "foolishness" and admitting: "It is possible that my idea is really a terrible one but my mind's eye is so distracted ... that I am unable to see things with my former precision" (*L II* 98).

Years later the suburban cottage would reappear in Joyce's writings. It is the site of Richard Rowan's homecoming in *Exiles*, a play whose title Joyce explained by declaring: "A nation exacts a penance from those who dared to leave her payable on their return" (*E* 114). And it is (self-mockingly) the "thatched ... dwellinghouse" (*U* 17.1504–05) of Bloom's pipedream in *Ulysses*. But in real life the cottage never got off the drawing-board. Joyce managed to hang on in Trieste until Stanislaus joined him there that autumn. When he plunged into depression again in early 1907 in Rome, going back to Ireland was no longer an option. Yet it had been a close call. Full of doubts about his life and his writing, the proud, self-exiled artist had almost returned to the center of paralysis.

The crucial conflict for Joyce had to do with being a subject, in both senses of the word.[9] He fled Ireland to avoid being the subject of an oppressive history, yet he needed to be the subject, or hero, of his own story. The crux was the interconnection between history and story. Children grow into history by assuming parts in ready-made stories of which they are the subjects; they are interpellated into these stories which, collectively, reflect the ideology of a given culture. The protagonists of *Stephen Hero* and *A Portrait* refuse two such narratives by turning down, respectively, a clerkship in a

brewery and the priesthood. Joyce not only rejected similar possibilities in his own life, but sought a perspective from which he could
turn the tables on Irish history and encompass it within his own
story. He sought some high, distant point affording a broad view
and the freedom and isolation to forge a counter-history. Exile
seemed to be such a place; in "The Holy Office," the broadside he
composed in Dublin shortly before his departure in 1904, he wrote:

> So distantly I turn to view
> The shamblings of that motley crew ...
> I stand the self-doomed, unafraid,
> Unfellowed, friendless and alone,
> Indifferent as the herring-bone,
> Firm as the mountain-ridges where
> I flash my antlers on the air. (*CW* 152)

Yet exile imposes hardships. Too much distance can be one of
them; and during that first year abroad, Joyce, struggling among
strangers to earn a living for himself and a companion who didn't
"care a rambling damn about art" (*L II* 78), felt isolated. He missed
his native flatlands even while he spurned them. He had misgivings
about his ability to live his chosen story, that of the exiled artist-as-
hero. And he must have had misgivings about his autobiographical
novel, *Stephen Hero*, whose protagonist was sure of his ground in
rebelling against Irish society in a way that his creator was not.
Joyce, who urgently needed both Nora and Ireland, must have
realized that his portrait of a self-possessed adolescent flinging
"disdain from flashing antlers" (*SH* 35) at his benighted compatriots
did not do justice to the complexities of his own growing up.

If Joyce's writings generally depict "culture ... as a fabulist,
whose institutions generate narratives with which various characters
must fall into line,"[10] then *Stephen Hero* stands as an exception.
Stephen resists such narratives so uncompromisingly that he eschews
the conventional counter-narrative of artist-rebel, prompting a
fellow student to ask: "If you are [an artist] why don't you wear
your hair long?" (*SH* 34). Most of the protagonists in *Dubliners*, in
contrast, seem unable to resist the authorized stories into which they
are pulled. Eveline, though enchanted by the romantic escapism of
The Bohemian Girl, follows a culturally sanctioned plot of womanly
self-sacrifice in staying at home. Bob Doran falls into line with Mrs.
Mooney's contrived but resonant tale of seduction and reparation.
And so forth. Only in the stories of childhood do we find protagon-

ists who question approved narratives to some extent and seem capable of growing into different histories. It is here, in the opening section of *Dubliners*, that Joyce explored the relationship between official culture and developing young minds in a way which, more than the crude oppositions of *Stephen Hero*, would help him create the Stephen of *A Portrait*.

In all three stories the hero resists the values of school and family only to experience disillusionment when the possibility of an alternative set of values crumbles. The unnamed boy in "An Encounter," for instance, rejects Father Butler's Roman History in favor of American detective stories and Westerns. The latter conjure up a world of "real adventures" (*D* 21) which he and his friend Mahony go forth to seek one morning, but their day of truancy ends unhappily with the victory of stories of law and order over narratives of escape. This victory is presaged at the outset by mock Indian battles that follow the same monotonous plot, leading to the inevitable triumph of Joe Dillon, a domineering young candidate for the priesthood. Father Butler, the boys' teacher, also insists on a hegemonic narrative, and reprimands Leo Dillon for reading *The Apache Chief* instead of Roman History. Leo stumbles over an opening formula, "*Hardly had the day dawned*," which could be a translation of phrases that commence several accounts of a day's campaigning in Caesar's *Commentaries on the Gallic Wars*.[11] With their stock phrases and predictable endings, these accounts of Caesar's victorious campaigns against the savage, unruly Gauls call to mind the boys' mock sieges and battles, ending always with Joe's chant of victory. The American Indians being "savages," too, their (presumed) glorification in *The Apache Chief* implies a rebellion against "civilization" – in this case Roman civilization, which paved the way for Christianity, but with overtones of England's subjugation of the wild Irish.

The tales inspiring the boys' flight from civilization are attributed to three popular periodicals published in England by Alfred C. Harmsworth (1865–1922). Harmsworth advertised them as "reform magazines that would replace sensational trash with good, clean, instructive stories of adventure for boys."[12] There is a mild historical irony in Irish schoolboys reading a magazine, put out in England by an Irish-born journalist, called *The Union Jack*. A similar irony lies in the certainty that, Father Butler to the contrary, the sanitized adventure tales printed in such publications were safe reading material – escapist yet not conducive to liberation. No doubt the heroes of these tales, such as the Apache chief, embodied the virtues of an ideal English public-school boy, among which physical prowess and moral purity would have stood foremost. These were prime virtues, too, for the Gaelic Athletic Association's and Padraic Pearse's brands of Irish nationalism, as well as for muscular Christians of both the Protestant and Catholic persuasions (such as Joe Dillon). Fittingly, then, the physically timid narrator, in search of "wild sensations" and "real adventures," turns away from Harmsworth's "pure healthy tales"[13] of the Wild West to stories featuring "unkempt fierce and beautiful girls" (*D* 21, 20). He needs a different kind of narrative, one recognizing the sexual impulses of his adolescent body and offering alternative values to those of colonial Dublin.

He finds such a narrative in his encounter with a strange elderly man who admires "the poetry of Thomas Moore [and] the works of Sir Walter Scott and Lord Lytton."

> I pretended that I had read every book he mentioned so that in the end he said:
> —Ah, I can see you are a bookworm like myself. Now, he added, pointing to Mahony who was regarding us with open eyes, he is different; he goes in for games.
> He said he had all Sir Walter Scott's works and all Lord Lytton's . . . Of course, he said, there were some of Lord Lytton's works which boys couldn't read. Mahony asked why couldn't boys read them – a question which agitated and pained me because I was afraid the man would think I was as stupid as Mahony. (*D* 25)

A minority community of supposedly shared intellectual tastes and special, implicitly sexual knowledge begins to develop between the narrator and the old man from which Mahony – aligned with the dominant community, which prizes physical prowess and sexual purity – is excluded. If we see the boy as being, like Stephen, an incipient artist, then the importance of an alternative community becomes clear. A somewhat older Stephen, in *A Portrait*, creates his own imaginative community of "subversive writers" in whose company all "the leisure time which his school life left him was passed" (*P* 78), and he defends the immoral Byron against a boy who champions Captain Marryat, an early Victorian writer of sea tales and boys' adventure stories embodying values similar to those of *The Union Jack*. Later he retreats to "the company of phantasmal comrades" instead of heeding various "voices" of his society that urge him to be "strong and manly and healthy" or "a gentleman" or "a good catholic" (*P* 83–84). At the end he invokes Daedalus as his spiritual father; and in *Ulysses* he communes with a host of heretics, philosophers, and writers.

For the boy in "An Encounter," however, the old man proves to be (like Father Flynn in "The Sisters") a disturbing spiritual guide who offers no viable alternative to the Philistine values of the larger community. Further, the works by Scott, Moore, and Bulwer-Lytton which he reads and rereads embody an outmoded second-hand culture such as Yeats saw in the early 1900s in Galway:

> In the shop-windows there were ... halfpenny comic papers and story papers, sixpenny reprints of popular novels, and, with the exception of a dusty Dumas or Scott ... and one or two little books of Irish ballads, nothing that one calls literature, nothing that would interest the few thousands who ... have what we call culture.[14]

In the context of *fin-de-siècle* Europe – when Baudelaire was long dead, Ibsen an old man, and Conrad entering his prime – the status of Dumas, Scott, Bulwer-Lytton, and Thomas Moore as representatives of culture might well be considered a symptom of paralysis. Similar symptoms were the popularity of sentimental poems such as "The Arab's Farewell to His Steed," recited by the uncle in "Araby," and "the cult of the *Bohemian Girl*," admired by Eveline, which for a time was as big a draw in Dublin as the imported "lunacies of the English music hall."[15] In *Stephen Hero* both popular and official culture make little impression on Stephen, who seems immune to the paralysis that their authorized narratives of human life engender in individuals who take them as models for their own lives. In contrast, the stories of *Dubliners* portray the power and seductiveness of such narratives. Joyce seems to have recognized, during his first year abroad, the necessity of evoking the vulnerability of the young artist to social forces that would reproduce in him received ideas and have him repeat history rather than create his own story. The first-person narratives of the anonymous boy(s) in *Dubliners* showed him a different, subtler way of depicting the relationships between history and story, between society and the artist.

Yet what *Stephen Hero*, *Dubliners*, and *A Portrait* have in common is an insistent portrayal of a society with no place for the artist. In another story dealing with Joyce's concern over his identity as an artist and his relationship with Ireland, the protagonist, a would-be poet, thinks: "If you wanted to succeed you had to go away. You could do nothing in Dublin" (*D* 73). "A Little Cloud" is mordantly ironic, and there are more differences than parallels between Joyce and Little Chandler, yet the story's closing imagery of confinement suggests that Chandler's prime failure is that he doesn't emigrate. Joyce, despite his early vacillations in Trieste, made no concession in his art to the possibility of living and writing successfully in Ireland. His conception of the artist as a solitary hero-rebel did not allow him to take part in the shared or allied efforts of any Irish school or community, even one so divided and variegated as that of the Literary Revival. He saw himself as belonging to a tradition of exiled or rebellious writers extending from Dante to Ibsen. Although Russell, Yeats, and Lady Gregory helped him, he preferred to view himself (like Stephen in *Ulysses*) as being indifferently excluded from their circle. Various forces – the Church, Irish nationalism, British imperialism, the Anglo-Irish literary establishment – were all arrayed against him. In *A Portrait*, Stephen's sense of persecution and isolation is not so finely honed as in *Ulysses*, but religion, nationalism, the Revival, his family, E. C., and his friend Cranly all have failed him. The novel barely hints at the existence of Yeats and other talented artists who recognized the force of Irish "paralysis" yet chose to stay in Ireland. If Joyce had greater need than the Anglo-Irish writers did to put distance between himself and his country's calamity-ridden past, exile was still not necessary or inevitable. It was, however, a response that grew out of his vision of Irish history – one he shared with many nationalists – as a series of betrayals culminating in the betrayal of Charles Stewart Parnell.

PARNELL AND IRISH POLITICS

Much of the passion informing Stephen's rejection of political activism stems from Joyce's self-identification with Parnell. Since a social chasm divided middle-class Catholic Dublin from the rural Anglo-Irish gentry, Joyce was necessarily selective in choosing the elements of this identification. But the artist could see a parallel between himself and the politician insofar as both had undertaken projects, in their respective callings, to liberate Ireland. According to the Parnellite martyrology passed down to Joyce from his father, most Irish Catholics had turned on the "Chief" ignobly and treacherously, thereby enacting one more in a series of betrayals of would-be liberators in Irish history. Joyce often discerned betrayal in his own life. In 1939 he explained his refusal to return to Ireland in a note to the proofs of Gorman's biography:

He has not even sought refuge there during the present calamitous events in Europe. Having a vivid memory of the incident at Castlecomer when quicklime was flung into the eyes of their dying leader, Parnell, by a chivalrous Irish mob, he did not wish a similar unfortunate occurrence to interfere with the completion of the book he was trying to write. (*JJ* 338)

Joyce also identified with Parnell's aloofness, defiance, and sense of personal destiny. He evoked their kinship in the image of a highland stag – a strong, noble, hunted creature – in "Gas from a Burner" and *Stephen Hero*. Perhaps he saw another parallel in their irregular (though monogamous) love relationships. He told Stanislaus that the "slightest disapproval on the part of my genteel pupils would . . . obtain for me dismissal and with my 'immorality' belled about the town [Trieste] I should find it next to impossible to get anything to do here" (*L II* 94). Defiance of convention coupled with a fear of persecution marks much of Stephen's behavior as a university student. He refrains from political activism because Parnell's martyrdom has proven the futility of such action. In refusing Davin's plea to join the nationalist cause, he replies:

No honourable and sincere man . . . has given up to you his life and his youth and his affections from the days of Tone to those of Parnell but you sold him to the enemy or failed him in need or reviled him and left him for another . . . When the soul of a man is born in this country there are nets flung at it to hold it back from flight. You talk to me of nationality, language, religion. I shall try to fly by those nets. (*P* 203)

Davin's credo of "Ireland first" provokes the retort: "Ireland is the old sow that eats her farrow" (*P* 203). The emotion behind this accusation is rooted not in any specific act of betrayal Stephen has experienced, but in Joyce's identification with Parnell, that is, the Parnell who played the part of tragic hero in the nationalist historical narrative Joyce learned from his father.

Joyce retold this narrative in "Home Rule Comes of Age" (1907) and "The Shade of Parnell" (1912), where, writing as a journalist in Trieste, he expressed views that infuse his fictional depictions of Parnell. (The publication in 1914 of Mrs. O'Shea's unintentionally deflating memoir of her lover, it is true, does seem to have contributed to the more human Parnell of *Ulysses*.) I would like to compare the picture of the Parnell era that emerges from these articles and (implicitly) from *A Portrait* with a few later accounts that have the advantage, which Joyce could not attain through exile, of emotional and temporal distance.

"Home Rule Comes of Age" opens with a dramatic sketch of the joy felt by Dubliners in April 1886 on hearing news that Gladstone had approved limited self-rule for Ireland. The second paragraph begins: "Seven years pass, and we are at the second Home Rule Act. Gladstone [has] in the meantime completed the moral assassination of Parnell with the help of the Irish bishops" (*CW* 193). The body of the article revolves around the fact that now, in 1907, twenty-one years after the first Home Rule Act, the return to power of the English Liberals has not brought Ireland any closer to Home Rule. Joyce criticizes the Liberal Party and the Vatican as "the most powerful weapons that England can use against Ireland" (*CW* 195). He treats the enmity of the Vatican as a given, and reasons that Conservatism is an "openly inimical doctrine" whereas (he implies) the hypocritical half-measures of the Liberals have raised false hopes and disarmed Irish separatists. He concludes by denouncing the Liberals' ally, the Irish Parliamentary Party, which after twenty-seven years of fruitless talk and agitation and fund-raising "has gone bankrupt" while its members have individually prospered. The newly rich Irish MPs, he claims ironically, "have given proof of their altruism only in 1891, when they sold their leader, Parnell, to the pharisaical conscience of the English Dissenters without exacting the thirty pieces of silver" (*CW* 196).

Published five years later, "The Shade of Parnell" responds to the passing of the third Home Rule Bill on 9 May 1912. The article has two parts. First Joyce portrays the bill as a product of duplicitous art designed to resolve the Irish question to England's advantage without vouchsafing much more than "an appearance of autonomy." He contrasts the limitations of the bill with the general rejoicing and predicts a celebration on the reopening of the old Irish Parliament that will be attended not only by the living, but by "the shade of Charles Parnell" (*CW* 224). The remainder of the article deals with Parnell himself. Joyce describes the "extraordinary personality" of this paradoxical Irish leader whose influence on his people "defies critical analysis" (*CW* 225). In contrast to Gladstone, an orotund statesman who tacked and veered in political winds, the taciturn, self-composed Parnell maintained both his "sovereign bearing" (*CW* 226) and a constant course whose goal was Home Rule. Only in the last third of his article does Joyce focus on the career rather than the man. The steady march of this "Moses, le[ading] a turbulent and unstable people from the house of shame to the verge of the Promised Land," he outlines in one paragraph. What really interests him is the sudden end of the march, in between the first and second Home Rule Bills:

Parnell's fall came . . . like lightning from a clear sky. He fell hopelessly in love with a married woman, and when her husband, Captain O'Shea, asked for a divorce, the ministers Gladstone and Morley openly refused to legislate in favour of Ireland if the sinner remained as head of the Nationalist Party. Parnell did not appear at the hearings to defend himself. He denied the right of a minister to exercise a veto over the political affairs of Ireland, and refused to resign.

He was deposed in obedience to Gladstone's orders. Of his 83 representatives only 8 remained faithful to him. The . . . clergy entered the lists to finish him off. The Irish press emptied on him and the woman he loved the vials of their envy. The citizens of Castlecomer threw quicklime in his eyes. He went from county to county, from city to city, "like a hunted deer" . . . Within a year he died of a broken heart at the age of 45. (*CW* 227–28)

The Irish, Joyce closes, "did not throw [Parnell] to the English wolves [but] tore him to pieces themselves."

The Christmas 1891 dinner scene in *A Portrait* sounds many of the same themes, but emphasis falls on the Church's intervention in the Nationalists' internecine struggle over Parnell. Inevitably the rhetoric of the episode aligns the reader with the Parnellites: the dour, fanatical Mrs. Riordan would not be a good advocate for any cause. She scarcely attempts to debate with the men. Rather she advances, over and over, the interlinked propositions that "God and religion and morality come first" and that the priests and bishops of the Church, the collective "apple of God's eye" (*P* 38), are the only arbiters of morality. Mr. Dedalus and Mr. Casey, a Fenian who has served time for his revolutionary activities, argue for the exclusion of politics from Dante's all-embracing categories of religion and morality: "We go to the house of God, Mr Casey said, in all humility to pray to our Maker and not to hear election addresses" (*P* 31). The issue of betrayal arises when Mr. Dedalus asks heatedly: "Were we to desert him at the bidding of the English people?" (*P* 32). He does not need to identify "him"; everyone at the table except Stephen knows already that the passion behind the general principles at stake derives from the recent events of Parnell's downfall and death. After a failed attempt to smooth things over, there is more invective, including Mr. Dedalus' aspersions on William Walsh, Archbishop of Dublin, and Michael Logue, Archbishop of Armagh – "Billy with the lip" and "the tub of guts up in Armagh" (*P* 33). Mr. Casey tells the story of how he spat tobacco juice in the eye of an anti-Parnellite woman who was taunting him after an election meeting. Stephen is confused:

He [Casey] was for Ireland and Parnell and so was his father: and so was Dante too for one night at the band on the esplanade she had hit a gentleman on the head with her umbrella because he had taken off his hat when the band played *God save the Queen* at the end. (*P* 37)

Continuing his attack on priests in politics, Mr. Dedalus makes a side thrust at the anti-Parnellite Nationalists, now dominant politically and economically, by describing his grandfather as "a good Irishman when there was no money in the job" (*P* 38). Dante angrily counters his gibe that the Irish are "an unfortunate priest-ridden race" by casting Parnell as a "traitor" to Ireland because of his adultery: "The priests were right to abandon him. The priests were always the true friends of Ireland" (*P* 37, 38). This claim provokes Mr. Casey to cite examples of the Church's interference in politics against the interests of Irish nationalism throughout the nineteenth century. Mr. Dedalus adds Paul Cullen, Archbishop of Dublin and later Cardinal, to his list of contemptible clerics. Then the scene rises to its highest pitch of passion, the issue between Dante and Mr. Casey boiling down to God vs. Ireland, and the Christmas dinner breaks up.

As reflected in his Trieste articles and in *A Portrait*, Joyce's case for Parnell rests on the following assumptions. Parnell was an extraordinary leader and human being. Whether or not Home Rule was really the Promised Land, he had led the Irish people to its border by the end of the 1880s. The uncontested verdict against him and Mrs. O'Shea in her husband's divorce suit aroused the puritanism of the English Protestant Dissenters (that is, Methodists and other dissenters from the Anglican Church of England). In response to their pressure, the inconstant Gladstone demanded Parnell's resignation as the price of another Home Rule Bill. The vast cowardly majority of the Irish Party turned on their leader. The Church, living up to its long history of sabotaging the nationalist cause, joined Parnell's betrayers in waging electoral war against him and driving him into his grave.

Joyce did not exaggerate in portraying Parnell as an extraordinary man. Even Parnell's enemies admitted his uniqueness. Newspaper accounts, political speeches, and word of mouth made him a living legend. R. Barry O'Brien's biography (1898), which appeared less than a decade after his death, codified what several historians have called "the Parnell myth." The tale of the Split and the fall of Parnell form "the main story line" of this myth.

The idea of the lonely, heroic figure, deserted by his party, fighting to the end against overwhelming odds, had a nobility which made an irresistible appeal to those – such as John O'Leary . . . – who saw the issue primarily in terms of the ancient struggle against England; to others, like Yeats, whose piety and indignation were stirred by the spectacle of greatness overthrown by mediocrity; and to such as Joyce, for whom the fall of Parnell symbolised the triumph of all that was . . . degrading in Irish life.[16]

Parnell's genius was thus subsumed by the Parnellite narrative of betrayal – by the legend of a "tragic hero hounded to death by English Liberal hypocrites and their allies, spiteful or weak Irish politicians and narrow-minded priests."[17] Anti-Parnellites could accept their opponent's greatness while resisting the notion that they had betrayed him, but they were working against a prototype narrative, the story of Christ, which reverberated powerfully in their society.

The idea of betrayal, in connection with Irish nationalism, predates the Parnell myth. Mr. Casey traces the Church's betrayals back to the Act of Union (1800), "when bishop Lanigan presented an address of loyalty to the Marquess Cornwallis" (*P* 38). Many Irish bishops did in fact favor the Union because of its promised rider: Catholic emancipation. Since the leaders of late eighteenth-century Irish nationalism, such as Henry Grattan and Wolfe Tone, had been Protestants, the bishops saw no unbreakable link between the Catholic cause and the nationalist cause. And if emancipation could be salvaged out of the wreckage of the rebellion of 1798, why not? Mr. Casey looks back at the Union from the perspective of the post-Parnell era, as Joyce did, and casts the bishops in the anachronistic light of traitors to a national movement of and for Irish Catholics that was not born until Daniel O'Connell's heyday.

A broken English promise set the stage for this movement. Facing domestic opposition, Pitt and Cornwallis could not deliver their end of the Union bargain to Irish Catholics. The latter

felt betrayed when the promised emancipation did not follow. The lines, which had been shifting for so long, soon became clear and hard again. "Protestant" and "Unionist" were to become virtually synonymous. Catholic rejection of the Union was to have various names, associated with different methods towards essentially the same end: "Repeal," "Home Rule," "Sinn Fein."[18]

The Church was first enlisted in Irish politics by O'Connell. He coerced the Church into joining the controversy, from 1809 to 1815, over permitting the Crown a veto in the appointment of Catholic bishops; and he drew it, in 1824, into alliance with the Catholic Association. This alliance achieved its goal after five years in the form of a Catholic Relief Act, which, without loosening England's grip on Ireland, lifted religious and civil restrictions against Roman Catholics throughout Great Britain. Mr. Casey refers to the act in asking: "Didn't the bishops and priests sell the aspirations of their country in 1829 in return for catholic emancipation?" (*P* 38). This rhetorical question repeats his first charge concerning the Irish prelates' support for the Union, and probably also contains an implied charge that the Church, having gained religious freedom in 1829, did not support Irish political emancipation during O'Connell's campaign in the early 1840s for repeal of the Union. Actually, the Irish clergy had backed O'Connell throughout the 1830s in his alliance with the English Whigs; this had seemed to offer more or less religious benefits, such as the abolition of tithes paid to the (Protestant) Church of Ireland[19] and increased civil power for Catholics. They found it harder to justify involvement in the repeal campaign, which had nakedly secular aims. "Yet fully two-thirds of the Irish bishops and a still higher proportion of the lower clergy eventually threw themselves into this agitation."[20] When the repeal movement collapsed, it did so because of stiff English resistance and O'Connell's failure of nerve, not because of clerical betrayal.

The Church was on delicate ground in backing agitation against an established government. The *Maynooth Catechism* quotes Holy Writ in advising: "The duties of subjects to the temporal powers are, *to be subject to them, and to honour and obey them . . . for so is the will of God.*"[21] Had O'Connell turned to force after the prohibition of his monster meetings, his clerical allies could not have followed him. A quarter of a century later the episcopate began censuring the nascent Fenian movement, taking a stand against revolutionary violence that it maintained consistently from 1858 to 1918. Mr. Casey angrily points out this fact: "Didn't they [the bishops and priests] denounce the fenian movement from the pulpit and in the confessionbox? And didn't they dishonour the ashes of [the Fenian] Terence Bellew MacManus?" (*P* 38).

Paul Cullen, the Irish Church's informal "pope" during the third quarter of the nineteenth century, was one of the Fenians' staunchest foes. In 1861 he refused to let the body of MacManus, a leader of the 1848 rebellion, lie in state in Dublin's Pro-Cathedral because the funeral smacked of "a Fenian publicity stunt."[22] Cullen and like-minded bishops argued against Fenianism on both religious and patriotic grounds. It was sinful to try to overthrow a legitimate government, or to join a secret society and pledge obedience to men of unknown or unacceptable religious beliefs. The Fenian paper, *The Irish People*, sought to spread socialism and to undermine ecclesiastical authority. Revolutionary extremism could only benefit England and Protestants; to Ireland and Irish Catholics it would bring bloodshed and ruination.[23] Often, in the Church's anti-Fenian campaign, individuals were asked – sometimes in the "confessionbox," as Mr. Casey implies – if they had taken the Fenian oath. The penitent had to renounce the organization in order to be absolved. Hence the dilemma of divided loyalties which pervades the Christmas dinner scene: how could one be both a Fenian and a good Catholic?

The conflict did not lead, however, to a final choice between Catholicism and Ireland, as it does for the impassioned Mr. Casey. Although the rhetorical battle between Church and Fenians became heated – Cullen called Fenianism "a compound of folly and wickedness wearing the mask of patriotism"[24] – the clerical stand was not monolithic:

In Dr. Cullen's own archdiocese Fenians would go to confession in the Jesuit Church in Gardiner Street, where the priests did not ask the awkward question about the oath. At Christmas and Easter [Fenians] in the diocese of Ross crossed over into the diocese of Cloyne where the bishop, Dr. Keane, had not insisted on withholding the sacraments ... There was many an instance where the interpretation of the episcopal censures by a sympathetic priest left a door open for the man who wanted to reconcile his Fenianism with his religious beliefs.[25]

One priest, Father Lavelle, achieved fame as a supporter of the Fenian cause and a preacher of what today would be termed liberation theology. While under attack by Dr. Cullen and the majority of Irish bishops, he was defended by his superior, Archbishop MacHale of Tuam. MacHale himself "assisted at the High Mass for the Manchester Martyrs [1867] when Cullen believed that the real object of these High Masses was to promote Fenianism."[26]

One reason why some clergymen broke ranks to help the Fenians was that virtually all parties to the conflict between the Church and Fenianism were patriots. Even Cullen, a deeply conservative ultramontanist, was not simply a "Castle-bishop."[27] The bishops' quarrel with the Fenians had to do with priorities, tactics, and power, not with the ultimate goal of a self-governing Ireland. Though their spiritual task remained paramount, the bishops had aligned themselves firmly with the constitutional wing of Irish Catholic nationalism in O'Connell's day. A thumbnail sketch of a clerical dinner in 1835, made by Alexis de Tocqueville, captures this alliance. Several prelates and priests expressed:

Distrust and hatred of the great landlords; love of the people and confidence in them. Bitter memories of past oppression ... A profound hatred of the Protestants ... Little impartiality apparent. Clearly as much the leaders of a Party as the representatives of the Church.[28]

Priestly power, as a rule, depended on the absence of lay. In the emancipation and repeal campaigns, the clergy followed O'Connell's lead, although they were essential to his plans and provided lower-level leadership. After his death, and after the famine and the abortive rising of 1848, priests and bishops filled a vacuum left by the breakdown of O'Connell's *de facto* national party. During the 1850s and 1860s, the clergy, headed by Cullen, tended to take the lead in forming Irish public opinion. In 1870 Isaac Butt's Home Government Association held its first meeting, officially launching the Home Rule movement. By the late 1870s Parnell had taken charge of this movement, and once again constitutional nationalism in Ireland had a towering leader whose natural allies and followers included the Catholic priests and bishops. The Church, from 1881 on, "was embedded in and integral to the Parnellite movement – subordinate ... but accorded the respect and accommodation earned by its indispensability as sanctioner of popular courses and local agent of the organisation."[29]

According to Joyce, the Church hitched its wagon to Parnell's star and then, over the issue of adultery, disengaged itself and viciously helped destroy both him and Ireland's best chance of Home Rule. This was the standard Parnellite position during the seemingly hopeless years of 1891–1916, when Joyce wrote his early fiction and his political journalism. There can be no doubt that Parnell led the Home Rule movement masterfully and that the Church joined some of his former subordinates in bringing him down. The question is: from today's perspective, after seventy-odd years of Irish self-government, what principles were at stake in this internecine nationalist conflict which the Parnell legend distorts?

Emmet Larkin, looking back at Parnell's rise and fall, sees him as the architect of the modern Irish state, which he created between 1878 and 1886 on the foundation of two political alliances. The first was the Clerical–Nationalist alliance, on which Parnell's state depended for stability. The second was the Liberal–Nationalist alliance, which Parnell needed to translate "his *de facto* state from reality to legality."[30] When conflict arose, Irish nationalists had to choose between these alliances and the man who had fashioned them.

The English Conservatives recognized the danger of these alliances and labored to undo them while in power (1886–92) between Gladstone's ministries. Their attempt to foil the Plan of Campaign illustrates the Church's loyalty to its Nationalist allies. The plan, devised by Irish Party members John Dillon and William O'Brien in 1886, was a response to agricultural distress. It resumed the struggle of the Land League, which had subsided after Gladstone's 1881 Land Act and the 1882 Kilmainham pact, by setting up a system through which hard-pressed tenant farmers could pressure landlords to accept a "fair" rent in lieu of the usual one. It also created a "campaign fund," consisting of proffered rents refused by landlords, to support evicted tenants, and it provided for boycotting anyone who took an evicted tenant's farm. The leading Irish clergyman, Archbishop Walsh of Dublin (Mr. Dedalus' "Billy with the lip"), declared the plan to be morally acceptable. Lord Salisbury's Conservative government retaliated with a severe Coercion Act; it also inveigled Pope Leo XIII into condemning the plan in his decree of April 1888.

The Irish Bishops, cruelly caught between their duty to the pope and their loyalty to their people, opted not to enforce the Roman condemnation . . . They told the pope . . . in a joint letter signed by twenty-eight of the thirty

Irish Bishops, that they knew more about the Irish situation than either he or his advisers and that the price . . . for making his will effective in Ireland would be the loss not only of their own power and influence but of millions of Irish Catholics at home and abroad.[31]

Thus the bishops, in effect, chose Ireland over the pope.

The Liberals held up their end of the alliance by opposing the Conservatives' efforts at coercion. The crisis precipitated by the plan, therefore, actually strengthened Parnell's hand. His English allies were still pledged to grant Home Rule, and the Irish Church had remained in the Nationalist camp in spite of papal pressure. The bishops resisted an added Conservative effort to pry them loose from the Nationalists with the lure of a government-subsidized university for Catholics. Archbishop Walsh declared "that no bargain on the education question could be struck . . . if it involved any abridgment of the aspirations of the Irish people with regard to either the land question or Home Rule."[32] Hence the bishops did the opposite of what Mr. Casey accuses their counterparts of having done in 1829 – that is, they did *not* "sell the aspirations of their country" (*P* 38). From 1886 through 1890 the Church stood firm: it upheld its partnership with the Nationalists in a *de facto* "constitutional arrangement"[33] which had emerged out of the Plan of Campaign crisis. During the summer and autumn of 1890, as the Liberals edged closer to regaining power in England, many people thought Ireland was poised on the brink of Home Rule. Then, on 17 November, an English divorce court delivered an uncontested verdict against Parnell and his mistress.

❀

The Split in Irish political life that arose out of Parnell's tacit admission of adultery was a complex phenomenon which is reduced, in the Christmas dinner scene, to a conflict between Parnell and the Church. Joyce ignores the sizable minority of MPs who remained loyal to Parnell; he allows the anti-Parnellite MPs to be dismissed as "the priests' pawns" (*P* 33–34) without offering any suggestion to the contrary. The competing principles in the quarrel appear clear-cut: nationalism and morality. Putting Ireland's secular interests first, Mr. Dedalus asks: "Were we to desert him at the bidding of the English people?" Dante asserts the primacy of morality, in particular a puritanical sexual morality: "He was no longer worthy to lead . . . He was a public sinner" (*P* 32). Joyce had good technical reasons for simplifying political issues in this scene; it grips us because of its dramatic, not its argumentative power. But he had ideological and emotional reasons as well.

Though everyone agrees on the crucial role of the Church in overthrowing Parnell – "The Bishops and the Party / That tragic story made," as Yeats says – the bishops at first neither desired nor thought it necessary to get involved in such a business. They expected Parnell to step down voluntarily and were silent, thus causing Gladstone to express his surprise "at the apparent facility with which the Roman Catholic bishops and clergy appear to take [Parnell's] continued leadership."[34] While the hierarchy and the English Liberals marked time, the most influential nationalist daily in Ireland, *The Freeman's Journal*, responded to Parnell's declaration to its London correspondent that he had no intention of relinquishing his position. Its editorial of 18 November articulated the two essential arguments of Parnellite loyalists: first, his leadership was a political, not a moral, question; and second, the question should be resolved by the Irish rather than the English people. But the bishops had no doubt that the leadership by an adulterer of any Irish organization, let alone a national party with which they had allied themselves, was a moral and religious problem. And the solution to the problem seemed obvious. Even a strong nationalist such as Archbishop Croke assumed that Parnell would have to disappear, at least for a time, from Irish politics. Thus the prelates, though stunned and dismayed by the divorce court's verdict, waited quietly through a week filled with public declarations of lay support for Parnell.[35]

During this week Michael Davitt, in *Labour World*, raised a major voice of dissent in calling for his former ally's retirement. He also wrote privately to Archbishop Walsh, in effect answering the Parnellite arguments advanced in *The Freeman's Journal*: "If Parnell persists in placing his own personality . . . above the cause of Ireland and insists upon remaining in his position, there is no . . . hope of Home Rule being won at the General Election."[36] The reason for Davitt's gloomy prediction was the pressure on Gladstone of the voters who formed the backbone of his English constituency, the Nonconformists. Many felt they couldn't support the Liberal Party if it remained in alliance with a party led by an unmasked sexual sinner. Despite the arguments of *The Freeman's Journal*, morality and English public opinion were inevitably involved from the start. Hence the cogency of Davitt's reasoning that the real choice lay between Parnell and Ireland's political future.

The second week following the divorce court's verdict began on 25 November with Parnell's reelection as chairman of the Irish Party. The bishops' continued silence on the moral issue drew criticism from Davitt's *Labour World*, but they hardly required reminding that morality in this case was not the province only of the English Nonconformists. So far the Irish Party's political machine had worked with spectacular success in marshaling public support for Parnell, with the result that the bishops, apart from their own mixed, unhappy feelings about the crisis, found themselves caught in a dilemma. As Archbishop Walsh wrote to Davitt before the 25th, the situation called for "grave deliberate action." Yet "we find a particular course publicly urged on the country with the greatest vehemence, so that all those who differ ... have to choose between effacing themselves and running the risk of causing a split."[37] After Parnell's reelection the bishops saw no alternative, both as moral leaders and nationalists, to taking this risk. They scheduled a special meeting for 3 December.

In the meantime a split began to develop without the bishops' help. Gladstone, prior to Parnell's reelection, had spoken to the influential Irish MP, Justin McCarthy, pointing out that Non-conformist pressure made it impossible for Parnell to continue as leader without jeopardizing Home Rule. On 24 November he put essentially the same advice in a letter to his adviser on Irish matters, John Morley, intending for Parnell to see it. Morley failed to find Parnell before the Irish Party meeting the next day; and McCarthy, though he apprised Parnell of his talk with Gladstone, did not tell the party. On the 26th the letter appeared in *The London Standard*. It focused the eyes of many Irish MPs on a prospect which they, unlike Davitt, had willfully overlooked, and at an emergency meeting that day they asked Parnell to "re-consider his position." He declined. Instead he responded with a "manifesto to the Irish people," published on 29 November, in which he assailed Gladstone and those MPs whose request for second thoughts had signaled "the first revolt" against his leadership.

Parnell's manifesto asserted: "The integrity and independence of a section of the Irish parliamentary party ha[s] been apparently sapped and destroyed by the wire-pullers of the English liberal party."[38] He blamed Gladstone's published letter as the immediate cause. R. Barry O'Brien also makes much of the letter, quoting various unidentified sources – "a distinguished Liberal," "an Irish

Nationalist," and "an old Fenian leader" – to show that publication
of Gladstone's views "suggested English dictation" and turned the
issue of Parnell's leadership into a "question ... between an
Englishman and an Irishman."[39] Joyce may have taken his cue from
O'Brien's account and added his own exaggerations in "The Shade
of Parnell" and the Christmas dinner scene. But the issue was not a
simple one of whether or not to "desert" a leader beset by the enemy.
Although Parnell was less a sexual transgressor than the Prince of
Wales, whose peccadilloes failed to stir up the Nonconformists, the
Prince had not been named an adulterer in an uncontested legal
action. What should amaze us, as Cruise O'Brien points out, is not
the intolerance of the English Dissenters, but rather the fact that the
equally austere members of the Irish Party rallied to Parnell's
support for a full week until the political implications of Gladstone's
letter made most of them reconsider.[40] With regard to the letter
itself, Gladstone undoubtedly *was* trying to force Parnell's resignation. But he and his fellow Liberals

> could have had no desire to destroy Parnell, who was their valued ally,
> until the news, most unwelcome to them, of the divorce-court verdict. Nor
> did they pretend that it was their reprobation of Parnell's adultery – about
> which they had known for eight years – which moved them to seek his
> retirement. Their action was based solely on ... English public opinion;
> they bowed before the moral indignation of the lower middle class, a force
> which hardly anyone in Victorian England ... could withstand for long.[41]

The Split, we can see, had already manifested itself as a hairline
fracture at the special party meeting on 26 November, a full week
before the Irish bishops held their own meeting to consider the crisis.
A Portrait, therefore, insofar as it highlights the Church's role in the
Split and reduces other anti-Parnellite forces to the function of a
cat's paw, is misleading. But granting that Gladstone's letter rather
than the Church's action prompted the first rebellious move against
Parnell, which escalated quickly into the break-up of the Irish Party
on 6 December, there remains the question of what part the Church
played once the two factions materialized. In the hierarchy of
betrayers in Joyce's Trieste articles and *A Portrait*, Gladstone takes
the lead, followed by the Irish clergy; the anti-Parnellite MPs are
minor players. I do not have space to investigate the complex goals
and actions of this last-mentioned faction, which included individuals of ability and high ideals (as well as the talented but
malicious T. M. Healy), but would like to look briefly at the bishops'

involvement in the ten months of strife between the beginning of the Split and Parnell's death.

Before the bishops caucused on 3 December, a few of them, notably Walsh and Croke, made a private effort to preserve the Clerical–Nationalist alliance. Croke was the hierarchy's most fiery nationalist, and had defended Parnell against the Pope, but felt no less firmly than his brethren that an adulterer could not continue as party leader. This conclusion was the premise rather than the point of advice he wired to Justin McCarthy in the wake of Parnell's manifesto:

All sorry for Parnell; but still, in God's name, let him retire quietly ...

If he does so the Irish Party will be kept together, our honourable alliance with Gladstonian Liberals maintained, success at general election assured, Home Rule certain.

But if he does not retire, alliance will be dissolved, election lost, Irish Party seriously damaged ... Home Rule indefinitely postponed, coercion perpetuated, evicted tenants hopelessly crushed, and the public conscience outraged.[42]

Croke, though angry, upset, and disillusioned, clearly was not engaged in what Joyce called "moral assassination." By the bishops' lights, Parnell had undone himself. Their main aim apart from morality (and their realization that the party's crisis was the Church's opportunity to regain equality in the Clerical–Nationalist alliance) was keeping Home Rule alive. These priorities, morality and nationalism, emerged in that order from the "Address" made public by the bishops following their meeting on 3 December. As Archbishop Walsh summarized the address in a telegram to McCarthy, Parnell was "unfit for leadership, first of all on moral grounds ... also in view of ... defeat at elections, wreck of Home Rule hopes, and sacrifice of tenants' interests."[43]

In Committee Room 15 at Westminster, the Irish Party debated while Parnell, in the chairman's seat, ruthlessly bent rules of parliamentary procedure to his own advantage. In a clever move he persuaded McCarthy to go on the fool's errand of asking Gladstone to guarantee the terms of a Home Rule bill that would follow on his retirement. Predictably, Gladstone refused to make such a compromising and possibly unfulfillable commitment. This refusal allowed John Redmond to develop the Parnellite theme that the Irish Party was giving up its chief in response to English pressure while receiving nothing in return: "If we are asked to sell our leader to preserve an alliance . . . we are bound to enquire what we are getting for the price we are paying." When Redmond said this, Parnell interjected: "Don't sell me for nothing . . . If you get my value, you may change me tomorrow."[44] Joyce, with his affinity for betrayal, made the most of this phrase, together with Parnell's injunction that he not be thrown to the English wolves. He uses the wolf imagery in "The Shade of Parnell" and conjectures that Parnell somehow knew that "one of the disciples who dipped his hand in the same bowl with him would betray him" (*CW* 228); decades later he links Parnell, Christ, and betrayal once more in the cry, "Do not flingamejig to the twolves!" (*FW* 479.14). But the debate in Committee Room 15 revolved around political principles rather than the issue of personal loyalty. When it was cut short by the forty-five anti-Parnellites who walked out on 6 December, Parnell had lost a power struggle but hardly had been betrayed.

The theater of what would become a bloodless nationalist civil war shifted to Ireland, where Parnell had decided to battle for his leadership by appealing directly to the Irish people. Again, Cruise O'Brien, Larkin, and other historians draw a picture of a man strikingly different from the rather passive victim depicted by Joyce. At the outset of his campaign Parnell not only had twenty-eight loyalist MPs as allies, but retained control of the Irish Party's machinery and funds. He had the fervent support of *The Freeman's Journal*. Intangible factors on his side, which *The Irish Catholic* pointed out with calculated rue on 27 December, included "his own high position . . . the charm of his prestige and name [and] the magnetic spell of his personality."[45] On the day of his return to Ireland he seized the initiative, taking control of the nationalist weekly, *United Irishman*, and making a powerful speech at the Rotunda. The next morning, after his foes had reoccupied the paper's offices, he led a party that forcefully evicted them. (Joyce reminds us of Parnell's aggressiveness by having Bloom remember returning the Chief's hat after it had been knocked off during this "historic fracas" [*U* 16.1497].) In disarray the anti-Parnellite MPs leaned on their strongest, best-organized ally, the Church, which suddenly was called by its former superior ally, the party, to the fore of political warfare.

The "roaring political animal [that] had been awoken in many priests and bishops"[46] half a century earlier, as a result of clerical involvement with O'Connell's emancipation movement, now reawakened with a vengeance. Led by Archbishop Walsh, the Church took on the major role in raising money, starting up a new daily newspaper, and building a political machine, doing this so effectively that by March 1891 the anti-Parnellites had the upper hand.[47] The Church also acted decisively in the series of by-elections that formed the cockpit of struggle in 1891. In the general election of 1892, in which Parnell's adherents fought on without him, it was no less conspicuous:

Parish priests or their curates collected money locally for the national election fund ... They comprised a significant proportion of the attendance at the county conventions held to adopt candidates ... [P]riests signed the nomination papers submitted to returning officers, most commonly as proposers ... Another role ... was that of local aide to the candidate ... Priests were also orators; hardly ever at a public meeting was one not to be found presiding, or at least speaking in support of the candidate. The preferred place and time for meetings was a spot adjacent to the catholic chapel at the close of mass or other office.[48]

All this clerical electioneering had a long tradition behind it, extending from O'Connell's day to the immediate past. The priests and bishops had exhorted their flocks on behalf of emancipation, repeal, and the Land League, and had preached against Young Ireland and the Fenians. They had carried out a wide variety of practical tasks, including fund-raising, nominating, poll-watching, and almost everything save running for office. By 1850 the priest in politics – "that terrible bogeyman of the nineteenth century," as O Faoláin calls him – was well established.[49] He was valued and used by conservative constitutional nationalists; feared and criticized by others. Though Mr. Dedalus and Mr. Casey raise the Parnellite / Fenian cry of no priests in politics, Parnell and his loyalists not only didn't object, prior to the Split, to the Church's political activism but depended on it. Although the Fenians could honestly decry clerical meddling, the Parnellites were hypocritical in doing so, since their real objection was not so much that the clergy were intervening as that they were intervening on the wrong side.

Beginning with North Kilkenny on 22 December 1890, the opposing forces backed their own candidates in several by-elections. Kilkenny – where the priests "preached a regular crusade"[50] and where the Parnellites lost heavily – set the tone for what was to follow:

The campaign ... was vicious on both sides ... *The Irish Catholic*, however, easily took the laurels for unbridled abuse in simplifying matters for its readers: "The fight which we have now to fight is a good, a holy, and a glorious one. It is a conflict into which ... men might go as Christian soldiers did of yore, crucifix on breast ... for it is a struggle in which are ranked powers of light and darkness, of Heaven and Hell, of Virtue and adultery!"[51]

A curate called Parnell "a man reeking with the filth and corruption of a London divorce court," and more than one priest preached against him from the altar. This intemperateness and lack of charity, Larkin comments, "was manifested to the very end of the bitter struggle by a noisy section of those opposed to Parnell."[52]

It is this virulent minority to which Joyce refers in "The Shade of Parnell" and in the Christmas dinner scene, where Mr. Casey recalls marching through an anti-Parnellite mob and being harassed by an old woman who "kept dancing along beside me in the mud bawling and screaming into my face: *Priesthunter! The Paris Funds! Mr Fox! Kitty O'Shea!*" (*P* 36). Such insults, which aligned Parnell with the priest-hunting Anglo-Irish of Penal Law days and portrayed him as a cowardly immoralist who had used the funds of the Irish Party to finance his affair with a slut (the meaning of "Kitty"), naturally inflamed the Parnellites. But Parnell's men cast their own slurs, for instance, Harrington's question "whether the opposition to Mr. Parnell's leadership sprang not from a love of morality but from an innate love of Whiggery in the hearts of men who were proclaiming themselves Nationalist today." Stung, Archbishop Croke replied to this charge with an indignant open letter. Not all the anti-Parnellites engaged in mudslinging. Two factions swiftly emerged within their ranks, with Healy leading the "war party" which, backed by the bishops, advocated no compromise. For a time the peace faction had its way and arranged negotiations, conducted by William O'Brien during the first six weeks of 1891, for Parnell's retirement as leader. But the talks broke down, apparently because Parnell was playing for time and trying to divide his opponents rather than negotiating in good faith. O'Brien attributed the breakdown to the lack of a "real truce" and the "appalling spirit of reckless determination ... on both sides to make it a War."[53] He and John Dillon belatedly joined the anti-Parnellites with the idea that driving Parnell out of the political arena as quickly as possible was the best way to keep the Nationalists from becoming "a Healy–

Bishops party." Thus the spirit of Kilkenny prevailed: war to the death, and beyond, resumed.

O'Brien's and Dillon's attempt to develop a "policy of moderation and decency [that] would not be ground down between a clerical right and an anticlerical left"[54] is another episode in the complex history of the Split that Joyce chose to overlook. So, too, was the breaking of clerical ranks in the diocese of Killala in North Sligo, where a by-election took place at the beginning of April. The bishop and many of his priests remained neutral during the campaigning, and he refused to rein in pro-Parnell clerics. In another diocese, dissension provoked Archbishop Logue (Mr. Dedalus' "tub of guts up in Armagh" [*P* 33]) to complain about "individuals among the clergy who are lukewarm or faithless,"[55] including such notables as the Guardian of the Franciscans and the Prior of the Augustinians. But the warlike spirit on both sides, which O'Brien lamented and which Joyce captures so tellingly, dominated.

Parnell's biographer describes the beginning of the end:

The fight went on, and not a ray of hope shone upon Parnell's path. In Ireland the Fenians rallied everywhere to his standard, but the whole power of the Church was used to crush him. In June he married Mrs. O'Shea, and a few weeks later "young" Mr. Gray, of the "Freeman's Journal," seized upon the marriage as a pretext for going over to the enemy, because it was against the law of the Catholic Church to marry a divorced woman. But Parnell, amid all reverses, never lost heart . . . He . . . continued to traverse the country, cheering his followers, and showing a bold front to his foes.[56]

Joyce may have embroidered this moderately partisan sketch in his own account ("The Shade of Parnell") of the broken-hearted Chief moving from venue to venue like a hunted deer. His view was not any more one-sided than that of many other Parnellites, however, whose emotions are reflected in the response in *United Irishman* to Parnell's sudden death on 6 October 1891. In counterpoint to *The Irish Catholic*, which suggested that God's hand could be seen in the unrepentant sinner's demise, the Parnellite paper keened: "They have killed him . . . under God we do solemnly believe they have killed him. Murdered he has been, as certainly as if the gang of conspirators had surrounded him and hacked him to pieces."[57]

Emotions ran just as high during the July 1892 campaign, with the clergy taking up cudgels (once literally) even more energetically than the year before and with Parnellite priests verging on extinction. The Parnellites tumbled into defeat, retaining only nine seats in Parliament. *United Irishman* blamed the debacle on "gross clerical intimidation, servile obedience to the priests on the part of the illiterate voters, [and] clergymen canvassing . . . in their parishes."[58] All these charges of clerical influence and activity were true except their premise that the Parnellites otherwise would not have been roundly defeated. They were in fact already a gravely weakened party that was contesting only half the seats for which the anti-Parnellites had nominated candidates, and "many catholics . . . voted against Parnellism without taking any advice from their priests."[59]

After this, both sides in the Split (later a third faction emerged out of a dispute among the anti-Parnellites) became frozen into the polarized positions dramatized in *A Portrait*. As an article of faith, loyalists such as Joyce's father believed that Parnell had been murdered by his enemies. The Christmas dinner scene captures the mingled grief and rage of Mr. Dedalus and Mr. Casey. The latter says:

It was one day down in Arklow, a cold bitter day, not long before the chief died. May God have mercy on him!

He closed his eyes wearily and paused. Mr Dedalus took a bone from his plate and tore some meat from it with his teeth, saying:

—Before he was killed, you mean. (*P* 36)

In "Ivy Day" an execrable poem by a die-hard Parnellite shows how, shortly after the reunification of the Nationalists and over a decade after Parnell's death, the myth of his martyrdom could still evoke real emotion. Even in the humming, twentieth-century world of *Ulysses* an invitation to "go round by the chief's grave" (*U* 6.919) conjures awe. Healy observed in 1891, after being assaulted by some young boys: "It appears as if we had the voters and Parnell had their sons."[60] He might have added that Parnell had the writers as well, as would be reflected soon enough in the literary Parnellism of Joyce, Yeats, and others. Parnell's hold on the Irish imagination translated into political power when, in 1900, the Split was closed by the Nationalist factions' acceptance of the leadership of the Parnellite Redmond. Without the man himself, though, the party lacked electricity, and was swept away in 1918 when "the emotional power of Parnellism rose again, without Parnell's policy, in Sinn Féin."[61]

There was right and wrong on both sides of the internecine struggle. In the crisis which his actions had precipitated, Parnell put himself before Ireland; like a romantic hero, he preferred to fight to the death rather than retire and let others carry on his policies.[62] Irish nationalists had good reason for asking him to step down. Having a stronger priority than nationalism, the Church would have opposed Parnell even had the English Nonconformists not raised their own moral hue and cry first. The bishops wisely refrained from intervention until the Split was an accomplished fact, but later a large minority of clergymen acted without generosity or common sense, contributing to bitter feelings that would last for a generation. The hysteria to which they succumbed had its roots in the French Revolution. Although Parnell was a conservative force in Irish domestic politics, many priests and bishops saw his moves to retain power, especially his alliance of convenience with the Fenians, in terms of a narrative in which he figured as the leader of a revolutionary Jacobin movement. Parnellites such as Harrington and the editors of *United Irishman* made this fantasy more plausible through angry attacks on the Church. Between these obdurate forces people of moderation found little room to maneuver.

Larkin concludes that Parnell's great achievement was the modern Irish state, which, depending on "an effective governing consensus of Leader, Party, and Bishops,"[63] survived him. Cruise O'Brien also identifies this as one of the lasting accomplishments of Parnell and his party, though he slights the Church's contribution. There are other shades of informed opinion, but most commentators would agree with Oliver MacDonagh that "the Church … proved itself indispensable politically"[64] through the first two decades of the twentieth century.

These and other accounts also confirm that both the Church and Redmond's reunited Nationalist party, working hand in glove, exerted a conservative social influence (apart from agrarian reform) much like that of the Clerical–Nationalist alliance of the 1880s. We find evidence for this in the career of Harrington, Parnell's bishop-baiting lieutenant during the Split (and John Joyce's friend). As Lord Mayor of Dublin in 1902 he led the Nationalist machine, with help from the clergy, in its electoral struggle against Labour and Socialist candidates. James Connolly identified him as an enemy of the working classes as early as 1898. Referring to the planned celebration that summer of the rising of 1798, Connolly praised Wolfe Tone and his fellow rebels but excoriated those who had united the centenary movement with what he called the bogus organisation associated with the name of Mr Tim Harrington, a reference to the association of the Parnellite MP with the foundation of the United Irish League. That organisation, Connolly declared, had distorted the meaning of "United Irishmen" into a "union of class and creed." How feasible was it to unite in one movement underpaid labourers and overpaid masters?[65]

When Connolly and other I.S.R.P. members ran for office in Dublin between 1899 and 1903, their "opponents were in the main nominees of the rank-and-file Home Rule organizations (after 1900 the United Irish League) supported by clergy and M.P.s."[66] A middleclass Parnellite Labour man, such as Hynes in "Ivy Day," was a rarity.

It is true that, during the Split, Parnell and his loyalist MPs picked up not only Fenian, but lower-class support. "The lower stratum of society," Archbishop Croke commented disgustedly, "is almost entirely for him. Corner boys, blackguards of every hue, discontented labourers, lazy and drunken artisans [and] Fenians . . . are at his back."[67] An English official, impressed by the nearly 100,000 sad-faced, sober, orderly people "out in defiance of the Priests" for Parnell's funeral, observed:

The most striking feature of the demonstration . . . was the fact that it was so entirely composed and controlled by the lower classes. Special trains ran from all parts of the Country and yet there were few if any farmers present. Townspeople and laborers – and Fenians – composed the multitude.[68]

In contrast, among the anti-Parnellite MPs virtually all the businessmen opposed Parnell.[69] The wealthiest of the lot, William Martin Murphy – who in 1913 would lead the employers' successful effort to crush the striking workers during the Dublin Lockout – advanced his own money to support his side's first organizing efforts. Yet the autocratic Parnell "was not only not a demagogue," as the Liberal Prime Minister Asquith wrote, "he was not . . . a democrat."[70] Still less was he a socialist or a physical-force revolutionary. Although at the end Parnell's political maneuvers and his charisma drew to him the Fenians and the urban working classes, the contest between Parnellite and anti-Parnellite was a middle-class struggle. The down-and-out poor in Dublin and other Irish cities never truly had a stake in the struggle. When the spirit of Parnellism resurfaced in Sinn Fein, another petty-bourgeois movement, they were still disenfranchised. Archbishop Walsh lived long enough to change his allegiance from the Irish Party to Sinn Fein, but, though courageous and decisive as a nationalist, he did not intervene courageously and decisively in the Lockout or other issues affecting the multitudes of ill-housed, ill-fed, and underpaid or unemployed citizens of his own city.

The drama of Parnellism, then, both in life and as reflected in Joyce's works, was that of a middle-class struggle over the principles of Irish nationalism. Catholic morality, once Parnell had made his fatal decision to hold onto the leadership, came into conflict with the need for a united, independent Irish Party. Given the virtual inter-changeability of Catholicism and Irish nationalism (with the ill-fated exception of Young Ireland and a few individual exceptions, such as Parnell and Douglas Hyde) from O'Connell's day on, the anti-Parnellites' final if incomplete victory could hardly have been in doubt. Joyce's depiction of the anti-Parnellite side is patently distorted. His dismissal of the Home Rule movement in his Trieste articles appears questionable, too, at least with regard to 1886–90. With men like Walsh, Croke, and Davitt behind him, Parnell might well have succeeded in making the Home Rule sun rise over Ireland – another of those intriguing might-have-beens of Irish history. What seems less speculative is the likelihood that a semiautonomous Ireland, with or without Parnell, would have been ruled by and for the middle classes through a Clerical–Nationalist alliance. Connolly made a similar point in 1897: "If you remove the English army tomorrow and hoist the green flag over Dublin Castle, unless you set about the organization of the Socialist Republic your efforts would be in vain."[71]

Joyce, an avowed socialist for many years, must have heard or read similar statements by Connolly and other left-wing thinkers. No doubt his socialist leanings tinge his scornful sketch of the post-1900 Irish MPs as "well-paid syndics, directors of factories and commercial houses, newspaper owners, and large landholders" (*CW* 196). In "Ivy Day" he adumbrates the conflict between the interests of labor and those of middle-class nationalism. But in general his felt beliefs reflected his upbringing in a middle-class Parnellite household, which led him to write about Parnell as if he were Ireland's last best hope and about the Split as if it were Ireland's deepest social divide. This phenomenon, in a writer who prided himself on his independence, is a tribute to the intertwined power of Irish nationalist ideology and of Parnell's personality, which served even after his death as a matrix in which the class conflicts built into that ideology were mystified.

STEPHEN'S WOMEN

The historical drama of Parnell's downfall features an all-male cast of major characters except for the offstage siren, Katherine O'Shea. In his fictive Christmas debate, however, Joyce assigns the role of spokesperson for the anti-Parnellites to a woman, Dante. The puritanical "spoiled nun" (*P* 35) and the adulterous Englishwoman are foils. A third woman, Mrs. Dedalus, ineffectually trying to make peace, also plays a part in the scene. We have here, then, what many critics have identified as the three feminine archetypes in Joyce's writings: the temptress, the virgin, and the mother.

Although in *Stephen Hero* and *A Portrait* these types stand out clearly, they are complex and often overlap. Another way of looking at Stephen's women would be to classify them in terms of their relationship to the established order of Catholic Ireland from which Stephen seeks to free himself. Those who belong to the biggest set – Dante, Mrs. Dedalus, Emma Clery – are products and upholders of Irish Catholic ideology; they oppose sexual and imaginative freedom. Outcasts, the woman in the black straw hat in *Stephen Hero* and the prostitute in *A Portrait* seemingly offer sexual freedom, albeit at a price. Mercedes and the bird-girl stand outside everyday social reality and spring largely from Stephen's imagination. Linked with imaginative liberation, they are idealized alternative realities. What all these female characters have in common is that Stephen sees them in terms of his needs or desires. They rarely appear as full-fledged, complex individuals who act in response to their own deep-felt apprehensions of the world. Further, there is little suggestion of other kinds of women who existed in Joyce's Dublin, either lower-class ones a good deal more oppressed than Stephen himself or women of his own class who were persons of principle and talent engaged in their own struggles against authority.

Stephen's mother and Emma, the key love objects in his life, go from being full-blooded characters in *Stephen Hero* to a shadowy half-life in *A Portrait*, yet remain firmly aligned with Church and state in both novels. The earlier Mrs. Dedalus "fulfill[s] her duties to [her husband] with startling literalness" (*SH* 110) and continues to defer to him even though he arrogantly shirks his own duty as a provider. She is what Stephen thinks his dying sister, Isabel, might have become: "a Catholic wife of limited intelligence and of pious docility" (*SH* 127). In *A Portrait* Mrs. Dedalus introduces her young son, with Dante's help, to the pressures of the social order by insisting that he apologize for saying he will marry his Protestant playmate. When he decides as a young man to leave the Church, she poses his only serious resistance, and remains convinced he will "come back to faith" (*P* 248).

Stephen needs to break away from his mother because she functions as an advocate of the social order,[72] the very order that victimizes her and that (in a different way) would victimize him. Yet his bond with the "Nice mother!" (*P* 9) whom he misses at Clongowes Wood, and who still washes his face after he has become a university student, is the most difficult of all his ties to sever. This difficulty has a basis in Irish culture apart from the normal affection inspired by any good-enough caretaker. Ideally, the Irish Catholic mother serves as

the spiritual and emotional foundation for the family, the source of love and affection and of moral values . . . She is also expected to protect and forgive her children, and display the virtues of humility, gentleness and mercy. It is an ideal which is clearly modelled on the image of Mary as mother of Jesus.[73]

This image, as Beauvoir points out, entails the mother's acceptance of her inferiority to her son; and it is the origin of the stereotypical overdevoted Irish mother who rears her son to believe he is more important than she or other women are, yet manipulates her bond with him to secure his emotional dependence on her.[74] Granting that May Dedalus seems to fit this mold, and that she seeks to reproduce Irish Catholic ideology in her son, Joyce's presentation of her is remarkably narrow. Only a few passages in *Stephen Hero* – notably, when she touchingly reveals that she was moved by *The Wild Duck* (*SH* 83–87) – and one in *A Portrait* remind us that she has an inner being. In the latter passage Cranly asks:

—Has your mother had a happy life?
—How do I know? Stephen said.
—How many children had she?
—Nine or ten, Stephen answered. Some died.   (*P* 240–41)

Joyce was aware of the burden on his own mother of serial pregnancies and child-rearing. He described her to Nora as the "victim" of a system, a system that half a century later was still causing "the tragedies of mothers no longer fit for childbearing who died giving birth, of family life destroyed because of the burden of too many children, of women driven to mental breakdown by the multiple pressures of their lives."[75] Yet little of this awareness creeps into his fiction.

There were also, no doubt, aspects of his mother's life to which Joyce remained oblivious. One of Stephen's diary entries recounts a discussion with his mother: "Subject: B.V.M. Handicapped by my sex and youth" (*P* 248). In this context their talk, which ends with her prediction that Stephen will return to the Church, represents another attempt to catch him in the net of religion. But an Irish Catholic housewife's relationship to the Blessed Virgin did not necessarily reflect a simple-minded adherence to authority. A contemporary Irishwoman complains of her schooldays: "The religious theme was that every woman was trying to imitate the Virgin Mary ... Women were supposed to sacrifice themselves." Yet Mary could also signify "a female presence in a male Church," and other women speak of relating to her as a "friend" and a fellow mother who "suffered [and] knew what it was to be human."[76] Such ideological complexities do not enter Joyce's sketches of any of Stephen's women.

The Emma Clery of *Stephen Hero*, though younger and livelier than Mrs. Dedalus, seems no less conventional, allowing for the difference between the two generations. Stephen meets her at one of the weekly at-homes of the Daniels family (modeled satirically after Joyce's friends, the Sheehys), who are Home Rule and cultural nationalists given to recitations that Stephen audits while eyeing "the picture of the Sacred Heart which hung right above ... the reciter's head" (*SH* 44). Emma, with her petty-bourgeois nationalism and piety, differs little from the Daniels girls except for her sexy figure. She becomes his virgin temptress, but he finds himself relegated to third place in her affections after religion and country. She signs her name in Irish, invites him to learn Irish and join the Gaelic League, and appears to include him in the "general scheme of her nationalising charm" (*SH* 48), although she also flirts decorously with a young priest, Father Moran. Stephen desires and dismisses her at once:

She treated femininely everything that young men are supposed to regard as serious but she made polite exception for Stephen himself and for the Gaelic Revival ... [H]e felt that even that warm ample body could hardly compensate him for her distressing pertness and middle-class affectations. (*SH* 67)

Emma appears to reciprocate Stephen's desire, but his proposition to share "a mad night of love" (*SH* 158) comes to naught. Stung, he tells himself that "it was a menial fear and no spirit of chastity which had prevented her from granting his request ... He cursed her burgher cowardice" (*SH* 210).

Both Stephen and his friend Cranly see middle-class Irish women as being, unlike themselves, hopelessly conventional. Joyce does not give us an inside view of Emma, yet we still can speculate as to reasons apart from "cowardice" why such a young woman might have rejected Stephen. First, she would have been brought up to deny her sexual feelings. Edna O'Brien (describing a younger self) has said: "I don't think I have any pleasure in any part of my body, because my first ... body thoughts were blackened by the fear of sin and therefore I think of my body as a vehicle for sin."[77] Once more we see the exemplary influence of Mary, who conceived without intercourse and remained a virgin after giving birth. This model denies the demands of the female body, which force themselves onto a woman's consciousness daily as well as during episodes such as menstruation, pregnancy, and menopause:

All these events are real and immediate and have strong effects on every woman's social and emotional life. Yet they are barely acknowledged in either the virginal image of the pure Catholic girl or in the ideal of the devoted mother.[78]

The contradiction between this model and her own upwelling desire could have led an unmarried woman such as Emma to invite a man's attentions unconsciously and spurn them, when offered, with genuine confusion and anger. But even if tempted to act on her desire, she almost surely would have known next to nothing about the mechanics of reproduction, let alone contraception. Women born five decades after Joyce left Ireland were still growing up "profoundly ignorant of sexual matters."[79] (Many young men did not know much either, as O Faoláin testifies in *Vive Moi.*)[80] Yet the penalty in Ireland for motherhood outside of wedlock would have been, and still is, draconian. Not until 1973 did the state introduce a welfare allowance for unmarried mothers. In 1984 a 15-year-old schoolgirl, Ann Lovett, went to the Grotto of Our Lady overlooking the small town where she lived and, alone and outdoors in the

January weather, gave birth. She and her infant died. Nobody in the town, save a single friend, admitted to knowing of her pregnancy. The episode illustrates "the atmosphere of shame, guilt, secrecy and punishment which surrounds women who are pregnant outside marriage," women whose treatment "is one of the scandals of Irish social history."[81] No wonder Emma turns Stephen down.

In *A Portrait* Emma becomes the shadowy E. C., losing her name and other details of her social identity, but takes on wider symbolic meaning. Davin has told Stephen of a young peasant woman who, in her husband's absence, all but begged him to spend the night with her. Stephen thinks of her "as a type of her race and his own" (*P* 183); later he thinks of Emma as a similar type and evokes her with the same metaphor: "a batlike soul waking to the consciousness of itself in darkness and secrecy and loneliness" (*P* 183, 221). In his imagination she becomes a composite figure, containing contradictions impossible in a single historical person but representing certain historical aspects of Irish Catholic women and of male attitudes toward them. She remains a middle-class Dubliner with "her fine dress and sash and long black stockings" (*P* 69). She also has links (like Stephen's childhood playmate, Eileen) with the Virgin Mary. He repeatedly remembers her wearing a shawl over her head like a "cowl" (*P* 69, 82, 222). After the retreat, stricken with shame over her role in his sexual fantasies, he imagines standing with her and being addressed by the Blessed Virgin: "Take hands, Stephen and Emma. It is a beautiful evening now in heaven. You have erred but you are always my children" (*P* 116). The reverie assumes that Emma, too, has sinned, for Stephen habitually melds together virgin and temptress. Though he wonders "[i]f her life were a simple rosary of hours," he pictures her "waking from odorous sleep, the temptress of his villanelle" (*P* 216, 223). Finally she becomes Everywoman, associated not just with whores and virgins and peasants, but with working-class girls such as "the flowergirl in the ragged dress . . . the kitchengirl in the next house . . . a girl who had laughed gaily to see him stumble . . . a girl . . . [who had] passed out of Jacob's biscuit factory" (*P* 220).

One historical reason why E. C. is such a composite, multivalent figure might be the "culture of male narcissism" that arises out of single-sex education. Male children learn to fear being feminine, to exaggerate gender differences, and to seek solace for separation from maternal care through self-aggrandizement: they become "vain, hypersensitive, invidious, ambitious ... and exhibitionistic."[82] They also develop a distorted view of girls. In their eyes girls represent the Other; they are

> stupid, 'silly eejuts', soft. Later on they become dangerous, desirable, tempting – anything but equal human beings. Three dominant images colour men's view of women: ... the virgin, the whore and the mother. They appear in stories, songs and religious imagery as well as in schoolboys' fantasies. They cause problems in a relationship when the man sees the woman as a combination of images instead of seeing her clearly as herself.[83]

In Joyce's day middle-class girls usually went to convent school, a pattern his mother followed, as preparation for marriage and motherhood. More ambitious young women, admitted through the Intermediate Act to university education and degrees only in 1878, attended separate colleges and had little to do socially with male students. They did, however, compete with them – quite success-fully, since by 1901 women were taking almost 30 percent of the honors, as Francis Skeffington noted in his essay (co-published with Joyce's "The Day of the Rabblement") on behalf of equal education for women.[84] At exam time, we learn in *Stephen Hero*,

> girl students were not the subject of the usual sniggers and jokes but were regarded with some aversion as sly enemies. Some of the young men eased their enmity and vindicated their superiority ... by saying that it was no wonder the women would do well seeing that they could study ten hours ... a day all the year round. (*SH* 130–31)

Joyce pokes fun at the insecure male students, yet he may have felt some ambivalence, since women were his own chief competitors in modern languages and since Hanna Sheehy and others took honors degrees whereas he scraped through with a pass. Later in life he confessed to Mary Colum that he hated intellectual women (*JJ* 529). At any rate, he depicted Stephen's women in terms of cultural stereotypes that seem traceable, in part, to single-sex schooling.

✳

In each of Joyce's early novels a woman beyond the pale of middle-class Dublin offers Stephen what he cannot get from Emma and so comes to stand for a kind of sexual-social liberation. After flirting with Emma in *Stephen Hero*, he walks away frustrated and encounters a homely whore wearing a rakish black hat; he hands her money and walks on. Later he informs Lynch of his decision not to see Emma anymore because she will not grant him "Love" (*SH* 190), that is, sexual love, even though she, too, wants it. Lynch reminds him that he "could get her ... [i]n marriage," but Stephen rejects this alternative because it does not accord with his revolutionary aims. He quotes Yeats's story, "The Adoration of the Magi": "When the immortals wish to overthrow the things that are today ... they have no-one to help them except one whom the things that are today have cast out" (*SH* 192). Who, he asks rhetorically, can help him but the woman in the black straw hat? His inept attempt to seduce Emma ensues. He criticizes her afterwards, saying that he likes "a woman to give herself," and adds:

A woman's body is a corporal asset of the State: ... she must sell it either as a harlot or as a married woman or as a working celibate or as a mistress. But a woman is ... a human being [whose] love and freedom is not a spiritual asset of the State ... The woman in the black straw hat gave something before she sold her body to the State. Emma will sell herself to the State but give nothing. (*SH* 202–03)

In transforming the woman in the black straw hat into an emblem of his revolt against his culture's sexual mores,[85] Stephen ignores the fact that prostitutes, no less than their middle-class sisters, were products of Dublin's established order. He also turns into a symbol a living person whose obvious degradation and suffering do not appear to cross his mind. She and Emma have more in common than he thinks: they are victims (in differing degrees due to their class differences) not only of patriarchy but of his limited imagination.

In *A Portrait* Joyce cuts out Stephen's intellectualizing on sex, focusing instead on his protagonist's emotional struggle to come to grips with his sexuality. Stephen is driven by his restlessness to the red-light district. There, in a sensual, dreamy, ritualistic scene – women, "leisurely and perfumed," walk from house to house in their "long vivid gowns," and "yellow gasflames" burn "against the vapoury sky ... as if before an altar" (*P* 100) – he is initiated by an alluring young woman who gives him joy and relief unavailable from respectable Dublin. Later Nighttown loses its romantic aspect. It becomes "the squalid quarter of the brothels" where, on his regular visits, his senses note keenly all that wounded or shamed them" (*P* 102). During the retreat his revulsion rises to a crescendo. In fear and shame he remembers "his sins, the jeweleyed harlots of his imagination," and "the sordid details of his orgies" (*P* 115).

Later he confesses to a priest his sins of impurity with himself and "with others" (*P* 144). These "others" are the women of Nighttown who, desired or rejected, glamorous or squalid, have no individuality for Stephen and are indistinct from his fantasies. Their lives do not impinge on him: they exist for his physical and emotional use, just as the woman in the black straw hat exists for his earlier incarnation's intellectual use.

Though few fictional or historical narratives remind us of this fact, the women of turn-of-the-century Dublin's red-light district all had personal histories as well as a broader social history. Few details of their individual lives have survived, but the historical determinants of their collective existence are clear. Contemporary attitudes varied. Joyce took their existence for granted; they were a necessary evil in a country where men and women could not give their bodies freely to each other. The Church and Dublin's many magdalen societies saw prostitution largely as a moral problem. Nationalists attributed the abundance of prostitutes in Dublin, not without some justification, to the presence of the British garrison there. A women's nationalist group, Inghinidhe na hEireann (Daughters of Erin), inaugurated in October 1900 under the presidency of Maud Gonne, took action by producing leaflets that warned girls against "consorting with the enemies of their country."[86] They handed the leaflets to girls seen walking with soldiers on O'Connell Street. As a result O'Connell Street echoed nightly to shouts and blows as angry soldiers threatened the nationalist women and fought their brothers or boyfriends or passers-by. But although the Inghinidhe were

imaginative propagandists, [they] revealed little awareness of the reasons why women were forced to resort to prostitution. However, a decade later, Maud ... appealed through the pages of *The Irish Worker* for men and women to come together "without any false modesty" in order to see what could be done to prevent the system where "women were forced to sell their body, mind and soul." She admitted that the Inghinidhe ... had simply "appealed to girls as sisters to keep out of temptation's way" ... [with] no alternative to offer – they couldn't get nonexistent, or atrociously paid factory jobs for the women.[87]

The problem of prostitution did indeed have socioeconomic roots. There was "massive unemployment and lack of opportunity facing females at all ages."[88] The pert girl coming out of Jacob's biscuit factory who catches Stephen's eye represents a lucky minority even though Jacob's, a very large, prosperous business by Irish standards, would have required her to work over fifty hours a week for wages on which she probably could not have lived by herself. The most unfortunate women were the lower-class unemployed, such as the flower-girl, really a beggar, who accosts Stephen, seeing him as a middle-class "gentleman" (*P* 183). Yet no adult worker

could have been more abused than the poor shop girls with their paltry 7s. to 10s. per week. Their condition was often offered as evidence for the prevalence of prostitution in large cities. James Larkin's *Irish Worker* was especially active in exposing the "slavery" imposed on these young girls in shops and laundries.[89]

Hardly paid better were several other classes of female employee, such as clerks and bookkeepers. Furthermore, paltry pay (always less than for comparable work by men) usually went hand in hand with long, enervating working hours. Various Factories and Workshops Acts supposedly regulated female and juvenile labor but put minimal checks on employers. The 1901 Act, allowing women and adolescents older than thirteen to do nontextiles work up to sixty hours per week, harbored loopholes permitting even longer hours. Nevertheless, employers routinely violated the Acts, which imposed only token penalties on the small proportion of offenders who were caught – for instance, 10s. on a newsagent for employing girls for seventy-four hours. Even some charitable and religious institutions (such as convent laundries) took part in this pervasive exploitation.[90] These conditions, combined with a repressive middle-class sexual ideology and the presence in Dublin of a large garrison as well as many civilian bachelors, guaranteed a continuing flow of recruits for the bordellos of Nighttown.

❋

Stephen's encounter with the prostitute reveals a complex dualism that extends to other women, mothers and virgins as well as whores. Before she accosts him, he "want[s] . . . to force another being to sin with him and to exult with her in sin" (*P* 99–100). His wish to impose his will on a female typifies males in a repressed society who resent the female's, especially the whore's, supposed sexual power over them.[91] This power produces ambivalence in men – desire coupled with a fear of submission which alternates with a will to assert mastery. In Stephen such mixed feelings are even more complicated because he associates women in general, as images of Ireland, with subjection. His ambivalence is crystallized in the question "to kiss or not to kiss."[92] As a new boy at the all-male

Clongowes Wood School, he wonders, after being teased, whether a regular fellow kisses his mother. He wants to kiss E. C., as she flirts with him on the tram, but holds back. And he hesitates to kiss the prostitute, who must take the initiative herself: "With a sudden movement she bowed his head and joined his lips to hers." The imagery of submission in this scene – Stephen, wishing "to be held firmly in her arms," "surrender[s] himself" in a "swoon of sin" (*P* 101) – suggests both projective identification with women and fear of their power, which his later identification with a powerful male, Daedalus, seems designed to counteract.

Stephen's revulsion from the women of Nighttown eventually propels him back to the Church and into the embrace of the Blessed Virgin. He becomes prefect of her sodality at college: "The glories of Mary held his soul captive" (*P* 105). Later, after a hellfire sermon scares him senseless, he confesses his sexual sins to a priest who advises him to pray "to our mother Mary" and "repent" (*P* 145). Obeying, he assumes once more the traditional woman's part in a sexualized act of submission: "The attitude of rapture in sacred art, the raised and parted hands, the parted lips and eyes as of one about to swoon, became for him an image of the soul in prayer, humiliated and faint before her Creator" (*P* 150). Later he considers an invitation to become a candidate for the priesthood. Pride moves him, and the prospect that he "would know . . . the sins . . . of others, hearing them murmured into his ears in the confessional under the shame of a darkened chapel by the lips of women and of girls" (*P* 159). He seems unable to avoid oscillating between the sexualized poles of submission and mastery.

The only women who do not threaten Stephen's independence, and whom he does not feel the need to flee from or subjugate, are those who exist largely or wholly in his imagination. The first such woman is Mercedes, heroine of *The Count of Monte Cristo*, in connection with whom he imagines himself playing the part of the self-renouncing hero, Edmond Dantes, "standing in a moonlit garden with Mercedes who had so many years before slighted his love, and with a sadly proud gesture of refusal, saying: – Madam, I never eat muscatel grapes" (*P* 63). There is no kiss here, and Stephen–Dantes seems master both of the situation and himself. Later, though, he broods upon Mercedes' image under the influence of "a strange unrest" (*P* 64). The stirrings of adolescence make him feel apart from other children: "He did not want to play. He wanted to meet in the real world the unsubstantial image which his soul so constantly beheld" (*P* 65). He does not recognize the sexual nature of his unrest, but dreams of encountering his feminine ideal in sexual terms – "They would be alone, surrounded by darkness and silence: and in that moment of supreme tenderness he would be transfigured" (*P* 65) – which foreshadow his encounter with the prostitute. Hence, though Mercedes acts as a model for that "idealized alternative reality"[93] which haunts Stephen from the green rose of his early schooldays onward, her image reflects the historical and biological determinants of his young life.

The bird girl whom Stephen watches at the strand also functions as a model for the imagined reality he seeks beyond "the dull phenomenon of Dublin" (*P* 78). Her beauty seems supernatural, like that of "one whom magic had changed into the likeness of a strange and beautiful seabird." As with Mercedes, he does not desire her physically. He values her as a symbol; a "wild angel ... of mortal youth and beauty" (*P* 172), she confirms his newly discovered vocation as artist. What might give us pause are her colors, blue and white and ivory, earlier linked with the Blessed Virgin. However, the bird girl has antecedents in Celtic myth. In Irish hero-saga the magic bird image is common. Further, the evocation of a crane-like woman, who confirms him in a vocation associated with flying and a hawklike man, places Stephen in both the tradition of "Irish tales of lovers who unite as birds" and that of mythic "heroes who marry their vocations in their union with magical women."[94] The bird girl also seems derived from the Gaelic *aisling* or vision poem, whose central situation revolves around a beautiful young woman from faery and a declaration of sensual joy. Thus Stephen

has progressed beyond the Catholic iconography of [the Blessed Virgin] to a sensual, pagan incarnation of the Celtic Otherworld ... The bird-girl / fairy-woman ... offers a vision of body and soul; she and Stephen suffer each other's gaze "without shame or wantonness" (*P* 171), the notion of Christian sin having no place in the fortunate isles.[95]

After this point in *A Portrait* the Blessed Virgin no longer plays a part in Stephen's life, although his mother and E. C. continue to do so. The question arises: how did Joyce intend his readers to react to Stephen's encounter with the bird girl? No doubt he meant to qualify the liberating aspect of the encounter by making an association between the girl and the Virgin Mary. The purple prose describing the scene is no doubt deliberate, too, reflecting Stephen's highly charged emotions and echoing previous passages. In an ironic novel structured by its protagonist's alternating falls and triumphs, a rapturous adolescent, even if he will someday be an artist capable of writing the novel himself, must be taken somewhat ironically. The touch-me-not sensuality of this episode must also be ironic, given Joyce's belief in the importance of sexuality. But what of the girl? Where would she have fitted in the Dublin of the 1890s? Actually, she would not have fitted: we must realize "how unlikely such a display of womanly flesh would have been in the petit-bourgeois precincts of a Dublin beach at the turn of the century."[96] Such exposure would have been acceptable, however, in the West of Ireland. In *The Aran Islands* (1907), a book Joyce knew, Synge described a typical island girl wading in the sea in terms that foreshadow Joyce's bird girl.[97] Hence another irony. Although Stephen has just adopted Daedalus, a European patron, while experiencing a "timeless" sensation that makes "all ages [seem] as one to him" (*P* 168), he quickly finds in the bird girl an Irish muse who stems from a specific Irish historical context.

This context was one of deprivation. The Aran Islanders led hard lives – a fact which Synge, in spite of the romantic glow in which he wraps them, makes clear. He compares his wading girls to exotic creatures – "Their red bodices and white tapering legs make them as beautiful as tropical sea-birds" – but states that they are washing clothes in the sea because it hasn't rained in nine days and the few springs do not reliably supply fresh water in hot weather. "This habit of using the sea water for washing causes a good deal of rheumatism on the island, for the salt lies in the clothes and keeps them continually moist." In the next few paragraphs he sketches the "continuous hard work" of preparing kelp to sell for its iodine content, a discouraging labor because formerly "good kelp would bring seven pounds a ton, now four pounds are not always reached."[98] Though Synge's washer girls are not individualized, they exist in a concrete social and economic world, whereas the bird girl has no socioeconomic existence at all. She doesn't even belong in Dublin. Her sole *raison d'être* derives from Joyce's artistic need to provide dramatic confirmation of Stephen's newly revealed vocation. She is not a likely historical reality but a projection of Stephen's imagination – an idealization bearing a family resemblance to other idealized female figures in his life.

The bird girl embodies a broad principle in Joyce's autobiographical novels: female characters represent the historical reality of turn-of-the-century Irish women only as filtered through the eyes of an intelligent, imaginative, middle-class Catholic boy. In the case of *A Portrait* this must be qualified further because Stephen's sexuality (reflecting Joyce's) is somewhat quirky and tinged with masochism. Nevertheless, Stephen's tendency to divide women into virgins, mothers, and temptresses seems fairly representative of Irish Catholic male attitudes in his day. Yet if the evocation of Stephen's inner life in *A Portrait* is an artistic triumph, one measure of its cost might be its exclusion of other viewpoints, especially feminine ones.

More than one critic, notably Bonnie Kime Scott, has lamented the loss involved in the reduction of Emma Clery, who shows signs of a life of her own in *Stephen Hero*, to the shadowy E. C. of *A Portrait*. Scott points out that Emma, one of a small band of Catholic women undergraduates in turn-of-the-century Ireland, "is participating in a genteel and quiet women's revolution."[99] Her intellectual and political interests, still more her acting upon them, make her unusual not only in the context of Joyce's writing but in Irish life at the time. Scott describes the obstacles in Emma's way, such as the inferiority in resources of the Catholic women's colleges to the Catholic men's colleges (which in turn were inferior to the Protestant men's preserve of Trinity College) and the women students' lack of access to cultural events due to curfews or outright prohibition. Emma would have been barred, for example, from listening to the paper Stephen is going to read at University College; the college's president, Father William Delaney, "strenuously opposed admitting women to his school's lectures."[100] Scott evokes "A Young Woman Walking Proudly Through the Decayed City" (the subtitle of her essay). The portrait is more hers than Joyce's, but her point resounds: there were Irishwomen of courage and intellectual distinction who wanted no less than Joyce to change a stultifying, unjust social system.

Foremost among these women, at least among Joyce's circle of acquaintances, was Hanna Sheehy. Five years older than Joyce, she was born to Catholic nationalist parents who raised their daughters on an unusual basis of equality with the sons. She won scholarships and took B.A. and M.A. degrees with honors. While still in school, she began her life's work in the service of a vision of Ireland that included elements of feminism, pacifism, socialism, and nationalism. In 1901, serving on a subcommittee of the Royal Commission on

University Education, she called for "absolute equality" between the sexes and "a complete system of co-education."[101] The next year, to further those goals, she took part in setting up the Irish Association of Women Graduates and Candidate-Graduates. She married Joyce's classmate, Francis Skeffington, in 1903. Though she attributed to him her interest in feminism, it had already taken tenuous root in Ireland in 1874, when the Dublin Women's Suffrage Society was founded. This was followed by the Irish Women's Suffrage and Local Government Association, formed in 1876 by Anna and Thomas Haslam, and in 1900 by Inghinidhe na hEireann.

She had joined the Haslams' group before her marriage. After this her activism blossomed slowly, but in 1908 she helped found the Irish Women's Franchise League, which would have a key role in the votes-for-women struggle in Ireland and bring out into the open the antagonism of the Parliamentary Party toward this struggle. On behalf of the I.W.F.L. she became a well-known journalist, public speaker, and militant (among other provocations to patriarchy, she shouted "Votes for Irishwomen!" during a speech by Winston Churchill). She served short prison sentences for her militancy, at times going on hunger strike. Reflecting an informal alliance between labor and the suffragists, she cooperated with Connolly and Larkin, and addressed recruiting meetings for the new Irish Women Workers Union in 1911. Besides all this, she edited and wrote for her husband's paper, *The Irish Nation*, a leading voice for feminism during this period. Like Joyce, she left the Church; and she declined to have her son baptized.

After her husband was murdered by a British officer during the 1916 Rising, Sheehy-Skeffington continued her work through the Troubles and in the Free State. I could go on, but the point is that Joyce, while he was composing *A Portrait*, knew quite well what she was doing. He had known her as a student when he visited her parents' house, and as a young married woman when he attended her and Francis' at-homes. Even in Trieste, letters and newspapers from Dublin would have kept him abreast of her activities. In the fiction of a writer devoted to portraying the significant realities of his country, the lack of recognition, even a nod, given to Sheehy-Skeffington and women like her amounts to a significant absence.

It is hard to say how much the historical distortions and gaps in the view of women presented in *Stephen Hero* and *A Portrait* stemmed from Joyce's artistic needs and how much from his own (rather than his protagonists') defects of vision. Beyond a doubt the lover of Nora Barnacle and the creator of Molly Bloom had some notion of women's lives. He recognized the oppression to which women (middle-class ones like his mother and Nora, anyhow) were subjected. Reportedly he said in middle age that feminine emancipation "has caused the greatest revolution in our time in the most important relationship there is – that between men and women; the revolt of women against the idea that they are the mere instruments of men."[102] Perhaps the Sheehy-Skeffingtons influenced him after all. Yet *Stephen Hero* and *A Portrait* barely give us an inkling of the problems facing women; nor do they suggest the possibility that women existed who were bravely and resourcefully tackling these problems. Joyce's handling of female characters in these novels implies that he shared, consciously and unconsciously, many of his culture's assumptions about women. He rebelled against Irish society, but saw it from a man's point of view; and he depicted, in *A Portrait*, the growing into history of a *male* artist. To Hanna Sheehy-Skeffington, if she ever thought about him in connection with the struggle for women's liberation in Ireland, he might well have appeared to be on the wrong side of the barricades.

CHAPTER 5

Ulysses *and the Great War*

The Great War was perhaps the last to be conceived as taking place within a seamless, purposeful "history" involving a coherent stream of time running from past through present to future.

Paul Fussell, *The Great War and Modern Memory*

Seemingly light years away from London, hub of Empire, or Paris, the *ville lumière*, the Dublin of *Dubliners* is a paralyzed colonial city on the fringe of Europe. The artist who grows up there in *A Portrait* eventually realizes that he must leave in order to fulfill himself. But in *Ulysses* the artist has returned, aimless and depressed, to a city that in contrast seems pretty lively. A state-of-the-art electric tram system whisks travelers here and there; newspapers shoot off presses; people talk freely and vividly about sports, politics, the arts, each other. On the whole, the Dublin of *Ulysses* – not only its human citizens, but its animals, machinery, and things – pulsates with energy. But why? The time is mid-1904, a little over a year after the period of Stephen's diary and within two years of the time of "Ivy Day" and "The Dead." In the meantime no revolution has transformed Ireland. James Connolly, unable to support body or soul there, has sailed for America. Sinn Fein is little more than a gleam in Arthur Griffith's eye. The Lord Lieutenant, whose cavalcade clatters through the downtown streets, stands for the foreign power that has dominated Ireland for centuries and still holds the reins. The New Woman, despite Hanna Sheehy-Skeffington, has barely manifested herself. What has changed?

Among other things, Joyce's relationship to Dublin had changed. Writing *Ulysses* between 1914 and 1921, he looked back on his homeland from the perspective of the Continent, where he had resided since 1904 – most of his adult life. Inevitably he had a different view of Ireland, one colored by a sense of her belonging to the larger, faster-paced world of Europe. He also was older, an internationally recognized writer, and more inclined to satirize his earlier self. But Europe had changed too, and, while working on *Ulysses*, he lived through its greatest upheavals – World War I and revolutions and wars in Russia and Ireland.

The guns of 1914 quelled whatever remained of Joyce's interest in movements such as socialism and anarcho-syndicalism. When Italy entered the war in May 1915 he declared to a friend:

My political faith can be expressed in a word: Monarchies constitutional or unconstitutional, disgust me. Kings are mountebanks. Republics are slippers for everyone's feet ... What else is left? Can we hope for monarchy by divine right? Do you believe in the Sun of the Future? (*JJ* 383)

His last question, alluding to the Italian socialist anthem, was a bitter one that month "when youth, spurred on by D'Annunzio [once the object of Joyce's admiration] and Marinetti, descended into the piazzas of Italy demanding war."[1] In June Joyce removed his family to neutral Switzerland. Remaining there until after hostilities ceased, he steered clear of politics and said little about the war. He made his only direct literary comment on the war with the scathing broadside, "Dooleysprudence." In Paris in 1920 he cast a cold eye on the retrospective adulation of the war dead: "Valery Larbaud said to him as they drove in a taxi past the Arc de Triomphe with its eternal fire, 'How long do you think that will burn?' Joyce answered, 'Until the Unknown Soldier gets up in disgust and blows it out'" (*JJ* 486).

For a pacifist and an already disappointed "socialistic artist" (*L II* 89) who had thought of socialism as an antidote to war, the spectacle of the European masses (including socialists) rushing eagerly into the first general European war in a century must have been the crowning disillusionment. But, as Manganiello and other critics have shown, Joyce was not so indifferent to politics during the war and after as he professed to be. The upheavals precipitated in 1914 affected every thoughtful person in Europe:

From its start, the war was a stimulus to the imagination ... Artists, poets, writers, clergymen, historians, philosophers, among others, all participated fully in the human drama being enacted ... Even the introvert Marcel Proust ... was spellbound by the spectacle: "As people used to live in God, I live in the war."[2]

Switzerland was a refuge from the fighting but not from other forms
of involvement. The country resembled "a beleaguered town,"
Joyce's friend, Budgen, recalls. "There was a perpetual ebb and flow
of grey blue men of all military ages between the interior and the
frontiers ... [A]ll Swiss talked war strategy and politics." He and
Joyce "watched the fortunes of the war change for the combatants."
The interval between their meeting in 1918 and the completion of
the "Cyclops" episode in 1919 "was ... packed with great events.
The Allies gathered themselves together after the great Ludendorff
offensive, took the offensive themselves on all fronts, and forced the
Germans to sue for peace."[3]

   Joyce did not live unmoved through this time of the breaking of
nations. He did translating work in Zurich for the neutralist *International Review*, a journal devoted to combating the belligerents'
"campaign of lies [and] the unholy legends that are forming around
us."[4] In October 1918 he said he was engaged in the "eternal
struggle" of the artist against the state, adding: "Naturally I can't
approve of the act of the revolutionary who tosses a bomb in a
theatre ... On the other hand, have those states behaved any better
which have drowned the world in a blood-bath?" (*JJ* 446). The war
touched him personally as well as intellectually. His brother Stanislaus spent four years in an Austrian internment camp, Triestine
friends disappeared into the army or across the border into Italy, and
a brilliant fellow student from University College, Thomas Kettle,
died on the Western Front in September 1916. Kettle had married
Mary Sheehy, for whom the adolescent Joyce had "conceived a small
rich passion" (*JJ* 51). He concluded his letter of condolence to her:
"I am grieved to learn that so many misfortunes have fallen on your
family in these evil days" (*L I* 96). He was alluding to the fact that
the family had lost another son-in-law, Francis Sheehy-Skeffington,
less than six months earlier during the Easter Rising. Skeffington had
ventured into the streets in a quixotic effort to discourage looters;
arrested, he was shot without trial by a firing squad. His death and
Kettle's – one was killed by soldiers in British uniforms; the other was
killed while wearing a British uniform – may have reminded Joyce of
the intimate ties between the Rising and the Great War.[5] In any
case, he found it harder to pretend indifference to the "evil days" at
home than to those in Europe:

Joyce followed the [Rising] with pity; although he evaluated [it] as useless,
he felt also out of things. His attitude towards Ireland became even more

complex, so that he told friends, when the British had to give up their plans to conscript troops in Ireland, "*Erin go bragh!*" and predicted that some day he and Giorgio would go back to wear the shamrock in an independent Ireland; but when this temporary fervor waned, he replied to someone who asked if he did not look forward to the emergence of an independent country, "So that I might declare myself its first enemy?" Would he not die for Ireland? "I say," he said, "let Ireland die for me." (*JJ* 399)

Still, Joyce remained remarkably silent on the subject of Irish as well as European politics while he was composing *Ulysses*. He made no pronouncements; he wrote no articles. Yet *Ulysses* does inevitably reflect the era and circumstances of its making. It constitutes a response, in content and form, not only to World War I, the Easter Rising, and other upheavals, but to the preceding quarter of a century – a period of intensified imperial and national rivalries, of technological innovation, of social change, and of the emergence in art of modernism. One reason why the Ireland of *Ulysses* appears different from that of *Dubliners* and *A Portrait* is that, seen in the retrospective light of 1914–21, it *was* different. The realization of its once unknown future had changed it. Dublin, in *Ulysses*, is still the deposed capital of an economically stagnant colony as in the earlier fiction, yet now it belongs to a larger, European-dominated world which, reflecting "the velocity of modern life" (*U* 17.1773), is moving and changing with violent energy. Although no one in *Ulysses* knows that Ireland and Europe are speeding toward convulsions from which they will emerge bloodily transformed, Joyce himself could not escape knowing this, and he had to rethink his attitudes toward both Irish and world history.

RUMORS OF WAR

Presumably even Joyce, with his acute ears, could not hear in Zurich the cannonading of the Western Front whose faint sound haunted Henry James across the English Channel. James, as a friend observed, "ate and drank, he talked and walked and thought, he slept and waked and lived and breathed only the War."[6] Joyce adopted the opposite strategy, that of willed indifference. Yet in his Swiss haven he could not ignore the cataclysmic clashes on the flatlands below him any more than could Hans Castorp, hero of Mann's *Magic Mountain*. His awareness of the war finds expression in *Ulysses* through themes and motifs that seem to arise solely out of the action of 16 June 1904, yet suggest what is to come in 1914 and what is actually going on during the composition of the novel.

Joyce was afraid of thunderstorms, loud noises, physical violence. He must have been appalled by accounts of crashing artillery assaults that could make their victims vanish from the face of the earth. In *Ulysses*, though no one dies violently or even suffers injury, there are remembered, reported, or imagined events which remind us that Dublin 1904 belongs to a world marked by violence past and present. History itself appears to Stephen in the "Nestor" episode as a blood-soaked nightmare. He pictures the scene as Pyrrhus comments on his costly victory at Asculum: "From a hill above a corpsestrewn plain a general speaking to his officers, leaned upon his spear. Any general to any officers" (*U* 2.16–17). Joyce composed "Nestor" during late 1917, an especially demoralizing year dominated by the idea that attrition would decide the war. The previous year a week-long artillery barrage had announced the battle of the Somme, "destined to be known among the troops as the Great Fuck-Up, [which] was the largest engagement fought since the beginnings of civilization."[7] Corpse-strewn plains and Pyrrhic victories, in 1917, were topical subjects.

Just after Stephen starts his history lesson by asking where Pyrrhus fought the famous battle, his mind conjures up an apocalyptic moment: "I hear the ruin of all space, shattered glass and toppling masonry, and time one livid final flame" (*U* 2.9–10). Later, at the climax of "Circe," virtually the same imagery recurs when Stephen smashes a lamp at Bella Cohen's brothel. This vision is overdetermined: it echoes recent Irish history – the campaigns of the Dynamitards and, in particular, the huge explosion set off by Fenians in 1867 at London's Clerkenwell prison – as well as anarchist bombings in Europe and the U.S. around the turn of the century. In the context of "Nestor," however, the Great War provides the primary reference. Stephen's vision evokes a topos of the war, the destruction of a building by artillery fire.[8] Although he is picturing not a battle but the end of the world, the unheard-of firepower loosed in 1914 actually did mark the end of a world. During a concentrated artillery attack on the Western Front,

there [was] usually one field gun for every ten yards under fire, and one heavy ... for every twenty yards. When the huge shells burst, they ravage[d] the earth with their violence, hurling trees, rock, mud, torsos, and other debris hundreds of feet into the air.[9]

The British used a 15-inch gun that fired a 1,400-pound shell, while the Germans' "Big Bertha" launched a projectile weighing over a ton: the "impact of this shell annihilate[d] buildings; it shatter[ed] windows in a two-mile radius."[10] Two notorious instances of toppling masonry and shattered glass were the destruction by the Germans of the Belgian city of Louvain, together with its ancient library, and of the cathedral at Reims in France. (Henry James called the bombardment of the Reims cathedral "the most hideous crime ever perpetrated against the mind of man.")[11] Joyce made no recorded comment on these atrocities; but by the time he started "Nestor," they must have been conflated in his mind with the devastation of the General Post Office and downtown Dublin caused by the use of artillery by British soldiers, some on leave from the Western Front, against the Irish rebels of Easter 1916. Although the burning, war-shocked city in "Circe" – "*Brimstone fires spring up. Dense clouds roll past. Heavy Gatling guns boom. Pandemonium. Troops deploy. Gallop of hoofs. Artillery. Hoarse commands*" (*U* 15.4661–63) – is identified as Dublin, the scene could just as well depict a Belgian or French town. So, too, could the scene at the end of the "Cyclops" episode, where the biscuit tin flung by the Citizen at Bloom turns into "an incandescent object of enormous proportions hurtling through the atmosphere at a terrifying velocity in a trajectory directed southwest by west." Its impact causes a "catastrophe ... terrific and instantaneous in its effect ... All the lordly residences in the vicinity of the palace of justice were demolished and that noble edifice itself ... is literally a mass of ruins beneath which it is to be feared all the occupants have been buried alive" (*U* 12.1879–81, 1858–69).

World War I struck many contemporaries, especially after 1915, as the apocalypse whose specter had been giving European thinkers bad dreams for the past generation. The huge Martian machines that threaten the earth in H. G. Wells's *The War of the Worlds* (1898) were the imaginary forerunners of tanks (first used in large numbers by the British in 1917) and artillery pieces such as the "twenty-ton monsters"[12] known collectively as Big Bertha. Wells closed *The Time Machine* (1895), a novel about a fatally divided future society, with his vision of a dying planet.[13] This link between apocalypse and the diseased state of society typifies a literary genre, which sprang up in the 1880s, on the decline and fall of modern civilization.[14] Although the most eloquent prophet of doom, Nietzsche, was vague about its form, artists did not hesitate to picture it. Often the apocalyptic moment involves an explosion resulting from the built-up pressures of a pathological social situation. Such moments, real or imagined, occur in major works written during or shortly after the war, including *Heartbreak House, Women in Love, Confessions of Zeno* (by Joyce's friend, Italo Svevo), *Time Regained, The Magic Mountain*, and *Tender Is the Night*.

Dublin in 1904 was in no danger of being blown up. Ireland was quiet, its middle classes more comfortable than ever before, and for a change calamities seemed to befall other countries. Throughout *Ulysses* we hear of an excursion boat that had caught on fire and sunk the previous day in New York's East River. Bloom thinks: "All those women and children excursion beanfeast burned and drowned in New York. Holocaust." Father Conmee passes "newsboards [which] told of a dreadful catastrophe in New York. In America those things were continually happening." Tom Kernan recollects a conversation: "Terrible affair that *General Slocum* explosion. Terrible, terrible! A thousand casualties ... Most brutal thing" (*U* 8.1146–47; 10.89–91, 725–27).

Just over a thousand passengers aboard the *General Slocum*, mainly women and children, died in twenty minutes.[15] The disaster figures in *Ulysses* partly because Joyce wanted to document the actualities of 16 June, but it serves another purpose as well. What impresses his characters is the scale of the loss of life – a "thousand casualties" – as well as the horrifying circumstances. The word "casualties" is used only one other time in the novel, when Bloom recalls his encounter with the Citizen at Kiernan's pub: "So far as politics themselves were concerned, he was only too conscious of the casualties invariably resulting from propaganda and displays of mutual animosity and the misery and suffering it entailed ... on fine young fellows, chiefly, destruction of the fittest" (*U* 16.1598–1602). While Joyce was composing *Ulysses*, the word "casualties" inevitably referred to or brought to mind the war, which was facilitating the destruction of fine young fellows in numbers inconceivable a few years earlier. The motif of the *General Slocum* "catastrophe" helps date the action of 16 June 1904 in more than one way; it reminds the reader of the gulf between that era and the one inaugurated by World War I. Eric Hobsbawm writes:

If the word 'catastrophe' had been mentioned among the members of the European middle classes before 1913, it would almost certainly have been in connection with the few traumatic events in which men and women like themselves were involved in the course of a lengthy, and in general tranquil, lifetime: say, the burning of the Karltheater in Vienna in 1881 ... or the sinking of the Titanic ...

After 1914 it is a safe bet that the word suggested other and greater calamities.[16]

Prior to the war, "virtually the only quantities measured in millions, outside astronomy, were populations of countries and the data of production."[17] The stunning casualty lists emanating from the Continent signaled something new in Western history. The Germans suffered a million dead and wounded in the first five months; the British, on the first day of their Somme offensive in 1916, lost 60,000 men. The appalled American ambassador wrote home from London, "When there's 'nothing to report' from France, that means the regular 5,000 casualties that happen every day."[18] The citizens of Joyce's Dublin think of the *General Slocum* as a catastrophe because they cannot imagine anything much worse.[19] A dramatic irony arises because the readers of *Ulysses* know, as Joyce did, what rough beast would be born in Europe only ten years later. Consequently the characters of *Ulysses* live not only in their fictive time frame but, as Robert Spoo demonstrates,[20] that of the world ushered in by the Great War.

The war manifests itself as a ghostly future presence most compellingly in "Nestor." Apart from Stephen's vision of apocalypse, several themes and images evoke both the slaughter on the Western Front and the combatants' reactions to it. The Anglo-Irish boys whom Stephen teaches in 1904 "will be officer material in ten years." Their hockey game foreshadows what they will face as young men: its imagery of "battling bodies" (*U* 2.314) and carnage "blends medieval warfare with the horrific accounts of trench conditions and bayonet-fighting."[21] The very idea of manly, competitive play and goals evokes the sports cult whose spirit pervaded early British attitudes toward World War I and is captured in Sir Henry Newbolt's poem, "Vitaï Lampada" (1898), which begins on a cricket pitch and ends on a blood-sodden battlefield.[22] Another theme to arise out of the war was the relationship between young men and older men, surrogate sons and fathers. The relationship had two opposing faces. On the one hand, there was the alienation that George Orwell recalls: "By 1918 everyone under forty was in a bad temper with his elders, and the mood of anti-militarism ... was extended into a general revolt against orthodoxy and authority."[23] This ill will continued during the first few years after the Armistice when veterans disappointed in civilian life blamed the "old men" for depriving them of their hard-won victory.[24] On the other hand, there was the bond, born out of the comradeship of the trenches, between some junior officers and the soldiers they commanded, which also took on paternal and filial nuances.

We see, as Spoo points out, both kinds of surrogate father–son relationship in "Nestor." Mr. Deasy, with his aggressive belief in the Orange cause and his teleological faith in providence, suggests one of the generals of World War I. He makes an unsatisfactory father / teacher for Stephen, who mistrusts him. At the same time Stephen stands between the old schoolmaster and his students somewhat as a young field officer stood between his higher-ups in the rear, the "staff-wallahs," and his own soldiers. Stephen's compassion for the boy named Sargent who stays behind in the classroom for help carries "overtones of the English officer's concern for his men, a concern which ... often resembled paternal responsibility."[25] Yet Stephen must send the boy out, hastened by Deasy's command, towards "the scrappy field where sharp voices were in strife" (*U* 2.184–85). He, too, is an ineffectual father, who cannot save his sons from the incubus of history.

Mr. Deasy serves in Joyce's scheme of Homeric analogues as the counterpart to Nestor, the garrulous old warrior who, in *The Odyssey*, counsels Telemachus and treats him to a history of the Trojan War. He is also a nineteenth-century "happy warrior ... full of hardy Victorian optimism and high-sounding imperialistic rhetoric, exactly the type who promoted and welcomed the war."[26] A proud unionist, one of history's blood-stained winners, Deasy makes Stephen think of the "corpses of papishes" produced by Protestant violence in Ireland. He refutes Stephen's comment about history being a nightmare by saying: "The ways of the Creator are not our ways ... All human history moves toward one great goal, the manifestation of God" (*U* 2.274, 380–81). Ideologically, he belongs to the same camp as British military leaders in the Great War such as Field Marshal Haig, who after victory in 1919 said: "We were fighting, not only for ourselves and for our own Empire, but for a world ideal in which God was with us."[27]

With his cynicism and his lack of belief even in his own ideas, Stephen brings to mind junior officers like Graves and Sassoon who returned from the war with their bodies but not their prewar ideologies intact. His gloomy passivity, which contrasts with Deasy's bellicosity, parallels attitudes remarked by T. E. Lawrence, who wrote: "The blood thirstiness of the old men – who did not fight – towards our late enemies is sometimes curiously relieved against the tolerance of those who have fought and wish to avoid making others fight again tomorrow."[28] Stephen, unlike Deasy, does not believe that the advancement of any community – racial, national, or imperial – justifies killing. Although he recalls a moment of murderous anger toward a uniformed man (a post office functionary) in France – "Shoot him to bloody bits with a bang shotgun, bits man spattered walls" (*U* 3.187–88) – he takes back his imagined assault and fantasizes shaking hands with the victim instead. During his confrontation with Private Carr he disavows fighting for his nation. He tells the private: "Let my country die for me" (*U* 15.4773). This seemingly bloody-minded statement has more of a metaphorical than a literal sense: Stephen, who earlier has said he must "kill the priest and the king" (*U* 15.4437) inside his head, now wishes to kill the internalized nation. For him, nations, empires, and other political communities are inextricably linked with the violence of history.

IMAGINED COMMUNITIES

Legally, in 1904, Leopold Bloom is every bit as Irish as the Citizen or any other Dubliner in *Ulysses*. That is, he lives in the United Kingdom, has the right to vote for a Member of Parliament, is subject to British law, and would carry a British passport if he traveled abroad. In other words, his Irishness does not receive recognition as an attribute of citizenship in an Irish nation-state. As far as British or international law is concerned, such a state does not exist. Even before the Act of Union (1800), Ireland had never been a nation-state, despite the beguiling flicker of semiautonomy invested in Grattan's parliament (1782–1800). After the Union it became part of the United Kingdom, its official status equivalent to that of Wales or Scotland or England. One parliament, one state, several – several what? Countries? Regions? Communities? Today, with the Irish component of the United Kingdom limited to that tragic appendage known as Northern Ireland, the ambiguity lingers. The United Kingdom retains "the rare distinction of refusing nationality in its naming"[29] – a distinction which, in 1904, when the prenational dynastic states of the nineteenth century had not yet fallen apart under the impact of World War I, was not so rare. The advantage of such nomenclature was that it could include subject nationalities, such as Irish Catholics, under the umbrella of a state controlled by a dominant nationality and uphold the official pretense that all citizens were equal regardless of where they lived.

Citizenship in this sense, for a subjugated group that would like to make its territory into a separate nation-state, is what Stephen suggests paternity may be – "a legal fiction" (*U* 9.844). On a practical level, everyone sees through the fiction. The talk in "Telemachus" illustrates this everyday acknowledgment of an officially ignored reality. A Celtic enthusiast, Haines is visiting Ireland to observe the natives and practice speaking their language in the same spirit in which Orientalists made journeys to more distant outposts of Empire. He addresses the old milkwoman in Gaelic, which she, being a deracinated product of colonization, not only doesn't understand but mistakes for French. Corrected, she asks if Haines comes from the west of Ireland. He replies without hesitation: "I am an Englishman." Mulligan confirms his identity: "He's English . . . and thinks we ought to speak Irish in Ireland" (*U* 1.431–32). A little later Stephen calls himself a "servant" – not a citizen – of the "imperial British state." Haines replies patronizingly, "An Irishman must think like that . . . We feel in England that we have treated you rather unfairly" (*U* 1.647–48). There is no mistaking an Irishman for an Englishman here, and no mistaking the coercion involved in having made Ireland a supposed partner in the so-called United Kingdom.

It seems arguable that Ireland in 1904 was a nation, like Hungary or Poland, aspiring to be a nation-state. Certainly, in the "retrospective arrangement" (*U* 14.1044) of history sponsored by the Irish state that did come into being, this is a given. We must ask, however, the same question that puts Bloom on the spot in "Cyclops": "But do you know what a nation means?" The question provokes this exchange:

—A nation? says Bloom. A nation is the same people living in the same place.
—By God, then, says Ned, laughing, if that's so I'm a nation for I'm living in the same place for the past five years.
So of course everyone had the laugh at Bloom and says he, trying to muck out of it:

—Or also living in different places.
—That covers my case, says Joe.
—What is your nation if I may ask? says the citizen.
—Ireland, says Bloom. I was born here. Ireland. (*U* 12.1422–31)

Most people think they know what a nation is, just as Haines knows he is English and not Irish; yet the concept eludes neat formulation. The *Oxford English Dictionary* defines "nation" as: "An extensive aggregate of persons, so closely associated with each other by common descent, language, or history, as to form a distinct race or people, usually organized as a separate political state and occupying a definite territory." The *OED* would exclude from nationhood, then, not only the barflies at Barney Kiernan's but also the United Kingdom, the Dual Monarchy, the Ottoman Empire, and Czarist Russia, among other states. In fact, it is only with some gyrations that turn-of-the-century Ireland could be made to fit such a definition. Most Irish people spoke English, not Irish, as the milk woman's inability to understand Haines points up. Ireland was not "a separate political state" – except insofar as the Coercion Acts punctuating its history during the nineteenth century showed that British law operated there differently from elsewhere in the United Kingdom. As an island, its territory was definite enough. But within that tight little island many inhabitants, concentrated in the north, gave their primary allegiance not to Ireland but to the Queen – and so fervently as to make civil war seem a threat in the event of a successful Home Rule Bill. (Any war talk in Britain during the early summer of 1914 – only ten years later – referred to the threat of conflict in Ireland.) Mr. Deasy's combativeness – "*For Ulster will fight / And Ulster will be right*" (*U* 2.397–98) – reminds us that both the United Kingdom and Ireland herself were disunited. Only a foreigner would have thought Ireland to be populated by a single "distinct race or people." Protestant avatars of cultural nationalism, such as Thomas Davis in the 1840s and Yeats in Joyce's day, valiantly pushed a concept of Irish nationality that downplayed differences in religion and ancestry. These are precisely the differences Bloom ignores in advancing his definition of a nation. For his Irish Catholic audience, however, they are crucial, and the Citizen angrily excludes Bloom from *his* Ireland.

Bloom's idea of a nation as the same people living in the same place is not so ludicrous as it might appear. The more specific one becomes in defining "nation," the more one is contradicted by the reality of nations that don't fit the definition. It does not help much, either, to look at how individual nations define themselves, since nationalisms are notable for "their philosophical poverty and even incoherence."[30] The author of *Nations and States* writes in frustration: "All that I can find to say is that a nation exists when a significant number of people in a community consider themselves to form a nation, or behave as if they formed one."[31] Though circular, this statement is useful because it emphasizes the role of the imagination in creating a nation. It leads us toward Benedict Anderson's more elegant definition of a nation as "an imagined political community." Anderson elaborates:

> It is *imagined* because the members of even the smallest nation will never know most of their fellow-members, meet them, or even hear of them, yet in the minds of each lives the image of their communion ...
>
> [I]t is imagined as a *community*, because, regardless of ... inequality and exploitation ... the nation is always conceived as a deep, horizontal comradeship.[32]

Anderson's formulation brings into sharper focus the issues of Bloom's verbal skirmish in the pub. Any nation differentiates its citizens from those of other nations in terms of certain shared traits, while it ignores inconvenient facts that tend to subvert the illusion of unity. Ernest Renan alluded to this illusion in writing: "The essence of a nation is that all its individuals should have many things in common, and also that they all should have forgotten many things."[33] Bloom offends the Citizen and his drinking companions because he is a walking paradox, a threat to the imagined unity of Ireland. The question – "[W]hy can't a jew love his country like the next fellow?" – spurs instant disavowals:

—Why not? says J.J., when he's quite sure which country it is.
—Is he a jew or a gentile or a holy Roman or a swaddler or what the hell is he? says Ned. Or who is he? No offence, Crofton ...
—We don't want him, says Crofter the Orangeman or presbyterian.
—He's a perverted jew, says Martin, from a place in Hungary and it was he drew up all the plans according to the Hungarian system. We know that in the castle ...
—That's the new Messiah for Ireland! says the citizen. (*U* 12.1630–42)

Even the rumor that "Bloom gave the ideas for Sinn Fein to Griffith" (*U* 12.1574) is disturbing, since it shows a foreign influence at the heart of the country's latest nationalist movement. With virtually one voice, the community of drinkers in Kiernan's rejects this bundle of contradictions whose political and religious affiliations are uncertain and whose father was a Hungarian Jew. (They would be even more disconcerted if they knew that Bloom's mother was one Ellen Higgins, very likely of Irish Catholic stock on her mother's side [*U* 17.536–37].) Ironically, though, this community itself reverberates with contradictions. The Citizen represents the blustery, public face of physical-force nationalism, yet cannot return to his rural hometown because other nationalists are "looking for him to let daylight through him for grabbing the holding of an evicted tenant" (*U* 12.1315–16). Cunningham, a Castle Catholic, works for the regime the Citizen would like to overthrow. Crofton is a Protestant Unionist. Most of the drinkers seem to embody Cruise O'Brien's "Fairyhouse tradition" – that is, they belong to the mass of citizens who passively accept the existing power structure. Yet, in spite of these differences, they all agree on a tacit definition of Irishness that includes themselves and excludes Bloom.

We see Bloom's status as a national outsider, a "dark horse" (*U* 12.1558), throughout *Ulysses*. In "Hades" the sight of an elderly Jew, by implication a pawnbroker, creates among Bloom's Gentile companions an instant community from which he is shut out. Mulligan, leaving the National Library with Stephen, warns him about the "wandering jew" (*U* 9.1209). The "Cyclops" episode begins with the scurrilous narrator's anecdote of a swindled Jewish merchant, is interspersed with slurs directed at Bloom, and ends with the Citizen's attempt to brain the "bloody jewman" (*U* 12.1811). In "Ithaca" Stephen, in Bloom's own kitchen, sings an anti-Semitic ditty about ritual murder. Here, ironically, the would-be artist-rebel represents the larger community; and Bloom, wanting acceptance, remains the outsider.

❈

The Jew, in Joyce's day, had long been Europe's "Other." The Citizen could be any European nationalist speaking of the Jews: "Swindling the peasants ... and the poor of Ireland. We want no more strangers in our house" (*U* 12.1150–51). Joyce first aired his idea for a story, "Ulysses," about a Dublin Jew named Alfred H. Hunter, in 1906. At this time, having resisted the efforts of Irish Catholic nationalism to enlist him in its imagined community and having adopted instead his own imagined transnational European community, he was discovering in self-exile what it meant to be an outsider in a world of nations and races. "The subject of the Jews . . . seized upon [his] attention as he began to recognize his place in Europe to be as ambiguous as theirs" (*JJ* 230). By 1914, when he started turning "Ulysses" into a novel, he had spent nearly eleven years in multinational Trieste, which belonged to the Austro-Hungarian Empire and at the same time to the imagined community known as *Italia irridenta*. This experience broadened him and impressed on him the ties between Irish nationalism and other European nationalisms. One tie was anti-Semitism.

As Stephen leaves Mr. Deasy's school, the old schoolmaster tells him a joke: "Ireland, they say, has the honour of being the only country which never persecuted the jews. Do you know . . . why?" Stephen does not, and Deasy explains: "Because she never let them in" (*U* 2.437–42). Deasy is wrong on both counts. Joyce was still in Dublin when, in January 1904, a priest incited a boycott of Jewish merchants in Limerick; there was violence, and the year-long boycott won the support of Griffith's *United Irishman*.[34] But in Ireland, unlike many European countries, the Jewish minority was tiny and normally unmolested. Joyce's introduction to Continental anti-Semitism, more virulent than the Irish strain, likely occurred in France:

He must have been affected . . . by the Dreyfus uproar in Paris, which continued from 1892 to 1906; it had reached one of its crises in September 1902, just before Joyce's arrival in Paris, when Anatole France, a writer he respected, delivered his eloquent oration at the funeral of Zola, whose *J'accuse* was still stirring up Europe. A connection between the Jew and his artist-defender may have been fixed in Joyce's mind by the connection between Zola, France, and Dreyfus. (*JJ* 373)

Undoubtedly Joyce saw a link between French right-wing nationalism, infected with anti-Semitism, and Irish nationalism. The link becomes explicit in "Proteus" when Stephen, remembering his meeting in Paris with the old Fenian, Kevin Egan, thinks of Egan's rambling talk of "Ireland . . . of hopes, conspiracies, of Arthur Griffith" and of "M. Drumont, famous journalist" (*U* 3.226–31). Edouard Drumont (1844–1917) was France's most influential anti-Semite, author of *La France juive* (1886), "a polemic compounded of Rothschilds and ritual murder,"[35] and co-founder of the National Anti-Semitic League. In 1892 he launched a newspaper, *La Libre Parole*, which explained Dreyfus's "treason" as being motivated by a desire to avenge himself for slights received and the desire of the Jewish race to ruin France. He paid for a claque to jeer outside the windows of the Palais de Justice where Zola was tried for libel in 1898; he was implicated in anti-Semitic riots; and he had a hand in anti-Dreyfusard agitation from the outset of the affair to its finale (Dreyfus's full vindication) in 1906. Though his star had begun to wane when Joyce first visited Paris in 1902, he remained powerful and famous. Egan's admiration may stem in part from Drumont's Anglophobia, yet the tie between Irish nationalism and anti-Semitism is suggested, nonetheless. Haines and Deasy earlier have expressed English and Anglo-Irish prejudices toward the Jews; Egan does so only implicitly, but later the Citizen will make Haines and Deasy sound tolerant. The upshot of his rantings is an attempt at violence, which, though farcical, again reminds us of the Dreyfus affair: the biscuit tin missile which he has hurled at Bloom destroys "the palace of justice . . . in which . . . important legal debates were in progress" (*U* 12.1865–67). Such a building did not exist in Dublin, but the one in Paris was the site of legal wrangling over Dreyfus.

Admittedly, even the Citizen's chauvinistic aggression pales when compared with the persecutions sponsored by Drumont. Still, Irish and French anti-Semitism did share a common vocabulary of mystification. Griffith, writing of the affair in the *United Irishman*, backed the anti-Dreyfusards; he focused on the Jew as an "alien" who "forms a nation apart,"[36] always a potential traitor. In France Zola, too, was denounced as a "foreigner": though born in Paris of a French mother, he had an Italian father. The novelist Maurice Barrès, in refusing to sign a protest after Zola had been convicted of libel, cited "the instinct of patriotism" and linked Zola, a "denaturalized Venetian," with the Jews. The latter, he said, "have no country as we understand it. For us our country is the earth of our ancestors, the land of our dead. For them it is the place of their best interest."[37]

Barrès's remarks illustrate the fact that nationalism "concerns itself with the links between the dead and the yet unborn, the mystery of re-generation."[38] The Citizen's mind shuttles between Ireland's past, at once great and tragic, and its shining if indefinite future. He recalls "the invincibles and the old guard and the men of sixtyseven" and the peasants who "were driven out of house and home in the black '47" (*U* 12.480–81, 1365–66). At the same time he invokes "the future men of Ireland" and the day "when the first Irish battleship is seen breasting the waves with our own flag to the fore" (*U* 12.1264, 1306–08). He evokes a vast imagined community, including "our greater Ireland beyond the sea" (*U* 12.1364–65), that comprises the dead, the living, and the yet unborn.

The Citizen's community is bound together by mystical ties of blood – especially the blood relationship of fathers and sons as a metaphor for the relationship between generations – and soil. Such ties, though cited passionately by believers, tend to evaporate in the light of actual day-to-day relations. I have already discussed a few of the internal divisions, reflected among the crew at Kiernan's pub, of Ireland in 1904. Even among "Irish nationalists" – a term which, conveying an illusory unity, covers Connolly's I.S.R.P., Parnellites, anti-Parnellites, rural G.A.A. athletes, white-collared urban Gaelic Leaguers, I.R.B. men, the Irish Literary Theatre, the women of Inghinidhe na hEireann, and countless overlappings among these groups and shades of opinion within them – variety and conflict were the norm. As for "Ireland beyond the sea," the actual Irish-American community was similarly fragmented, and its Fenians were still recovering from a murderous split that had occurred in 1889 just before the more famous Split that traumatized constitutional nationalism in Ireland herself. But the *ideal* of an essential national community, stretching backward and forward in time, had power to command the loyalty of people more thoughtful than Michael Cusack, the real-life analogue of the Citizen. It had power, in fact, to triumph over the realities of division and change and mortality, and to bring to life as a political entity what previously had only an imagined existence.[39]

Just such an incarnation had begun to take place in Ireland as Joyce was writing *Ulysses*. He acknowledged this most recent, surprising manifestation of the power of Irish nationalism through the proleptic anachronism of making Sinn Fein and Arthur Griffith, "the coming man" (*U* 18.385–86), unrealistically prominent for 1904. "Sinn Féin, founded in 1905, reached its pre-war high-water mark in 1908, after that declining to such an extent that its historian has said, 'From 1910 to 1913 the Sinn Féin movement was practically moribund.'"[40] The blood-letting not so much of Easter 1916 but of the ensuing executions resuscitated the movement, which had attracted Joyce during its earlier heyday, and paved the way for its electoral landslide in December 1918 and the Anglo-Irish War of

1919–21. But while he must have been impressed and to some extent pleased by Sinn Fein's resurgence, its principle of Irish essentialism and its invocation of dead heroes and a romanticized national history no doubt confirmed his earlier mistrust of nationalism, whose dark power was convulsing Europe as he worked on *Ulysses*.[41]

Joyce alludes to this dark power throughout *Ulysses* but especially in "Cyclops." An emblematic scene occurs when the Citizen breaks off his debate with Bloom over patriotism and "Wolfe Tone . . . and Robert Emmet and die for your country" (*U* 12.498–500):

—The memory of the dead, says the citizen taking up his pintglass and glaring at Bloom . . .
—You don't grasp my point, says Bloom. What I mean is . . .
—*Sinn Fein!* says the citizen. *Sinn fein amhein!* The friends we love are by our side and the foes we hate before us. (*U* 12.519–24)

The Citizen cannot tolerate debate because he is actuated not by reason but by mystical concepts of race and nationality. Similar feelings motivated the anti-Dreyfusards and vast numbers of citizens of the Great Powers in August 1914. Their foes, like the Citizen's, stood for the Other, whose opposition or prominence or mere existence constituted an affront to the nation.

✲

The irrationality of nationalists, racists, and empire-builders is intertwined in *Ulysses* with violence and the cult of death. We see this most vividly in the theme of heroticism as illustrated in Joyce's treatment of Robert Emmet, the Croppy Boy, and Joe Brady. But in the dual time frame of *Ulysses* these hero-martyrs also foreshadow their political descendants, Padraic Pearse and the leaders of the Easter Rising. Pearse wrote in 1913: "We must accustom ourselves to the thought of arms, to the sight of arms, to the use of arms. We may make mistakes in the beginning and shoot the wrong people; but bloodshed is a cleansing and a sanctifying thing."[42] Pearse's "rhetoric of blood"[43] had distinctive Irish roots yet also had much in common with contemporary political writing. In fact, heroticism and the idea of spiritual purification through bloodshed, conjoined with a sense of innate moral superiority, crossed European boundary lines from the late nineteenth century through the second year of the Great War.

Nationalism, racism, and imperialism are not identical phenomena, but among the European powers prior to 1914 they tended to merge and shared a mystical rationale which, however much it flowed from and cloaked the hard realities of economic competition, had a life of its own. Barbara Tuchman writes of the poet and imperialist W. E. Henley:

No Teutonic homage to the master race could outshout his celebration of "England, My England," whose "mailed hand" guides teeming destinies, whose "breed of mighty men" is unmatched, whose ships are "the fierce old sea's delight," who is:

> Chosen daughter of the Lord
> Spouse-in-Chief of the ancient Sword.[44]

Joyce takes potshots in *Ulysses* at the evils and pretensions of European (mainly British) imperialism – for example, in his depiction of Haines, in a reference to Roger Casement's exposé of atrocities in the Belgian Congo, and in two parodic passages in "Cyclops" dealing with Queen Victoria and her empire. But his chief target remains Irish nationalism, which he presents as a mirror image of British attitudes.

Henley's paean to England finds its counterpart in the gigantesque description of the Citizen as a monument to ancient Irish glory – "From his girdle hung a row of seastones which jangled at every movement of his portentous frame and on these were graven with rude yet striking art the tribal images of many Irish heroes and heroines of antiquity" (*U* 12.173–76) – and in the Citizen's bombast about Ireland's great past and her great future. The difference is that Henley could gaze in self-congratulation on the present, whereas the Citizen must take satisfaction from past and future glories. As Declan Kiberd writes:

Like all colonised peoples whose history is a nightmare, the Irish have no choice but to live in the foreglow of a golden future. For them history is a form of science fiction, by which their scribes must rediscover in the endlessly malleable past whatever it is they are hoping for in an ideal future.[45]

But the Citizen's vision of the revival of Irish commerce and of a battleship steaming under the Irish flag suggests his philosophical alignment with the English imperialists whom he excoriates. After reading about the visit of a Zulu chief to a cotton factory in the Midlands, he comments: "That's how it's worked ... Trade follows the flag" (*U* 12.1541). What he wants is not freedom for all oppressed peoples but Ireland's own place in the sun – a view shared by Griffith, who resisted the idea that non-European races had the same right to self-determination as the Irish.

Joyce was hardly fair to Irish nationalism in making the Citizen its representative figure. It is true that one could mistake Pearse's rhetoric for the Citizen's:

> By the bloody wounds of Tone,
> By the noble blood of Emmet,
> By the Famine corpses,
> By the tears of Irish exiles,
> We swear the oaths our ancestors swore,
> That we will free our race from bondage.

In a free Ireland there will be work for all the men and women of the nation. Gracious and useful rural industries will supplement an improved agriculture. The population will expand in a century to twenty millions... Towns will be spacious and beautiful.[46]

Yet unlike the Citizen or Griffith, he was not a latent imperialist, especially after he fell under Connolly's influence. And his death in a fusillade of British bullets had, for many Irish Catholics, including those angered by the Rising, a redeeming effect that made up for his occasional silliness.

Dying for one's country, as Pearse did, is traditionally the highest expression of nationalism. The willingness to sacrifice oneself for the extended national community "suggests a strong affinity with religious imaginings" and differentiates "the nationalist imagining" from, say, Marxism or liberalism – neither of which concerns itself much with death or immortality.[47] Clearly a person ready to die for his or her imagined community identifies with that community, and does so based on a belief in its metaphysical virtues (in which the individual shares) rather than on a desire to defend or gain territory. National wars and revolutions, from this perspective, have overriding cultural or "spiritual" imperatives, in addition to economic aims. Again, this is one of the parallels, which Joyce surely noted, between the Great War and the Easter Rising.

In August 1914, for instance, German soldiers marched to war with a sense of purpose derived from editorials and speeches that advanced their country's "moral superiority" and "moral right." Most Germans "regarded the armed conflict they were entering in spiritual terms"; it was "the supreme test of spirit ... a test of vitality, culture, and life." The Germans felt encircled by hostile, decadent powers, among which Britain – seen as a nation of shop-keepers and bourgeois respectability – was "the foremost representative of a life-denying order that Germany had to break out of." In striking the first blow, Germany would be starting a war of liberation – a war to free German culture, the German soul. Three days after the declaration of war on Russia an article in the *Berliner Tageblatt*, entitled "Moral Victory," declared: "And even if a catastrophe were to befall us such as no one dare imagine, the moral victory of this week could never be eradicated."[48]

Pearse and his fellow rebels did not share the faith in technology which was part of Germany's sacred *Kultur*, nor did they expect military victory. Many, however, did believe in "the divinity of our people" and in Irish nationalism as a "Splendid and holy cause."[49] They felt a sense of moral superiority toward England, toward what they perceived as middle-class English materialism and hypocrisy. And, in spite of hopes for a landing of German arms, they aimed at what the writer for the *Berliner Tageblatt* emphasized – a divinely sanctioned moral victory. If the German slogan was *Gott mit uns*, the signers of the Proclamation of the Irish Republic declared: "We place the cause of the Irish Republic under the protection of the Most High God, Whose blessing we invoke upon our arms." Pearse's reading of the Proclamation on the steps of the General Post Office ended on a lofty note reminiscent of the August 1914 rhetoric of Germany: "In this supreme hour the Irish nation must, by its valour and discipline and by the readiness of its children to sacrifice themselves for the common good, prove itself worthy of the august destiny to which it is called."[50] Thus the Great War and the Easter Week Rising both resulted from spiritual projects, so to speak, launched on behalf of imagined political communities.

Joyce must have been dumbfounded to learn that his former Irish teacher was the leading figure in the Rising. He attempted to take Pearse's measure in *Ulysses*, most particularly in the theme of the hero-martyr, and generally in his depiction of the collision between Bloom and Irish nationalism in "Cyclops." As I have tried to show, his insights into the nature of nationalism were acute. Yet at bottom the figure of the hero-martyr doesn't sum Pearse up. Yeats's notion of the "terrible beauty" of Easter 1916 perhaps serves as a corrective, though this idea itself calls out for a corrective. Pearse's most recent biographer concludes: "He wrote, acted and died for a people that did not exist; he distorted into his own image the ordinary people of

Ireland, who lacked his own remarkable qualities, but who had perceptions and complexities of their own that he could never understand."[51] One might say of Joyce that, although he brilliantly analyzed the pathology of nationalism, he failed to understand the perceptions and complexities of its human agents.

The absence from *Ulysses* of any Irish nationalists except those who are grotesquely funny, pernicious, or ineffectual indicates the limitations of Joyce's point of view. And if his response to Pearse was inadequate, what can we say about his response – or lack of one – to that altogether more complex and tragic nationalist, James Connolly? Joyce may have lumped him with those socialists who marched off to war in 1914, yet his life and death raise crucial issues for anyone concerned with the relationship between nationalism and social justice. Bloom's Fabian ideal – "all creeds and classes *pro rata* having a comfortable tidysized income . . . in the neighbourhood of £300 per annum" (*U* 16.1133–35) – does not address these issues. Nor does anything in *Ulysses* address the question: what "authentic qualities"[52] of Irish nationalism impelled Connolly, after two decades of combating the oppression of lower-class Irish Catholics by middle-class Nationalists, to throw himself and his Citizen Army into the Easter Rising? Like all of Joyce's fiction, *Ulysses*, a novel whose characters represent a narrow stratum of the petty bourgeoisie, has a middle-class frame of reference. Politically, it explores the pathologies of nationalism, racism, and imperialism, but not that of class exploitation.

No doubt the mayhem of 1914–21 confirmed Joyce's predisposition to see nationalism as Europe's direst plague. In spite of his anger at British misrule in Ireland, even imperialism struck him as a lesser evil. As a refugee in Zurich, he dismissed

all talk of democratic Utopias with the remark that he had never been happier than under the lax rule of the Austro-Hungarian emperor in Trieste. "They called it a ramshackle empire," he said later to Mary Colum, "I wish to God there were more such empires." (*JJ* 389)

Yet he didn't really care for empires any more than nation-states. Budgen identified Joyce's "patriotism [as being] that of a citizen of a free town in the middle ages. He has told me that he would rather be burgomaster of a city like Amsterdam than emperor of any empire; for a burgomaster is somebody among people he knows, while an emperor rules over unknowable people in unknown territories."[53] In other words, Joyce felt attachment to the "knowable community"[54] of a small city – that of a Dublin or a Trieste, as opposed to the imagined community of a nation. He associated the latter with what Bloom decries at Kiernan's pub – with "Persecution" and "national hatred among nations" (*U* 12.1417–18). The Citizen's concept of the Irish community – absurd, narrow, and shot through with contradictions – has broad implications when set against the backdrop of 1914–21. It is "such limited imaginings," Anderson says, that have made it possible in the twentieth century "for so many millions of people, not so much to kill, as willingly to die."[55] Joyce's own imaginings, though they do not do justice to the rich ambiguities of nationalism, evoke its incoherence and violence.

"FUNDAMENTALS OF SEXOLOGY" (*U* 15.2423)

Nationalism. War. Masculine aggressiveness. Joyce's three main characters all have negative feelings toward these phenomena, but each stands in a different relationship to them.

Molly expresses her sentiments in a rumination prefaced by scornful references to "them Sinner Fein" and to "that little man ... Griffiths":

I hate the mention of their politics after the war that Pretoria and Ladysmith and Bloemfontein where Gardner lieut Stanley G 8th Bn 2nd East Lancs Rgt of enteric fever he was a lovely fellow in khaki ... Im sure he was brave too he said I was lovely the evening we kissed goodbye ... they could have made their peace in the beginning or old oom Paul and the rest of the other old Krugers go and fight it out between them instead of dragging on for years killing any finelooking men there were ... I love to see a regiment pass in review the first time I saw the Spanish cavalry at La Roque it was lovely ... the lancers theyre grand. (*U* 18.387–402)

Military displays and handsome young men in uniform excite Molly, but she deplores politics and the resulting wars which kill the young men. She is thinking of the Boer War in particular. Her regret, however, that the old men didn't "fight it out between them instead of [the war] dragging on for years killing any finelooking young men" suggests a woman looking back on the Great War. Later she muses: "Itd be much better for the world to be governed by the women in it you wouldnt see women ... killing one another and slaughtering" (*U* 18.1434–36).

Molly's notion of petticoat government rejects the existing order and yet, since she does not intend to do anything, acquiesces in it. The question, then, is: to what extent does she represent an alternative to the sexual polarization of patriarchal societies that produces warriors, hero-martyrs, and bereaved women? Richard Brown compares her to the Anne Hathaway of Stephen's theory of Shakespeare as evidence that *Ulysses* advances "a radical interpretation of masculinity and feminity":

Stephen . . . give[s] women a central position in Shakespeare's plays and in his life. It is 'female' theory, elevating the figure of Anne Hathaway from her traditional position of obscurity to a central role . . . Stephen makes her into a powerful, sexually aggressive, deceitful woman, just as Joyce redefines the classic image of a faithful 'Penelope' to present a self-possessed, adulterous Molly Bloom.[56]

But we can grant that *Ulysses* subverts received concepts of gender without necessarily seeing Molly as a strong, self-possessed woman who rises above stereotypes of femininity.

Molly's bossiness toward Bloom, for instance, does not reflect autonomy. As Beauvoir comments, "the tyranny exercised by woman [over her husband] only goes to show her dependence . . . because she is alienated in him – that is, her interests as an individual lie in him."[57] Molly shows initiative in pursuing a singing career, yet does not seem inclined to give up the middle-class comfort of her home with the financially secure Bloom. Her life revolves around men, who validate her by responding to her physical attractiveness. When she thinks about her vocation, it tends to be in the context of encounters with amorous males: "He [Bartell D'Arcy] commenced kissing me on the choir stairs after I sang Gounod's Ave Maria" (*U* 18.274–75). Her lover, Blazes Boylan, has arranged her upcoming concert tour. On 16 June she commits a socially defiant act of self-assertion in starting her affair with Boylan. But, as Elaine Unkeless argues: "At the same time that her love-making represents a kind of freedom for Molly, it is indicative of her limitations: although she is rebellious against Bloom and social mores, in her affair she is still dependent on Boylan's approval."[58]

Admittedly, in the last two pages of *Ulysses* Molly is transfigured. Her imagination enlarges and her language becomes lyrical; she accepts people and life and the entire world – "the Spanish girls laughing in their shawls and . . . the Greeks and the jews and the Arabs and the devil knows who else" (*U* 18.1586–88). Here she lives up to the symbol of the "Penelope" episode, the Earth, and is the

great reconciler of contraries in an antimilitarist novel devoted to
the undermining of polarized, potentially antagonistic identities.
Yet she fulfills this role only as a symbol, not as a realistic character.
No matter how much we focus on her archetypal aspect,[59] there
remains her everyday existence as a woman shot through with
Joyce's and middle-class European society's stereotypes of femininity. Though she appreciates Bloom's sensitivity, she takes as a lover
an aggressive man (suggesting the heroes of the pulp romances she
reads) whose love-making carries overtones of assault. Abstractions
bore her. In dismissing politics she consigns it to the male sphere of
action. In such ways she is, as Unkeless argues, a conventional
woman; and so – unlike a handful of actual women of her day, such
as Hanna Sheehy-Skeffington and Emily Hobhouse (a feminist
protester against the Boer War)[60] – she reflects rather than resists
patriarchal notions of gender identity.

❋

What is wrong with Stephen in *Ulysses*? As a writer he appears to be
impotent. He has no genuine friends, feels alienated from his family,
and wards off a surrogate father (Bloom). A thunderclap terrifies
him. He thinks often of death. A chance encounter with his sister,
Dilly, plunges him into despair: "She is drowning. Agenbite. Save
her. Agenbite . . . She will drown me with her, eyes and hair. Lank
coils of seaweed around me, my heart, my soul. Salt green death"
(*U* 10.875–77). This imagery suggests the death of Ophelia, whose
love Hamlet, another troubled young man, could not return. It
recalls, too, the drowned man in "Proteus," whom Stephen has
associated with another literary drowning, that of Edward King, a
symbol of untimely death in Milton's "Lycidas." Its most freighted
emotional link, however, is with Stephen's mother, who has merged
in his musings that morning with the drowned man: "His human
eyes scream to me out of horror of his death. I . . . With him down
together . . . I could not save her." The dead woman seems linked
also to the grandmother buried by the fox in Stephen's riddle in
"Nestor," an image that recurs when the dog in "Proteus" digs on
the strand, "vulturing the dead" (*U* 3.328–30, 363–64). Vivid
memories of her wasted body trouble him during the day, and at
night, in "Circe," she appears to him in a horrifying vision.

Obsession with corpses. Hallucinations. Inability to work. Survi-
vor guilt. Fear of intimacy. Fear of loud noises and dying young. A
British Army psychiatrist during the later stages of the Great War,

seeing this constellation of symptoms in a soldier, would likely have diagnosed a condition known variously as "anxiety neurosis," "war strain," "soldier's heart," but most popularly as "shell shock." The controversy in medical and military circles over the eruption of such a condition among mainly front-line troops, the flower of Britain's manhood, had to do with its resemblance to the "female" disease of hysteria. "Built on an ideology of absolute and natural difference between women and men," English psychiatry, Elaine Showalter explains, found "its categories undermined by the evidence of male war neurosis." The multiplying cases of shell shock (80,000 *official* ones in all) upset military commanders not only because they threatened Britain's ability to fight, but because they undermined received norms of masculine and feminine behavior, norms enshrined in English psychiatric thinking. The constant flow into military hospitals of the "wounded in mind," including ruling-class officers, shockingly controverted "the heroic visions and masculinist fantasies" of 1914. It turned the Great War into "a crisis of masculinity and a trial of the Victorian masculine ideal"[61] which had survived intact until then.

Showalter suggests that shell shock was not simply a reaction to traumatic stress but a form of resistance to the wartime ethic of masculine violence:

While epidemic female hysteria in late Victorian England had been a ... protest against a patriarchal society that enforced confinement to a narrowly defined femininity, epidemic male hysteria in World War I was a protest against the politicians, generals, and psychiatrists. The heightened code of masculinity that dominated in wartime was intolerable to ... large numbers of men.[62]

Stephen has not been to war, but its correlative, for him, is history. He feels oppressed by history, which he sees as the record of the world's battles and conquests and assassinations, and which he associates with the brute fact of death, especially his mother's. His resistance to history takes several forms; in particular, however, he resists the aggressive masculine code of history's combatants, from Pyrrhus to Private Carr.

Stephen also resists the masculine norms of peacetime. He shuns sports, for instance, in contrast with the manly Buck Mulligan, a fine swimmer. In *A Portrait* his earlier self, too, is alienated from the sports culture. During his first year at Clongowes Wood, Stephen hovers at the edge of a football match, "out of the reach of the rude feet, [feeling] his body small and weak" (*P* 8). Football exemplified the sporting spirit which many British leaders, during the Great War, seriously thought had made their countrymen good empire-builders and now made them good soldiers.[63] Yet Irish nationalists, in the mirror-imaging that goes on between oppressor and oppressed, similarly praised sports for helping to mold the ideal young Irishmen who would someday set their country free. The infiltration of the Gaelic Athletic Association by I.R.B. men reflected this nexus of sporting and military virtues, which Stephen mocks in referring to Davin's "mak[ing] the next rebellion with hurley sticks" (*P* 202) and which underlies the Citizen's dual role in "the Gaelic sports revival" and in "building up a nation once again" (*U* 12.880, 891). Stephen consciously refuses, as a young man, to live up to the code of aggressive, athletic, conformist masculinity shared by British imperialists and Irish nationalists alike. Hence his resemblance to a victim of shell shock goes only so far. His "unmanly" traits – his distaste for sports, his pacifism, his anti-patriotism – differentiate him from most soldiers who served in the Great War, shell-shocked or "healthy," as well as from Irish nationalists. At the same time they ally him with Leopold Bloom. Bloom, though an Irishman and a father, subverts nationalist and patriarchal codes of masculinity in ways Stephen cannot even imagine, and so potentially offers him a lesson unavailable from other father figures in *Ulysses*.

❋

One aspect of Bloom's status as an outsider relates to his supposed feminine traits. After complaining of anti-Jewish persecutions, he is challenged:

—Right, says John Wyse. Stand up to it then with force like men.
   That's an almanac picture for you. Mark for a softnosed bullet. Old lardyface standing up to ... a gun. Gob, he'd adorn a sweepingbrush, so he would, if he only had a nurse's apron on him. (*U* 12.1475–77)

Like Stephen, Bloom is a pacifist; and when, collapsing "as limp as a wet rag," he disavows force and hatred, he discloses what his auditors view as unmanliness.

   But their doubts about Bloom's masculinity cut deeper. A discussion of his nationality, which establishes his exclusion from the *echt* Irish community, leads to the Citizen's sarcastic epithet, "the new Messiah for Ireland." Martin Cunningham says:

—Well, they're still waiting for their redeemer . . .
—Yes, says J.J., and every male that's born they think it may be their
Messiah. And every jew is in a tall state of excitement . . . till he knows if
he's a father or a mother . . .
—O, by God, says Ned, you should have seen Bloom before that son of his
that died was born. I met him one day in the south city markets buying a
tin of Neave's food six weeks before the wife was delivered . . .
—Do you call that a man? says the citizen.
—I wonder did he ever put it out of sight, says Joe.
—Well, there were two children born anyhow, says Jack Power.
—And who does he suspect? says the citizen.
    Gob, there's many a true word spoken in jest. One of those mixed
middlings he is. Lying up in the hotel Pisser was telling me once a month
with headache like a totty with her courses. (*U* 12.1644–60)

Bloom represents the Other, to the Citizen and his cronies, not just
because he is Jewish but because he strikes them as unmanly and
even feminine. They find his sexuality, like his nationality, ambiguous. This perception links them with other European nationalists,
who believed that Jewish men "exhibit[ed] female traits" and "were
endowed with excessive sexuality, with a so-called female sensuous-
ness that transformed love into lust."[64] Although other groups could
be tarred with the same brush – "for many Germans, the French
lacked manliness"[65] – the Jews, as a "mixed middling," posed a
special threat to nationalists who insisted on a unitary concept of
identity within their own land.

    In Nighttown we see Bloom accused of or performing acts of lust
that reflect nationalist fantasies. Gertie MacDowell, who earlier, on
the strand, joined him in a voyeuristic masturbation *à deux*, "*shows
coyly her bloodied clout*" and says: "You did that. I hate you." A bawd
spits out a sexual-racial insult: "Jewman's melt!" (*U* 15.373–76,
534). After the Watch stops him, it becomes plain that he is under
suspicion of sexual misconduct when a card printed with the name
"Henry Flower" – his alias in his epistolary affair with Martha
Clifford – falls out of his hat. Martha herself appears, accusing him
of breach of promise. A trial ensues, and the Blooms' ex-servant,
Mary Driscoll, charges him with sexual harassment but at the same
time puts down his manhood: "(*Scornfully*) I had more respect for the
scouringbrush, so I had" (*U* 15.892). This double image of Bloom,
lustful yet unmanly, is augmented by the chief witnesses for the
prosecution, a set of aggressively pure-minded Anglo-Irish ladies
who allege that he has mailed them improper suggestions. When

they threaten to chastise him bodily, he *"quails"* and *"pants"* (*U* 15.1085) in a caricature of masochistic female sexual excitement.

Bloom's trial ends with the finding of his guilt. Described as having "no fixed abode" – a phrase suggesting his lack of a fixed national or sexual identity – he is found guilty both of being a "cuckold" and of engaging in the "white slave traffic" (*U* 15.1159, 1167). Again we see the impugning of Bloom's virility, coupled with the "racist commonplace that Jews were ... given to corrupting Christian girls."[66] Finally Bloom is denounced by the American evangelist, Alexander J. Dowie, as a "disgrace to christian men" and a "fiendish libertine." The Mob cries: "Lynch him! Roast him! He's as bad as Parnell was" (*U* 15.1754, 1762). Joyce alludes here not only to Parnell's sexual misconduct, which required that he be cast out of Ireland's nationalist movement, but to the lynching in Dowie's homeland which the pub loungers read about in a newspaper: *"Black Beast Burned in Omaha, Ga."* (*U* 12.1324). The sexual motivation behind lynchings of black men was essentially the same as that behind the imagined burning of Bloom; his accusers call him a "kaffir," a "beast" (twice), a "mormon," and an "Anarchist" (*U* 12.1552; 15.845, 1717, 1156), linking him both with blacks and with groups whose sexual practices (polygamy and free love) threaten the mores of the dominant majority. In describing the new Bloomusalem, Bloom himself, temporarily triumphant over the "patriotism of barspongers," says what he stands for: "Union of all, jew, moslem and gentile" and "Mixed races and mixed marriage" (*U* 15.1686–99). This miscegenist vision leads to condemnations by Father Farley, a Catholic priest, and Dowie. After more revelations of his sexual sins and abnormality, he is prepared for death. His execution reflects the dark underside of the "kind of nationalism which for so many [British] boys meant public service at home or in the Empire, [but which] in the world of schoolboy adventure [stories] meant torturing a 'dago' bartender ... or hanging a Jewish jewel thief because he had tried to paw a British girl."[67] In Bloom's case, the outraged parties are international but mainly Irish Catholic, and it is the Citizen who says "Thank heaven!" (*U* 15.1933) once the Dublin Fire Brigade has set the offender alight.

The fantasia of "Circe" does not always reflect Bloom's thoughts or actions, but the central theme of his sexual guilt suggests the way many outsiders "[seem] to accept the stereotype of themselves." Similarly, his attempts to defend himself suggest the way victims of discrimination "[seek] to transcend it by integrating themselves into the existing order."[68] When first accosted by the Watch, for instance, he tries to placate the constables by adopting an air of hearty masculinity: "Lady in the case. Love entanglement. (*he shoulders the second watch gently*) Dash it all. It's a way we gallants have in the navy. Uniform that does it." In the eyes of European nationalists he thus would have been guilty of attempting to hide his Jewish origins by associating himself with the military, the epitome of nationalist manhood. This cover is stripped away when a mysterious being declares: "The Castle is looking for him. He was drummed out of the army" (*U* 15.742–50). Joyce may not have been aware of Drumont's campaign during the 1890s to purge the French army of Jewish officers, but he did know about the most famous Jew to be drummed out of that army, Captain Dreyfus. There is another allusion to the affair when Bloom responds to Martha Clifford's reproaches. He claims, "Mistaken identity ... I am wrongfully accused," and again tries to wrap himself in the mantle of military-nationalist virtue, mentioning his father-in-law, "a most distinguished commander ... Majorgeneral Brian Tweedy," and claiming to have served in the Boer War: "I'm as staunch a Britisher as you are, sir. I fought with the colors for king and country" (*U* 15.760–95). Later he recollects taking part in a Tennysonian cavalry charge and "sabr[ing] the Saracen gunners to a man" (*U* 15.1525–30). (A poster from the days of Zola's trial "shows Drumont ... in shining armor, driving the latter-day Jewish Saracens from the banks and the Bourse.")[69] Yet his efforts to embody middle-class nationalist manhood always fail, just as the assimilative efforts of European Jews like Dreyfus tended to fail. He gives himself away or is unveiled by accusers; acting out the latter's fantasies, he becomes more Jewish or more radical or more unmasculine than he really is. When this happens, though, the characteristic usually exaggerated is his heterodox sexuality, as if this above all threatens society and marks him as the Other.

Twice in "Circe" Bloom's shaky masculine identity is reversed. One sex change takes place at the hands of Bella Cohen, a burly madam who feminizes him in a fantasy of submission and domination. Bella becomes Bello, a masculine being who places a heel on Bloom's neck, squeezes his testicles, and commands: "Henceforth you are unmanned ... Now for your punishment frock. You will shed your male garments ... and don the shot silk" (*U* 15.2966–67).

Bloom is dressed in frilly clothes and trained to be a sexual object. Protesting but enjoying, (s)he suffers escalating abuse by Bello that culminates in physical violation.

The role reversals in this sadomasochistic *pas de deux* reflect the bipolar sexual norms of European society, norms which solidified at the same time as national and middle-class stereotypes.[70] Bloom and Bella take on androgynous traits, but their androgyny lacks the positive features that the concept once carried. George Mosse observes:

The fate of the image of the hermaphrodite or androgyne ... during the nineteenth century is the most startling illustration of the importance of fixed and unchanging sex roles as part of the fabric of society and of the nation. In the first half century, the androgyne was still being praised as a public symbol of human unity. But by the end of the century the image, with its confusion of sex roles, had turned into a monster.

The *fin-de-siècle* androgyne – "perceived as a monster of sexual and moral ambiguity" and "often identified with other 'outsiders'"[71] – contributes to the characterization of both Bloom and Bella (whose surname suggests that she, too, is Jewish). Androgyny of this sort involves the exaggeration of traits supposedly typical of the opposite sex; masculine aggressiveness becomes sadism in Bello, while feminine passivity becomes masochism in Bloom. Like creatures of carnival, they violate social norms, yet they also reflect the binary oppositions built into their society's straitened idea of normality. These oppositions typify notions of nationality as well, as I have been arguing. No insider exists without an outsider, no "broad-shouldered deepchested stronglimbed ... sinewyarmed hero" without a "fellow that's neither fish nor flesh" (*U* 12.152–55, 1055–56).[72]

Bloom's other sexual transformation occurs during his trial after sex specialists testify on his behalf. Dr. Mulligan pronounces him to be "bisexually abnormal"; then Dr. Dixon describes him as "a finished example of the new womanly man," and announces that "He is about to have a baby." Bloom's wish – "O, I so want to be a mother" (*U* 15.1775–1817) – promptly comes true, and he gives birth to eight children. This fantasy reflects a different androgyny from that which we see in the scenes with Bella-Bello, and appears related to Bloom's genuine fellow feeling for women. He feels compassion for Mina Purefoy when he hears of her prolonged confinement: "Sss. Dth, dth, dth! Three days imagine groaning on a

bed with ... her belly swollen out ... Phew! Dreadful simply!"
(*U* 8.373–75). Afterwards he repeatedly thinks about her and child-
birth, finally going to inquire at the lying-in hospital, "for he felt
with wonder women's woe in the travail that they have of motherhood" (*U* 14.119–20). He is attuned to other aspects of the female
reproductive cycle. Often he puts himself in what he imagines to be
the woman's position, both physically – "Fill me. I'm warm, dark,
open" – and emotionally, as when he thinks of the jocular caretaker
at Glasnevin Cemetery: "Fancy being his wife" (*U* 11.974; 6.746).
Even Molly, recalling what first attracted her to him, testifies to his
empathy: "I saw he understood or felt what a woman is"
(*U* 18.1578–79). If Beauvoir is right in identifying the root problem
of gender relations as man's inability to see woman as an independent self – "He is the Subject, he is the Absolute – she is the Other"[73]
– then Bloom's imaginative efforts to take part in womanhood would
seem to be a step toward resolving the problem. Bloom's ability to
empathize with women, his sensitivity toward the feelings of others,
his distaste for force – all these traits constitute a healthy androgyny,
unlike the exchange of sadomasochistic sexual stereotypes enacted
between him and Bello. In comparison, the supermasculinity of
Blazes Boylan, the Citizen, and Private Carr reflects a pathological
polarization of the sexes. Gerty MacDowell, the barmaids at the
Ormond Hotel, and the whores of Nighttown represent the opposite
extreme, a superfemininity determined outwardly by legal and
economic injustice and inwardly by ideas internalized from the
Church, the schools, popular magazines, advertising, and so on.
Both extremes make for an unhealthy society, but the overriding
danger of the supermasculine ideal is its link to aggression and to
war. We see this link in Boylan, the "conquering hero" (*U* 11.340),
whose sexual aggressiveness carries militaristic overtones. And we
see it in the all-male setting of the Burton restaurant, which Bloom
surveys squeamishly: "Men, men, men ... Every fellow for his own,
tooth and nail ... Eat or be eaten. Kill!" (*U* 8.653–703).

The all-male context *par excellence* is the military, which many
British officers, J. B. Priestley recollects, "hailed with relief [as] a
wholly masculine way of life uncomplicated by Woman."[74] I take
this quotation from Fussell's discussion of war and sexuality, in
particular "homoeroticism," a term he uses "to imply a sublimated
... form of temporary homosexuality."[75] Homosexuality of this kind
(related to Joycean "heroticism") was by no means alien to martial

virtue, for the lover of his fellow soldiers could still be "blood-thirsty and forever thinking how to kill the enemy,"[76] as a British officers' manual described the ideal platoon commander. Sassoon's fighting spirit won him the nickname "Mad Jack." For Henry de Montherlant "the war exemplified the possibility of leading a truly masculine way of life with its heroism and beauty of [the male] body."[77]

What Montherlant, Sassoon, and Owen had in common with heterosexual comrades was their upbringing in milieus marked by extreme oppositions between male and female, among other polarities, and their participation in an enterprise – the Great War – that encouraged the fullest expressions of both masculine bonding and masculine belligerence. If woman was intrinsically different, so was the "enemy" whom they had to destroy. The aggression toward the Other released in sexual intercourse could be released in combat. As Fussell reminds us, the "language of military attack – *assault, impact, thrust, penetration* – has always overlapped with that of sexual importunity."[78] The German soldier and writer, Ernst Jünger,

used explicit sexual vocabulary to describe battle. The feeling of ecstasy as the bayonet sank into the white flesh of a French or English soldier was likened to an orgasm. When the battle was over, the sober new storm trooper left behind the "disheveled bed of the trenches" ... Jünger's storm trooper can satisfy his sexual needs in much the same manner against the enemy in battle or against women when the battle is done.[79]

This transformation of enemy soldiers and women into the Other requires the denial, however, of a fundamental kinship. For the enemy is a fellow male actuated by similar "masculine" values of patriotism, aggressiveness, and fortitude, while soldiers' tenderness and caring for each other and fear are "feminine" values shared with women.

The Great War, then, reflected a split self. The split did not originate in the war but in civilian life. As an English officer commented, "the Army with its male relationships was simply an extension of my public school."[80] This divided mentality, which treats woman as the Other from both the heterosexual and homoerotic male point of view, characterized Ireland perhaps even more than England or France or Germany. What Joyce seems to offer in *Ulysses* in the person of Bloom is an alternative to the split male self which made possible that "apocalypse of masculinism,"[81] the Great War. More than Stephen, who prides himself on his own tool of masculine aggression – the "cold steel pen" (*U* 1.153) – Bloom bridges the gap between male and female. As the "new womanly man" (*U* 15.1798-99), as Jew and non-Jew, as Irishman and outsider, he transcends the narrow oppositions of middle-class nationalism.

THE CONTENT OF THE FORM

Joyce, as he was walking with Budgen down the Universitätstrasse, said of *Ulysses*: "I want ... to give a picture of Dublin so complete that if the city one day suddenly disappeared from the earth it could be reconstructed out of my book."[82] His pre-1914 self probably never imagined that dull, solid, colonial Dublin was in danger of vanishing. But after the Easter Rising, the Russian Revolution, and the continuing slaughter of the Great War, many things once thought permanent were receding into memory or had taken on an air of mortality. As Dick Diver mourns while touring the battlefields of the Somme, "All my beautiful lovely safe world blew itself up here."[83]

The Great War struck contemporaries as being unprecedented, yet was prefigured and prepared by the world which it destroyed. Symbolist poets and anarchist bomb-throwers were dreaming about apocalypse before the turn of the century. Although British power and self-confidence seemed at their apogee on 22 June 1897, when a magnificent parade of native soldiers from all corners of the empire marched through London to celebrate the queen's diamond jubilee, even the arch-imperialist Kipling saw "a certain optimism ... that scared me."[84] His monitory poem, "Recessional," with its vision of a vanished empire "one with Nineveh and Tyre," appeared in *The Times* the next morning. The festivities belied a growing awareness of challenges to British hegemony from the United States, Japan, France, and above all Germany. A sense of danger led many ordinary people to support the international peace conference proposed by Czar Nicholas II. In *A Portrait* MacCann (modeled after Skeffington) recruits for the peace movement, lecturing on "the Csar's rescript [and] general disarmament" (*P* 196). With fanfare, the first Hague Peace Conference commenced in May 1899 against the backdrop of the Dreyfus affair and recent wars between Spain and the United States, Turkey and Greece, and China and Japan; it achieved little more than a face-saving agreement to set up a powerless tribunal to arbitrate disputes. Three months after the conference British troops embarked for South Africa. From 1900 to 1914 the march toward a general war quickened. European and American soldiers put down the Boxer Rebellion. In 1904 Russia ("The Russians, they'd only be an eight o'clock breakfast for the Japanese" [*U* 4.116–17]) entered into a short, losing war with Japan. The next year Germany precipitated a crisis by challenging French ambitions in Morocco. In 1908 Austria-Hungary annexed Bosnia and Herzegovina from the Ottoman Empire. France's occupation of Fez sparked the second Morocco crisis in 1911, while Italy seized a sphere of influence in Libya. In 1912 the Balkan peoples initiated two wars against Turkey. And in Ireland the Curragh mutiny and the Larne gun-running seemed to cast over the British Empire, during the summer of 1914, a more troubling shadow than anything that might happen in the faraway Balkans.

But other forces besides national and imperial rivalries contributed to what the narrator of "Ithaca" calls "the velocity of modern life" (*U* 17.1773). Europeans first connected this velocity with technology when railroads started to become a regular means of transport in the mid-nineteenth century; by the end of the century technological change, and resultant social change, had become a feature of everyday urban life. In response, in 1900, Henry Adams formulated his "Law of Acceleration in History." Driving down the Champs Elysées, he wrote, he always expected an accident; standing near an official, he expected a bomb to be thrown. "So long as the rate of progress held good, these bombs would double in force and number every ten years . . . Power leaped from every atom . . . Man could no longer hold it off. Forces grasped his wrists and flung him about as though he had hold of a live wire or a run-away automobile."[85]

Adams sensed the alliance between civilian and military technology in speeding the pace of life and making the present historical moment ever more evanescent. At the International Exposition of 1900 in Paris, this interrelationship could be seen in microcosm. Visitors to the Civil Engineering Palace could admire, three years before the Wright brothers' flight, a model airplane with a fifty-foot wingspan. Inside the Optical Palace the curious could look at the moon through the world's most powerful telescope. Other exhibits included gigantic steam hammers, a crane that could hoist forty-five tons, and models of steamships. A double moving sidewalk circled the grounds. But the two biggest single exhibits were Schneider-

Creusot's monstrous cannon, over fifteen meters long, and Vickers-Maxim's display of machine guns. In a "conspicuously large" Palace on the Seine, tourists could also view "the latest explosives, torpedoes ... armored trains, pontoon bridges, motor cars, airplanes and wireless equipment."[86]

Joyce had an opportunity in April 1903 to see first-hand the ties between speed, capitalist technology, and international competition when he interviewed the French racing-car driver, Henri Fournier, for *The Irish Times*. The focus of the interview was the same invention, the automobile, which Adams chose as the embodiment of his law of historical acceleration. Joyce and Fournier talked at Paris-Automobile, a motor-car company managed by Fournier, amidst the noise of a thriving modern business: "The voices of workmen, the voices of buyers talking in half-a-dozen languages, the ringing of telephone bells, the horns sounded by the 'chauffeurs' as the cars come in and go out" (*CW* 106–07). Plainly uneasy in this brave new world, the young interviewer posed his questions on speed and horsepower tentatively; the racer-businessman fielded them crisply. Fournier was scheduled to compete in the second Gordon Bennett Cup race, hosted by Ireland that July, which forms the background of "After the Race." Featuring German, French, English, and American drivers in cars from their respective countries, the race mirrored political rivalries, especially given the military and economic implications of automotive technology. In only a dozen years this technology would produce tanks and armored cars and trucks (the last two would be used in the Anglo-Irish as well as the Great War). *The Irish Times* emphasized the race's aspect as a competition among the leading industrial powers. Its two articles on the race are flanked by more serious discussions of international rivalry – for example, the alarming moves of the German warship *Panther* and the need for a British "Army big enough 'to fight the Russians, or the Germans, or the French.'"[87]

On 16 June 1904, in the European backwater of Dublin, Stephen Dedalus can speak of how "rare ... a motorcar is now." Only one auto actually appears in *Ulysses*; through the eyes of Tom Kernan we see "[t]he windscreen of that motorcar in the sun there. Just a flash like that" (*U* 9.441; 10.759). The machine may or may not be moving, but in any event generates an image of rapid movement, "a flash." A modern technology more central to the city is its electric tram system. The newspaper episode begins:

IN THE HEART OF THE HIBERNIAN
METROPOLIS

Before Nelson's pillar trams slowed, shunted, changed trolley, started for Blackrock, Kingstown and Dalkey, Clonskea ... The hoarse Dublin United Tramway Company's timekeeper bawled them off:
—Rathgar and Terenure!
—Come on, Sandymount Green!
Right and left parallel clanging ringing a doubledecker and a singledeck moved from their railheads, swerved to the down line, glided parallel.
—Start, Palmerston Park! (*U* 7.1–13)

The purpose of the "timekeeper," of course, is not to hold or capture time but to keep his machines moving in conjunction with time. Later that morning the tramcars briefly stand "still, becalmed in short circuit," while the older technology of hackney cars, cabs, mailvans, and other horse-powered vehicles continues to rattle "rapidly" (*U* 7.1047, 1049) through the streets. Such a mixture of technologies – for instance, horse-drawn wagons and tanks – marked the Great War as well, and it was when rebels in the G.P.O. fired on a British cavalry troop that the Easter Rising began.

For Henry Adams the symbol of the new machine technology, propelling society at an ever faster pace, was the Dynamo. In "Wandering Rocks" Stephen encounters the dynamos that power the tramway. Their hum "urge[s him] to be on. Beingless beings. Stop! Throb always without you and the throb always within. Your heart you sing of. I between them. Where? Between two roaring worlds" (*U* 10.822–24). He associates his heart with the power-house: the new technology has invaded his sense of his own body. Though he imagines smashing these mechanistic forces – "Shatter them, one and both. But stun myself too in the blow" – he recognizes that the outcome would be stasis. Frightened, he retracts his rebellious impulse, praising what he cannot destroy: "Yes. Quite true. Very large and wonderful and keeps famous time" (*U* 10.828). Both he and his society have internalized the time-sense of the Dynamo, and depend on it to keep going. The power failure that stalls the trams earlier in the day, though momentary, foreshadows the menacing, intolerable stoppages of the future – not only Larkin's 1913 strike against the Dublin United Tramway Company, but the stasis of trench warfare on the Western Front, where the wonderful machines unveiled or presaged at the Paris Exposition failed to achieve anything other than killing thousands of men each day. If the speed of modern life was frightening, the prospect of its forward rush being halted was terrifying.

✳

At the National Library Stephen tells himself: "Hold to the now, the here, through which all future plunges to the past" (U 9.89). The theme of devouring time was ancient even when Shakespeare, the subject of Stephen's disquisition at the library, addressed it. But what worries Stephen is the acceleration of time in his own historical moment. It concerns him especially as an artist, and it concerned his creator, too. One of Joyce's motives in writing Ulysses was a desire to preserve some part of himself and the world of his youth, yet he was working in a period of wars and revolutions which pushed the Dublin of 1904 further and further into a naïve, doomed past. How could he capture the felt present of that past, chronologically recent but fast receding, without hopelessly dating his novel?

One way of looking at Joyce's technical problem is in terms of anachronism. As Thomas Greene says, "all products come into being bearing the marks of their historical moment and then, if they last, are regarded as alien during a later moment because of these marks." He contrasts such "pathetic" or "tragic" anachronism with "creative" anachronism, which allows a text to deal with its own datedness – with "the pathos of its potential future estrangement" – through "a deliberate dramatization of historical passage, bringing a concrete present into relation with a specific past and playing with the distance between them."[88] Greene is speaking of a text that acknowledges its historicity by looking backward from its dramatized present to the past. In Ulysses Joyce does this constantly: he does so with regard to events, as when Kernan looks at a motor-car and then at the corner where "Emmet was hanged, drawn and quartered" (U 10.764), and with regard to language, as when Stephen ponders linguistic change in "Proteus" and when a series of styles in "Oxen of the Sun" parodies the development of English. But Joyce also reverses the process by embedding in his text the future events of 1914–22. The ironies that arise from this tactic help the text transcend its ostensible limited perspective of 1904 and earlier; they allow it to enter into dialogue with what would be otherwise the "estranging future"[89] of the Great War, the Easter Rising, and related upheavals.

Joyce's impulse to preserve expresses itself in other ways besides his forward and backward glances in time. The sheer bulk of Ulysses and its accretion of painstakingly verified naturalistic detail contribute to the reader's sense that 16 June 1904 has indeed been recreated. The famous Odyssean framework also serves Joyce's recreative purpose, at least insofar as it provides what Eliot hailed as a way of giving shape and significance to the anarchy of contemporary history. But Joyce's somewhat mechanical mythicizing and naturalism do not save *Ulysses* from pathetic anachronism. Rather, it is the novel's form which militates against anachronism and makes it appear fresh, new, and innovative even today.

Hugh Kenner argues that Joyce's formal experimentation does not really get underway until the "Sirens" episode. If the novel had ended with "Wandering Rocks," we "should have ... a moderately orthodox novel of under 100,000 words ... The interior monologue ... would be its striking technical feature: that and a certain penchant for abrupt scene-shifting."[90] Kenner knows better than this, and includes the qualification, "by contrast with the book we know." Except from the perspective of a literary professional, *Ulysses* is a challenging novel from the start, and only becomes more so as it unfolds; the change after "Wandering Rocks" is more of degree than kind. Ask any educated person who has not studied modernism in a graduate seminar for an opinion on reading *Ulysses*, and you will likely be told that from "Proteus" on it is a difficult, disorienting experience.

The *avant-garde* form of Joyce's novel seems not to go with his subject-matter. There was nothing *avant garde* about the Dublin of 1904 except its tram system; it was a border outpost of European culture. The center of that culture was Paris, a city pulsing with novelty – with new forms of art and new forms of technology. Drawn by the same magnet as Moore and Synge, the young Joyce traveled to Paris as soon as possible. The landmark he would have seen most often during his stay there – its gossamer iron framework poked into the sky above the rooftops – was the Eiffel Tower. Completed in 1889 for the World's Fair, it was a symbol of the new and a triumph of the engineer, Gustave Eiffel, over the stodginess of Beaux-Arts architecture. Artists and enthusiasts of the *avant garde*, such as Apollinaire, praised the tower; yet it also had a mass audience:

Millions of people, not the thousands who went to the salons and galleries to look at works of art, were touched by the feeling of a new age that the Eiffel Tower made concrete. It was the herald of a millenium ... And in its height, its structural daring, its then-radical use of industrial materials for the commemorative purposes of the State, it summed up what the ruling classes of Europe conceived the promise of technology to be: Faust's contract, the promise of unlimited power over the world and its wealth.[91]

By the turn of the century the motor-car had become the avatar of the future – a future which Joyce encountered in 1903 during his thought-provoking visit to Paris-Automobile. The motor-car symbolized the *avant garde* not just because of its wondrous technology but because of the different view it created of the world. A similar defamiliarizing effect had been provided for over a decade by the viewing platform (and photos taken from it) atop the Eiffel Tower. "The sight of *Paris vu d'en haut*," Robert Hughes comments, "was as significant in 1889 as the famous NASA photograph of the earth from the moon ... would be eighty years later."[92] The new experience offered by the motor-car was speed. The continuous unfolding of the world which was the common experience of turn-of-the-century pedestrians and passengers in horse-drawn vehicles became, in a speeding motor-car (more so than in a track-bound train) a series of disjunctive images. Although few people had a chance to ride in motor-cars and fewer still owned them, they elicited interest everywhere – witness the campaign to bring the Bennett Cup race to Ireland – and carried a universal symbolic valence: technology, power, rapid movement, the new.

The automobile rode the crest of the *avant-garde* wave for a while. In 1909 Louis Blériot flew the English Channel and another icon took precedence. In triumph, his little wooden machine was carried through the streets of Paris and housed in a deconsecrated church. But the motor-car and the airplane were only two among many inventions – the box camera, the cinematograph, the X-ray, the gramophone disc – that contributed to the accelerating tide of change which swept across Paris and other centers of the leading industrial countries during the three decades prior to World War I. A wave of new ideas in the hard and social sciences also washed over the intellectual elites of Europe. The discoveries of Planck, Einstein, and other scientists demolished the old Newtonian universe and the mechanics theory that had dominated the second half of the nineteenth century. Freud led the way in a shocking re-evaluation of the human interior universe. William James wrote about the rule of chance; Bergson about the importance of becoming rather than being; Croce about the plasticity of the historical past. In a multitude of ways, the European world whose capital was Paris looked different almost from year to year.

One question which this phenomenon of constant technological and social transformation posed for the *avant garde* of art was how to compete. With the triumph of the machine, and with everyday middle-class life in the cities changing so swiftly, how could new art avoid taking on the marks of the past almost as soon as it was produced?

This problem – that of escaping pathetic anachronism – was tackled by many artists besides Joyce. One such artist was Wagner (whose works Joyce knew well). In his day, before the middle classes belatedly embraced his music, the German composer had been a grand revolutionary. His revolution lay in his creation of a "total art" – poetry, music, drama. Such art could deliver an overwhelming, synesthetic experience more than equal to whatever strange new sensations were filling everyday life, even in Kaiser Wilhelm's Germany, the industrial wonderland of the later nineteenth century.

Wagner represented an *avant garde* of the past, but his art influenced the revolutionary artists who became his successors after the turn of the century.[93] Several different currents flowed through the works and proclamations of the new modernist *avant garde*. There remained Wagner's heritage of the "search for the *Gesamtkunstwerk* – for the holy grail that is the total art form."[94] This heritage was reflected in the première of *L'Après-midi d'un faune* (1912), whose credits might have read: poem, Mallarmé; music, Debussy; choreography and dancing, Nijinsky; sets and costumes, Bakst. Another current was an odd, offensive realism, utterly different from the nineteenth-century kind, which shared the same goal as surrealism and abstraction. This goal was to render the human experience of the world, daily growing stranger, as vividly as possible, using forms and objects formerly unheard-of in art. Richard Strauss (building on Wagnerian opera, which called for a live horse to accompany Brunhilde on stage) used a wind machine in *Don Quixote* to suggest the turning sails of windmills. He accompanied such ultra-realism with musical innovations that to the conventional ear were full of discords and dissonances – for example, muted brasses to suggest the bleating of sheep and "battle music" to depict Don Quixote's mental confusion. The critics attacked, and after the public rejected *Elektra* (1911), Strauss retreated to more conventional grand opera.

Just as Strauss defected from the *avant garde*, certain painters – the Cubists – were beginning to expand and defamiliarize what Stephen Dedalus calls the "modality of the visible" (*U* 3.1). The credo of the Cubists preceded them; Gauguin's friend, Maurice Denis, stated it in 1890: "A picture – before being a warhorse, a nude woman, or some sort of anecdote – is essentially a surface covered with colours arranged in a certain order."[95] Going a step further, Braque began mixing "non-art" materials – sand, sawdust, iron filings – with his paint. And Picasso incorporated into a painting, "Still Life with Chair Caning" (1912), a recognizable slice of everyday life, a fragment of oilcloth designed to cover a café table. Again, art was becoming at once more "realistic" and yet further removed from conventional representations of the "real" world. Strauss's wind machine and Picasso's factory-made oilcloth not only acknowledged the technology that was transforming everyday life, but subsumed it in works of art that competed with such inventions as the gramophone, the X-ray, or the cinematograph in their invitations to listen to or look at the world differently.

Such works of art, if not too radical, sometimes aroused excitement, amazement, enthusiasm. In 1909 the Ballets russes de Diaghilev took Paris by storm, generating what Proust called a "fever" which he compared to that of the Dreyfus affair. But some works shook people up, set their teeth on edge, infuriated them. This happened on 29 May 1913, the opening night of *Le Sacre du printemps*. Stravinsky's theme was provocative. He tried to evoke the primeval bursting forth of the Russian spring through a series of pagan rites culminating in the mindless, jerky dance, suggesting both a primitive human being and a machine, of a sacrificial maiden. The ballet celebrated renewal, sexual fertility, energy; civilization, reason, morality went by the board. But what elicited howls and hisses from the audience was the form of the ballet – its dissonant, unornamented, violently loud music and especially the jumping and the knock-kneed contortions of Nijinsky's choreography. Here the conflict between middle-class society and artists who saw themselves as pioneers of the spirit, as liberators whose art superseded social and moral codes, exploded into controversy. The creators of *Le Sacre* didn't have to fear anachronism. Rather, they had carried their passion for the new, the jarring, and the provocative too far, and had moved forward at a quicker pace than their audience could handle.

The *avant garde* had to be ahead of its time so as to avoid being made anachronistic by the future which was plunging (as Stephen puts it) ever faster into the past. The past, as the Futurist Marinetti declared in 1913, was "necessarily inferior to the future." The modern artist's task was to "deny the obsessing splendour of the dead centuries, and [to] cooperate with the victorious Mechanics that hold the world firm in its web of speed."[96] Although *The Rite of Spring* may seem far removed from the world of the internal combustion engine that obsessed the Futurists, its radically new techniques – its explosive sounds and jolting movements and raw power – suggest artists who were at least competing, if not cooperating, with the "victorious Mechanics."

❋

In August 1914 the Great War manifested itself as that future toward which Europe, propelled by national rivalries and technological innovation, had been rushing. Some artists managed to draw inspiration from the war and its transformations. After all, the First Futurist Manifesto (1909) had announced: "We will glorify war – the world's only hygiene." In 1917 Marinetti sketched a one-act ballet in which a girl performed "The Dance of the Machine-Gun." An awareness of the war's sterile sexuality animated the "mechano-sexual images" of Marcel Duchamp and other painters. Dada was born in Joyce's Zurich in 1916 as a response, wrote the Dadaist Jean Arp, to "the slaughterhouses of the world war . . . We searched for an elementary art that would . . . save mankind from the furious madness of these times."[97]

Even before the war Joyce had given up making political pronouncements. Yet, only a decade removed from the young author who had hoped to reform the Irish people by letting them see themselves in the looking-glass of his stories, he no doubt still believed, together with the Dadaists and many other artists,

in the power of art to "save mankind" from political abominations; the central myth of the traditional *avant-garde*, that by changing the order of language, art could reform the order of experience and so alter the conditions of social life, had not yet collapsed.[98]

Joyce shared little else with the Futurists and the Dadaists, but, like them, he did respond through his art to the acceleration of modern life and to its violent crack-up in World War I. Although his innovations as a writer began with *Dubliners*, even *A Portrait* offered no hint of the experiments to come in *Ulysses*. It was as if the war inspired a delayed reaction, a passion for the new arising out of the destruction of the old. As European painters, composers, choreographers, and other artists of the *avant garde* had been doing before the war, Joyce now began aggressively innovating, creating a novel whose form marked a radical break with tradition.

Let me delve briefly into the "content" of a few of Joyce's innovations. As Kenner says, the salient technique of the early chapters is the interior monologue. This technique evokes the flux of an individual's mental life. Among other things, it represents a response to the change in the concept of human consciousness brought about with stunning speed (the first psychoanalytical congress took place in 1908) by Freud and his allies. The mind no longer seemed to be a passive mirror of the world, or a stable container of discrete ideas, memories, and impressions; rather, it had become a dynamic reflector / shaper of reality whose constant movement and flux could be organized, at best, in the form of recurrent themes. Dynamism was a key feature of Freud's psychology, and its transformation of the individual's inner world matched in some respects the transformation of the outer world by scientific discoveries and technology. Though the mind's power as a transforming agent had been recognized in the past (for instance, by the Romantics), now it had a new scientific basis.

Joyce, who was familiar with Freudian thought, must have been struck by the creative power it attributed to even the most ordinary mind. We see the mind's ability to transform the conventional everyday world throughout *Ulysses*. Stephen imagines two women on the strand to be midwives lugging in their bag a "misbirth with trailing navel cord," then combines biological and technological forms of connection in picturing the cord as a link to Eve, the first mother, and a telephone cable to Eden: "Hello! Kinch here. Put me on to Edenville. Aleph, alpha: nought, nought, one" (*U* 3.39–40). An image of the Sacred Heart at Glasnevin Cemetery prompts Bloom to think of a more technologically advanced way to remember the dead: "Have a gramophone in every grave or keep it in the house. After dinner on a Sunday. Put on poor old greatgrandfather" (*U* 6.963–64). The most radical transformations occur in "Circe." Here the technique is "Hallucination,"[99] and an unsettling question arises: *who* is having the hallucinations? Often the relationship between the episode's hallucinations, such as the Bloom-Bello interlude, and any immediate reality or any character's actual thoughts seems vague or nonexistent. To rephrase the question: under the influence of what mind do "Circe's" magical transformations take place?

David Hayman suggested an answer in 1970 when he formulated the concept of the "Arranger," an arranging consciousness – not a narrator or an implied author – responsible for many of the most striking (and disconcerting) formal aspects of *Ulysses*. He writes of a passage in "Telemachus" (*U* 1.512–19), where we cannot separate Stephen's mental reality from Mulligan's actions and words:

> We have a sense that the two individuals are momentarily and magically joined by the narrator whose procedures are more comprehensible on the thematic and analogical levels than on the mimetic. In this way he has foreshadowed the more emphatic miracle by which Bloom and Stephen are joined in Circe's looking-glass ... The narrator is obliging us to accept another order of reality ... He is also asserting his independence ... By the book's second half he will have become ... a larger version of his characters with a larger field of vision and many more perceptions to control.[100]

It is the Arranger, then, who generates the hallucinations in "Circe," the asides in "Cyclops," the fugue structure of "Sirens," and so forth. But where does the Arranger come from?

Above I pointed out the often-remarked link between Joyce's innovation of the interior monologue and the development of psychoanalysis. The Arranger, however, represents a collective – not an individual – consciousness. Moreover, it manifests itself in a variety of forms besides interior monologue, though its concerns seem always to relate to the mechanics of *Ulysses* – the novel's techniques of representation and the ordering of its material. Historical influences other than psychoanalysis seem to lie behind the Arranger.

Take the Arranger's focus on the material (that is, language) of *Ulysses*. If novelists traditionally have seen their task as that of using language to represent human experience, then something odd is happening as early as the first page. Buck Mulligan whistles, "his even white teeth glistening here and there with gold points. Chrysostomos" (*U* 1.25–26). Looking up this last word in Thornton's *Allusions*, the reader learns that "Chrysostomos, 'golden-mouthed,' is a common epithet for orators."[101] We can ascribe this odd addition to a hitherto realistic mix of description and dialogue to Stephen's obscure learning, perhaps, which provides him with a word that evokes both Mulligan's oratory and his gold-filled white teeth. In that case the term rings ironically. Such playful linguistic creativity also dominates the "Proteus" chapter yet remains, however loosely and implicitly, attributable to Stephen's perceiving mind. But in the newspaper episode, language, riddled with intrusive rhetorical devices, starts to become autonomous. It is strikingly autonomous in the overture to "Sirens," even though it returns to the task of representation in the rest of the chapter. Finally, in "Oxen of the Sun," language has become the hero: the progression of parodic styles from Anglo-Saxon to the slangy commercial-religious lingo of an American evangelist, imitating the growth of an embryo, overshadows the representation of any felt human reality.

Why has the Arranger become so focused on language, on signifiers in themselves as opposed to what they represent? Let's go back to 1890, when the painter Denis defined a picture as being "essentially a surface covered with colours and arranged in a certain order." Apply this definition to the novel and you get the working principle of Joyce's Arranger: a written narrative, before being a story about people or events, is a series of pages covered with words and arranged in a certain order: "Signs on a white field" (*U* 3.415), as Stephen thinks. In "Proteus" Stephen meditates not on what art imitates, but on what it consists of physically and how it is ordered. The "modality of the visible" is that in which objects, as in paintings and sculpture, exist "*Nebeneinander*" or next to one another; the "modality of the audible" is that in which sounds, such as those of music and spoken poetry, exist "*Nacheinander*" (*U* 3.1–15) or after one another. Stephen's interests are both esthetic and scientific, and he echoes Lessing and Aristotle. But startling investigations into the substance and order of art and nature were going on in Joyce's own era, and it is these which underlie both the Arranger's and Stephen's concerns with language.

I have mentioned, besides the innovations of artists, the discoveries of Planck and Einstein. But the social sciences also were transformed during this era, and one, linguistics, has special reference to the Arranger's obsession with language. The linguist Fernand de Saussure died in 1913, little known outside his field; yet within three years "his name became a household word in all interested circles,"[102] which presumably would have included Joyce, living in Saussure's native Switzerland from 1915 to late 1919. Saussure, in redefining linguistics as the study of how conventional systems generate meanings, made three seminal distinctions:

1. The distinction between language (*langue*) as an abstract, suprapersonal system and language (*parole*) as the concrete, personal manifestations of language in speech or writing.
2. The distinction between studying language diachronically and synchronically – i.e, as a system that has developed through time and as a system existing at a particular moment in time.
3. The distinction between the signification and the value of a word – that is, between overall "meaning" and that portion of the meaning which derives from the word's use in a given context.

Joyce's Arranger functions somewhat like a mad linguist who tries to illustrate Saussure's ideas within the miniature verbal universe of a single book. As such, the Arranger is imbued with the suprapersonal consciousness of language as system (*langue*) and at the same time seems to control and record every manifestation (*parole*) of that system. In "Sirens," for instance, we are told: "As said before he ate with relish the inner organs, nutty gizzards," and other foods. This reverts to our introduction to Bloom: "Mr Leopold Bloom ate with relish the inner organs of beasts and fowls. He liked thick giblet soup, nutty gizzards" (*U* 11.520; 4.1–2). As Kenner remarks of these passages: "Some mind ... keeps track of the details of this printed cosmos, and lets escape from its scrutiny the fall of no sparrow."[103] Elsewhere the Arranger's monitoring eye is less intrusive, yet the repetition of key words and phrases, by or in connection with characters who couldn't know their previous contexts, reminds us of this constant presence, which seems to be manipulating the significations and context-generated "values" of these words and phrases. The Arranger also attempts to capture the diachronic within the synchronic through the use of archaic or obsolete words suggesting the continuous flux and evolution of language, as in "Proteus," and through the stylistic parodies that mimic the growth of English in "Oxen of the Sun."

There is something alien from everyday individual experience in both Saussure's abstract system of communication and the Arranger's world of autonomous or semiautonomous words. Yet the suprapersonal consciousness of the Arranger suggests more than merely a personification of Saussurean linguistics. It reflects not one but many of the new ways of perceiving the world that had developed in Europe and the United States over the two generations prior to World War I. *Avant-garde* art and the social sciences were not the only matrixes of these new modes of perception. Above all there was technology, especially as used in industries affecting masses of people.

Consider the newspaper industry. "Aeolus," which takes place primarily at the offices of *The Evening Telegraph*, impresses on us the technology of newspaper production. The chapter is full of technical terms, such as "galleypage" and "caseroom" (*U* 7.161, 196), and offers repeated glimpses of technicians and machinery at work. We meet a foreman, a dayfather, "a typesetter neatly distributing type" (*U* 7.205). Bloom walks through "a lane of clanking drums," glances at "obedient reels feeding in huge webs of paper," and watches as "[t]he nethermost deck of the first machine jogged forward its flyboard with sllt the first batch of quirefolded papers" (*U* 7.74, 136, 174–75). Early in the chapter he thinks:

This morning the remains of the late Mr Patrick Dignam. Machines. Smash a man to atoms if they got him caught. Rule the world today. His machineries are pegging away too. Like these, got out of hand: fermenting. Working away, tearing away. And that old grey rat tearing to get in. (*U* 7.80–83)

Apart from suggesting the Great War, with its man-smashing artillery, rotting corpses, and rats, this passage links the triumph of machines with the acceleration of time. As in Stephen's encounter with the dynamos, the machine's violent tempo has entered the human body. But what is more significant in this episode, technology also governs historical change. History becomes a product of capitalist newspaper production as reflected in the chapter's format of headlines, subheads, and captions – MEMORABLE BATTLES RECALLED, THE GRANDEUR THAT WAS ROME (*U* 7.358, 483) – followed by brief stories. Thus the Arranger manifests itself in "Aeolus" as the suprapersonal consciousness of modern journalism, which orders the world and particularly time ("Sufficient for the day is the newspaper thereof" [*U* 7.736]) in its own specialized way.

Another technology, that of photography, also seems to play a part in "Aeolus," some of whose chapter titles suggest captions under photographs.[104] But by 1904 the still photograph did not excite wonder anymore; it is mentioned matter-of-factly that Milly Bloom has a job as a "Photo girl" (*U* 1.685). In contrast, the moving picture, invented around 1890, was a sensation still changing people's view of the world when Joyce started work on *Ulysses*:

The triumph of the cinema was ... unparalleled in its speed and scale ... [S]hort films were first shown as fairground or vaudeville novelties in 1895–6, almost simultaneously in Paris, Berlin, London, Brussels, and New York. Barely a dozen years later ... 26 million Americans ... went to see motion pictures *every week* ... [E]ven in backward Italy there were by then almost five hundred cinemas ... By 1914 [films] were ... big business.[105]

Joyce himself had a small pioneering role in this mass business /art form. In 1909, as a partner in a miniature multinational business venture, he helped set up the first regular cinema in Ireland. It failed, but he remained interested in the medium and in 1924 suggested translating *Ulysses* into film.

Joyce's interest in motion pictures expressed itself in another of the Arranger's manifestations, that is, as a camera eye. In "Proteus," which deals with change, flux, and the protean nature of reality, one of many transformations is "a reversal of motion brought about by the old silent-movie technique of reprinting a section of film in reverse order."[106] Stephen's fantasy of blowing a rude usher into bits is retracted when he reassembles his victim – "Bits all khrrrrklak in place clack back" (*U* 3.189) – and shakes hands with him. Here the camera's eye, subordinated to Stephen's point of view, serves a humanistic purpose. In "Wandering Rocks" it becomes a supra-personal consciousness which mechanistically orders space and time in a way remote from felt individual experience. Its cinematic technique is that of montage. Generally speaking, montage involves the juxtaposition of two distinct "shots," so that the action on the screen jumps or "cuts" from one shot to the next. As a self-conscious technique, montage grew out of the Russian Revolution (and the Great War) in tandem with Russian literary formalism. Sergei Eisenstein saw montage as a technique whose aim is "the creation of ideas, of a new reality, rather than the support of narrative, the old reality of experience."[107] He stressed, in other words, dynamism and becoming. Montage, as he viewed it, is an ongoing dialectic of creation through conflict; it works through the collision of images that often seem dissonant or unrelated in meaning but together produce a new meaning. He compared this process in a film to the continuing series of explosions in an internal combustion engine – that symbol of the triumph of the machine. Such a comparison seems on the mark when we remember that Eisenstein represented the *avant garde* in a new art form made possible by technological advances.

Eisenstein's *Battleship Potemkin* (1925), which showed spectacularly what montage could do, postdates *Ulysses*. But an early form of the technique appeared during the first two decades of the century in the movies of D. W. Griffiths, to which Eisenstein acknowledged his debt and which the cinema-going Joyce family probably saw. Moreover, throughout his career, Eisenstein "praised Joyce for having pushed literary limits in ways strikingly similar to his own pathbreaking activities in the cinema."[108] We seem, then, to be dealing with parallel developments in two different arts responding to the same overall historical circumstances – war, revolution, and the ascendancy of the machine.

In "Wandering Rocks" we see Joyce's literary montage harnessed to a peculiar, machine-like task. Like "Aeolus," the chapter presents a disjointed appearance, containing nineteen sections separated by asterisks. The sections offer vignettes of various characters' actions as they move around downtown Dublin between 3 and 4 p.m. The "flat," realistic narrative surface, which gives way only occasionally and discreetly to interior monologue, mimics what a movie camera might "see," and generates meaning through the camera's (that is, the Arranger's) montage of different scenes and parts of scenes. The characters in these scenes often do not know or are unaware of each other, yet are related through the montage; they function less as citizens in a knowable community than as creatures of a complex, misleading, sometimes ironic space–time continuum. This is especially true of Joyce's adaptation of "parallel montage." Developed by Griffiths, this cinematic technique interpolates into each section of a story an action or actions, occurring simultaneously but distant in space, taken from other sections.

The procedure suggests the binding of the vignettes onto a common time frame by a sort of temporal "riveting." Similarly, Joyce uses two devices which convert the space of Dublin itself into two species of clock: from time to time he "cuts" to a throwaway of Elijah, floating down the river Liffey, its progress charting the passing of time as well as movement through space; and at the end of the episode, he recapitulates its time and space by following a viceregal procession across Dublin, as it intersects most of the places and characters we have seen.[109]

Ironies arise when a scene and an interpolation represent significantly parallel or contrasting actions of which the characters involved are unaware. For example, the sentence – "A darkbacked figure under Merchants' arch scanned books on the hawker's cart"

(*U* 10.315–16) – suddenly interrupts a description of Boylan buying fancy fruit to send to Molly before their assignation. The irony: the dark figure, we learn elsewhere, is Bloom, also seeking a gift for Molly.

Montage serves a larger purpose in "Wandering Rocks." On the whole, the chapter constitutes a study of time and space to which considerations such as character development, plot, theme, and even cinematic technique are subordinate. Budgen recalls: "Joyce wrote the *Wandering Rocks* with a map of Dublin before him ... He calculated to a minute the time necessary for his characters to cover a given distance of the city."[110] Clive Hart, who retraced all the characters' routes with watch in hand, confirms that they (and even the throwaway floating down the Liffey) could have realistically followed their itineraries in the time allotted.[111] The question is: what does it mean when a work of art, or part of one, is constructed as a time and motion study? In many ways such studies lie at the heart of modern science and technology. Although Joyce "liked factories" (*JJ* 302), he did not portray one in *Ulysses*, perhaps because Dublin had so few. But the Arranger's measuring of human movements through time and space in "Wandering Rocks" suggests a basic tool – the time-and-motion study of procedures performed by assembly-line workers – for measuring productivity in a factory. And it suggests the dependence of most technologies on finely measured temporal–spatial relationships. Examples include transportation networks (Dublin's tram system), engines (the dynamos that remind Stephen of a watch), and missiles (the artillery shell whose precisely calibrated "trajectory" [*U* 12.1881] causes it to land on central Dublin in "Cyclops").

In its very form, then, "Wandering Rocks" represents a response to the acceleration of history in Joyce's era and its attendant danger for the artist of pathetic anachronism. The "content" of the form is its reflection through the Arranger of a distinctively modern consciousness or way of looking at the world, one that breaks reality down into space–time relationships which are minutely realistic yet are also abstract in their removal from the individual's everyday felt experience. In other words, the chapter's radical form and its suprapersonal mechanistic consciousness at once reflect and attempt to contain history. Like other manifestations of the Arranger, they are aimed at matching the strangeness and newness of the present with their own strange new forms even while, paradoxically, they serve to recreate a world made old by the swift pace of historical change.

❋

A closing thought on the form of *Ulysses* and its period of production. The Great War (and the revolutions it triggered in Ireland, Russia, and defeated Germany) symbolized a combined destruction and liberation which long had been the goal of *avant-garde* art. "The Faustian moment that Wagner and Diaghilev and other moderns sought to achieve in their art forms had now arrived for society as a whole."[112] The middle classes who had dismissed *Elektra* and hooted *The Rite of Spring* were killing each other. They were doing so in the "theater of war" – a phrase whose resonance Fussell explores. In creating a totally absorbing new reality, the war achieved what *avant-garde* artists had been looking to achieve before 1914 and what Joyce attempted afterwards. The war was a *Gesamtkunstwerk*, combining elements of what some of its soldier-actors called a "screaming farce," a "melodrama," a "pantomime," a "grotesque comedy."[113] Among its hallmarks were dissonance, bursts of energy, jerky movements, the violence of machines, and transformation. Many soldiers described the war in terms of the "transformation scene," a staple of Georgian theater whose "effect was equivalent of 'dissolve' or 'mix' in cinema," only far more impressive. Presiding over the ensemble was a stage-manager / God with a taste for "ironic action"[114] such as victories that turn into defeats and for accidents of time and space such as the shell whose trajectory causes it to miss (or hit) a given soldier.

Ulysses, especially in the phantasmagoria of "Circe," seems to vie with the Great War as a *Gesamtkunstwerk*. In Nighttown Bloom denounces machines as "manufactured monsters for mutual murder" (*U* 15.1393) – one of the novel's frequent allusions to the horror of 1914–18. Yet the "Circe" chapter, written as a play, has built into it most of the striking features of the actual theater of war; it is filled with ironies, disjunctions, jerky energy, and hallucinatory violence and transformations. It also seems to be stage-managed by its own version of the organizing mind of the war – that omniscient intelligence, indifferent to human well-being, whose bizarre logic (Cecil Lewis called the trench system "a fantastic caricature of common sense")[115] many soldiers and civilians alike sensed in the weird, unpredictable twists and turns of the fighting. I refer, of course, to the Arranger. Hart, in discussing this aspect of Joyce's narration in another chapter, "Wandering Rocks," writes of "the narrator's dominant, privileged position and his playful but also ruthless handling of the characters ... The mind of this city is both mechanical and maliciously ironic."[116] The playfully malicious intelligence of the Arranger turns *Ulysses*, in some respects, into a black comedy, a Hardyesque "satire of circumstance"[117] – which was how the war, in its later stages, appeared to some thoughtful observers.

All Joyce's narrative innovations in *Ulysses* serve his twin goal of recreating the Dublin of 16 June 1904 and saving his narrative from pathetic anachronism. But this link aside, the Arranger differs drastically from Joyce's other major innovation, the internal monologue. The latter evokes the flux of individual consciousness; it approximates what Bergson calls *la durée*, or time-as-experience, which he locates in our experience of our personalities flowing through time. The Arranger, however, reflects a suprapersonal consciousness. It suggests ways of seeing the world, and objectifying and quantifying it, that arose out of the scientific and technological advances of prewar Europe and found their apotheosis in the Great War. The ironic arranging mind that so many people sensed during the war was in large part the functioning, in the theater of mass technological warfare, of these new modes of perceiving and ordering the world. That an analogue to this mind should be embedded in the very form of *Ulysses* – an antiwar novel concerned with depicting the richness of individual consciousness – is one of the novel's great contradictions.

CHAPTER 6

Reforming the wor(l)d

The war is in words and the wood is the world.
(Joyce, *Finnegans Wake* 98.34–35)

A foul act has taken place in Phoenix Park. But is it fact? And whether fiction or fact, what exactly happened? Who are the malefactors? Who the victim? Why did they do it? If they did it. Do we have evidence to convict?

Whom? Of what?

Such questions arise when we try to define the central event in *Finnegans Wake*. Some recall the questions which revolved around an actual outrage in the park – the assassination of two officials carried out by the Invincibles on 6 May 1882. References in the *Wake* link the two incidents. Although we never learn precisely who the "foenix culprit[s]" (*FW* 23.16) are, one account implicates an unknown person who "was ... posted at Mallon's at the instance of watch warriors of the vigilance committee" (*FW* 34.3–4); the meaning is vague but evokes the ambiguous world of police, spies, crooks, and rebels inhabited by Detective Superintendent Mallon and the Invincibles. The crime takes place on "Ides of April morning" (*FW* 35.3) – bringing to mind the tools (knives) and the season (spring) of the killings. One H. C. Earwicker (HCE) happens to be walking through the park that morning. He is "carrying his overgoat under his schulder, sheepside out" – a complex image melding guilt (Ger. *Schuld*) together with a goatskin coat, which suggests both scapegoat and Skin-the-Goat, the Invincibles' decoy getaway driver. On being asked for the time by a pipe-smoking cad whose "watch was bradys" (*FW* 35.19–20) – the sense is "broken" but the association is with the knife-wielding Joe Brady – Earwicker fears for his life. Later the cad, like the Invincibles, celebrates his "happy escape" (*FW* 38.1) at a pub. Conflicting versions of HCE's misadventure in the park float about afterwards, but, as is true of the

214

assassinations, no definitive history can be told: "The unfacts, did we possess them, are too imprecisely few to warrant our certitude" (*FW* 57.16–17). Yet, in spite of this lack of certainty, "Madam's Toshowus" mounts a "lifeliked" exhibit, reminding us of the tableau of the Invincibles at Madame Tussaud's in London.

Once again, as in *Ulysses*, the Phoenix Park murders seem to have stimulated a Joycean meditation on the interrelatedness of history and story, of fact and fiction. The factoid of the Tussaud exhibit in "our notional gullery" (*FW* 57.20–21) suggests the status of the Invincibles, in Irish nationalist legend, as "the pork martyrs" (*FW* 617.12); it also recalls the contrary English version of the Invincibles as monstrous murderers. The vagueness and error of popular memory – illustrated by Bloom and Crawford – is paralleled in the *Wake* by a pervasive narrative murk in which actions and actors become hopelessly blurred or self-contradicting. Earwicker, for instance, may seem to be the victim of the pipe-smoking cad; yet he treats the cad's mysterious words as an accusation, and protests (with suspicious vehemence) his innocence. Another account of the Park incident has him molesting two girls. All versions, however, are confusing as to issues of guilt and innocence and the boundary line between victim and perpetrator.

Before we explore the meaning of this narrative murk, I would like to glance at other historical episodes which figure distortedly but prominently in the *Wake*. Many of these episodes are violent; often they involve military conflict or power struggles. Book I opens with the Fall initiating human history, a pageant of warfare and wailing:

What clashes here of wills gen wonts, ostrygods gaggin fishygods [Ostrogoths vs. Visigoths]. Brékkek Kékkek Kékkek Kékkek! Kóax Kóax Kóax! Ualu Ualu Ualu! Quaouauh! (*FW* 4.1–3)

The battles of Clontarf, Balaclava, and Waterloo form major motifs. There are references to the Great War: HCE's coffin turns into a submarine amid imagery of a "T.N.T. bombingpost," an "aerial thorpeto," a "minefield," and "ground battery fuseboxes" (*FW* 77.5–11). There are foreshadowings of a new impending war: a Czech radio station announces that soldiers are on the march through "the danzing [Danzig] corridor" (*FW* 333.8). Throughout the text Irish natives and invading colonizers clash. And the Irish – "Freestouters and publicranks ... swearing threaties" [Free State forces and Republicans split by the 1921 Anglo-Irish Treaty and its oath of allegiance] (*FW* 329.31–32) – fight among themselves.

The career of Parnell is another prominent motif. Parnell often becomes mixed up with other figures when the topic of betrayal or of a great man's fall arises. In "The Ballad of Persse O'Reilly" Parnell–HCE is the lost leader ("He was one time our King of the Castle/ Now he's kicked about like a rotten old parsnip" [*FW* 45.7–8]) who, unlike the noble ghost of "Ivy Day" and *A Portrait*, does not deserve to be resurrected because of his (HCE's) silliness and knavery. The phrase "Argentine in casement" (*FW* 559.4) – Roger Casement was executed for trying to smuggle German arms to Irish rebels during the Great War – brings Parnell to mind through the silver ("Argentine") paid to Judas for betraying Christ, an image in Joyce's article, "Home Rule Comes of Age." Like Parnell, Casement was supposedly a victim of forged documents.[1]

Forgery, always carrying overtones of Parnell, is one of the *Wake*'s great themes. Along with other themes, it reverberates with echoes of the sinister event in Phoenix Park. Parnell had been accused in 1887, in a series of articles run by *The Times* on Parnellism and crime, of having condoned the Invincibles' crime. His prolonged trial before a special commission ended in 1889 with the unmasking of Richard Piggott as the forger of incriminating letters ascribed to Parnell; Piggott gave himself away in the witness-box by repeating a misspelling – "hesitency" for "hesitancy" – that appeared in one of the letters. The section of the *Wake* that begins "Remarkable evidence was given" takes place in "Deadman's Dark Scenery Court" (*FW* 86.32; 87.33), based on Probate Court No. 1 where the Parnell Commission sat.[2] And the word "hesitency" recurs throughout the *Wake*, suggesting, besides the Parnell trial, a nexus of meanings that I will investigate later.

Parnell and the issue of forgery are connected with a more notorious historical episode, the Dreyfus affair. At the heart of the affair lay the conundrum of an incriminating document, the *bordereau*, attributed to Dreyfus but actually written by an army officer. Joyce alludes to it in an atypically naked passage:

Closer inspection of the *bordereau* would reveal a multiplicity of personalities inflicted on the documents or document and some prevision of virtual crime or crimes might be made by anyone unwary enough before any suitable occasion for it or them had so far managed to happen along. (*FW* 107.23–28)

Here the question is not just "[who] wrote the durn thing ...?" (*FW* 107.36) but also: how do we interpret it?

The problem of interpretation crops up in regard to another historical event, the Irish Civil War. During a denunciation of HCE by customers at his pub, two documents – "ducomans nonbar one" and "decumans numbered too" (*FW* 358.30; 369.24–25) – are cited. In this context they are part of the usual ambiguous, self-contradicting evidence with which we must decipher events in the *Wake*. But they also refer to the treaty that terminated the Anglo-Irish War. A large minority of the young Irish parliament, Dail Eireann, rejected the treaty. The minority leader, Eamon de Valera, argued for changes in terms and terminology which he embodied in an alternative called "Document No. 2." One issue was partition. Led by Arthur Griffith and Michael Collins, the treaty negotiators had agreed to exclude six northern counties from the Free State, interpreting the treaty's boundary clause to mean that Ulster citizens – including Catholic majorities in several areas – would soon vote on reunification; they expected the results to make a separate Ulster government untenable. De Valera demurred; years later he was vindicated when the British interpretation (no vote was held) proved to be the opposite of Griffith's. These conflicts in interpretation contributed to two momentous events: the partitioning of Ireland and the Civil War.

Another problem with interpretation (at least as Joyce saw it) led to a less momentous but emblematic tragedy in a murder trial held in 1882. One night in August of that year, in an isolated area of County Galway called Maamtrasna, a farmer named John Joyce and four members of his family were slaughtered. Supposedly they were police informers in the war, raging in the countryside, between landlords and tenants. Local people accused ten men, all Irish-speakers, of the killings; two of the accused became "approvers" or state witnesses. Because officials saw the crime as an act of political terrorism sponsored by the Land League, a change of venue was effected (by virtue of a coercion bill engendered by the Phoenix Park murders) from the Irish-speaking Maamtrasna area to Dublin. The court provided interpreters for the defendants. All of them, except the approvers, were summarily convicted; three were hanged in December at Galway jail, even though two of the condemned men had sworn to a magistrate that the third, Myles Joyce, was completely innocent.

Joyce describes this miscarriage of justice in "Ireland at the Bar," an article ("L'Irlanda alla Sbarra") published in Trieste in 1907. His account begins:

In a lonely place ... called Maamtrasna, a murder was committed. Four or five townsmen, all belonging to the ancient tribe of the Joyces, were arrested. The oldest of them, the seventy-year-old Myles Joyce, was the prime suspect. Public opinion at the time thought him innocent and today considers him a martyr. Neither the old man nor the others accused knew English. The court had to resort to the services of an interpreter ... The magistrate said:

"Ask the accused if he saw the lady that night." The question was referred to him in Irish, and the old man broke out into an involved explanation ... Then he quieted down [and] the interpreter ... said:

"He says no, your worship."

"Ask him if he was in that neighbourhood at that hour."

The old man again began to talk, to protest, to shout, almost beside himself with the anguish of being unable to understand or to make himself understood, weeping in anger and terror. And the interpreter, again, dryly:

"He says no, your worship." (*CW* 197–98)

The sketch concludes with Myles Joyce's hanging: "The story was told that the executioner, unable to make the victim understand him, kicked at the miserable man's head in anger to shove it into the noose."

Joyce drew on popular history in his account of the Maamtrasna murders and, as John Garvin has shown,[3] made several factual errors. But, although contemporary records don't reveal that Myles Joyce complained of failing to understand or being misunderstood, the pivotal fact remains: an Irish-speaker was wrongfully condemned by an English-speaking court and hanged by an English executioner. Hence, for Joyce, the victim became a "symbol of the Irish nation at the bar of public opinion" (*CW* 198). He must have been impressed, too, by the parallels between the Maamtrasna and the Phoenix Park killings. They occurred only a few months apart (in the resonant year of Joyce's birth); they involved nationalism, politics, and informers; and the same English hangman, Marwood, did his grisly work at the end. Unlike the Invincibles, however, Myles Joyce was an unambiguous, defenseless victim of colonialism. As such he provided Joyce with a counter-image to British representations "of the Irish as highwaymen with distorted faces" (*CW* 198). Joyce needed such an image for "Ireland at the Bar," a forceful defense of Ireland against British claims of Irish lawlessness. The article, significant for its linkage of the language question and colonialism, is also significant for its focus on the Irish countryside, usually absent from Joyce's writings. No doubt a handful of key details in the folk history of the Maamtrasna episode – a man named Joyce, caught up in the ongoing war between Irish nationalism and British imperialism, was victimized in a foreign court which misconstrued his language – awakened in Joyce a sense of kinship. At any rate, the episode inspired him to write sympathetically about an embodiment of a type, the Irish peasant, which he normally did his best to ignore.

In *Finnegans Wake* the pathetic last words of Myles Joyce, "I am going" (*tá mé ag imtheacht*), seem to be echoed when Anna Livia fades away – "I'm going!" (*FW* 215.7) – and at other key moments of departure.[4] But most details of the Maamtrasna affair are interwoven with the trial of Festy King, an *alter ego* of HCE's son, Shaun. Suddenly Book I shifts its focus from HCE and the event in Phoenix Park to a new alleged misdeed:

Little headway ... was made in solving the wasnottobe crime cunundrum when a child of Maam, Festy King, of a family long and honourably associated with the tar and feather industries, who gave an address in old plomansch Mayo ... was subsequently haled up at the Old Bailey ... under an incompatibly framed indictment. (*FW* 85.21–27)

The accused defended himself "in the royal Irish vocabulary" while "the crown [attempted] to show that King ... once known as Meleky" (*FW* 86.1, 7–8), attended a certain country fair under disguise. Obvious links to the Maamtrasna murders include the key word "Maam," the place-name "Mayo" (also in the rural West), the Irish-language defense, and the phrase "tar and feather industries" – tarring and feathering was a traditional punishment for informers.

Myles Joyce, though identified with Festy King, is not the clear symbol that he was in "Ireland at the Bar." Like all Wakean figures, Festy has multiple levels, and his associations reach far beyond Maamtrasna. "Meleky" alludes to Malachy, an ancient High King of Ireland.[5] The "clanetourf" with which Festy is accused of disguising himself suggests the Battle of Clontarf (1014), where another High King, Brian Boru, defeated Viking invaders. A motif of conflict – Irish vs. foreigners, Irish vs. Irish, Boers vs. English – runs through this section. The trial itself becomes conflated with the Parnell Commission when a witness called "W. P." (*FW* 86.34) – a reversal of the abbreviation P. W. for "Parnell Witness" in summaries of testimony before the Commission[6] – testifies in "Deadman's Dark Scenery Court." Hence Festy King ties together the Maamtrasna and the Phoenix Park murders against the backdrop of Ireland's violent history.

We can dig up many other historical episodes out of the matrix, or midden heap, of *Finnegans Wake*; the book is a compendium of references to world history. A Wakean politics could be inferred from such references. The *Wake* pictures history as a dynamic, violent process (not unlike Stephen's vision of history in "Nestor"), yet it continually undermines the notion of heroes or great men as agents of that process.[7] In "The Ballad of Persse O'Reilly," HCE– Humpty Dumpty–Parnell not only falls but becomes an object of ridicule. The assassins of Phoenix Park are merely the "Ignorant invincibles, innocents immutable" (*FW* 361.20–21); the result of their efforts, and the efforts of other Irish hero-martyrs (including the fratricidal heroes of the Civil War), is merely "our wee free state" (*FW* 117.34). If wars, assassinations, intrigues, and all manner of politics end in nothing much to celebrate, then the *Wake* might be seen as an argument for political quietism – for the course of action pursued by the antihero of "Dooleysprudence" who goes home to paddle his own canoe while the European nations rush off to war. It might also be taken, especially as a work written during the ominous interval between the two world wars, as a plea for peace; the last book begins ringingly with three words – "Sandhyas! Sandhyas! Sandhyas!" (*FW* 593.1) – that suggest the Sanskrit for "peace." But this is too clear, and too superficial, an interpretation. To understand the *Wake*'s politics, we must plumb its narrative murk and look for meaning in its revolutionary form.

THE DISUNITED KINGDOM OF THE SUBJECT

> You have reared your disunited kingdom on the vacuum of your own most intensely doubtful soul.
>
> (*FW* 188.16–17)

One problem with trying to decode Joyce's "take" on any particular historical figure or event, in *Finnegans Wake*, is the fact that these figures and events metamorphose out of the mist and are barely constituted before they start blurring and mixing with other figures and events or dissolving back into the mist. The *Wake*'s handling of

Parnell, for instance, simply does not lend itself to analysis in the manner of "Ivy Day" or *A Portrait*. Or consider the Maamtrasna murders as the background of Festy King's trial. Like Myles Joyce, Festy is the defendant, and his alleged crime involves violence toward fellow Irishmen; specifically, he is accused (under the name of Hyacinth O'Donnell) of having "sought ... to sack, sock, stab and slaughter another two of the old kings" (*FW* 87.15–17). Yet, whereas Irish popular history and Joyce's article rest on a crystal-clear assumption of Myles's innocence, the *Wake* connects Festy ("feisty," "fisty") with a variety of conflicts – the Battle of Clontarf, a "middlewhite [middle-weight] fair" (*FW* 86.11), the attacks on the other old kings – in which his role is not at all clear. Maybe the charges against him are false. Then again, the ancient Irish kings did battle each other as well as outsiders. In any case, Festy–Shaun–Hyacinth is not a single, unitary character who can be evaluated as such. We cannot answer, simply and definitively, the question: who is Festy King? His identity floats, picking up here and there aspects of other Wakean figures which themselves are floating constellations of traits and attributes. Nor can we answer the question: what specifically is the trial of Festy King all about? Like their agents, actions in *Finnegans Wake* – sins, crimes, inquests, battles – merge and intermix with each other. Myles Joyce stands in "Ireland at the Bar," in the daylight of Joyce's journalistic prose, as a distinct figure with a particular historical meaning. But in the *Wake* he materializes, as though at a seance, out of a dim, crowded, spirit world, speaks in someone else's voice, then fades against a shifting background of other shapes and voices. We can discuss this ghostly manifestation, to be sure, and relate it to history, yet not without acknowledging that basic Wakean question, "Who is he?" (*FW* 261.28).

One way of reading the slipperiness of identity in *Finnegans Wake* is as an attack on essentialism. Continually, in the *Wake*, rivalries and conflicts spring up that suggest differences between nations or differences as to self-definition within a nation. This is especially true of clashes between natives and foreign invaders. The arrival in Ireland of HCE – a Protestant of Scandinavian descent – is associated with that of Strongbow, who led Henry II's invasion force as an ally of the disaffected king of Leinster: "He landed in ourland's leinster ... off Lipton's strongbowed launch." Yet HCE–Strongbow is also that benevolent invader, St. Patrick, who "converted [Ireland's] nataves" (*FW* 288.13–15, 16) and became an emblem of Ireland. Over and over the *Wake* destabilizes the borderline between alien and native. When HCE as Roderick O'Connor, the last Irish High King before the triumph of the Anglo-Normans (themselves the hybrid product of invasion), contemptuously entertains a party of earlier colonists – "the unimportant Parthalonians with the mouldy Firbolgs and the Tuatha de Danaan googs and the ramblers from Clane" (*FW* 381.4–6) – we are reminded that although the most recent successful interlopers may despise previous ones, they will neither remain in power nor remain pure. Inevitably, they too will be displaced and make their own contribution to "the confusioning of human races" (*FW* 35.5) which is part of the historical process.

Not only do native and outsider frequently merge or switch roles, but the cyclical nature of conflict in the *Wake* tends to reduce their identity to a side issue. When a native "attackler" engages an intruding "Adversary" at the mouth of the Liffey, that ancient route of Viking invaders, we are told:

The boarder incident prerepeated itself. The pair (whethertheywere Nippoluono engaging Wei-Ling-Taou or de Razzkias trying to reconnoistre the general Boukeleff, man may not say), struggled apairently for some considerable time, (the cradle rocking equally to one and oppositely from the other on its law of capture and recapture). (*FW* 81.33–82.2)

Here the Battle of Waterloo, a major motif, reappears. Or maybe it isn't Waterloo; as the dreamer-narrator remarks, no one can say whether the belligerents are Napoleon and Wellington or some other pair. The point is not who is fighting but that such struggles are "prerepeated" – are predestined to happen over and over in a world in which history "moves in vicous cicles yet remews the same" (*FW* 134.16–17). In this Viconian world combatants merely enact historical law. For Vico, individuals make history; their individuality, however, is merely the local incarnation of the universal, and their actions in history are both individual and supra-individual. In the *Wake*'s recycling of Vico, conflict propels the historical process; the specific identity of the contestants – France and England, Free Staters and Republicans, Shem and Shaun – matters little.

This universal law of conflict affects individual psyches, too, which often split into opposed or warring halves. During our tour of the "Willingdone Museyroom" (Wellington Museum), we view relics and representations of Waterloo. These include not only

"Lipoleum" (Napoleon) but his mitotically reduplicated self, the "lipoleums," two of whom are locked in perpetual fatal combat: "This is the bog lipoleum mordering the lipoleum beg" (*FW* 8.24). Another identity of these Irish ("bog") combatants is Shem and Shaun, the two young brothers to whom their parents' intercourse, secretly witnessed, suggests a military conflict (Waterloo). The brothers – with their overtones of Cain and Abel, Jacob and Esau, and other fraternal enemies – are arch-opponents. In their incarnation as Dolph and Kev, a political disagreement leads to Kev (Shaun) knocking Dolph (Shem) down. Later a dialogue on unity and diversity ends abruptly when Juva (Shaun) hurls a death-wish at Muta (Shem); the ominous one-word paragraph "Shoot" (*FW* 610.33) follows. Yet, like other opposites in the *Wake*, the brothers periodically merge. Their mother, Anna Livia Plurabelle (ALP), complains about their contrariness and at the same time notes their virtual interchangeability:

Them boys is so contrary ... Unless they changes by mistake. I seen the likes in the twinggling of an eye. Som. So oft. Sim. Time after time. The sehm asnuh. Two bredder as doffered as nors in soun. When one of him sighs or one of him cries 'tis you all over. No peace at all. (*FW* 620.12–18)

The brothers' north-south differences disappear as they twin-mingle. By becoming the same anew ("sehm asnuh" – a variant of a Wakean leitmotif), they illustrate Viconian history; and, as ALP remarks ("'tis you all over"), they are a recycling of a single person, their fractious father.

HCE's own conflicted psyche is on display throughout the *Wake*. A Protestant Irishman, he "is unhesitent in his unionism and yet a pigotted nationalist" (*FW* 133.14–15). These contradictory, perhaps fraudulent (as the double allusion to Richard Pigott implies) allegiances are suggested also in the context of the Phoenix Park murders: "Quary was he invincibled and cur was he burked" (*FW* 132.32–33). HCE is linked to Burke, the Chief Secretary's deputy (and Britain's Irish watchdog), whom the Invincibles assassinated; and he is linked to the assassins themselves through the person of the Invincible James Carey. Such a linkage – which we see repeatedly in *Ulysses*, for instance, between the Citizen and Major Tweedy – suggests the interdependence of opposites in producing and maintaining each other's supposedly separate identity. And the fact that Carey informed on his fellow conspirators points up the illusory unity of the Invincibles, and of Irish nationalists in general, as well as another fault line in HCE's disunited character. The description of HCE as "partitioned Irskaholm, united Irishmen" (*FW* 132.33–34) again balances the illusion of national(ist) unity against the actuality of division. The historical references here are dense. Though the United Irishmen, a nationalist movement co-founded by Wolfe Tone in 1791, joined together Catholic and Protestant, the alliance was fragile; after the debacle of the 1798 rising, the historical crevasse separating the two religious groups – camouflaged by the movement's name – became a chasm and made nationalism, despite the valiant work of Protestant cultural nation-alists such as Davis and Hyde and Yeats, largely a matter of religion. A little over a century later, both the political and military arms of the nationalist forces in the Anglo-Irish War bore names declaring a unitary identity – Sinn Fein (roughly, "we ourselves") and the Irish Republican Brotherhood. Yet the efforts of these latter-day "united Irishmen," Joyce suggests, led to a double split: first, the sundering of their own ranks into a Free State army and a Republican army in the Civil War; and second, the partitioning of the Irish island ("Irskaholm" – Dan. *Irsk*, Irish, and *holm*, islet)[8] into north and south as a result of the Anglo-Irish Treaty. Inevitably, the breaking asunder of the nationalist forces brings to mind other divisions of "Irrland's split little pea" (*FW* 171.6): notably the Split between Parnellites and anti-Parnellites during the 1890s, and the ongoing rivalry between the two principal political parties that arose out of the Civil War. The fact that all these conflicts reflect cleavages in HCE's psyche subverts essentialism – the notion of a pure, essential, undivided Irishness – at the most basic level, that of the individual subject.

The stakes involved in the *Wake*'s assault on essentialism are made clear in *Ulysses*. Recall the pub scene where the chauvinist Citizen first questions Bloom's Irishness and then, amid echoes of the great artillery barrages of World War I, hurls a biscuit tin at him. The Citizen's flesh-and-blood counterpart was Michael Cusack (1847–1906), co-founder in 1884 of the Gaelic Athletic Association. Cusack's concept of an essential Irishness passed on from father to son, but imperiled by English colonial rule, permeates his leading article of 3 January 1885 in *United Irishman*. The piece lauds Arch-bishop Croke, patron of the G.A.A., as a leader whose "marvellous influence over the Irish race" stems from his racial understanding:

He ... knows what every Irish priest must know about his people [and] he cries out indignantly against the vile thing [the curfew law that effectively banned many Irish sports and pastimes] which is creeping over us and threatening our chief racial characteristics with destruction ... He knows the unparalleled nerve-strength and power of endurance which is developed by the system of physical culture and amusements handed down to us by our fathers; and he is desirous that we should hand that precious inheritance, uninjured and unsullied, to the next generation.[9]

Cusack, though a cultural nationalist and probably not a Fenian, saw a natural alliance between the two groups; and Fenians did use the G.A.A. as a recruiting ground. An editorial on the establishment of the Association in *The Irishman* expresses his views and those of the many G.A.A. members whom Joyce personified in the hurley-wielding Davin in *A Portrait*:

While fighting the enemy in the byeways which are called constitutional, we must maintain a ... readiness to meet our enemy in the field ... Our politics being essentially National so should our athletics. We must maintain a stout physique and cultivate a hardy constitution. A townsman unexercised in the field is stiff-limbed, short-winded, and unable to endure hardship and privation ... This defect would tell heavily against the townsman in a war with any recognised army.[10]

Cusack himself made this cultural-military linkage in his "Address to the Irish People" published in the first edition (1885) of the G.A.A. rules. His thumbnail sketch of the history of hurling claims: "It was the training of the hurling-field that made the men and boys of the Irish Brigade."[11] In this parallel to the English notion that Britain's battlefield victories were won on the playing fields of Eton, we see the Shem–Shaun mirror-imaging that goes on between enemies, such as imperialists and colonized subjects, locked in conflict. The two foes, however, rarely acknowledge their mutual resemblance; rather, each side acts on the basis of an essentialist self-definition that depends, paradoxically, on the other's existence, that is, on the existence of an opponent viewed as inherently different. Hence the unconscious alliance, implied in *Ulysses*, between Irish nationalists and English imperialists – for example, the Citizen and Major Tweedy. And hence the associations, within the novel's double time frame, between the struggle in Ireland and the Great War.

For an essentialist such as Cusack, both national and personal identity depend on a belief in the undivided subject. He undoubtedly would have agreed with Pearse's declaration: "Like a divine religion, national freedom bears the [mark] of unity ... for it contemplates the nation as one [and] it embraces all the men and women of the nation."[12] In *Ulysses* the Citizen relies on mystical nationalism, exclaiming at one point the mantra *"Sinn Fein!"* (*U* 12.519) in his effort to meld his heterogeneous fellow boozers into a single bloc in opposition to Bloom. The *Wake* alludes to Cusack in Shaun–Sordid Sam's wish: "Now let the centuple celves of my egourge as Micholas de Cusack calls them ... by the coincidance of their contraries reamalgamerge in that indentity of undiscerni- bles" (*FW* 49.34–50.1). This bent to amalgamate all political cells and individual selves into a magical indenture/identity typifies nationalist and racial discourses, especially when a perceived danger looms from outside the community.

Yet always there exists a counter-tendency to divide, subdivide, and fragment. The G.A.A. exhibited this tendency from the start. A minor infraction of the rules by the Dublin Grocers' Assistants' Clubs – they decided, during the summer of 1887, to use their own handi- capper at an athletic meeting instead of the G.A.A.'s official handi- capper – led to the distribution around Dublin of the following poster:

NATIONALISTS OF DUBLIN – Down with dissension! Discountenance disu- nion! Support not the would-be wreckers of the G.A.A.! Down with the men who would disgrace the Association that has for its patrons the tried, true, and illustrious Irishmen – Archbishop Croke, C. S. Parnell, Michael Davitt, and John O'Leary. Who are those men who try to prove that Irishmen are not worthy of self-government? The Grocers' Assistants' Sports Committee. Do not by your presence at their meeting commit an act of treason to Ireland. God save Ireland![13]

Before a compromise finally quelled this tempest in a teapot, Croke, Davitt, and Parnell all had become involved. Another quarrel, never resolved, led to the choleric Cusack's break with the G.A.A. executive board in 1886. He founded *The Celtic Times*, a newspaper which he turned into a launching-pad for "attacks full of vigour, sarcasm, and banter at the expense of 'the vile, grabbing imitators'" of the G.A.A. Executive, "whose extermination ... he demanded weekly"[14] for over a year until the paper folded. In response the G.A.A. started up its own journal, *The Gael*. This did not save it, however, from dividing in 1887 into Fenian and clerical factions – a split that left the association virtually moribund until the first years of the next century.

Such cracks in the wished-for undivided subject appeared in all nationalist groups, and warnings against division punctuate their literature. In "A Song for the Gaelic Athletic Clubs," John O'Leary's sister Ellen urged: "By no harsh word let strife be fanned,/ Forbear with one another./'Tis for the right you all unite."[15] A faction of the Irish Literary Theatre, led by actor-playwright Padraic Colum, seceded for patriotic reasons and set up the rival Theatre of Ireland in 1906. A remaining loyalist, producer Frank Fay, wrote to Lady Gregory in regard to his discussions with Colum: "I fear if some of the directors don't come to my rescue, I shall be found some fine morning knocking loudly on the door of the Richmond Asylum asking, What is Nationality? What is a Nationalist? and do two Nationalists make one Nationality?"[16] Countess Markievicz sought to turn the suffrage movement into a force for nationalist unity. In her pamphlet, *Women, Ideals and the Nation* (1900), she argued in regard to the male inclination "to fight and squabble" over partisan issues:

Now here is a chance for our women. Let them remind their men, that their first duty is to examine any legislation proposed not from a party point of view, not from the point of view of a sex, a trade, or a class, but simply and only from the standpoint of their Nation.[17]

Padraic Pearse, often a divider in his youth – as a 19-year-old he had hoped "to strangle [the Irish Literary Theatre] at its birth" because of its "Irish literature in English idea"[18] – stressed unification later on. Commiserating with Hanna Sheehy-Skeffington in May 1915 over a government ban on Irish attendance at the Women's International Peace Congress, he suggested: "The present situation will do good if it ranges more of the women definitely with the *national* forces."[19] He was alluding to the gap, formed in 1912, between feminist and nationalist women over the issue of whether a votes-for-women platform would jeopardize the passing of a Home Rule bill. The gap had widened when Cumann na mBan (Irishwomen's Council) was born as the women's auxiliary of the Irish Volunteers;[20] its manifesto of 8 August 1914 concluded: "We call on all Irishwomen who realise that our national honour and our national needs must be placed before all other considerations, to join our ranks."[21] As for the Volunteers, they were conceived, like the United Irishmen before them, as a body that would join together patriots of divergent political beliefs. Soon, however, they came under fire both from Redmond's Parliamentary Party and from Larkin's (soon Connolly's) Irish Citizen Army. Speaking for the I.C.A., Sean O'Casey warned workers tempted to join the Volunteers that "there can be no interests outside of those identified with your own class"; he asked rhetorically: "Are you going to rope Ireland's poor outside to the boundaries of the Nation?"[22] Only desperation and great imagination enabled the Citizen Army, the Irish Republican Brotherhood, and the Volunteers to come together to ignite the Easter 1916 Rising; and even that performative discourse on unity, Pearse's Proclamation, had to acknowledge "the differences" among Irishmen which it attributed to the careful fostering of "an alien government."[23]

The sacred goal of solidarity and the fact of difference were polarities that the nine-year-old Joyce grappled with in his first known work, "Et Tu, Healy," which dealt with the Split. Though he remained a passionate Parnellite for another two decades, his wariness of group identities grew early, especially in relation to nationalism. The aloofness expressed in "The Day of the Rabblement" toward the Irish Literary Theatre extended to other groups whose blandishments, or threats, the protagonists of *Stephen Hero* and *A Portrait* spend much of their energy resisting. In *Ulysses* Joyce critiqued Irish and European essentialism, which he connected with World War I, by pointing up the imagined nature of nationalist Ireland and nations in general; more radically, he also set about destabilizing our notion of the individual subject – what D. H. Lawrence, alluding in 1914 to the pre-Freudian era, called "the old stable *ego*."[24] The received historical identity of the Invincible, Skin-the-Goat Fitzharris ("assuming he was he" [*U* 16.985]), begins to lose its firm outlines in juxtaposition with the keeper of the cabman's shelter who may or may not be Fitzharris in old age. Similarly in "Circe" the once familiar character of Bloom becomes less familiar, and somewhat problematic, in juxtaposition with fantasized Blooms who in most respects are not any more fictional than the "real" Bloom.

In *Finnegans Wake*, composed during the menacing period of *l'entre deux guerres*, Joyce takes his critique of the undivided subject much further. The *Wake* does not simply destabilize identity; its centripetal force whirls away the elements of any narrational center, such as Festy King, almost as soon as they come together. We can only loosely call these centers "characters," for they lack the bounds and temporal continuity of characters. Boundedness and continuation through time are also crucial traits of the "magic nation" (*FW* 569.29–30). Benedict Anderson writes: "The nation is imagined as *limited* because even the largest of them ... has finite ... boundaries, beyond which lie other nations." And the nation, which always concerns itself with generational ties, speaks "in a language of 'continuity.'"[25] In the fluid, non-sequential universe of *Finnegans Wake*, nations have no place, even though the book resounds with echoes of "boarder incidents" and long-time national rivalries. The *Wake* deconstructs not just the individual but the national subject. A product of Joyce's engagement with both Irish and European history, it is a profoundly anti-nationalist, anti-racist, and (as Sollers points out) anti-Fascist work.

UNDERSTANDING NAT LANGUAGE

[I]n the Nichtian glossery which purveys aprioric roots for aposteriorious tongues this is nat language at any sinse of the world.

(*FW* 83.10–12)

Like their masculine counterparts, feminine entities in the *Wake* merge with one another and split into multiple selves. James Atherton has suggested that Issy, HCE and ALP's daughter, is based on the famous "Christine Beauchamp" of Dr. Morton Prince's study of a case of multiple personality. She takes on the voices, at various times, of Jonathan Swift's Stella and Vanessa, of Lewis Carroll's Alice and the mirror-Alice, and of Tristan's beloved, Iseult.[26] But if feminine and masculine subjects resemble each other in having an illusory unity which we can deconstruct into contradictions and differences, gender itself appears to be a fairly consistent aspect of identity for most voices in the *Wake*. One of the few borderlines left largely undeconstructed in Joyce's text is that between the sexes. Feminine voices, in fact, are usually aligned with the *Wake*'s deconstructive project, and function as subverters of phallocentric authority.

Like *Ulysses*, *Finnegans Wake* "ends" (before it begins again) in a flow of woman's words. Anna Livia's swansong, which carries us in its all-embracing sweep down the Liffey and out to sea, contrasts with Earwicker's stutter. HCE's stutter manifests itself when he answers the apparent accusation leveled at him by the pipe-smoking cad. A symptom of repression, this speech impediment suggests a fatal flaw at the heart of phallocentric language, a flaw connected with HCE's sexual guilt and the incident in the park. According to one repeated version of this incident, HCE was homosexually "annoying Welsh fusiliers"; according to another, he was spying on two girls – "the saucicissters … (peep!) meeting waters most improper" (*FW* 33.26–27; 96.13–14) – as they urinated. Whatever his sexual sin may be, it represents a fall – the Fall – and the beginning, in his stuttered response to the cad, of language.

In the Viconian world of the *Wake*, all languages evolve from the stammering onomatopoeic efforts of the ancient patriarchs to name the Thunderer, the divine creator and punisher: "The sibspeeches of all mankind have foliated … from the root of some funner's stotter" (*FW* 96.30–31). Language is thus, at its root, both patriarchal ("some funner's stotter" suggests Ibsen's *Samfundets Støtter* [*Pillars of Society*])[27] and fundamentally flawed. Its flaw lies in its inability to reflect reality directly or naturally. The persistent drive in phallocentric discourse to repress this flaw is an attempt, then, to deny *différance*. In its secondary sense, that of deferral – the deferral of meaning resulting from the absence of a direct or natural link between signifier and referent – *différance* is a hesitation, like a stutter. Hence HCE's stutter is associated with the motif of "hesitency," Pigott's misspelling in the forged letters attributed to Parnell. Immediately after the cad's query-threat-charge the dreamer observes: "Hesitency was clearly to be evitated [avoided]" (*FW* 35.20). But in his reply HCE develops a stutter, just as later, in another life-or-death emergency – he is a fox fleeing the hunt – he slows down due to "the spoil of hesitants, the spell of hesitency" (*FW* 97.25). The fox identification reinforces the tie with Parnell, who used the alias of Mr. Fox in his affair with Mrs. O'Shea. At the same time it reinforces the tie between "hesitency," or the flaw of phallocentric language, and the Fall, which introduced mortality into the world, since Parnell – who suffered from a slight stutter – fell from power following the revelation of his adultery and died soon after. HCE's impediment thus suggests a repressed recognition not only of a sexual fall whose consequence is death, but of linguistic phallacy whose consequence is dearth – a dearth or absence of intrinsic connectedness between words and referents.

Earwicker is linked, too, with Ibsen's *Master Builder*, Solness, that ill-fated asserter of phallic power. As "Bygmester Finnegan of the

Stuttering Hand," he erects "a skyerscape" whose "baubeltop" (*FW* 4.18, 36; 5.2) identifies it as the Tower of Babel – an emblem of phallocentric failure, since its confusion of mutually incomprehensible tongues exposes the arbitrariness of the link between word and referent. Later, in "The Ballad of Persse O'Reilly," he falls from a height:

> Have you heard of one Humpty Dumpty
> How he fell with a roll and a rumble
> And curled up like Lord Olofa Crumple
> By the butt of the Magazine Wall,
>   (Chorus) Of the Magazine Wall,
> Hump, helmet and all? (*FW* 45.1–6)

Another version of the Fall in the Park, this one occurs just after a repetition of the divine thunder-word; it is a reminder, like the Tower of Babel, of the illusoriness of phallocentric mastery. The following exchange takes place in *Through the Looking-Glass*:

"When *I* use a word," Humpty Dumpty said, "it means just what I choose it to mean – neither more nor less."

"The question is," said Alice, "whether you *can* make words mean so many different things."

"The question is," said Humpty Dumpty, "which is to be master – that's all."[28]

Humpty's claim that he can "manage" words, and force them to mean one thing, is betrayed by slippage – his fall off the wall and the slippage of meaning illustrated by his portmanteau words.

Carroll's Humpty Dumpty brags of his relationship with a king, yet uneasily represses an apparent awareness of his coming fall and the futility of efforts by the king's horses and soldiers to restore him. He seems relieved that Alice's information about him merely comes from a book, which he dismisses as a "History,"[29] not realizing that he will soon enact the narrative of that history – that is, the nursery rhyme which Alice has whispered to herself. Joyce's Humpty–HCE also has kingly and military associations. Helmeted, he falls off the wall of a disused fort in Phoenix Park "like Lord Olofa Crumple" (Oliver Cromwell). His ballad, that of Persse O'Reilly, brings to mind both Pearse and the O'Rahilly, fallen heroes of Easter 1916. Further, he enacts the narratives of several texts – the nursery rhyme, *Through the Looking-Glass*, and the ballad. The ur-narrative is that of the Fall itself. The *Wake*'s early warning – "Phall if you but will, rise you must: and none so soon either shall the pharce for the nunce come to a setdown secular phoenish" (*FW* 4.15–17) – seems to offer a double lesson, both historical and linguistic. History is a series of phallic rises and falls brought about by the warfare which rages after the first occurrence of the thunder-word: "What clashes here ... " (*FW* 4.1). The phallic will to rise and conquer asserts itself repeatedly, yet always ends in detumescence, defeat, death – a "setdown ... phoenish [finish]." Not only the made-up Humpty Dumpty and HCE follow this pattern, but so do Cromwell, Parnell, Pearse, and other historical figures: they act out a "pharce" with a predetermined plot. If the "phoenish [phoenix]" implies another rising, it also, according to script, implies another fall.

Humpty Dumpty's repression, in *Through the Looking-Glass*, of the nursery rhyme foretelling his fall suggests his subliminal awareness that he does not really exercise mastery over words. Even his name – he says, "*my* name means the shape I am,"[30] taking pride in the relationship between signifier and referent – betrays him insofar as it points to his fragility. Joyce's Humpty–HCE is similarly betrayed by his own words, which constantly give rise to contradictory meanings and, in particular, point to his fallibility and the fact of his fall in the Park. In response to the cad, a challenging younger man ("cadet") with a pipe (Fr. *pipe*, slang for "penis"), he asseverates, "I am woo-woo willing to take my stand, sir, upon the [Wellington] monument, that sign of our ruru redemption." But his stammer, that symptom of linguistic phallacy, tells another tale. And even his unspoken sign gives him away:

In greater support of his word [he stood] full erect ... with one Berlin gauntlet chopstuck in the hough of his ellboge (by ancientest signlore his gesture meaning: ∃!) pointed at an angle of thirty-two degrees towards his duc de Fer's overgrown milestone as fellow to his gage. (*FW* 36.7–19)

The number 32 brings to mind the rate at which falling bodies accelerate – 32 feet per second per second (a motif in *Ulysses*) – and undermines the phallicism of both his gesture and its taller counter-part, the Wellington (*duc de fer*: Iron Duke) Monument. The sign of his "ru ru redemption," then, is also the sign of his fall.

The politico-military associations of Humpty Dumpty, HCE, and the Wellington Monument (the Duke was a prime minister as well as a general) remind us that Joyce's deconstruction of phallocentric language has the same roots as his deconstruction of the unitary

subject. In large part it is a response to the violence of Irish and
European history. More particularly, it is a response to the linguistic
phallicism which colored editorials and political speeches
throughout Europe during his lifetime, especially before World War
I. In the pre-1914 economic and military competition between the
great powers, expansion and bigness were constant concerns. "I
understand by a world policy," explained the German chancellor,
von Bülow, in 1900, "the support and advancement of the tasks that
have grown out of the expansion of our industry, our trade, the
labour power, activity and intelligence of our people."[31] In 1903 the
Irish Times (identifying with England and Empire) declared:

We do not agree with Mr. CHURCHILL that the regular Army at home
should only be a very small one – "an Army big enough to send to fight the
MAHDI of the MAD MULLAH" – but not an Army big enough "to fight the
Russians, or the Germans, or the French."[32]

Even in Ireland expansion was a theme, with Arthur Griffith proclaiming that an independent Ireland had a right to colonies, and
with Pearse imagining an Irish homeland whose population would
"expand to twenty millions."[33]

Another theme was the ancient tie between military might and
manhood. Pearse equated wielding a rifle with manliness – "the
thing which cannot defend itself, even though it may wear trousers,
is no man" – and asserted that "the nation which regards [blood-
shed] as the final horror has lost its manhood."[34] More ominous
were expressions of a need for a purging orgasmic explosion. Such
expressions were not new in Europe: anarchists had been voicing
them, and acting on them spectacularly, during the 1890s. In the
early years of the twentieth century, in Italy, the Futurists celebrated nationalism, war, and orgasmic male energy. In France in 1910
Charles Péguy claimed:

The Dreyfus Affair can only be explained by the need for heroism which
periodically seizes this people, this race ... When a great war or great
revolution breaks out it is because a great people, a great race needs to
break out ... It always means that a great mass feels and experiences a
violent need, a mysterious need for a great movement ... a sudden need for
glory, for war, for history, which causes an explosion, an eruption.[35]

As the armies mobilized in the euphoric days of August 1914, such
language could be heard, at least on the Continent, on all sides.

Finnegans Wake deconstructs more than just the linguistic gigantism and heroticism parodied in the "Cyclops" chapter of *Ulysses*. It subverts what the young Joyce called, in his 1902 review of a nationalist poet, "those big words which make us so unhappy" (*CW* 87). He was referring in particular (as Arthur Griffith pointed out in the *United Irishman*) to the word "patriotism." No doubt he had Irish history primarily in mind. Later, in *Ulysses*, he deconstructed the word "nation" against the backdrop of the Great War and the lofty abstractions offered to justify its carnage. Other writers also reacted against the language of the war – Owen in "Dulce et Decorum Est," Sassoon in "On Passing the New Menin Gate," and Hemingway in his famous passage in *A Farewell to Arms*: "Abstract words such as glory, honor, courage, or hallow were obscene beside the concrete names of villages, the numbers of roads, the names of rivers, the numbers of regiments and the dates."[36] But Joyce's reaction in *Finnegans Wake* went immeasurably beyond any other artist's; he set about creating a new, self-deconstructing language in which binary oppositions such as honor/dishonor, virtue/sin, and right/wrong could find no purchase. This night or dream language, which is "nat [not] language" in the usual phallocentric mode, is fatal to the linguistic absolutes and opposites which dominate public discourse in time of war. Though the *Wake* echoes throughout with conflict, the conflicts always come down to words ("The war is in words and the wood [word] is the world") whose meanings slip and dissolve endlessly into counter meanings that render oppositions nugatory. The word glory, embedded in the "Sanglorians" (*FW* 4.7) mentioned in the opening sketch of world conflict after the Fall, suggests glorying in blood and fighting without (*sans*) glory. The word "hero," in connection with Festy King's "heroes in Warhorror [Valhalla]" (*FW* 91.29–30), takes on sharply ambiguous overtones. A quest for metaphysically privileged words in the *Wake* leads nowhere; we become "lost in ... a puling sample jungle of woods [pure and simple jumble of words]"[37] (*FW* 112.2–3) whose overriding principle of *différance* and conflict, like the principle of conflict in the world itself, stems from the Fall.

❋

But what about the women? The first sustained feminine voice in the *Wake* belongs to Kathe, an old woman who conducts the tour of the "Wallinstone national museum" (*FW* 8.1–2), erected in Phoenix Park on the spot of Finnegan–HCE–Wellington's fall. Kathe gives visitors a practiced spiel on the Battle of Waterloo. Punctuated with exclamations, her talk brims with phallic and military imagery; it centers on the exploits of "the big Sraughter Willingdone, grand and magentic" with his "big ... mormorial tallowscoop [telescope]" (*FW* 8.15–16, 34–35). All the grand action and drama of Wellington's assertion of his will over "Lipoleum," however, is contained in Kathe's words, and is framed by prosaic references to the museum setting: "This way to the museyroom. Mind your hats goan in!" and "This way the museyroom. Mind your boots goan out" (*FW* 8.9; 10.22–23). Thus, for all his phallic achievements, England's Iron Duke is reduced like the Invincibles to a waxwork ("tallowscoop") in a museum. And he is brought back to life only in the well-rehearsed speech of an old woman (Ireland – the Poor Old Woman[38] – and also fate) which brings the tale of his famous battle to the same end over and over, thus suggesting the effects not of phallic will but of historical necessity in a fallen world.

The next feminine manifestation is that of ALP as a "peacefugel," or bird of peace, who picks over the ruins of a world catastrophe. References to munitions workers, an armistice, and a Christmas truce (such a truce occurred in 1914) establish that the disaster is not only the biblical flood but the Great War. In her "nabsack" she stashes "all spoiled goods," mainly the refuse of war, such as "curtrages [cartridges] and rattlin buttins, nappy spattees and flasks [flags] of all nations" (*FW* 11.18–20). A "peri potmother" ("fairy godmother" and Gk. *peri potmon*: "concerning fate"),[39] she is associated like Kathe with destiny. The dreamer comments:

How bootifull and how truetowife of her, when strengly forebidden, to steal our historic presents from the past postpropheticals so as to will make us all lordy heirs and ladymaidesses of a pretty nice kettle of fruit. She is livving in our midst of debt ... (her birth is uncontrollable) ... Gricks may rise and Troysirs fall (there being two sights for ever a picture) for in the byways of high improvidence that's what makes lifework leaving. (*FW* 11.29–36; 12.1–2)

She salvages for us both our preordained history after the Fall – the kettle of fruit we inherit – and our postlapsarian language with its "historic present" tense. In regenerating both world and word, she is a life force as well as fate. She makes life worth living, and her reproductive capacity cannot be controlled by death ("debt") or contraception or male attempts (the Trojan War) to possess her. She causes and survives phallic rises and falls ("Gricks": Greeks, pricks, bricks; "Troysirs": men of Troy, trousers). And, like Helen – "Let young wimman run away with the story" (*FW* 12.2–3) – she gives rise not only to events but to history in the sense of stories about the events. But, as the product of a fallen world, men's words have no more authority over her than men themselves, "there being two sights [sides, views] for ever a [for every] picture." Implicitly, ALP is linked to the endless production of meanings which thwarts the phallocentric drive to pin down, define, and control. Neither patriarchal society nor phallocentric language can achieve mastery over her.

The feminine principle as genetrix of "history" in the sense of stories or words permeates the *Wake*. Personified by Anna Livia (both as herself and as an aspect of all other feminine beings), this principle produces one of the book's central mysteries, the letter scratched by Biddy the hen out of the middenheap of history. The notion of history as a collection of fragments which are also words begins on the first page with the thunderword that marks the Fall. It is elaborated in Kathe's tour of the museyroom, in ALP's scrounging among the *disjecta membra* of war, and in the dialogue between Mutt and Jute (Shem and Shaun). Recognizing the stranger, Jute, as one of Ireland's perennial invaders, Mutt tries to teach him a lesson about the island's cyclical history of rises and falls. He points out a tumulus that contains the remains not only of earlier natives and invaders – "And thanacestross mound have swollup them all" – but of words: "(Stoop) if you are abcedminded, to this claybook, what curios of signs ... in this allaphbed! Can you rede ... its world?" (*FW* 18. 3–4, 17–19). An allusion to the fall of Troy ("Fiatfuit!") links this passage to ALP on the battlefield. Here, though, the earth itself embodies the feminine principle ("thanacestross": death, ancestress), generating the histories (the "meandertale") of the dead warriors and history-makers whom it embraces.

The midden mound reappears as a "filthdump near the Serpentine in Phornix Park" scavenged by Kate Strong. A widow reminiscent of Kathe, Kate provides a museum-like tableau – a "picture ... in a dreariodreama [diorama, Drury Lane, drama, dream] setting" – of the earliest history of Dublin and HCE. The dreamer suggests that the dump, once a military camp, would be a subtle place to "hide a leabhar [Ir. "book"] ... or a loveletter" (*FW* 80.6; 79.27–28; 80.14). Sure enough, we learn later that the mound had been covering the "untitled mamafesta" (*FW* 104.4) of ALP. Scratched up by that "original hen" (*FW* 110.22), Biddy, the letter-manifesto proves to be a history like Kathe's talk or Kate's tableau. It "is but an old story" of famous figures which ends with a woman, Kate, "tak[ing] charge of the waxworks" (*FW* 113.21–22) – that is, she takes over the waxwork museum of history, and also the moldable and remoldable words of historical narratives.

The mamafesta confuses the *Wake*'s four historians, "those gloompourers who grouse that letters have never been quite their old selves again since that weird weekday ... when to the shock of both, Biddy Doran looked at literature" (*FW* 112.24–27). Poring and bickering over the unsigned manuscript, the Four can determine neither its authorship nor its meaning. The letter's words seem at first to move "in comparative safety" along the "ruled barriers" of the lined paper on which it is written, but the writing becomes confusing, "with lines of litters slittering up and louds of latters slettering down" (*FW* 114.17–18). Finally the Four agree that the letter must be authoritative:

While we in our wee free state, holding to that prestatute in our charter, may have our irremovable doubts as to the whole sense of the lot, the interpretation of any phrase in the whole, the meaning of every word of a phrase so far deciphered out of it, however unfettered our Irish daily independence, we must vaunt no idle dubiosity as to its genuine authorship and holusbolus authoritativeness. (*FW* 117.34–118.4)

But here the letter becomes conflated with a fatally ambiguous historical document, the Anglo-Irish Treaty, whose misinterpretation by Griffith and Collins led to the fettering of Ireland's independence, her permanent partition, and the smallness of the Free State. Once again, then, woman is associated with the slipperiness of language, which constantly frustrates the desire of patriarchal authority to delimit and define it within "ruled barriers."

Later versions of the letter goad the four old men to further cogitations on the never-to-be-resolved question of what it means, particularly in relation to the incident in the park. In their role as judges at the inquest and trial concerning HCE's alleged crime, they cannot determine if the evidence clears or convicts him. But the very indeterminacy of the evidence, which is all words, points to the fact of a fall – not just HCE's fall, but "an overthrew of each and ilkermann of us" (*FW* 356.2). It is the persistent echo of the Fall, down through history, with which feminine voices – Anna Livia's, Issy's, Nuvoletta's, Margareen's – are associated in the *Wake*. They

themselves are not immune to the effects of the Fall. ALP gives voice
to the *Wake*'s most moving words in her farewell to life and desire
and illusion: "First we feel. Then we fall" (*FW* 627.11). In her
sadness she recognizes what HCE and his male *alter egos*, such as
Wellington and Parnell, will not permit to rise to consciousness: the
immanence of guilt, failure, division, death. Yet as the feminine
principle she is aligned with what the men repress, in particular with
the *Wake*'s "natlanguage" in whose web of endlessly creative and
deconstructive words all history-makers and historians are caught.

As many critics have noted, both *Ulysses* and *Finnegans Wake* end
in a flow of woman's words. The image of Molly Bloom as Penelope,
weaving and then unweaving her work each day, adumbrates Anna
Livia's association with language. Each figure subverts patriarchal
efforts to control and define her, and each provides the closing
perspective. Yet the extent to which Molly escapes her society's
stereotypes of femininity is debatable. Against Brown's notion of a
powerful, "self-possessed" woman we may set Unkeless' picture of a
conventional woman whose self-esteem derives largely from men's
responses to her.[40] When we turn to ALP, we can hardly speak of
self-possession or conventionality since she is not a distinct character
situated in a finely articulated social setting. But Joyce's concept of
ALP and other feminine figures in the *Wake* certainly has a historical
component, some aspects of which may be recoverable.

A photograph of Joyce at age six shows him kneeling and leaning
on his mother, who holds an open book in her lap; his father and
maternal grandfather flank them (*JJ* Plate 1). Adrienne Munich
has shown that this picture reappears in "The Dead" with the men
cropped out and with Gabriel Conroy's brother in the same pose as
Joyce with his mother. She argues that the story has two subtexts
relating to this photo.[41] One has to do with Gabriel's ultimately
futile attempts to assert a masculine dominance over women,
women's words, and his mother, who in his family functioned as
name-giver and initiator of her children into the world of language
and culture. The other has to do with Joyce's achievement, as
author of "The Dead," of his own masculine identity as an artist,
which he had set out to confirm when he sailed into self-exile in
October 1904. We see his triumph more clearly in light of *A Portrait*,
at the end of which Stephen's decision to pursue his art abroad
signifies a rejection not only of Ireland herself but of real and
symbolic women associated with Ireland. Most of all, he rejects his

mother, for whom he had danced and recited a poem as the infantile
artist of the opening; he replaces the maternal muse with a father
figure, the mythical artificer Daedalus. At a slightly later period in
his own life, while preparing to quit Ireland for good, Joyce used
"Daedalus" as a pen name in his letters and his first published
stories. But during his first year abroad, notably in July 1905 (*L II*
99), he expressed serious doubts about his vocation. Only in 1907,
after recovering from a fever and a fit of apathy toward his writing,
did he achieve a new, liberating view of both Ireland and himself in
that masterpiece and artistic jumping-off point, "The Dead."

If *A Portrait* confirms Joyce's achievement, his last two novels
bring out the earlier work's limitations. *Ulysses* reveals the super-
ficiality of Stephen's emancipation from his mother and reminds us,
through Molly, that Joyce took a woman with him when he left
Ireland to forge his identity. Both novels counter masculine artistic
and intellectual power with a subversive feminine force. Yet Joyce's
concept of this force grew out of an essentialist notion of femininity
that had roots in the patriarchal culture of nineteenth-century
middle-class Europe and that helped shape his characterization not
only of Molly but of ALP.

In 1907 Joyce told Stanislaus: "I have an Irish way of looking at
women. I can't take them seriously in anything they do."[42] Living
with Nora, a mistress-mother from whom he could scarcely bear to
be apart for a single night, taught him to take women seriously
enough in some respects. His predisposition to see women as fundamentally different and inferior, however, was reinforced by his
reading of Otto Weininger's *Sex and Character* (1903). Weininger
theorized that, although human beings contain within them both
masculine and feminine elements,[43] men and women are separated
by innate, radical differences. Preoccupied with their sexuality,
women, unlike men, remain restless children all their lives. They are
incapable, he argued, of playing an important part in any of the
essential activities of civilization, such as science, art, religion, commerce, or politics.[44] Joyce accepted much of this pseudo-scientific
nonsense, and "was always laboring to isolate female characteristics,
from an incapacity for philosophy to a dislike for soup" (*JJ* 463). He
took Nora (who had better sense than to regard herself as a model
for all women) as his principal object of study. Thus her distaste for
household chores, her dislike of highbrow culture, her indifference
to politics – these became "feminine" traits writ large.

One of Nora's most striking traits, for Joyce, was her tendency to write sentences with few punctuation marks or capital letters. This contributed to his idea of the feminine mind as a flow (in contrast with the analytic thinking and "hesitencies" of the masculine mind) and entered his portrayals of Molly and Anna Livia (*JJ* 376). But more than any single characteristic, Nora's otherness as a woman impinged on Joyce in her attitudes toward his writing and his sense of his own uniqueness. At least intermittently, throughout their relationship, her indifference to the creations of his phallic pen stung him. Almost at the start he recognized ruefully that she "didn't care a rambling damn about art" (*L II* 78). Later, in that crisis-fraught letter of 7 July 1905, he complained: "With one entire side of my nature she has no sympathy and will never have any." She withheld acknowledgment of his genius (perhaps for the good reason that she didn't understand his writing) even after *Ulysses* had made him a cult figure in Paris (*JJ* 377). In her unselfconscious autonomy she effortlessly pricked his grandiosity, much as the feminine principle pricks the grandiosity of male master-builders in *Finnegans Wake*. It was not that she dismissed him as ALP finally dismisses HCE: "You're only a bumpkin. I thought you the great in all things, in guilt and in glory. You're but a puny" (*FW* 627.22–24). Rather, the fallenness of language in the *Wake* renders all linguistic productions suspect, and it is females who point this up. We see this with Shem the Penman, who is the closest thing in the book to Joyce's artistic *alter ego*. Shem's literary training involves insinuating himself into model households and studying "how cutely to copy all their various styles of signature so as one day to utter an epical forged cheque on the public for his own private profit." Forging an epic entails not only self-aggrandizement but forgery, that is to say, verbal trickery. But even a lowly female domestic (Nora had been working as a chambermaid when Joyce met her) can see through Shem's pretensions; and it is "the Dustbin's United Scullerymaid's and House-help's Sorority" that "[turns] him down and [boots] the source of annoyance out of the place altogether" (*FW* 181.14–20).

The lack of distinction Nora made between Joyce and other men also piqued him. He saw her failure to recognize his specialness as a form of infidelity, and liked to brood over past or imagined rivals such as Sonny Bodkin or Vincent Cosgrave (whom he pictured as Robert Hand to his Richard Rowan in a real-life version of *Exiles*). Emotional or physical, infidelity became for him another feminine trait, even though Nora resisted in distress his perverse desire for her to prove this by having an affair. The central act performed in *Ulysses* by Molly Bloom – that representative, as he described her to Budgen, of "amoral fertilisable untrustworthy engaging shrewd limited prudent indifferent *Weib*" (*L I* 170) – is the consummation of her affair with Boylan. When we turn to *Finnegans Wake* the situation differs since ALP makes love with HCE, but she and the feminine principle are, nonetheless, associated with infidelity of a sexual-textual kind. The male's insistence on complete authority – over a woman or over words – is thwarted by the woman's or language's resistance to being finally defined and owned. The feminine, in this dialectic, becomes that which is unfaithful to masculine desire, whether it be an individual man's need for sexual possession or the striving of phallocentric language for semantic possession.

TOWARD THE POSSIBILITY OF AN "IDEAREAL HISTORY"
(*FW* 262.7–8)

One of the great themes of *Finnegans Wake* is the possibility of freedom within history. It becomes conflated, however, with the possibility of freedom within language. History and story, the world and the word: these categories merge. Further, a third category – identity – is interlinked with the first two. In the Lacanian universe of the *Wake*, the mind is structured like a language; neither world nor self comes into being without the word. Thus, if the "allnights newseryreel" (*FW* 489.35) of Wakean world history takes place within the dreaming mind of HCE, its re-echoing implicit question – what happened in the Park? – might be restated: who is HCE? Or, to put it another way: who is the historian? In any case, the problem of finding freedom within history and language also becomes the problem of finding freedom within the confines of a subjectivity which has been shaped, in ways we can never fully realize, by both history and language.

At first glance, a book based partly on Vico's cyclical philosophy and partly on Christian cosmology would hardly seem to be the place to look for liberation within history. The world, in *Finnegans Wake*, seems to go round and round without arriving anywhere. It "millwheel[s]" through various stages – prehistory, gods, heroes, men – on its "vicociclometer" (*FW* 614.27) and, after many revolutions, "rearrive[s]" (*FW* 3.5) at its starting-point. Against the backdrop of these cycles even the most powerful agents – kings, diplomats, generals – merely act out their predestined roles. Further, the pervasive influence of the Fall sets limits on the freedom of all individuals. As the ur-event which initiates Wakean history, the Fall preordains key aspects – guilt, loss, diminishment, death – of individual experience within that history.

Yet, as Joyce suggests, our fall into history may be a fortunate fall – a *felix culpa*. In order to explore this possibility, we must return once more to Phoenix Park and those "phaymix cupplerts" (*FW* 331.2–3), the Invincibles. Once news of the Park murders broke, late in the evening of 6 May 1882, more than a few people saw them as an eruption of inexplicable evil and as a national fall. Parnell, reacting both to the killings' horror and to their threat to the Kilmainham treaty, asked Davitt: "What is the use ... of men striving as we have done ... if we are to be struck at in this way by unknown men who can commit atrocious deeds of this kind?"[45] On 11 May an article in *The Evening Telegraph* declared:

They [the murders] are offences not only against society and humanity, but, as they affect the future of the country ... they are of almost super-natural guilt – crimes of the same blackness as the conspiracy of the fallen angels against the eternal welfare of man.[46]

Decades later, in Gorman's biography of Joyce, the murders not only would reappear in a similar apocalyptic light, but would be linked to Joyce's birth. This extraordinary passage (no doubt prompted by Joyce)[47] begins by describing the excitement of life in Dublin in the 1880s, that period of cultural revival and Parnell's ascendancy. But Vichian thunder, signifying a new cycle of history, rumbles in the background:

The times were heavy with thunder and startled by unexpected flashes of cruel lightning ... 1882 was an année terrible in the annals of Irish history. On May fifth (when James Joyce was three months and three days old) there was the famous torchlight procession through the streets of the city, a procession celebrating the liberation of Parnell and Michael Davitt from Kilmainham Jail and loud with optimism for the future. The next day Lord Spencer, the new viceroy, made his state entry into Dublin. And in the twilight of this day ... Joe Brady and his Invincibles left the public house near the gates of the Lower Castle Yard, drove to the Phoenix Park and there slaughtered the Chief Secretary for Ireland, Lord Frederick Caven-dish, and the Permanent Under-Secretary, Thomas Henry Burke ... [I]t is easy enough to imagine [the] excitement that shook all Dublin and kept the streets full of people waiting for the midnight edition of the *Evening Telegraph*. James Joyce, sleeping quietly in his crib, was mercifully unconscious of the fact that he had been born in a black period. That he was to find out for himself in the years to come. But Dublin ... knew that Joe Brady, Carey, Kelly, Fagan, and the other Invincibles had changed the history of Ireland in a moment's ferociousness.[48]

In other words, the future artist had been born virtually at the inauguration of a new, dismal cycle in Irish history – a cycle set into motion by a mysterious crime, about which rumors soon would fly, committed in Phoenix Park.

The relationship between Joyce and the murders in the park boils down to the relationship between the artist and history. As I discussed in Chapter 1, Joyce, in *Ulysses*, links the Invincibles to the cycles of futile, mutually feeding violence between colonizer and colonized. A large part of his ambivalent rejection of Irish nationalism stemmed from its association with such violence and the worship of it in the form of heroticism. But he rejected it equally because of its narratives – its histories – and the claims they made not only on his allegiance but on his identity. In *A Portrait*, in his debate with Davin, the G.A.A. athlete and likely I.R.B. recruit, Stephen sloughs off these claims fairly easily by pointing out betrayal as the fault-line in the wished-for image of nationalist unity. His defense of his Irishness, however, points to his own identity problem. He tells Davin to check his father's name, that odd Greek patronymic, in the register at Dublin Castle. Yet in embracing Daedalus as his spiritual father he substitutes one masculine myth for another – the potency of the word for the potency of the weapon. As a phallocentric signifier, the name Daedalus serves a purpose not unlike that of Davin's *caman* or Joe Brady's knife or the rifle without which Pearse thought an Irish nationalist could not be a man. Thus, though Stephen's mythologizing of his identity points us toward the "ideareal history" of *Finnegans Wake*, it does not resolve the complexities of his relationship to Irish history.

In *Ulysses* Stephen faces the failure of the paternal identification that brings *A Portrait* to a seemingly successful close. Thoughts of his biological father, and of rebels and heretics who constitute alternative father figures, run through his mind. This theme of paternity entwines itself around the broader themes of identity and history. In Stephen's obsessed musing on anarchs and heresiarchs we see another stage in the development of ideareal history. They represent possibilities cancelled by actual events, by the march of history's victors. Yet in his imagination they live, suggesting alternatives both to the history which has come to pass and to his own identity as it has been shaped by history. If paternity is a "legal fiction" (*U* 9.844), then we can imaginatively choose our own fathers. Yet, unlike the hero of *A Portrait*, Stephen does not simply replace his blood-and-flesh father with a mythical one. Rather, the "All too Irish" (*U* 16.384) Simon Dedalus coexists dialogically with various paternal possibilities, including Bloom, the would-be surrogate father whom Stephen fails to recognize.

In a like manner, *Ulysses* suggests that the dark annals of Irish and world history coexist with those "possibilities they have ousted" (*U* 2.51). History, the past – Aristotle's "that which has been" – is in fact defined by "that which might have been," those possibilities which never materialized. Stephen himself, grappling with the nightmare of historical closure in the form of his mother's death, can do no more than theorize the opening up of history (and his own identity) through such dialogues. As his concept of "the lancet of [his] art" and Mulligan's nickname for him – "Kinch, the knife-blade" (*U* 1.55) – imply, he remains caught up in fantasies of phallic self-assertion. But *Ulysses* itself realizes what Stephen can only adumbrate. In its evocation of the nation as an imagined community, and in its deconstruction of the Invincibles, it reveals the imaginative component of history. And in so doing it offers an alternative to an unchanging, blood-stained past in which historical agents, represented in fixed subject positions like the waxwork Invincibles at Madame Tussaud's, perform over and over the one act they could have done from the beginning of time. It offers, then, an escape – even though a partial, provisional one – from the male-dominated history of winners and losers whose emblem in *Ulysses* is the knife.

In *Finnegans Wake* the possibility of ideareal history centers not so much in imagination as in language. Language itself becomes the prime creative and deconstructive force, acting as such whether generated by artists (Shem the Penman) or solid citizens (Shaun the Post). It constantly forms and reforms the world, history, identity. Because of the Fall – because, in particular, of the resulting gulf between signifier and referent – nothing generated by language is singular, unitary, unambiguous. To assert is to deny; to construct is to deconstruct; to rise is to fall. Through *différance* the closure of

history which threatens Stephen in *Ulysses* is opened up; history
becomes a receding horizon of endless difference. In this way the
Invincibles' murderous assertion of Irish identity in Phoenix Park,
like HCE's response to the cad, dissolves into a welter of contradictory meanings such as we saw in the various interpretations of the
murders in Chapter 1. Similarly, assumptions of English linguistic
superiority, tied to the judicial murder of Myles Joyce, dissolve in
the melting-pot of the *Wake*'s English-based but many-tongued
"messes of mottage" (*FW* 183.22–23). No kind of mastery – whether
of the phallic kind asserted with weapons or the phallocentric kind
asserted with words – succeeds in the *Wake*. Even the artist must
abandon dreams of mastery, of imposing a fixed, authoritative mark
on the raw material of words. Like Shem the Penman, he or she produces forged documents with multiple meanings which inevitably
ramify beyond the forger's intent or control.

Language in *Finnegans Wake*, then, points to the possibility of
freedom from mastery by being that force which reveals any unitary
identity, whether that of master or servant, to be an illusion. The
linguistically constituted subject is divided – both subject and other
– from the moment of self-awareness. From the point of view of historiography, this implies a scary yet potentially liberating bond
between the historian and those complex, conflicted, ambivalent
agents of history which historians (at least the best ones) write
about. When we weave a historical narrative, we leave imprinted
on our material the marks of our own dividedness. This has several
consequences. First, no history – for instance, the history a nation-
state requires its citizens to learn at school – can be authoritative or
(in the Rankean sense) objective. Second, our dividedness can be
read historically, so that any narrative about history becomes itself
a historical document. (In other words, even though our dividedness
has roots in what the *Wake* depicts as a prehistorical fall – a fall
which serves as a metaphor for the preverbal eruption-rupture of
the self – those myriad fault-lines which divide and subdivide the
self are acted out and expressed historically.) Third, we need to be
adept at reading the subtexts, or the latent content, of histories.
Like all texts, histories harbor conflicts, contradictions, and
ambiguities which reflect unfulfillable desire – the desire arising at
the moment of the fall into history and selfhood and dividedness –
and which express themselves in disguised or hidden form. *Finnegans
Wake*, by taking the shape of a dream about history which is also the

history of the dreamer, emphasizes this need for attunement to the repressed.

The scary part of the situation I have just outlined above has to do with the loss of the historian's privilege, authority, and stable identity. As readers we must look for the unconscious contradiction or double meaning which points to psychic division and verbal slippage. As historians we must write, like the dreamer in *Finnegans Wake*, without assurance that we know exactly who we are as historical subjects or that our words will say exactly what we want them to say. In fact, we must write with the opposite assurance. And herein lies the liberating aspect of language as Joyce presents it to us in the *Wake*. Because there are no inherently stable subject positions, we not only can escape the historical closure feared by Stephen in *Ulysses*, but have the opportunity to take part self-consciously in the ongoing process of making and remaking the self. History is not a tableau, frozen in the past, but "a collideorscape" (*FW* 143.28) – a kaleidoscope of meanings in constant, shifting dialogue with one another. Our fall into history is a fortunate fall insofar as we can move away from the illusion of an unchanging self, predestined to have its fixed desires disappointed, toward a more flexible sub-jectivity.

We make this move, so far as I understand the *Wake*'s implied history lesson, by recognizing and aligning ourselves with the creative-deconstructive power of language as a shaper of human reality. Though history acts on us, we can act on history. Language reveals that seemingly immutable subject positions are imagined insofar as they depend on repression of alternative positions which define them. By re-imagining these positions – as when we (re)write history – we may change them. Even in reading someone else's history we can reform the world, and reform ourselves, to the extent that our awareness of language allows us to enter a free flow of meanings which bypasses or overflows both our own and the his-torian's well-dug, narrow channels.

Hence, within the seemingly deterministic cycles of Vichian history, *Finnegans Wake* offers a vision of freedom based on language. Joyce's concept of language as the shaping force of ideareal history comes from Vico, too. Vico made it the cornerstone of his *New Science*:

Our Science therefore comes to describe ... an ideal eternal history traversed in time by the history of every nation in its rise, development, maturity, decline, and fall. Indeed, we make bold to affirm that he who meditates this Science narrates to himself this ideal eternal history ... For ... this world of nations has certainly been made by men, and its guise must therefore be found within the modifications of our own human mind. And history cannot be more certain than when he who creates the things also narrates them.[49]

There is, however, an ambiguity in Vico about the boundary line between world and word; and in the *Wake* the line disappears. The world collapses into the word, and so we face a paradox. However exhilarating it may be to read the *Wake*, and whatever it teaches us of potential liberation, the book tends to become a prisonhouse of words in the very endlessness of its play of meanings. To live and act in the world, we must slow down the kaleidoscope of history, however arbitrarily, simply to maintain our sanity. We can take our awareness of dividedness and the slipperiness of language only so far. We can remake our histories and ourselves only so much, only so fast. Thus *Finnegans Wake*, that meditation on freedom and limitation, has its own limits as a history lesson. Far ahead of its time, perhaps immune to pathetic anachronism, it offers us radical insights into the problem of our historicity. Yet as a historical product itself, it remains rooted in its own time; and it conveys thoughts on language, history, and gender which are conditioned not only by Joyce's subject position but by our own positions as readers within history.

CHAPTER 7

Afterword: Language and history

I am always sorry when any language is lost, because languages
are the pedigree of nations.

Samuel Johnson, quoted in Boswell, Tour to the Hebrides

The language of the conqueror in the mouths of the conquered
is the language of slaves.

Tacitus, quoted in "Irish Language Notes," United Irishman
(1896)

What, in the fallen world of a colonized country whose native
tongue has been usurped by the conqueror's tongue, is the relationship between language and history? In the first paragraph of "The
Sisters" the boy unknowingly puzzles over this problem as he repeats
the words *paralysis, gnomon,* and *simony.* What can they tell him about
his friend, a dying priest? Their inefficacy as signifiers is implied
when he must rely on his dreams – on nonverbal dream language –
for a felt response to Father Flynn's death. The adults in the story
seem afflicted with a similar linguistic inadequacy. Old Cotter trails
off as he tries to explain why the friendship between priest and boy
was unhealthy. Prone to malapropisms, Eliza gropes and falters as
she attempts to analyze her brother's sad history. The story ends
with one of her pauses, signaled by an ellipsis, a gap implying the
failure of words, of the Word, in relation to his "crossed" (*D* 17) life.

Father Flynn's frustrated career, and his breakdown and death,
represent the ruin of what should have been a success story and a
model for a fatherless, lower middle-class Catholic boy living in
turn-of-the-century Dublin. Flynn's journey from Irishtown to a
seminary in Rome constitutes a remarkable escape from his likely
future, that of a slum child born not long before colonial Ireland's
worst disaster, the famines of the late 1840s. One of the changes
Joyce made to the story was specifying the year of Flynn's death as
1895. Given his age, sixty-five, this makes it possible that the year of

his birth was also the year of Catholic Emancipation, 1829. His rise, then, loosely suggests that of the Church itself.[1] In nineteenth-century Catholic Ireland the alternative authority to the British Crown (we recall that the first version of "The Sisters" appears just above two advertisements citing appointments to the king) was the Church. The Irish Church offered a different history, a different order of language, and a different father from those of colonialism. Father Flynn, with his stories and his instruction in Latin, has served this function in relation to his young protégé. Yet, obscurely, he has frightened the boy; and the fear which the boy associates with the word *paralysis* has something to do not with the priest's authority but rather its absence.

Joyce's additions to the *Homestead* version of "The Sisters" emphasize the verbal nature of Flynn's, and the Church's, authority. The priest has taught the boy how to pronounce Latin "properly"; he has explained that "the fathers of the Church had written books as thick as the *Post Office Directory* and as closely printed as the law notices in the newspaper" (*D* 13). Embodying Irish Catholic patriarchy, he is associated with the authority of the phallocentric word. He also exemplifies what Declan Kiberd calls "the problem of the Irish male as inadequate father,"[2] a problem with roots in Ireland's history as an oppressed colony. The identity Father Flynn offers the boy betrays, underneath its imposing verbal-symbolic structure, its own hollowness, its absence of connection to spiritual referents. The significance of the dropped chalice has to do with what it did *not* contain, that is, the Eucharistic wine's referent, the blood of Christ. In the fallen world of Joyce's *Dubliners* the ceremony lacks authority, symbols and words lack linkage to any ultimate reality, and sons lack fathers. Thus Father Flynn does not offer the boy an alternative language or history or identity. He becomes instead an emblem of entrapment, and remains entrapped within Irish colonial history, as the date of his death – 1 July, the anniversary of the Battle of the Boyne – and his residence in Great Britain Street suggest. Foreshadowing the aftermath of phallocentric assertion in *Finnegans Wake*, his history, after his fall and death, is told by an old woman. Eliza's ellipses, punctuating her hesitant account, embody the hole in his life and the gap between word and referent. As in the *Wake*, women reveal the emptiness of men's pretensions – in particular, the emptiness of masculine verbal constructs asserting unity, authority, and identity.

The young author of "The Sisters" was not yet able to identify the creative-deconstructive power of language as a source of freedom from history, nor was he ready to link this power to women. In *Dubliners*, women (Mrs. Dillon, Mangan's sister, Eveline's mother, Annie Chandler, Ada Farrington, the Morkan sisters) tend to represent acquiescence in the established order of paralyzed, colonial Dublin. And language always emanates from that same order even when it seems to promise escape. In "An Encounter" the narrator is inspired by tales of the Wild West to try "to break out of the weariness of school-life." But, as I discussed in Chapter 3, these "chronicles of disorder," published in British boys' magazines, mirror the prevailing colonial order as much as their apparent dialogic opposite, Father Butler's Roman History. The "wild sensations" and "escape" (*D* 21) which they seem to offer turn out to be an encounter with another unsatisfactory father figure whose impotence takes linguistic form not just in his tendency to perform empty verbal rituals, but in the inadequacy of his literary heroes (two British lords and a lord-loving Irishman) as the source of an alternative identity for a young Irish Catholic boy. The narrator's quest in "Araby" runs into a similar dead end. The referent of the word *Araby*, which "cast[s] an Eastern enchantment" over the boy, proves to be a mundane charity bazaar. The bazaar's "magical name" (*D* 32, 34), the allusion to James Clarence Mangan (a celebrator in his poetry of the mysterious East), and the sentimentality of the uncle who tipsily recites "The Arab's Farewell to His Steed" – these all reflect the escapist orientalism, and the colonialism to which it was tied, of middle-class Western Europe in the late nineteenth century.

In "The Dead," Joyce's coda to *Dubliners*, the pattern of linguistic seduction, thwarted escape, and return to a historically determined paralysis differs somewhat. Gabriel seems to have dealt successfully with the problem of his subject position in a colonized country by choosing a cosmopolitan identity based in part on language – that is, on his disavowal of Irish, his ability to speak French and German, and his writing of book reviews without regard for nationalist politics. Yet the words of two women associated with the West, site of Ireland's severest colonial trauma, undo his cosmopolitanism and his sense of verbal mastery over women and Ireland. Shaken by his encounters with Molly and Gretta, Gabriel, in sleepy reverie, imagines himself "set[ting] out on his journey westward." His recognition of mortality, and the influence of the dead on the living, coincides with his recognition of the West of Ireland – which he connects with "that region where dwell the vast hosts of the dead" (*D* 223) – and the part it has played in shaping Gretta's and his own lives. This notion of the West as a land of ghosts is not merely metaphorical. It has roots in the great famine of the 1840s and the nineteenth-century dislocations and emigrations, accelerated by the famine, which turned the "Congested Districts" into the haunted, empty spaces we still find in the West today. Gabriel's epiphany, then, has a powerful historical component. This element remains latent, however, and is mystified by the universalizing imagery and poetic cadences of the story's ending. Entranced with rhetoric even as he drifts off to sleep, Gabriel cannot break through language to the repressed national history which has helped mold him any more than he can break through his psychic defenses to the fear of his mother and feminine power which has helped shape his masculine identity.

If none of the characters in *Dubliners* avoids entrapment in historically determined modes of language and thought, the artist himself does make an escape of sorts in that we cannot identify him with a single voice or level of discourse among the many marking the stories. In *A Portrait*, too, polyphony distances the artist from Stephen's various phases and their related idioms. There is an implied disavowal of identification with the history-bound protagonist, a disavowal even to some extent of the stable, undivided subject. Yet the novel depicts Stephen's search for a strong masculine creative identity, one which he ties to the same father figure, Daedalus, whose name the young Joyce himself adopted. Stephen's imagined filial kinship to the mythical artificer provides him with a countervailing force not just to female reproductive power, allied in *A Portrait* with family, country, and religion, but to opposing models of masculine identity: priest, king, and nationalist hero-martyr. Though one can only speculate, I think that the surrogate fathership of Daedalus (conflated with other male creators such as Dante and Ibsen) must have represented to Joyce a source of similar strength in 1904–05 when he first seriously pursued his artistic vocation. But in one sense this notion of the male artist-hero does not differ from other forms of masculine identity such as Joyce had rejected in refusing (as Stephen refuses) to join the priesthood or the nationalist movement. It shares with them an emphasis on phallocentric mastery exercised by an undivided subject. At the end of *A Portrait*, wrapped in Daedalus' mantle, Stephen hopes through such mastery to reform Irish consciousness and so change the course of Irish history. Joyce, however, by the time he started transmuting *Stephen Hero* into *A Portrait*, had long abandoned Daedalus as *his* father. He was developing concepts of language, history, and subjectivity, incompatible with phallocentric mastery, which infuse his writing as early as "The Sisters" but which *Ulysses* would give him far more scope to formulate than the stories or the autobiographical novel.

Ulysses ranges beyond the earlier works in several respects. First, it sets about deconstructing the notion of a stable, unified subject. It does this in "Circe," for instance, with its various versions of Bloom, each of them no less "true" and no more fictional than the other. Second, it deconstructs the boundary between history and fiction. It does this, with a view to opening up seemingly closed historical possibilities, through its portrayal of the Invincibles and especially Skin-the-Goat Fitzharris, a fictional character whose dubious status as a historical figure implies the imagined component of all historical agents and the narratives in which they function (see Chapter 1). Third, *Ulysses* suggests and embodies a creative mode based not on phallocentric mastery but on a feminine generative principle, similar to the creative aspect of Derrida's *différance*, that subverts all forms of mastery.

This principle actuates *Ulysses* throughout but does not become salient until "Proteus." Here Stephen strolls along Sandymount Strand and finds correspondences between the creative power of nature and that of language. Unlike the expectant young artist of *A Portrait*, this Stephen has suffered a creative and emotional fall relating to the death of his mother. He connects her death with the violence and closure of history, and with his own problematic subject position, which he links to the Fall and a half-mystical, half-biological determinism:

Spouse . . . of Adam Kadmon: Heva, naked Eve . . .
   Wombed in sin darkness I was too, made not begotten. By them, the man with my voice and my eyes and a ghostwoman with ashes on her breath. They did the coupler's will. (*U* 3.41–47)

As he walks on the beach, though, his meditations on natural and linguistic transformation suggest a way of dealing with both biological and historical closure. In his guilt over his mother's death, he

identifies her with a drowned man in Dublin bay whom he in turn
associates with "Lycidas" and a song ("Full fathom five thy father
lies") from *The Tempest*. Both poems transcend the harsh reality of
drowning by transmuting it into art; the bones and eyes of the father
in Ariel's song, for instance, have become coral and pearls in an
underwater paradise where sea-nymphs musically ring his knell. As
though inspired by the poems, Stephen, imagining minnows
nibbling on the corpse in the bay, thinks: "God becomes man
becomes fish becomes barnacle goose becomes featherbed mountain" (*U* 3.477–79). This series of transformations begins with the
supernatural, proceeds through the physical, and ends with linguistic metamorphosis. The unexpected addition of the word "mountain" – Featherbed Mountain is the name of a hill southwest of
Dublin Bay – removes us from the expected continuation of the
natural chain of consumer and consumed. It reminds us that all the
items in this series of changes are words. Nature's power of transformation is thus paralleled and subsumed by the creative-
deconstructive power of language; and the masculine order of God
the Father is replaced, as a response to the problem of change and
mortality, by a feminine verbal order.

The "femininity" of this verbal order arises out of its link to the
transformational power of the sea. The sea's maternal nature is
established early: Mulligan calls her the "great sweet mother" and
"Our mighty mother" (*U* 1.77–78, 80, 85), while Dublin Bay
reminds Stephen of his own mother. In "Proteus" a gypsy woman
trekking across the beach sparks a meditation on the sea, femininity,
and a mysterious vampire:

She trudges, schlepps, trains, drags, trascines her load. A tide westering,
moondrawn, in her wake. Tides, myriadislanded, within her, blood not
mine, *oinopa ponton*, a winedark sea. Behold the handmaid of the moon. In
sleep the wet sign calls her hour, bids her rise. Bridebed, childbed, bed of
death, ghostcandled. Omnis caro ad te veniet. He comes, pale vampire,
through storm his eyes, his bat sails bloodying the sea, mouth to her
mouth's kiss. (*U* 3.392–98)

This rich passage connects woman through her menstrual flow with
lunar tides. It also ties her in the first sentence to a playful linguistic
creativity or *jouissance* which elsewhere in "Proteus" manifests itself
as a property of the sea: "Listen: a fourworded wavespeech: seesoo,
hrss, rsseeiss, ooos" (*U* 3.56–57). The only male element is the
vampire, associated with Stephen and his creativity; later, between

this time and his visit to the newspaper office, he works the vampire imagery into a quatrain which is his only formal artistic product that day.

This passage offers us a key to the shift that Stephen seems to be trying to make, and that Joyce already has made, from phallic to feminine creativity.[3] The passage turns female blood, especially menstrual blood – "the wet sign" – into the essential marker of sexual difference. Drawn by her blood, the pale vampire comes to the woman not only to replenish himself but to absorb her femininity and actually become a woman – a wish fulfilled in Stephen's quatrain, which evokes the woman's point of view:

> *On swift sail flaming*
> *From storm and south*
> *He comes, pale vampire,*
> *Mouth to my mouth.*   (*U* 7.522–25)

This sequence illustrates a psychological mechanism – identifying with a significant object by orally incorporating it – which goes back to a stage in human development when the infant is still breast-feeding and before it has entered the world of fathers. In his guilty grief Stephen seems to have regressed to this early, mother-centered time. Yet the regression can also be seen as a further step in his search for an artistic identity that will enable him to cope with history. His mother's death has brought about the Icarus-like fall foreshadowed when the protagonist of *A Portrait*, denying maternal bonds, adopted Daedalus as artist-father. Now, in the role of the mother's vampire-son, Stephen seeks unconsciously to take on her reproductive power, which is also the creative-deconstructive power of nature (symbolized by the sea) and language. He seeks a fluid, "feminine" subjectivity, which constantly makes, undoes, and remakes itself. In this way he can avoid the phallic rises and falls, the rigidity, and the closure of possibility which he associates with "masculine" subjectivity and with history itself. He can align himself with that principle which subverts history, or at least history as exemplified in the careers of Pyrrhus, Parnell, and other father figures who have fallen through the agency of women. History, in *Ulysses*, is always masculine, always a chronicle of power and control whose paradigm is colonization. Feminine writing, then, becomes for the colonized subject the language of liberation.

The 22-year-old Stephen is not yet ready to complete his incipient shift from masculine to feminine modes of thinking and writing. But *Ulysses* points to the likelihood that Joyce himself had already moved in this direction, however unconsciously and conflictedly. His "hero," a destablizing revision of the ancient patriarchal idea of the hero, is an androgynous man. And the novel closes with a feminine point of view expressed in the flowing thoughts and words of an adulterous, hence subversive woman. *Ulysses* reflects Joyce's discovery of a principle more powerful than anything to be found in the history of nations, races, and languages.

It is this principle toward which Joyce was groping in "Ireland, Island of Saints and Sages" (1907) when he wrote:

What race, or what language ... can boast of being pure today? Nationality (if it really is not a convenient fiction ...) must find its reason for being rooted in something that surpasses and transcends and informs changing things like blood and the human word. (*CW* 165–66)

Later his wariness of nationality and national languages deepened: they struck him as being inseparable from phallic power struggles and domination. He acknowledged the displacement of Irish Gaelic by English as a loss – a loss whose result was the kind of alienation Stephen feels in his conversation with the dean of studies – yet refused from his student days on to support the revival of Gaelic. He must have felt vindicated when the Free State imposed Irish on reluctant teachers and students, which it did with authoritarian harshness after De Valera took power in 1932.[4] At this time Joyce himself was using an unprecedented number of Irish and Irish-based words. They were embedded, however, in the polyglot matrix of *Finnegans Wake*, where no single tongue could claim mastery. The *Wake*'s heteroglossia (a development of the ever more varied voices of the earlier works) undermines positions of dominance among national languages much as its deconstructive use of words in general undermines phallocentric privilege.

Finnegans Wake embodies Joyce's final concept of the artist's relationship to history. As a teleological progress toward one great goal (whether it be the British Empire or an Irish Republic), history involves winners and losers, oppression, and the closure of possibilities relating not just to politics but to individual identity. History in this sense is "masculine" because of its association with fact and power. By aligning himself with imagination and the creative-deconstructive power of language, the artist assumes a subversive, "feminine" position, one of perpetual resistance to history. Joyce thus discovered the political potential of *jouissance* and *différance* long before deconstruction was a gleam in Derrida's eye. The playful, anarchical elusiveness of language threatens all fixed, hegemonic positions.

Yet if we need narratives to live by – if human beings are story-making creatures, as Jameson suggests – then we cannot adopt a politics pure and simple of deconstructive resistance. Even the notion of such resistance implies a narrative and the constraints of a more or less fixed subject position: the role of the Shakespearean fool, say, who turns the words of the powerful inside out yet remains on the periphery of the drama. To be perpetually marginal and subversive (or "feminine," in the *Wake*'s dialectic) is to close off certain historical possibilities by limiting our ability to intervene in history. Such a position also inevitably reflects the historical circumstances of its production, and is no escape from history; it harbors its own political unconscious. This is a major limitation of Joyce's politics, particularly in *Finnegans Wake*. Yet the deconstructive openness of all Joyce's fictions encourages the opening up of other narratives, especially those of history. It impels us to think in new ways about ourselves as historical agents. And, by opening up unlikely or unconsidered historical possibilities, it suggests new ways of enacting and writing the history of the future.[5] For this reason alone Joyce's works are worth all all our tears and trouble as readers, and are worth the effort of introducing them to nonspecialists and nonacademics, since it is all of us who will shape future history together.

Notes

INTRODUCTION

1 Aristotle, *Poetics*, 234–35.
2 Gossman, "History and Literature," 4.
3 Quoted in the *OED* under "History."
4 White, *The Content of the Form*, 147.
5 Jameson, *The Political Unconscious*, 35.
6 Quoted in Krieger, *Ranke: The Meaning of History*, 4 and 5.
7 Quoted in Finley, *Ancient History*, 54.
8 Quoted *ibid.*, 52.
9 Quoted *ibid.*, 53.
10 Collingwood, *The Idea of History*, 237.
11 Gossman, "History and Literature," 31–32.
12 Collingwood, *The Idea of History*, 317.
13 Collingwood, "The Pleasures of Doubt," 521.
14 Collingwood, *The Idea of History*, 248.
15 Hirst, *Marxism and Historical Writing*, 51.
16 Barthes, "The Discourse of History," 18.
17 Hirst, *Marxism and Historical Writing*, 56.
18 Williams, *Marxism and Literature*, 54.
19 Finley, *Ancient History*, 4, 104, 105.
20 Jameson, *The Political Unconscious*, 10.
21 On history as a transcendent category in Marxian thought, cf. Eagleton, *Criticism and Ideology*, 95: "Ideological space is curved like space itself, and history lies beyond it as only God could lie beyond the universe."
22 White, *The Content of the Form*, 150.
23 White, "The Historical Text as Literary Artifact," 50.
24 Jameson, *The Political Unconscious*, 19.
25 *Ibid.*, 9.
26 *Ibid.*, 10 and 49.
27 See Derrida, *"Différance,"* 12: "We will designate as *différance* the movement according to which language, or any code, any system of referral in general, is constituted 'historically' as a weave of differences."

28 Ryan, *Marxism and Deconstruction*, 213.
29 Bennett, "Texts in History," 65.
30 Bennett recommends, with minor reservations, Ernesto Laclau's argument: "Marxism ... should conceive of itself as a set of discursive interventions ... which must prove their validity through their effects rather than by claiming any ... prior ontological privilege" ("Texts in History," 68).

1 THE MURDERS IN THE PARK

1 Quoted in Corfe, *The Phoenix Park Murders*, 247.
2 Brown, *The Politics of Irish Literature*, 284.
3 Corfe, *The Phoenix Park Murders*, 135.
4 Tynan, *The Irish National Invincibles*, 325.
5 Corfe, *The Phoenix Park Murders*, 142–43.
6 *Ibid.*, 192.
7 Quoted *ibid.*, 193.
8 *Ibid.*, 194.
9 *Ibid.*, 136.
10 *Ibid.*, 195.
11 *Ibid.*, 196.
12 *Ibid.*, 266.
13 *Ibid.*, 143.
14 Brown, *The Politics of Irish Literature*, 275.
15 Corfe, *The Phoenix Park Murders*, 190.
16 Brown, *The Politics of Irish Literature*, 276.
17 *Ibid.*, 272.
18 Corfe, *The Phoenix Park Murders*, 192.
19 Brown, *The Politics of Irish Literature*, 274.
20 O'Brien, *A Concise History of Ireland*, 114.
21 Adams, *Surface and Symbol*, 162.
22 Thornton, *Allusions in* Ulysses, 85.
23 Adams, *Surface and Symbol*, 162–63.
24 Corfe, *The Phoenix Park Murders*, 256.
25 Quoted in Brown, *The Politics of Irish Literature*, 280.
26 *Ibid.*, 281.
27 Corfe, *The Phoenix Park Murders*, 244.
28 *Ibid.*, 256.
29 Brown, *The Politics of Irish Literature*, 282–83.
30 *Ibid.*, 279; cf. *FW* 614.35.
31 *Ibid.*, 283–84.
32 Radford, "King, Pope, and Hero-Martyr," 314–15.
33 Jameson, *The Political Unconscious*, 35.
34 Tynan, *The Irish National Invincibles*, xiv.
35 Bakhtin, *The Dialogic Imagination*, 291–92.

36 Tynan, *The Irish National Invincibles*, 256 and 257.
37 *Ibid.*, xvii.
38 O'Casey, *Autobiographies*, Vol. I, 421.
39 Kaplan, "The Case of the Grassy Knoll," 418.
40 Barthes, "The Discourse of History," 17.
41 I use the term "prototype narratives" in a narrower sense than that of Jameson's "master narratives." It refers to the narrativizations of conceptual frameworks for grasping events, relationships, and other phenomena (such as wars and national histories).
42 Brown, *The Politics of Irish Literature*, viii.
43 "Cultural revolution" (*The Political Unconscious*, 95–98) is Jameson's term for this ongoing dialectic which produces ideology.
44 Deane, "Retrospective Review," 1.
45 Brown, *The Politics of Irish Literature*, 17.
46 Deane, "Joyce and Nationalism," 179.
47 Curtis, *Apes and Angels*, 43.
48 See Curtis's *Apes and Angels* for a comparison of opposed Celtic stereotypes in nineteenth-century English and Irish cartoons.
49 Brown, *The Politics of Irish Literature*, 282.
50 Deane, "Joyce and Nationalism," 181.
51 Deane, "History as Fiction," 137.

2 LITERARY POLITICS

1 Seeley, *The Expansion of England*, 10.
2 Tennyson, "Ulysses."
3 Kipling, "The White Man's Burden."
4 Newbolt, "Vitaï Lampada."
5 Garvin, "James Joyce's Municipal Background," 556.
6 *Ibid.*, 557.
7 Lyons, *Ireland since the Famine*, 192.
8 Brown, *The Politics of Irish Literature*, 17.
9 Brown, "Dublin in Twentieth-Century Writing," 7.
10 Mercier, "Dublin Under the Joyces," 286.
11 Brown, "Dublin in Twentieth-Century Writing," 11.
12 Joyce, in his essay on Fenianism, anachronistically attributes the rescue attempt at Clerkenwell prison to the Invincibles (*CW* 190) – a symptom perhaps of his obsessive interest in the Invincibles.
13 Dangerfield, "James Joyce, James Connolly and Irish Nationalism," 16.
14 Delany, "Joyce's Political Development," 258.
15 Manganiello, *Joyce's Politics*, 126.
16 Joyce, *My Brother's Keeper*, 170.
17 Manganiello, *Joyce's Politics*, 70.
18 Joyce, *The Complete Dublin Diary*, 54.

19 Bigazzi, "Joyce and the Italian Press," 54–66.
20 Budgen, *James Joyce and the Making of* Ulysses, 187.
21 Manganiello, *Joyce's Politics*, 128.
22 *Ibid.*, 71.
23 Marx and Engels, *Ireland and the Irish Question*, 149 and 336.
24 Ellmann, *The Consciousness of Joyce*, 82–83.
25 Manganiello, "Anarch, Heresiarch, Egoarch," 108.
26 Feshbach, Review of *Joyce's Politics*, 213.
27 Borach, "Conversations with James Joyce," 326.
28 Manganiello, "Anarch, Heresiarch, Egoarch," 107–08.
29 Deane, "Joyce and Liberalism," 17.
30 Quoted in Power, *Conversations with James Joyce*, 74.
31 Joyce, "A Portrait of the Artist," 84–85.
32 Deane, "Joyce and Liberalism," 18.
33 Ellmann, "Prologue: Two Perspectives on Joyce," 9.
34 Deane, "Joyce and Liberalism," 19.
35 Manganiello, "Anarch, Heresiarch, Egoarch," 114.
36 Gorman, *James Joyce*, 183.
37 MacCabe, *James Joyce and the Revolution of the Word*, 160.
38 Feshbach, Review of *Joyce's Politics*, 212.
39 Manganiello, *Joyce's Politics*, 70.
40 Wilde, "The Soul of Man under Socialism," 162–63.
41 Manganiello, *Joyce's Politics*, 218.
42 Benstock, *The Undiscover'd Country*, 78–79.
43 Budgen, *James Joyce and the Making of* Ulysses, 30 and 31.
44 Manganiello, *Joyce's Politics*, 219.
45 Shelley, *The Defence of Poetry*.
46 Melchiori, "The Language of Politics."
47 Ironically, the dean is ignorant of his own heritage: Shakespeare wrote
   of "filling a bottle with a Tunne-dish" in *Measure for Measure* (III.ii.182).
   But since Shakespeare's sense is a sexual one, it seems fitting that the
   dean doesn't know the word. During the span of history in which
   "tundish" fell from common to what the *OED* calls "Now *local*" usage,
   England changed from a small bawdy nation-state into a prurient
   imperial power, and it is as a representative of the latter that the dean
   speaks.
48 Garvin, *James Joyce's Disunited Kingdom*, 158–69.
49 *Ibid.*, 168.
50 MacCabe, *James Joyce and the Revolution of the Word*, 28 and 32.
51 Bakhtin, *Problems of Dostoevsky's Poetics*, 4.
52 Bakhtin, *The Dialogic Imagination*, 314.
53 *Ibid.*, 307–08.
54 *Ibid.*, 311–12.
55 MacCabe, *James Joyce and the Revolution of the Word*, 14.
56 Sollers, "Joyce & Co.," 109.

57 Vico, *The New Science*, par. 331.
58 Bahti, "Vico, Auerbach and Literary History," 106.
59 Vico, *The Autobiography of Giambattista Vico*, 167.
60 Vico, *The New Science*, par. 161.
61 Mali, "Mythology and Counter-History," 41–42.
62 *Ibid.*, 43.
63 *JJ* 340; Manganiello, "Vico's Ideal History and Joyce's Language," 199.
64 Deane, "Retrospective Review," 1.
65 Mali, "Mythology and Counter-History," 44.
66 Eliot, "*Ulysses*, Order and Myth," 177.
67 Kelley, "In Vico's Wake," 136.
68 Ellmann, *The Consciousness of Joyce*, 90.
69 Deane, "Joyce and Nationalism," 181.

3 THE PARALYZED CITY

1 Fitzpatrick, *Dublin*, 279.
2 *Ibid.*, 278.
3 Ghiselin, "The Unity of Joyce's *Dubliners*," 58.
4 Kenner, *Dublin's Joyce*, 48.
5 Magalaner and Kain, *Joyce*, 77, 76, 67.
6 Gorman, *James Joyce*, 184.
7 Freyer, "A Reader's Report on *Dubliners*," 457.
8 O'Brien, "1891–1916," 13 and 14.
9 Lyons, "James Joyce's Dublin," 7 and 9.
10 *Ibid.*, 20 and 22.
11 *Ibid.*, 24.
12 *Ibid.*, 12.
13 *Ibid.*, 7.
14 Lyons, *Ireland since the Famine*, 90.
15 A Town Clerk named Henry (later Sir Henry) Campbell provided his friend, John Joyce, with electoral work that was "fairly regular and comparatively well-paid" (Garvin, "Joyce's Municipal Background," 557).
16 The relative comfort of clerical life prompted George Moore's story, "A Letter to Rome," in which a crackbrained rural priest sends the pope his solution to the problem of Ireland's declining population: let those men who can best afford large families – the priests – marry and beget.
17 Lyons, *Ireland since the Famine*, 7.
18 *Ibid.*, 57, 90, 275–76.
19 *Ibid.*, 275.
20 Quoted in O'Brien, "*Dear Dirty Dublin*," 133.
21 Russell, "An Open Letter to the Employers," 228.
22 James, *The Art of the Novel*, 5.

23 O'Connor, "James Joyce," 490.
24 Cairns and Richards, *Writing Ireland*, 60; Daly, *Dublin, the Deposed Capital*, 133.
25 ó Laoi, *Nora Barnacle Joyce*, 8 and 11.
26 Apart from *Stephen Hero*, "The Dead," and a few passages in *A Portrait*, the countryside – so central to Irish politics and to cultural nationalism – barely exists in any of Joyce's works. I don't argue that this elision simply reflects a reaction formation to the trauma of the great famines. There were several reasons why middle-class Catholic Dubliners should have wished to ignore a rural Ireland whose peasantry they "associated ... with a strong and debilitating sense of cultural inferiority" (Hirsch, "The Imaginary Irish Peasant," 1127). I would suggest, though, that the horror of the famine years contributed to this aversion.
27 Gifford, *Joyce Annotated*, 70.
28 Wall, "Joyce's Use of the Anglo-Irish Dialect of English," 131.
29 Joyce, *English as We Speak It in Ireland*, 151.
30 See Brandabur, *A Scrupulous Meanness*, 62; ó Hehir, *A Gaelic Lexicon*, 333–34; Tindall, *A Reader's Guide to James Joyce*, 22; and Torchiana, *Backgrounds for* Dubliners, 75.
31 McCormack, *Ascendancy and Tradition*, 259.
32 Daly, *Dublin, the Deposed Capital*, 138. See also pp. 112 and 268 regarding the superiority of the farm laborer's diet over the Dublin working-class diet, which may account for the slavey's healthy appearance.
33 O Faoláin, "Love Among the Irish" (1953), quoted in Walzl, "*Dubliners*: Women in Irish Society," 35.
34 Connery, *The Irish*, 192.
35 Walzl, "*Dubliners*: Women in Irish Society," 34.
36 Norris, "Narration under a Blindfold," 206 and 208.
37 Walzl, "Joyce's 'Clay': Fact and Fiction," 134.
38 Hart, "'Eveline,'" 52.
39 Quoted in MacCurtain, "Woman, the Vote and Revolution," 51.
40 Connolly, *James Connolly: Selected Writings*, 292–97.
41 San Juan, *James Joyce and the Craft of Fiction*, 74.
42 Herring, *Joyce's Uncertainty Principle*, 48.
43 *Ibid.*, 50–53.
44 Torchiana, *Backgrounds for Joyce's* Dubliners, 68–75.
45 Walzl, "*Dubliners*," 196.
46 Gifford, *Joyce Annotated*, 31.
47 Suggested by John Kelleher to Torchiana, *Backgrounds for Joyce's* Dubliners, 22.
48 Walzl, "*Dubliners*," 196.
49 Gifford, *Joyce Annotated*, 57.
50 Daly, *Dublin, the Deposed Capital*, 72 and 80.
51 Walzl, "*Dubliners*," 198.

52 Scarry, "The 'Negro Chieftain' and Disharmony in Joyce's 'The Dead,'" 182.
53 Power, "Femmes de *Dubliners*/Femmes de Dublin," 514; my translation.
54 *Ibid.*, 516; my translation.
55 *Ibid.*, 516.
56 Benstock, "'The Dead,'" 160.
57 Adams, *Surface and Symbol*, 177–81.
58 Torchiana, *Backgrounds for Joyce's* Dubliners, 205 and 213.
59 Quoted *ibid.*, 219. Noon defends Vaughan in "James Joyce: Unfacts, Fiction, and Facts," 272–73.
60 Daly, *Dublin, the Deposed Capital*, 92–93.
61 Quoted *ibid.*, 93.
62 *Ibid.*, 114.
63 Quoted *ibid.*, 115.
64 *Ibid.*, 94.
65 Gifford, *Joyce Annotated*, 104.
66 Quoted in Daly, *Dublin, the Deposed Capital*, 94–95.
67 Daly writes: "It seems possible by virtue of the social background of members and of the emphasis ... placed on the practice of religious duties that middle class families in distress, or those working class families who subscribed to Catholic middle-class mores ... were more readily assisted than the hard core of destitute working class" (*ibid.*, 95).
68 Gifford, *Joyce Annotated*, 65.
69 Gwynn, *Dublin Old and New*, 159.
70 Torchiana, *Backgrounds for Joyce's* Dubliners, 116.
71 Gwynn, *Dublin Old and New*, 116.
72 Connery, *The Irish*, 171.
73 Torchiana, *Backgrounds for Joyce's* Dubliners, 93–104.
74 Joyce, *My Brother's Keeper*, 205–06.
75 Kee, *The Green Flag*, 437.
76 O'Brien, *"Dear Dirty Dublin,"* 73, 95.
77 *Ibid.*, 34.
78 *Ibid.*, 34.
79 *Ibid.*, 200.
80 Ryan, *James Connolly*, 19.
81 O'Casey, *Autobiographies*, vol. I, 411–19.
82 *Ibid.*, 365.
83 O'Brien, *"Dear Dirty Dublin,"* 84.
84 "Home Rulers and Labour," *The Workers' Republic* 4 (October 1901), 11.
85 *Ibid.*, 2.
86 O'Brien, *"Dear Dirty Dublin,"* 88.
87 "Dublin Municipal Elections," *The Irish Times*, 7 January 1902, 6.
88 Daly, *Dublin, the Deposed Capital*, 218.

89 Greaves, *The Life and Times of James Connolly*, 137–38; "Municipal Elections," *The Workers' Republic* 4 (March 1902), 6–7.
90 Daly, *Dublin, the Deposed Capital*, 218.
91 O'Brien, *"Dear Dirty Dublin,"* 188.
92 Lyons, *Culture and Anarchy*, 80.
93 Daly, *Dublin, the Deposed Capital*, 82.
94 Gifford, *Joyce Annotated*, 93.
95 Daly, *Dublin, the Deposed Capital*, 218.
96 "Dublin Corporation Scandal," *The Irish Times*, 2 January 1903, 9.
97 Daly, *Dublin, the Deposed Capital*, 219.
98 Garvin, "James Joyce's Municipal Background," 569.
99 Kee, *The Green Flag*, 492.
100 Daly, *Dublin, the Deposed Capital*, 289.
101 "Home Thrusts," *The Workers' Republic* 5 (March 1903), 1.
102 "Home Ruler and Tory," *The Workers' Republic* 5 (March 1903), 1.
103 "The Lord Mayoralty," *The Irish Times*, 10 January 1903, 9.
104 Letter, *The Irish Times*, 9 January 1903, 6.
105 Deane, "History as Fiction," 132.

4 GROWING INTO HISTORY

1 Suggested by Hugh Kenner in a talk at the 1986 Joyce Symposium.
2 Radford, "Daedalus and the Bird Girl," 253.
3 Gifford, *Joyce Annotated*, 132–33.
4 Radford, "Daedalus and the Bird Girl," 253–54.
5 Gifford, *Joyce Annotated*, 133.
6 Bauerle, *The James Joyce Songbook*, 183–85.
7 Rossman, "The Reader's Role," 32.
8 *Ibid.*, 32–33.
9 Herr, *Joyce's Anatomy of Culture*, 25.
10 *Ibid.*, 25.
11 Gifford, *Joyce Annotated*, 36.
12 *Ibid.*, 35–36.
13 Quoted from *The Union Jack*'s self-description *ibid.*, 36.
14 Yeats, "SAMHAIN 1906: Literature and the Living Voice," 203.
15 O'Brien, *"Dear Dirty Dublin,"* 45.
16 Lyons, *The Fall of Parnell 1890–91*, 309.
17 Murphy, *The Parnell Myth and Irish Politics 1891–1956*, 113.
18 O'Brien, *A Concise History of Ireland*, 98.
19 Under the colonial regime in Ireland, the Anglican Church, or Church of England, became the state-sponsored "Church of Ireland." Hence, until 1829, the Catholic majority paid tithes to support a Protestant religious establishment.
20 MacDonagh, *States of Mind*, 91.

21 *Maynooth Catechism*, 37; quoted in Gifford, *Joyce Annotated*, 149.
22 Quoted in McCartney, "The Church and Fenianism," 17.
23 *Ibid.*, 15–16.
24 Quoted *ibid.*, 21.
25 Quoted *ibid.*, 17.
26 *Ibid.*, 19.
27 *Ibid.*, 16.
28 Quoted in MacDonagh, *States of Mind*, 91.
29 *Ibid.*, 91. I draw on MacDonagh for my sketch of the Church's political activity in the 1800s.
30 Larkin, *The Roman Catholic Church in Ireland*, xvii.
31 *Ibid.*, xix–xx.
32 *Ibid.*, xx–xxi.
33 *Ibid.*, xx.
34 Quoted in O'Brien, *Parnell and His Party 1880–90*, 283–84.
35 *Ibid.*, 283–84.
36 Quoted in Larkin, *The Roman Catholic Church in Ireland*, 211.
37 Quoted *ibid.*, 212.
38 Quoted in O'Brien, *Parnell and His Party 1880–90*, 298 and 307.
39 O'Brien, *The Life of Charles Stewart Parnell 1846–1891*, 251 and 252.
40 O'Brien, *Parnell and His Party 1880–90*, 296–97.
41 *Ibid.*, 294.
42 Quoted in Larkin, *The Roman Catholic Church in Ireland*, 222.
43 *Ibid.*, 229.
44 Quoted in O'Brien, *Parnell and His Party 1880–90*, 316.
45 Quoted in Larkin, *The Roman Catholic Church in Ireland*, 233–34.
46 MacDonagh, *States of Mind*, 91.
47 Larkin, *The Roman Catholic Church in Ireland*, 234.
48 Woods, "The General Election of 1892," 293–94.
49 MacDonagh, *States of Mind*, 91.
50 Quoted in Larkin, *The Roman Catholic Church in Ireland*, 241.
51 *Ibid.*, 240.
52 *Ibid.*, 240.
53 Quoted *ibid.*, 245, 252, 253.
54 *Ibid.*, 278.
55 Quoted *ibid.*, 269.
56 O'Brien, *The Life of Charles Stewart Parnell 1846–1891*, 340–41.
57 Quoted in Larkin, *The Roman Catholic Church in Ireland*, 285.
58 Quoted in Woods, "The General Election of 1892," 306.
59 *Ibid.*, 319.
60 Quoted in O'Brien, *Parnell and His Party 1880–90*, 334.
61 *Ibid.*, 334.
62 *Ibid.*, 348–49.
63 Larkin, *The Roman Catholic Church in Ireland*, 289.

64 MacDonagh, *States of Mind*, 91.
65 Greaves, *The Life and Times of James Connolly*, 87; cf. ó Broin, *Revolutionary Underground*, 90.
66 Boyle, *The Irish Labor Movement in the Nineteenth Century*, 201.
67 Larkin, *The Roman Catholic Church in Ireland*, 249.
68 *Ibid.*, 285 and 286.
69 O'Brien, *Parnell and His Party 1880–90*, 328.
70 Quoted *ibid.*, 354.
71 Connolly, *James Connolly: Selected Writings*, 124.
72 Henke, "Stephen Dedalus and Women," 83.
73 Beale, *Women in Ireland*, 50–51.
74 *Ibid.*, 52.
75 Connery, *The Irish*, 201.
76 Beale, *Women in Ireland*, 51.
77 Quoted in Connery, *The Irish*, 206.
78 Beale, *Women in Ireland*, 92.
79 *Ibid.*, 89.
80 Connery, *The Irish*, 208.
81 Beale, *Women in Ireland* 57–58.
82 Slater, *The Glory of Hera*, 416; quoted in Henke, "Stephen Dedalus and Women," 86–87.
83 Beale, *Women in Ireland*, 71.
84 Scott, "Emma Clery in *Stephen Hero*," 61.
85 Scott, "The Woman in the Black Straw Hat," 409.
86 Ward, *Unmanageable Revolutionaries: Women and Irish Nationalism*, 54.
87 *Ibid.*, 54.
88 O'Brien, *"Dear Dirty Dublin,"* 200.
89 *Ibid.*, 205.
90 *Ibid.*, 207.
91 Beale, *Women in Ireland*, 73.
92 See Grayson, "'Do You Kiss Your Mother?,'" 119–26.
93 Rossman, "The Reader's Role," 32.
94 Radford, "Daedalus and the Bird Girl," 264 and 265.
95 Roche, "'The Strange Light of Some New World,'" 329.
96 *Ibid.*, 328.
97 *Ibid.*, 328.
98 Synge, "The Aran Islands," 120.
99 Scott, "Emma Clery in *Stephen Hero*," 58.
100 *Ibid.*, 60.
101 Levenson and Natterstad, *Hanna Sheehy-Skeffington: Irish Feminist*, 13.
102 Quoted in Power, *Conversations with James Joyce*, 35.

5 *ULYSSES* AND THE GREAT WAR

1 Wohl, *The Generation of 1914*, 170.

2 Eksteins, *Rites of Spring*, 208–09.
3 Budgen, *James Joyce and the Making of* Ulysses, 30, 31, 37, 166.
4 Manganiello, *Joyce's Politics*, 139.
5 In 1921, during the Anglo-Irish War, another friend from UCD days, George Clancy, was murdered by the Black and Tans (British auxiliary forces).
6 Quoted in Eksteins, *Rites of Spring*, 209.
7 Fussell, *The Great War and Modern Memory*, 12.
8 Epstein, "Nestor," 22.
9 Eksteins, *Rites of Spring*, 140.
10 *Ibid.*, 140.
11 Quoted *ibid.*, 158.
12 *Ibid.*, 139.
13 A reviewer, referring to the ominousness of the 1890s, called Wells's vision "that last *fin de siècle*" (quoted in Bergonzi, "*The Time Machine*: An Ironic Myth," 54).
14 Hobsbawm, *The Age of Empire 1875–1914*, 258.
15 Nolan, "'04 Ship Fire Fatal to 1,000," 3B.
16 Hobsbawm, *The Age of Empire 1875–1914*, 328–29.
17 *Ibid.*, 329.
18 Quoted in Eksteins, *Rites of Spring*, 155.
19 Something far worse than the burning of the *General Slocum* had, of course, occurred in Ireland within three generations of 1904 – the great hunger of the 1840s. This calamity sets Ireland apart from other western European nations during the nineteenth century; yet it seems to have faded, or been repressed, from the folk memory of Joyce's Dubliners except as an item in the Citizen's catalogue of great and tragic events in Irish history.
20 Spoo, "'Nestor' and the Nightmare," 142.
21 *Ibid.*, 145.
22 See Fussell, *The Great War and Modern Memory*, 25–28 and Eksteins, *Rites of Spring* 120–26.
23 Orwell, *The Road to Wigan Pier*, 170.
24 Wohl, *The Generation of 1914*, 223.
25 Spoo, "'Nestor' and the Nightmare," 145.
26 *Ibid.*, 141.
27 Quoted in Eksteins, *Rites of Spring*, 191.
28 Quoted in Wohl, *The Generation of 1914*, 267.
29 Anderson, *Imagined Communities*, 12.
30 *Ibid.*, 14.
31 Seton-Watson, *Nations and States*, 5.
32 Anderson, *Imagined Communities*, 15–16.
33 Quoted *ibid.*, 15; my translation.
34 Nadel, *Joyce and the Jews*, 60. Nadel points out the "distinctly Mr Deasy tone" of Griffith's anti-Semitism.

35 Tuchman, *The Proud Tower*, 183.
36 Quoted in Nadel, *Joyce and the Jews*, 60 and 64.
37 Quoted in Tuchman, *The Proud Tower*, 202–03.
38 Anderson, *Imagined Communities*, 18.
39 Deane, "Joyce and Nationalism," 181.
40 Mansergh, *The Irish Question 1840–1921*, 260.
41 Stanislaus Joyce writes of his brother as a very young man: "He thought that fanned nationalisms, which he loathed, were to blame for wars and world troubles" (*My Brother's Keeper*, 170).
42 Quoted in Edwards, *Patrick Pearse*, 179.
43 *Ibid.*, 179.
44 Tuchman, *The Proud Tower*, 248–49.
45 Kiberd, "Anglo-Irish Attitudes," 95.
46 Edwards, *Patrick Pearse*, 162 and 338.
47 Anderson, *Imagined Communities*, 18.
48 Eksteins, *Rites of Spring*, 91 (quotation), 90, 200, 93 (quotation).
49 Pearse, "The Coming Revolution," 234 and "At the Grave of O'Donovan Rossa," 238.
50 Proclamation, 246.
51 Edwards, *Patrick Pearse*, 343.
52 Deane, "History as Fiction, Fiction as History," 132.
53 Budgen, *James Joyce and the Making of* Ulysses, 151.
54 Williams, *The Country and the City*, 165.
55 Anderson, *Imagined Communities*, 16.
56 Brown, *James Joyce and Sexuality*, 102.
57 Beauvoir, *The Second Sex*, 481.
58 Unkeless, "The Conventional Molly Bloom," 153.
59 French suggests that Joyce intended Molly to be seen primarily as an archetype (*The Book as World*, 258–59.)
60 See Koss, *The Anatomy of an Antiwar Movement: the Pro-Boers*, xxxvi and 198–207.
61 Showalter, *The Female Malady*, 167–68, 169, 171.
62 *Ibid.*, 172.
63 Fussell, *The Great War and Modern Memory*, 25–28.
64 Mosse, *Nationalism and Sexuality*, 36.
65 *Ibid.*, 25.
66 *Ibid.*, 144.
67 *Ibid.*, 85.
68 *Ibid.*, 151.
69 Romein, *The Watershed of Two Eras: Europe in 1900*, 89.
70 Mosse, *Nationalism and Sexuality*, 16.
71 *Ibid.*, 19 and 104.
72 The resemblance between Bello and the Citizen reinforces this link between nationalism and sexual stereotypes. Cf. Boone, "A New Approach to Bloom as 'Womanly Man,'" 77.

73 Beauvoir, *The Second Sex*, xvi.
74 Quoted in Fussell, *The Great War and Modern Memory*, 273–74.
75 *Ibid.*, 272.
76 Quoted in Showalter, *The Female Malady*, 175.
77 Mosse, *Nationalism and Sexuality*, 128–29.
78 Fussell, *The Great War and Modern Memory*, 270.
79 Mosse, *Nationalism and Sexuality*, 124.
80 Quoted in Fussell, *The Great War and Modern Memory*, 273.
81 Showalter, *The Female Malady*, 173.
82 Budgen, *James Joyce and the Making of* Ulysses, 67–68.
83 Fitzgerald, *Tender Is the Night*, 57.
84 Quoted in Tuchman, *The Proud Tower*, 55.
85 Quoted *ibid.*, 268.
86 Romein, *The Watershed of Two Eras: Europe in 1900*, 303.
87 Quoted in Fairhall, "Big-Power Politics and Colonial Economics," 7.
88 Greene, *The Vulnerable Text*, 223.
89 *Ibid.*, 222.
90 Kenner, *Ulysses*, 61.
91 Hughes, *The Shock of the New*, 11.
92 *Ibid.*, 14.
93 Hobsbawm suggests that the next *avant garde*, which succeeded that of the *fin de siècle*, came into its own "some time between 1900 and 1910 ... In the last few years before 1914 virtually everything that is characteristic of the various kinds of post-1918 'modernism' is already present ... [T]he *avant garde* henceforth found itself marching in directions the main army of the public was neither willing nor able to follow" (*The Age of Empire 1875–1914*, 235).
94 Eksteins, *Rites of Spring*, 25.
95 Quoted in Hughes, *The Shock of the New*, 14.
96 Quoted in Hobsbawm, *The Age of Empire 1875–1914*, 219.
97 Hughes, *The Shock of the New*, 43, 51, 61.
98 *Ibid.*, 61.
99 Gilbert, *James Joyce's* Ulysses, 313.
100 Hayman, Ulysses: *The Mechanics of Meaning*, 92–93.
101 Thornton, *Allusions in* Ulysses, 12.
102 Romein, *The Watershed of Two Eras: Europe in 1900*, 444.
103 Kenner, *Ulysses*, 64.
104 Hodgart, "Aeolus," 129.
105 Hobsbawm, *The Age of Empire 1875–1914*, 238–39.
106 Morse, "Proteus," 48.
107 Monaco, *How to Read a Film*, 309.
108 Tifft, "Eisenstein's Montage," 1.
109 *Ibid.*, 4–5.
110 Budgen, *James Joyce and the Making of* Ulysses, 124–25.
111 Hart, "Wandering Rocks," 200.

112 Eksteins, *Rites of Spring*, 93.
113 Quoted in Fussell, *The Great War and Modern Memory*, 194–201.
114 *Ibid.*, 203 and 7.
115 Quoted *ibid.*, 201.
116 Hart, "Wandering Rocks," 193.
117 Fussell, *The Great War and Modern Memory*, 3.

6 REFORMING THE WOR(L)D

1 Gordon, *A Plot Summary*, 32.
2 Atherton, *The Books at the Wake*, 101.
3 Garvin, *James Joyce's Disunited Kingdom*, 164–68.
4 *Ibid.*, 168. Garvin notes (p. 167) that these were only the first of Myles Joyce's last words, which an Irish-speaking journalist recorded.
5 *Ibid.*, 160.
6 *Ibid.*, 161.
7 Joyce had rejected the idea of the hero (save Parnell) in young manhood; he wrote to Stanislaus on 7 February 1905: "The whole structure of heroism is . . . a damned lie" (*L II* 81).
8 McHugh, *Annotations to* Finnegans Wake, 132.
9 Quoted from *United Irishman* (3 January 1885) in O'Sullivan, *Story of the G.A.A.*, 13. O'Sullivan notes that the article "was probably written by Michael Cusack."
10 Quoted from *The Irishman* (8 November 1884) in O'Sullivan, *Story of the G.A.A.*, 12
11 Quoted *ibid.*, 18.
12 Quoted in Edwards, *Patrick Pearse*, 253.
13 Quoted in O'Sullivan, *Story of the G.A.A.*, 44.
14 *Ibid.*, 45.
15 Quoted *ibid.*, 11.
16 Quoted in Kohfeldt, *Lady Gregory*, 181.
17 Quoted in Cullen Owens, *Did your granny have a hammer???*, 22.
18 Quoted in O'Leary, "Uneasy Alliance," 144.
19 Quoted from Pearse's letter of 9 May 1915 in Cullen Owens, *Did your granny have a hammer???*, 20.
20 Maud Gonne's Inghinidhe na hEireann merged at this time with Cumann na mBan.
21 Quoted in Cullen Owens, *Did your granny have a hammer???*, 21. Later the Republican Mary MacSwiney stated the Ireland-first position more bluntly; she declared that her former feminist sisters "were British first, suffragettes second and Irish women a bad third!" (p. 20).
22 Quoted in Edwards, *Patrick Pearse*, 207–08.
23 Pearse, Proclamation, 246.
24 Moore, *Collected Letters of D. H. Lawrence*, 282.
25 Anderson, *Imagined Communities*, 16 and 18–19.

26 Atherton, *The Books at the Wake*, 117.
27 McHugh, *Annotations to* Finnegans Wake, 96.
28 Carroll, *Through the Looking-Glass*, 247.
29 *Ibid.*, 242.
30 *Ibid.*, 241.
31 Quoted in Hobsbawm, *The Age of Empire*, 302.
32 Untitled editorial, *The Irish Times*, 20 January 1903, 4.
33 Edwards, *Patrick Pearse*, 338.
34 Pearse, "The Coming Revolution," 237.
35 Quoted in Tuchman, *The Proud Tower*, 172.
36 Hemingway, *A Farewell to Arms*, 185.
37 McHugh, *Annotations to* Finnegans Wake, 112.
38 Kathe's identification with Ireland doubles the irony that Wellington's life is encompassed in a woman's words. Asked if he were Irish, he replied: "If a gentleman happens to be born in a stable, it does not follow that he should be called a horse" (quoted in McHugh, *Annotations to* Finnegans Wake, 10). The many references to his horse, and his description as a "bornstable ghentleman" (*FW* 10.17–18), underline this irony.
39 McHugh, *Annotations to* Finnegans Wake, 11.
40 Brown, *James Joyce and Sexuality*, 102; Unkeless, "The Conventional Molly Bloom," 153.
41 Munich, "'Dear Dead Women,'" 126–33.
42 Quoted in Ellmann, "Prologue," 7.
43 Weininger asserted that Jewish men show a preponderance of feminine qualities – an argument that contributed to Joyce's portrayal of Bloom as a womanly man (*JJ* 463).
44 Mosse, *Nationalism and Sexuality*, 145.
45 Quoted in McCarthy, Beja, and Seesholtz, "James Joyce and the Phoenix Park Murders," 83–84.
46 Quoted *ibid.*, "James Joyce and the Phoenix Park Murders," 88–89.
47 Seesholtz quotes this passage, and notes Joyce's likely influence on it, *ibid.*, 86–88.
48 Gorman, *James Joyce*, 18–19.
49 Vico, *The New Science*, par. 349.

7 AFTERWORD: LANGUAGE AND HISTORY

1 Torchiana, *Backgrounds for Joyce's* Dubliners, 21.
2 Kiberd, "The War against the Past," 46.
3 I draw here on Froula, "History's Nightmare, Fiction's Dream," 864–70.
4 See MacDonagh, *States of Mind*, 123–24.
5 Cf. Herr, "Ireland from the Outside," 778.

Bibliography

PRIMARY SOURCES – JOYCE

Joyce, James. *Chamber Music.* In *Collected Poems.* New York: Viking, 1957, pp. 9–44.

The Critical Writings of James Joyce. Eds. Ellsworth Mason and Richard Ellmann. New York: Viking, 1959.

Dubliners. Ed. Robert Scholes in consultation with Richard Ellmann. 1914. New York: Viking, 1967.

Finnegans Wake. 1939. New York: Viking, 1939.

Letters of James Joyce. Vol. 1. Ed. Stuart Gilbert. New York: Viking, 1957.

Letters of James Joyce. Vols. 2 and 3. Ed. Richard Ellmann. New York: Viking, 1966.

A Portrait of the Artist as a Young Man. 1916. New York: Viking, 1964.

A Portrait of the Artist as a Young Man: A Facsimile of Epiphanies, Notes, Manuscripts, and Typescripts. The James Joyce Archive. Eds. Michael Groden *et al.* New York and London: Garland, 1978.

Stephen Hero. Eds. John J. Slocum and Herbert Cahoon. New York: New Directions, 1963.

Ulysses. 1922. Eds. Hans Walter Gabler *et al.* New York and London: Garland, 1984.

SECONDARY LITERATURE

Adams, Robert M. *Surface and Symbol.* New York: Oxford University Press, 1962.

Anderson, Benedict. *Imagined Communities: Reflections on the Origin and Spread of Nationalism.* London: Verso, 1983.

Arensberg, Conrad M. and Solon T. Kimball. *Family and Community in Ireland.* 2nd edn. Cambridge, MA: Harvard University Press, 1968.

Aristotle. *Poetics.* In *The Rhetoric and the Poetics of Aristotle.* Trans. W. Rhys Roberts and Ingram Bywater. New York: Modern Library, 1954, pp. 219–66.

Arnold, Matthew. *On the Study of Celtic Literature.* London, 1867.

Atherton, James. *The Books at the Wake*. New York: Viking, 1960.

Bahti, Timothy. "Vico, Auerbach and Literary History." In *Vico: Past and Present*. Vol. 2. Ed. Giorgio Tagliacozzo. Atlantic Highlands, NJ: Humanities, 1981, pp. 97–114.

Bakhtin, M. M. *The Dialogic Imagination*. Trans. Caryl Emerson and Michael Holquist. Austin: University of Texas Press, 1981.

Problems of Dostoevsky's Poetics. Trans. R. W. Rotsel. N.p.: Ardis, 1973.

Bardon, Jonathan and Stephen Conlin. *Dublin: One Thousand Years of Wood Quay*. Belfast, 1984; Dover, NH: Longwood, 1985.

Barthes, Roland. "The Discourse of History." Trans. Stephen Bann. In *Comparative Criticism: A Yearbook*. Ed. E. S. Shaffer. Cambridge University Press, 1981, pp. 3–20.

Bauerle, Ruth, ed. *The James Joyce Songbook*. New York: Garland, 1982.

Beale, Jenny. *Women in Ireland*. Bloomington: Indiana University Press, 1987.

Beauvoir, Simone de. *The Second Sex*. 1949 (*Le Deuxième Sexe*). Trans. and ed. H. M. Parshley. New York: Knopf, 1971.

Bennett, Tony. "Texts in History." In *Post-Structuralism and the Question of History*. Eds. Derek Attridge, Geoff Bennington, and Robert Young. Cambridge University Press, 1987, pp. 63–81.

Benstock, Bernard. "'The Dead.'" In Hart, *Joyce's* Dubliners, pp. 153–69.

The Undiscover'd Country. Dublin: Gill and Macmillan; New York: Barnes and Noble, 1977.

Bergonzi, Bernard. "*The Time Machine*: An Ironic Myth." In *H.G. Wells: A Collection of Critical Essays*. Ed. Bernard Bergonzi. Englewood Cliffs, NJ: Prentice-Hall, 1976, pp. 39–55.

Bigazzi, Carlo. "Joyce and the Italian Press." In Melchiori, pp. 52–66.

Boone, Joseph Allen. "A New Approach to Bloom as 'Womanly Man': The Mixed Middling's Progress in *Ulysses*." *JJQ* 20 (Fall 1982): 67–85.

Borach, Georges. "Conversations with James Joyce." Trans. Joseph Prescott. *College English* 15 (March 1954): 325–27.

Boyle, John W. *The Irish Labor Movement in the Nineteenth Century*. Washington, DC: Catholic University of America Press, 1988.

Brandabur, Edward. *A Scrupulous Meanness*. Urbana: University of Illinois Press, 1971.

Brown, Malcolm. *The Politics of Irish Literature*. Seattle: University of Washington Press, 1972.

Brown, Richard. *James Joyce and Sexuality*. Cambridge University Press, 1985.

Brown, Terence. "Dublin in Twentieth-Century Writing." *Irish University Review* 8 (Spring 1978): 7–21.

Budgen, Frank. *James Joyce and the Making of* Ulysses. 1934. Bloomington: Indiana University Press, 1960.

Butler, Samuel. *Erewhon*. London, 1872.

Cairns, David and Shaun Richards. *Writing Ireland: Colonialism, Nationalism and Culture.* Manchester University Press, 1988.

Canary, Robert H. and Henry Kozicki, eds. *The Writing of History.* Madison: University of Wisconsin Press, 1978.

Carroll, Lewis. *Through the Looking-Glass.* 1871. New York: Modern Library, n.d.

Catechism Ordered by the National Synod of Maynooth, The. Dublin, 1883.

Clarkson, J. Dunsmore. *Labour and Nationalism in Ireland.* New York: n.p., 1925.

Collingwood, Robin. *The Idea of History.* 1946. New York: Oxford University Press, 1956.

"The Pleasures of Doubt." Abridgement of "The Limits of Historical Knowledge" (1920) in Winks, pp. 514–22.

Connery, Donald S. *The Irish.* New York: Simon and Schuster, 1968.

Connolly, James. *James Connolly: Selected Writings.* Ed. P. Berresford Ellis. New York and London: Monthly Review, 1973.

Labour in Ireland. Dublin and London: Maunsel, 1917.

Corfe, Tom. *The Phoenix Park Murders.* London: Hodder and Stoughton, 1968.

Cullen Owens, Rosemary. *Did your granny have a hammer??? A History of the Irish Suffrage Movement 1876–1922.* Dublin: Attic, 1985.

Curtis, Jr., L. Perry. *Apes and Angels: The Irishman in Victorian Caricature.* Washington, DC: Smithsonian Institution, 1971.

Daly, Mary E. *Dublin, the Deposed Capital.* Cork University Press, 1984.

Dangerfield, George. *The Damnable Question.* Boston: Atlantic Monthly, 1976.

"James Joyce, James Connolly and Irish Nationalism." *Irish University Review* 16 (Spring 1986): 5–21.

The Strange Death of Liberal England. 1935. New York: Capricorn, 1961.

Deane, Seamus. "History as Fiction, Fiction as History." In Melchiori, pp. 130–41.

"Joyce and Nationalism." In *James Joyce: New Perspectives.* Ed. Colin MacCabe. Brighton: Harvester; Bloomington: Indiana University Press, 1982, pp. 168–83.

"Masked with Matthew Arnold's Face: Joyce and Liberalism." *Canadian Journal of Irish Studies* 12 (June 1986): 11–22.

"Retrospective Review." *James Joyce Broadsheet* 4 (February 1981).

Delany, Paul. "Joyce's Political Development and the Aesthetic of *Dubliners.*" *College English* 34 (November 1972): 256–66.

Derrida, Jacques. "*Différance.*" In *Margins of Philosophy.* Trans. Alan Bass. University of Chicago Press, 1982, pp. 1–27.

Dickens, Charles. *Little Dorritt.* London, 1855–57.

Eagleton, Terry. *Criticism and Ideology.* 1976. London: Verso, 1978.

Edwards, Ruth Dudley. *Patrick Pearse: The Triumph of Failure.* 1977. New York: Toplinger, 1978.

Eksteins, Modris. *Rites of Spring*. Boston: Houghton Mifflin, 1989.
Eliot, T. S. "Tradition and the Individual Talent." 1919. In *Selected Prose of T.S. Eliot*. Ed. Frank Kermode. New York: Harcourt Brace Jovanovich/Farrar, Straus and Giroux, 1975, pp. 37–44.
"*Ulysses*, Order and Myth." 1923. In Eliot, pp. 175–78.
Ellis, P. Berresford. "Introduction." In Connolly, pp. 7–53.
Ellmann, Richard. *The Consciousness of Joyce*. New York: Oxford University Press, 1977.
James Joyce. 1959. New York: Oxford University Press, 1982.
"Prologue: Two Perspectives on Joyce." In *Light Rays: James Joyce and Modernism*. Ed. Heyward Ehrlich. New York: New Horizon, 1984, pp. 1–12.
Epstein, E. L. "Nestor." In Hart and Hayman, pp. 17–28.
Eyler, Audrey S. and Robert F. Garratt, eds. *The Uses of the Past*. Newark: University of Delaware, 1988.
Fairhall, James. "Big-Power Politics and Colonial Economics: The Gordon Bennett Cup Race and Joyce's 'After the Race.'" *JJQ* 28 (Winter 1991): 387–97.
"Colgan-Connolly: Another Look at the Politics of 'Ivy Day in the Committee Room.'" *JJQ* 25 (Spring 1988): 289–304.
Feshbach, Sidney. Review of *Joyce's Politics*, by Dominic Manganiello. *JJQ* 19 (Winter 1982): 208–13.
Finley, M. I. *Ancient History*. 1985. New York: Viking, 1986.
Fitzgerald, F. Scott. *Tender Is the Night*. New York: Scribner's, 1933.
Fitzpatrick, Samuel A. Ossory. *Dublin: A Historical and Topographical Account of the City*. London: Methuen, 1907.
French, Marilyn. *The Book as World: James Joyce's "Ulysses."* Cambridge, MA: Harvard University Press, 1976.
Freyer, Grattan. "A Reader's Report on *Dubliners*." *JJQ* 10 (Summer 1973): 455–57.
Froula, Christine. "History's Nightmare, Fiction's Dream: Joyce and the Psychohistory of *Ulysses*." *JJQ* 28 (Summer 1991): 857–72.
Fussell, Paul. *The Great War and Modern Memory*. New York: Oxford University Press, 1975.
Garvin, John. *James Joyce's Disunited Kingdom and the Irish Dimension*. Dublin: Gill and Macmillan, 1976; New York: Barnes and Noble, 1977.
"James Joyce's Municipal Background." *Administration* (Dublin) Vol. 33, No. 4 (1985): 551–72.
Ghiselin, Brewster. "The Unity of Joyce's *Dubliners*." *Accent* 16 (Spring 1956 and Summer 1956): 75–88 and 196–213.
Gifford, Don. *Joyce Annotated*. 1967. Berkeley: University of California Press, 1982.
Gilbert, Stuart. *James Joyce's Ulysses*. 1930. Rev. edn. New York: Vintage, 1955.

Gordon, John. Finnegans Wake: *A Plot Summary*. Syracuse, NY: Syracuse University Press, 1986.

Gorman, Herbert. *James Joyce*. 1939. New York: Octagon, 1974.

Gossman, Lionel. "History and Literature: Reproduction or Signification." In Canary and Kozicki, pp. 3–39.

Grayson, Janet. "'Do You Kiss Your Mother?': Stephen Dedalus' Sovereignty of Ireland." *JJQ* 19 (Winter 1982): 119–26.

Greaves, C. Desmond. *The Life and Times of James Connolly*. 1961. New York: International, 1971.

Greene, Thomas M. *The Vulnerable Text*. New York: Columbia University Press, 1986.

Gwynn, Stephen. *Dublin Old and New*. New York: Macmillan, 1938.

Hart, Clive. "'Eveline.'" In Hart, *Joyce's Dubliners*, pp. 48–52.

"Wandering Rocks." In Hart and Hayman, pp. 181–216.

Ed. *James Joyce's Dubliners: Critical Essays*. New York: Viking, 1969.

Hart, Clive and David Hayman, eds. *James Joyce's Ulysses: Critical Essays*. Berkeley: University of California, 1974.

Hayman, David. Ulysses: *The Mechanics of Meaning*. 1970. Rev. edn. Madison: University of Wisconsin Press, 1982.

Hemingway, Ernest. *A Farewell to Arms*. New York: Scribner's, 1929.

Henke, Suzette. "Stephen Dedalus and Women: A Portrait of the Artist as a Young Misogynist." In Henke and Unkeless, pp. 82–107.

Henke, Suzette and Elaine Unkeless, eds. *Women in Joyce*. Urbana: University of Illinois, 1982.

Herr, Cheryl. "Ireland from the Outside." *JJQ* 28 (Summer 1991): 777–89.

Joyce's Anatomy of Culture. Urbana: University of Illinois, 1986.

Herring, Phillip F. *Joyce's Uncertainty Principle*. Princeton University Press, 1987.

Hirsch, Edward. "The Imaginary Irish Peasant." *PMLA* 106 (October 1991): 1116–33.

Hirst, Paul Q. *Marxism and Historical Writing*. London and Boston: Routledge and Kegan Paul, 1985.

Hobsbawm, Eric. *The Age of Empire 1875–1914*. New York: Pantheon, 1987.

Hodgart, M. J. C. "Aeolus." In Hart and Hayman, pp. 115–30.

Hughes, Robert. *The Shock of the New*. New York: Knopf, 1981.

James, Henry. *The Art of the Novel*. Ed. R. P. Blackmur. New York: Scribner's, 1947.

Jameson, Fredric. *The Political Unconscious*. Ithaca, NY: Cornell University Press, 1981.

Joyce, P. W. *English as We Speak It in Ireland*. London: Longmans, Green, 1910.

Joyce, Stanislaus. *The Complete Dublin Diary*. Ed. George H. Healy. Ithaca, NY: Cornell University Press, 1971.

My Brother's Keeper. New York: Viking, 1958.

Kaplan, John. "The Case of the Grassy Knoll." In Winks, pp. 371–419.

Kee, Robert. *The Green Flag*. New York: Delacorte, 1972.

Kelley, Donald R. "In Vico's Wake." In Verene, pp. 135–46.

Kenner, Hugh. *Dublin's Joyce*. 1956. Boston: Beacon, 1962.

Ulysses. London: Allen and Unwin, 1980.

Kiberd, Declan. "Anglo-Irish Attitudes." In *Ireland's Field Day*. Field Day Theatre Company. 1983. South Bend, IN: University of Notre Dame, 1986, pp. 83–105

"The War Against the Past." In Eyler and Garratt, pp. 24–54.

Kipling, Rudyard. *Kim*. Ed. Edward W. Said. 1901. Harmondsworth: Penguin, 1987.

"The White Man's Burden." 1899.

Kohfeldt, Mary Lou. *Lady Gregory*. New York: Atheneum, 1985.

Koss, Stephen, ed. *The Anatomy of an Antiwar Movement: The Pro-Boers*. University of Chicago Press, 1973.

Krieger, Leonard. *Ranke: The Meaning of History*. University of Chicago Press, 1977.

Larkin, Emmet. *The Roman Catholic Church in Ireland and the Fall of Parnell, 1888–1891*. Chapel Hill: University of North Carolina Press, 1979.

Levenson, Leah and Jerry H. Natterstad. *Hanna Sheehy-Skeffington: Irish Feminist*. Syracuse, NY: Syracuse University Press, 1986.

Levin, Richard and Charles Shattuck. "First Flight to Ithaca." *Accent* 4 (Winter 1944): 75–99.

Lifton, Robert Jay. *Death in Life*. New York: Random, 1967.

Lyons, F. S. L. *Culture and Anarchy in Ireland 1890–1939*. Oxford: Clarendon, 1979.

The Fall of Parnell 1890–91. London: Routledge and Kegan Paul, 1960.

Ireland Since the Famine. New York: Scribner's, 1971.

"James Joyce's Dublin." *Twentieth Century Studies* (November 1970): 6–25.

Lyons, F. S. L. and R. A. J. Hawkins, eds. *Ireland under the Union*. Oxford: Clarendon, 1980.

MacCabe, Colin. *James Joyce and the Revolution of the Word*. London: Macmillan, 1979.

MacCurtain, Margaret. "Woman, the Vote and Revolution." In *Women in Irish Society*. Eds. Margaret MacCurtain and Donncha ó Corráin. 1978. Westport, CN: Greenwood, 1979, pp. 46–57.

MacDonagh, Oliver. *States of Mind: A Study of Anglo-Irish Conflict 1780–1980*. London: Allen and Unwin, 1983.

Maddox, Brenda. *Nora: The Real Life of Molly Bloom*. Boston: Houghton Mifflin, 1988.

Maertin, Donald. "When Digging Has Its Place." *Military History* 4 (October 1987): 12–16.

Magalaner, Marvin. "The Other Side of James Joyce." *Arizona Quarterly* 9 (Spring 1953): 5–16.

Time of Apprenticeship. London: Abelard-Schuman, 1959.

Magalaner, Marvin and Richard M. Kain. *Joyce: The Man, the Work, the Reputation*. New York University Press, 1956.

Malcolm, Elizabeth. "Temperance and Irish Nationalism." In Lyons and Hawkins, pp. 69–114.

Mali, Joseph. "Mythology and Counter-History." In Verene, pp. 32–47.

Manganiello, Dominic. "Anarch, Heresiarch, Egoarch." In Melchiori, pp. 98–115.

Joyce's Politics. London and Boston: Routledge and Kegan Paul, 1980.

"Vico's Ideal History." In Verene, pp. 196–206.

Mann, Thomas. *The Magic Mountain*. 1924 (*Der Zauberberg*). Trans. H. T. Lowe-Porter. New York: Knopf, 1968.

Mansergh, Nicholas. *The Irish Question 1840–1921*. 3rd rev. edn. London: Allen and Unwin, 1975.

Marx, Karl and Friedrich Engels. *Ireland and the Irish Question: A Collection of Writings by Karl Marx and Frederick Engels*. Ed. R. Dixon. New York: International, 1972.

McCarthy, Patrick, Morris Beja, and Mel Seesholtz. "James Joyce and the Phoenix Park Murders." In *Irish Renaissance Annual 4*. Ed. Zack Bowen. London and Toronto: University of Delaware and Associated University Presses, 1983, pp. 76–93.

McCartney, Donal. "The Church and Fenianism." In *Fenians and Fenianism*. Ed. Maurice Harmon. 1968. Seattle: University of Washington Press, 1970, pp. 13–27.

McCormack, W.J. *Ascendancy and Tradition*. Oxford: Clarendon, 1985.

McHugh, Roland. *Annotations to* Finnegans Wake. Baltimore: The Johns Hopkins University Press, 1980.

Melchiori, Giorgio, ed. *Joyce in Rome: The Genesis of* Ulysses. Rome: Bulzoni, 1984.

"The Language of Politics and the Politics of Language." *James Joyce Broadsheet* 4 (February 1981).

Mercier, Vivian. "Dublin under the Joyces." In *James Joyce: Two Decades of Criticism*. Ed. Seon Givens. 1948. Augmented edn. New York: Vanguard, 1963, pp. 285–301.

Mercier, Vivian and David H. Greene, eds. *1000 Years of Irish Prose*. 1952. New York: Grosset and Dunlap, 1961.

Mitchell, Arthur. *Labour in Irish Politics 1890–1930*. Dublin: Irish University Press, 1974.

Monaco, James. *How to Read a Film*. New York: Oxford University Press, 1977.

Moore, George. *The Untilled Field*. 1903. London: Heinemann, 1915.

Moore, Harry T., ed. *Collected Letters of D.H. Lawrence*. Vol. 1. New York: Viking, 1962.

Morse, J. Mitchell. "Proteus." In Hart and Hayman, pp. 29–49.

Mosse, George L. *Nationalism and Sexuality*. New York: Howard Fertig, 1985.

Munich, Adrienne A. "'Dear Dead Women,' or Why Gabriel Conroy Reviews Robert Browning." In *New Alliances in Joyce Studies*. Ed. Bonnie Kime Scott. Newark: University of Delaware Press, 1988, pp. 126–34

Murphy, William Michael. *The Parnell Myth and Irish Politics 1891–1956*. New York: Peter Lang, 1986.

Nadel, Ira B. *Joyce and the Jews*. Iowa City: University of Iowa Press, 1989.

Newbolt, Sir Henry. "Vitaï Lampada." 1898.

Nolan, James. "'04 Ship Fire Fatal to 1,000 All But Forgotten by US." *Journal of Commerce* (11 June 1987): 3B.

Noon, William T., S. J. "James Joyce: Unfacts, Fiction, and Facts." *PMLA* 76 (June 1961): 254–76.

Norris, Margot. "Narration under a Blindfold: Reading Joyce's 'Clay.'" *PMLA* 102 (March 1987): 206–15.

O'Brien, Conor Cruise. "1891–1916." In *The Shaping of Modern Ireland*. Ed. Conor Cruise O'Brien. London: Routledge and Kegan Paul; University of Toronto Press, 1960, pp. 13–23.

Parnell and His Party 1880–90. 1957. Oxford University Press, 1964.

O'Brien, Joseph B. *"Dear Dirty Dublin": A City in Distress, 1899–1916*. Berkeley: University of California Press, 1982.

O'Brien, Máire and Conor Cruise O'Brien. *A Concise History of Ireland*. 3rd edn. London: Thames and Hudson, 1985.

O'Brien, R. Barry. *The Life of Charles Stewart Parnell 1846–1891*. 1898. 2 vols. New York: Haskell, 1968.

ó Broin, Leon. *Revolutionary Underground: The Story of the Irish Republican Brotherhood 1858–1924*. Totowa, NJ: Rowman and Littlefield, 1976.

O'Casey, Sean. *Autobiographies*. Vol. 1. New York: Carroll and Graf, 1984.

O'Connor, Frank. "James Joyce." *The American Scholar* 36 (Summer 1967): 466–90.

The Lonely Voice. New York: World, 1963.

ó Hehir, Brendan. *A Gaelic Lexicon for* Finnegans Wake, *and Glossary for Joyce's Other Works*. Berkeley: University of California Press, 1967.

ó Laoi, Padraic. *Nora Barnacle Joyce: A Portrait*. Galway: Kennys Bookshops and Art Galleries, 1982.

O'Leary, Philip. "Uneasy Alliance: The Gaelic League Looks at the 'Irish' Renaissance." In Eyler and Garratt, pp. 144–60.

Orwell, George. *The Road to Wigan Pier*. London: Gollancz, 1937.

O'Shea, Katharine (Mrs. Charles Stewart Parnell). *Charles Stewart Parnell: His Love Story and Political Life*. 2 vols. New York: George H. Doran, 1914.

O'Sullivan, Thomas F. *Story of the G.A.A.* Dublin: n.p., 1916.

Owen, Wilfred. *Poems*. London: Chatto, 1920.

Peake, C. H. *James Joyce: The Citizen and the Artist*. Stanford University Press, 1977.

Pearse, Padraic. "The Coming Revolution" (1913) and "At the Grave of

O'Donovan Rossa" (1915). Rpt. in Mercier and Greene, pp. 234–37 and 238–39.

Power, Arthur. *Conversations with James Joyce*. Dublin: Cahill, 1974.

Power, Mary. "Femmes de *Dubliners*/Femmes de Dublin." In *James Joyce*. Eds. Jacques Aubert and Fritz Senn. Paris: L'Herne, 1985, pp. 512–27.

Proclamation of the Irish Republic. 1916. Rpt. in Mercier and Greene, pp. 245–46.

Proust, Marcel. *Remembrance of Things Past*. 1913–27 (*A la recherche du temps perdu*). Trans. C. K. Scott Moncrieff. New York: Random, 1934.

Radford, F. L. "Daedalus and the Bird Girl: Classical Text and Celtic Subtext in *A Portrait*." *JJQ* 24 (Spring 1987): 253–74.

"King, Pope, and Hero-Martyr: *Ulysses* and the Nightmare of Irish History." *JJQ* 15 (Summer 1978): 275–323.

Roche, Anthony. "'The Strange Light of Some New World': Stephen's Vision in 'A Portrait.'" *JJQ* 25 (Spring 1988): 323–32.

Romein, Jan. *The Watershed of Two Eras: Europe in 1900*. Trans. Arnold J. Pomerans. Middletown, CN: Wesleyan University Press, 1978.

Rossman, Charles. "The Reader's Role in *A Portrait of the Artist as a Young Man*." In *James Joyce: An International Perspective*. Eds. Suheil Badi Bushrui and Bernard Benstock. Totowa, NJ: Barnes and Noble, 1982, pp. 19–37.

Russell, George (AE). "An Open Letter to the Employers." 1913. Rpt. as "The Dublin Strike" in Mercier and Greene, pp. 228–30.

Ryan, Desmond. *James Connolly*. Dublin and London: n.p., 1924.

Ryan, Michael. *Marxism and Deconstruction*. Baltimore: The Johns Hopkins University Press, 1982.

San Juan, Jr., Epifanio. *James Joyce and the Craft of Fiction*. Rutherford, NJ: Fairleigh Dickinson University Press, 1972.

Scarry, John M. "The 'Negro Chieftain' and Disharmony in Joyce's 'The Dead.'" *Revue des langues vivantes* 39 (1973): 182–83.

Scott, Bonnie Kime. "Emma Clery in *Stephen Hero*: A Young Woman Walking Proudly Through the Decayed City." In Henke and Unkeless, pp. 57–81.

James Joyce. Atlantic Highlands, NJ: Humanities Press International, 1987.

"The Woman in the Black Straw Hat: A Transitional Priestess in *Stephen Hero*." *JJQ* 16 (Summer 1979): 407–16.

Seeley, Sir John Robert. *The Expansion of England*. 1883. London: Macmillan, 1911.

Seton-Watson, Hugh. *Nations and States*. Boulder, CO: Westview, 1977.

Shakespeare. *Measure for Measure*. 1604.

Shelley, Percy Bysshe. *The Defence of Poetry*. 1821.

Showalter, Elaine. *The Female Malady*. New York: Pantheon, 1985.

Slater, Philip E. *The Glory of Hera*. 1968. Boston: Beacon, 1971.

Sollers, Philippe. "Joyce & Co." In *In the Wake of the* Wake. Eds. David Hayman and Elliott Anderson. Madison: University of Wisconsin Press, 1978, pp. 107–21.
Spoo, Robert E. "'Nestor' and the Nightmare: The Presence of the Great War in *Ulysses*." *Twentieth Century Literature* 32 (Summer 1986): 137–54.
Stewart, J. I. M. *Eight Modern Writers*. New York: Oxford University Press, 1963.
Synge, John Millington. *The Aran Islands*. 1907. Abridged as "The Aran Islands" in Mercier and Greene, pp. 94–141.
In the Shadow of the Glen. Dublin, 1903.
Tennyson, Lord Alfred. "Ulysses." 1842.
Thom's Official Directory of the United Kingdom of Great Britain and Ireland. Dublin: Alexander Thom and Co., 1904.
Thornton, Weldon. *Allusions in* Ulysses. Chapel Hill: University of North Carolina Press, 1968.
Tifft, Stephen. "Eisenstein's Montage and the Wandering Rocks of Modernist Narrative." Unpublished talk. Annual Meeting of the Midwest MLA, St. Louis, November 1985.
Tindall, William York. *A Reader's Guide to James Joyce*. New York: Farrar, Straus, and Giroux, 1959; London: Thames and Hudson, 1960.
Torchiana, Donald T. *Backgrounds for Joyce's* Dubliners. Boston: Allen and Unwin, 1986.
Tuchman, Barbara. *The Proud Tower*. New York: Macmillan, 1966.
Tynan, Patrick J. P. *The Irish National Invincibles and Their Times*. London: Chatham, 1894.
Unkeless, Elaine. "The Conventional Molly Bloom." In Henke and Unkeless, pp. 150–68.
Verene, Donald P., ed. *Vico and Joyce*. Albany: State University of New York Press, 1987.
Vico, Giambattista. *The Autobiography of Giambattista Vico*. Trans. Max Harold Fisch and Thomas Goddard Bergin. Ithaca, NY: Cornell University Press, 1963.
The New Science. 3rd edn. 1744. Trans. Max Harold Fisch and Thomas Goddard Bergin. Ithaca, NY: Cornell University Press, 1968.
Wall, Richard. "Joyce's Use of the Anglo-Irish Dialect of English." In *Place, Personality and the Irish Writer*. *Irish Literary Studies*. Vol. 1. Ed. Andrew Carpenter. New York: Harper and Row, 1977, pp. 121–35.
Walsh, Nicholas, S. J. *Woman*. Dublin: Gill, 1903.
Walzl, Florence L. "*Dubliners*." In *A Companion to Joyce Studies*. Eds. Zack R. Bowen and James F. Carens. Westport, CN: Greenwood, 1984, pp. 157–228.
"*Dubliners*: Women in Irish Society." In Henke and Unkeless, pp. 31–56.
"Joyce's 'Clay': Fact and Fiction." *Renascence* 35 (Winter 1983): 119–37.
Ward, Margaret. *Unmanageable Revolutionaries: Women and Irish Nationalism*. London: Pluto, 1983.

Warren, Robert Penn. "The Use of the Past." In *A Time to Hear and Answer: Essays for the Bicentennial Season*. Franklin Lectures in Sciences and Humanities, 4th Ser. University of Alabama Press, 1977, pp. 3–35.

Watson, G. J. "The Politics of *Ulysses*." In *Joyce's* Ulysses. Eds. Robert D. Newman and Weldon Thornton. London and Toronto: University of Delaware and Associated University Presses, 1987.

White, Hayden. *The Content of the Form*. Baltimore: The Johns Hopkins University Press, 1987.

"The Historical Text as Literary Artifact." In Canary and Kozicki, pp. 41–62.

Wilde, Oscar. "The Soul of Man under Socialism." 1891. In *The Works of Oscar Wilde*. Vol. 14. New York and London: Putnam's, n.d., pp. 121–73.

Williams, Raymond. *The Country and the City*. New York: Oxford University Press, 1973.

Marxism and Literature. Oxford University Press, 1977.

Winks, Robin W., ed. *The Historian as Detective*. New York: Harper Colophon, 1970.

Wohl, Robert. *The Generation of 1914*. Cambridge MA: Harvard University Press, 1979.

Woods, C. J. "The General Election of 1892: The Catholic Clergy and the Defeat of the Parnellites." In Lyons and Hawkins, pp. 289–319.

Yeats, William Butler. *Cathleen ni Houlihan*. Dublin, 1902.

"SAMHAIN: 1906. Literature and the Living Voice." In *Explorations*. 1962. New York: Collier, 1973, pp. 202–21.

Index

283